Rome

JAMES LACEY

Rome

Strategy of Empire

OXFORD
UNIVERSITY PRESS

Oxford University Press is a department of the University of Oxford. It furthers
the University's objective of excellence in research, scholarship, and education
by publishing worldwide. Oxford is a registered trade mark of Oxford University
Press in the UK and certain other countries.

Published in the United States of America by Oxford University Press
198 Madison Avenue, New York, NY 10016, United States of America.

Library of Congress Cataloging-in-Publication Data
Names: Lacey, James, 1958- author.
Title: Rome : strategy of empire / James Lacey.
Description: New York, NY : Oxford University Press, [2022] |
Includes bibliographical references and index.
Identifiers: LCCN 2022003249 (print) | LCCN 2022003250 (ebook) |
ISBN 9780190937706 (hardback) | ISBN 9780190937720 (epub)
Subjects: LCSH: Strategy. | Rome—Military policy. | Rome—Army. |
Rome—History, Military.
Classification: LCC U35 .L33 2022 (print) | LCC U35 (ebook) |
DDC 355.009456/32—dc23/eng/20220223
LC record available at https://lccn.loc.gov/2022003249
LC ebook record available at https://lccn.loc.gov/2022003250

DOI: 10.1093/oso/9780190937706.001.0001

9 8 7 6 5 4 3 2 1

Printed by Lakeside Book Company, United States of America

Dedicated to Thomas and Jordan Saunders for their support of learning and their love of country

CONTENTS

THE EMPIRE'S TIMELINE

27 BCE	The Senate confers on Octavian the title of Augustus
23 BCE	The Senate grants Augustus the powers of *imperium proconsulare maius* and *tribunicia potestas* for life, thereby ending the Roman Republic
9 CE	Tiberius ends the Pannonian Revolt
9 CE	Roman army under Varus annihilated in the Teutoburg Wald
14–37 CE	Tiberius becomes emperor
14–16 CE	Germanicus campaigns in Germany
37–41 CE	Caligula becomes emperor
39–40 CE	Caligula launches an abortive campaign against Germania and Britain
41–54 CE	Claudius becomes emperor
43–44 CE	Britain brought under Roman rule
54–68 CE	Nero becomes emperor
68–69 CE	Year of the Four Emperors
69–79 CE	Vespasian becomes emperor; start of the Flavian dynasty
79–81 CE	Titus becomes emperor
81–96 CE	Domitian becomes emperor
96 CE	Domitian murdered; Nerva becomes emperor
98 CE	Trajan becomes emperor
101 CE	Trajan campaigns on the Danube
104 CE	Trajan conquers Dacia

114–117 CE	War with Parthia adds Armenia, Mesopotamia, and Assyria as new provinces
117 CE	Hadrian becomes emperor and makes peace with Parthia
138–161 CE	Antoninus Pius becomes emperor
161 CE	Death of Antoninus; Marcus Aurelius becomes emperor with Verus as co-emperor
162–166 CE	Parthian War
166 CE	Start of the Antonine Plague
167–175 CE	First Marcomannic War on the Danube
167 CE	Marcus Aurelius attacks the Quadi
168 CE	Marcus Aurelius becomes sole emperor
169–179 CE	Marcus Aurelius campaigns in Pannonia
175 CE	Avidius Cassius revolts
175–180 CE	Second war on the tribes along the Danube
180 CE	Commodus becomes emperor and makes peace with the Danubian tribes
192 CE	Death of Commodus
193–194 CE	A second Year of Four Emperors
193–211 CE	Septimius Severus becomes emperor, starting the Severan dynasty
195–196 CE	Parthian campaign
208–211 CE	Septimius Severus heads the campaign in Britain and dies there
211–217 CE	Caracalla becomes emperor
212 CE	Caracalla confers citizenship on all free men in the Empire
216 CE	War breaks out again in Parthia
218–222 CE	Elagabalus becomes emperor
222–235 CE	Alexander Severus becomes emperor
224–241 CE	Artaxerxes I reigns over a new Persian dynasty, the Sassanids
235–238 CE	Gordianus I and II become co-emperors
238–244 CE	Gordianus III becomes emperor
241–271 CE	Sapor I becomes ruler of Persia
242–243 CE	Victorious Roman campaigns against the Persians
244–249 CE	Philip the Arab becomes emperor
248 CE	Rome celebrates its millennium
248–251 CE	Decius becomes emperor
251 CE	Decius killed in battle by Goths
251–253 CE	Trebonianus Gallus becomes emperor

253–260 CE	Valerian and his son Gallienus become co-emperors
253 CE	Persians invade and take Antioch
260 CE	Valerian captured by Persians
260–268 CE	Gallienus becomes sole emperor
260–272 CE	Zenobia seizes most of the Eastern Empire and Egypt but is defeated by Aurelian
274 CE	Postumus establishes a new empire in Gaul (261–268), ruled by Tetricus (270–274)
268–270 CE	Claudius II (Gothicus) becomes emperor
270–275 CE	Aurelian becomes emperor
276–282 CE	Probus becomes emperor
282–283 CE	Carus becomes emperor
283–285 CE	Carinus becomes emperor
283 CE	Carus campaigns in Persia
284–305 CE	Diocletian and Maximian become co-emperors
293 CE	Diocletian creates the tetrarchy with himself and Maximian as co-Augusti and Galerius and Constantius as co-Caesars
297 CE	The Empire is divided administratively into twelve dioceses
301 CE	The Edict of Maximum Prices is published
305 CE	Diocletian and Maximian abdicate; Galerius and Constantius become co-Augusti
306 CE	Constantine is declared co-Augustus after death of his father, Constantius
306 CE	Maxentius, son of Maximian, revolts against Constantine
308 CE	An imperial conference, held by Diocletian, starts a new round of civil wars
312 CE	Constantine's victory at Milvian Bridge give him control of Rome
313 CE	Constantine and his eastern rival, Licinius, reconcile and become co-emperors
313 CE	The co-emperors issue the Edict of Milan, ending the persecution of Christians
314 CE	A ten-year series of civil wars erupts
324 CE	Constantine becomes sole emperor
325 CE	The Council of Nicaea makes Christianity the official religion of the Empire
326 CE	Constantine makes Byzantium the Empire's new capital and renames it Constantinople

337 CE	Constantine dies
337 CE	The Empire is divided among Constantine's three sons, Constantine II (Western), Constans (Middle), and Constantius (Eastern)
338 CE	Constantius fights war against Persia's Sapor II; first siege of Nisibis
340 CE	Constans and Constantine II fight; Constantine II is killed at the Battle of Aquileia
344 CE	Persian victory at Singara
346 CE	Second unsuccessful siege of Nisibis by Sapor II
350 CE	Third siege of Nisibis. Because of trouble on his other frontiers, Sapor II makes a truce with Constantius. A usurper, Magnentius, murders Constans and becomes emperor in the west
351 CE	Magnentius defeated by Constantius II at the Battle of Mursa
352 CE	Italy recovered; Magnentius in Gaul
353 CE	Final defeat and death of Magnentius; Constantius becomes the Empire's sole ruler
356 CE	Julian dispatched as Caesar to Gaul, where he successfully fights the Alemanni, Quadi, and Sarmatians
357 CE	Challenge by Sapor II
359 CE	Sapor II invades Mesopotamia; Constantius goes to the east
360 CE	Julian and the Gallic army revolt
361 CE	Constantius dies; Julian becomes emperor
363 CE	Julian killed, and his army disastrously defeated by Persians; army proclaims Jovian emperor
364 CE	Jovian dies; Valentinian becomes emperor in the west, leaving his brother Valens to rule in the east
368 CE	War of Valens with Goths
369 CE	Peace with Goths
369–377 CE	Huns conquer the Ostrogoths
375 CE	Valentinian dies, and Gratian now rules in the west
377 CE	Valens allows Goths to settle on the south bank of the Danube in Moesia
378 CE	Gratian defeats Alemanni; Visigoths revolt; Valens is killed at the disaster at Adrianople
380 CE	Gratian replaces Valens with Theodosius

382 CE	Theodosius makes a treaty with the Goths allowing them to stay within the Empire
394 CE	Theodosius makes his son Honorius the western Augustus, with Stilicho as his military commander
395 CE	Theodosius dies; Arcadius and Honorius become co-emperors
396 CE	Alaric's Visigoths overrun the Balkans
397 CE	Alaric is militarily checked by Stilicho and is given Illyria in the terms of peace
402 CE	Alaric invades Italy but is checked by Stilicho
403 CE	Alaric retires after defeat at Pollentia; Ravenna becomes the imperial capital
405–406 CE	Germans led by Radagaisus invade Italy
406–407 CE	Alans, Sueves, and Vandals invade Gaul
407 CE	Constantine II revolts and establishes the Gallic Empire
408 CE	Honorius puts Stilicho to death; the youth Theodosius II succeeds Arcadius; Alaric invades Italy and makes Rome pay a ransom
409 CE	Alaric proclaims Attalus emperor
410 CE	Attalus deposed; Alaric sacks Rome
411 CE	Athaulf succeeds Alaric as king of the Visigoths; Constantine III is crushed by Constantius, ending the Gallic Empire
412 CE	Athaulf withdraws from Italy to Narbonne
417 CE	Visigoths establish themselves in Aquitania
420 CE	Ostrogoths settle in Pannonia
425 CE	Honorius dies; Valentinian III becomes emperor
427 CE	Revolt of Boniface in Africa
429 CE	Boniface invites the Vandals, under Geiseric, to migrate from Spain to Africa
433 CE	Aetius rises to power in Italy
434 CE	Attila becomes king of the Huns
439 CE	Geiseric takes Carthage, breaking the Roman tax spine
440 CE	Geiseric invades Sicily
441 CE	Attila crosses the Danube to attack Thrace
443 CE	Attila makes peace with the Eastern Empire under Theodosius II; the Burgundians settle in Gaul
447 CE	Attila invades the eastern provinces a second time
449 CE	Attila makes a second peace in return for a large tribute

450 CE	Marcian become eastern emperor and immediately halts payments to the Huns
451 CE	Attila invades Gaul, where he is defeated by Aetius and the Goths, under Theodoric I, at Châlons
452 CE	Attila invades Italy but spares Rome
453 CE	Attila dies; Theodoric II becomes king of the Visigoths
454 CE	The Hunnic Empire is overthrown by the subjected barbarians at the Battle of Netad; Valentinian III murders Aetius
455 CE	Murder of Valentinian II; Geiseric invades Italy and sacks Rome
456 CE	The Empire is dominated by the masters of the soldiers, Aspar the Alan (east) and Ricimer the Sueve (west)
457 CE	Ricimer deposes Avitus and makes Majorian emperor, while Aspar makes Leo the eastern emperor
460 CE	Destruction of Majorian's fleet off Cartagena
461 CE	Majorian deposed; Libius Severus becomes emperor.
465 CE	Libius Severus dies; Ricimer rules as patrician; Asper falls from power in the east
466 CE	Euric, king of the Visigoths, conquers Spain
467 CE	Leo appoints Anthemius western emperor
468 CE	Leo's great expedition under Basiliscus, sent to crush Geiseric, is destroyed
472 CE	Ricimer deposes Anthemius and set up Olybrius; death of Ricimer and Olybrius
473 CE	Glycerius becomes western emperor
474 CE	Julius Nepos becomes western emperor; Leo dies and is eventually succeeded in the east by Zeno the Isaurian
475 CE	Romulus Augustus becomes the last western emperor
476 CE	Odoacer deposes Romulus Augustus and ends the Roman Augustus of Constantinople; end of the Western Empire.

Introduction

Standing on the Shoulders of Giants

S IMILAR TO BOOKS on the battles of Gettysburg and Waterloo, the market for new works on the Roman Empire seems inexhaustible. In books, movies, plays, and just about any other media, writers and producers labor to meet an unquenchable thirst for retellings of all or part of the story of the glory of Rome. In fact, the night before I wrote this chapter, I fell asleep watching Amazon Prime's series *Britannia*. As I drifted off to sleep, I heard a character repeatedly shouting, "Behold the power of Rome." Still, demand for new works on the Roman Empire does not justify adding to the thousands of works already in print. That would require the historian to have uncovered new information or to have interpreted existing finds and evidence in a new way. I believe this work falls into the latter category.

The story of ancient Rome has always fascinated me, and over the years I have tried to keep up with the most important works published on the topic. But I am at heart and by training a military historian. Furthermore, although I am a scholar, I do not have an established specialty. Most historians, even military historians, are encouraged to specialize in one specific area, such as World War II or seventeenth-century warfare. Many of these historians maintain an interest in other areas, but the overwhelming thrust of the research in writing is in their selected specialty. Historians whose research and writing range from Plato to NATO are increasingly rare.

Moreover, I have spent decades in the military world as an infantry officer, with my time spent equally in the active forces and reserves. Upon retirement, I moved into the strategic world, first at the Institute for Defense Analyses—a think tank catering to the United States military's Joint Staff and Office of the Secretary of Defense—and then on to become a professor of strategic studies at the Marine Corps War College. Finally, I was appointed to the Marine Corps University's Horner Chair of War Studies. In each of these roles I have been involved in examining current and future strategic policy for the United States military. But I remain a historian who has been able to make good use of my studies of the past as a prism for peering into the future, for the past is always prologue. Moreover, if I do have a sub-specialty, it is in the economics and financing of great-power competition and conflict, factors upon which the foundation of any practicable strategy must be built.

I hope that my combination of over two decades as a military officer, fifteen years as a professional strategic analyst, and a lifetime of studying strategy and warfare will allow me to bring a unique viewpoint to the study of Roman strategy. I have been studying and teaching courses on the economics of strategy for fifteen years and wrote my dissertation on the economic foundations of World War II. While *Strategy of Empire* is not a book on Roman economics, I am convinced that without some grounding on the economic realities of the Empire, it is impossible to comprehend Roman strategic decision-making or the course of Roman history. Moreover, economics, the foundation of all strategy, is an area often neglected by historians and strategists including Edward Luttwak, who in his *Grand Strategy of the Roman Empire* failed to address the topic.[1] One wonders, given the importance of economics for formulating and implementing strategy, why it is absent from so many historical works. The best explanation I can offer is that political economy and finance are so removed from the expertise of historians and today's strategists that they ignore the topic. For instance, several years back I attended a conference focused on grand strategy at the Naval War College in Newport, Rhode Island. In the first moments of the opening speaker's talk, he said: "If we are here to talk about grand strategy or even strategy we must talk about economics, for if we are not discussing economics, we are not talking about strategy." This comment was loudly applauded by the approximately two hundred participants. But after the applause had quieted, the topic was never again addressed during the remaining four days of the conference.

One, however, must tread carefully when discussing economic and financial topics in the ancient world. For, as Everett Wheeler long ago warned me: "We know nothing about Roman economics; it is all assumptions and guesses piled atop of other assumptions and guesswork." I do not believe Wheeler was right when he said this to me, and he is certainly wrong now.

Over the last few decades, scholars in the field, including Peter Temin, Paul Erdkamp, Walter Scheidel, Ian Morris, Richard Saller, Andrew Wilson, Elio Lo Cascio, William Harris, Alan Bowman, and many others, have accomplished tremendous work. Building on the pioneering work of M. I. Rostovtzeff, Tenney Frank, and Richard Duncan Jones, scholars have greatly enlarged our knowledge and understanding of the Roman economy. Consequently, I do not have to be an expert on the foundational written, epigraphical, or archeological evidence on which these scholars base their conclusions, as I have the luxury of standing atop their shoulders. *Strategy of Empire*, therefore, does not break any new ground when discussing the economy of ancient Rome. Rather, it integrates the consensus of findings of those listed above into a wider examination of Roman strategic thinking, as well as how the economy impacted strategic decisions and their execution.[2]

Economics is not the only area of Roman scholarship where I get to stand on the shoulders of giants. In recent decades there has been an explosion of masterful works that have employed new research tools, methodologies, and discoveries to remake the field of Roman studies. I became aware of this explosion in the mid-2000s when I was listening to a cafeteria conversation between two well-known historians that was heading in the direction of a heated argument. The topic was the fall of the Western Roman Empire, and one participant heatedly declared the other's interpretation of events wrong.

The reply came back: "Have you read Wickham or Heather?" To which the first professor answered, "I have read Gibbon from cover to cover, and that's enough."

The exasperated reply came back: "If you have not read Wickham and Heather then you don't know anything about the topic . . . and I'm wasting my time." He then stood and stalked off. I excused myself soon after and went and ordered Peter Heather's and Chris Wickham's books and pored over them. That started fifteen years of reading works by great historians: David Potter, Fergus Millar, Benjamin Isaac, Noel Lenski, Michael Kulikowski, A. D. Lee, Hugh Elton, C. R. Whittaker, J. E. Lendon, Kenneth Harl, A. Cameron, Ward Perkins, Philip Sabin, Hans Van Wees, Michael Whitby, and a host of others. So, although I also read the works of all the great historians who wrote during the Empire, from Livy to Procopius, I did not have to interpret them or try and discover where they erred, exaggerated, or made stuff up. Others much better versed in the intricacies and pitfalls of dealing with ancient sources have already done the heavy lifting in that regard. So, although the *Historia Augusta* is a fascinating read, one must be extremely careful in its use, as much of it is clearly fabricated. Separating truth from fiction in the *Historia* has been the work of scholars who have dedicated their professional lives to the study of ancient Rome. It cannot be done by dedicated amateurs such as myself.

My contribution is to take the work of these scholars and add value in areas where I have a degree of expertise that these scholars do not typically possess or do not claim as a specialty. This includes practical knowledge of military planning and execution, strategic studies, and military history as a specialty.[3] Is it fair to ask what makes this approach valuable? My response rests upon the reception that most, but not all, historians of ancient Rome gave to Luttwak's *Grand Strategy of the Roman Empire.* He stole a march on many historians when he published his dissertation on Roman grand strategy by taking on a topic that had been generally neglected. Since then, a huge number of scholars have entered the fray. A few, very few, have supported Luttwak's interpretations, while most have condemned his findings and replaced them with their own interpretations of Roman motives and actions. The resulting historical consensus is that the Romans did not act on any preconceived strategic plan. Rather, their approach was always one of ad hoc responses as a succession of crisis events unfolded. In this scholarly paradigm, not only did Rome lack a grand strategy, but its ruling elites were incapable of even thinking in strategic terms.

I contend that the Romans were, for their time, very sophisticated strategic thinkers who possessed all the tools to plan long-term strategies and to act according to those plans. I will lay out my basic argument for this contrary opinion at the start of the book before delving into the specifics of Roman strategy during various periods of the Empire's history. In laying out my initial argument I take a contradictory position to many of the greatest historians in the field of ancient history. By no means should my comments on strategy be viewed as attacks on their scholarship, nor on their interpretations of the ancient sources. In fact, my narrative relies on their work. Where I take exception to their findings is in one narrow portion of their studies where scholars have made incorrect generalizations and interpretations in an area I have spent my professional life studying and employing in practice.

My two fondest hopes for this book are that many of you will find the creation and execution of Roman strategy as fascinating as I have, and that this book may spark a new round of debate as passionate and as fruitful as that provoked by Luttwak when he first addressed the topic.

PART I | Themes and Topics

CHAPTER 1 | Could the Romans Do Strategy?

B EFORE ADDRESSING THE question posed in the title of this chapter, we must take a short definitional diversion. Over the past few decades, an astonishing number of historians and modern strategic thinkers have tied themselves in knots arguing over whether the concept of strategy even existed before the end of the eighteenth century, when the word "strategy" finally made it into the lexicon. In this rendering, the notion of strategic thinking is a by-product of the Enlightenment, when learned persons placed great faith in man's ability to understand the world through empirical science and reason. War, the greatest of all human endeavors, was not excepted from this movement. This is really a matter of semantic interest, in much the same way as one can ask whether those who made "Greek fire" were employing chemistry, which was not generally recognized as a science until Antoine Lavoisier published *Elements of Chemistry* in 1787. Others were certainly thinking about strategy and acting on their ideas long before Enlightenment thinkers began to systematize our mental approaches to the topic.

In any event, strategy is always and everywhere a matter of ends, ways, and means, as seen through the prism of "risk." Half of the professional strategic thinkers reading this will scoff upon finishing that last sentence. The reasons for doing so are numerous, starting with the accusation that the very simplicity of the "ends, ways, means" paradigm just leaves out too much that is required to develop a firm understanding of the topic.[1] Still, the basis of any good model is simplicity, although we must keep in mind that simplicity seldom implies a lack of depth. Einstein's theory of relativity, for instance, has often been summarized on a postage stamp. In the case of defining strategy, as with $E = mc^2$, the complexity increases the more one ponders the practical realities of strategic thinking and execution.

If we can torture the analogy to Einstein's theory just a bit further, one might note that, despite its continuing relevance in explaining the macro universe, much of the theory's elegance has been overthrown by the weird chaos of the quantum world. Similarly, even the best-considered, most well-planned strategy will quickly fall into shambles once confronted by the chaotic challenges of the real world. Thus, the best strategies endure despite chaos because resilience and the capacity for rapid adaption were built into the strategy from the start. As Helmuth von Moltke the Elder, the general most responsible for winning the wars that united Germany into a single state, once said, "Strategy is a matter of expedients that takes it far beyond the realm of mere scholars."[2]

Typically, strategy, when applied to the interactions of states, is narrowly defined as the bridge between an established policy and the military aims necessary to achieve it. This is clearly what is meant by the term "military strategy." But a state's aims are not always achieved through military force, and a strategy focused entirely upon military affairs, without taking account of the economic, political, social, and diplomatic structures that underpin and support it, is doomed. This broader concept of strategy—commonly referred to as "grand strategy"—seeks to align all the resources and institutions of the state toward specific policy goals. At its highest level, the primary goal of any state is survival. What else a state can accomplish within a strategic global context rests upon the distribution of power within the system and must always be judged in relative terms.

Still, many a large forest has been sacrificed in order to publish works that define strategy, such that there are now thousands of definitions differentiated only by such subtleties that would bewilder Thomas Aquinas and the scholastics who surrounded him. So I am going to offer two sets of definitions. The first are those proposed by my own institution—the Marine Corps War College.

> In its simplest form, strategy is a theory on how to achieve a stated goal. . . . Another way to think about strategy is to consider how to get from a current state or condition to a desired state or condition.[3]

In Joint Publication 3.0—Joint Operations, the Joint Chiefs of Staff offer their definition of strategy.

> Strategy—A prudent idea or set of ideas for employing the instruments of national power in a synchronized and integrated fashion to achieve theater, national, and/or multinational objectives.[4]

American strategists also employ the DIME paradigm in their strategic thinking. DIME is an acronym for the process of integrating a myriad of diplomatic, informational, military, and economic strategies and concerns into a coherent grand strategy aimed at protecting and enhancing our national values and interests.

The interesting thing about strategy is that, like the nature of war, the purposes underlying its methodologies never change. Rome never came up with a fancy acronym for the lists of interests influencing grand strategy. Nor did they ever express their strategic thinking in terms of the "ends, ways, means" mode. But if they were doing any strategic thinking and acting on those thoughts, they were employing precisely these concerns and methods. The crucial question, therefore, is whether the Romans were capable of thinking about the future in strategic terms. This question has riled the field of Roman studies for two generations, and now that we have defined the terms, we can turn to the details of that debate.

In Book 1 of *Rhetoric*, Aristotle lists the subjects that all politicians and statesmen must be familiar with: "[They are] five in number: ways and means, war and peace, national defense, imports and exports, and legislation."[5] According to Aristotle, policymakers must, as part of mastering "ways and means," be familiar with the extent of the state's resources and their sources. Further, they must be thoroughly acquainted with how revenues are being expended by the state so that they are not wasted on superfluous pursuits.[6]

In terms of war and peace, Aristotle urges politicians to apply themselves to comprehending the extent of a state's actual and potential military strength, as well as that of enemy states. The philosopher also makes a strong case for the importance of studying military history to comprehend how states have waged war in the past, as well as specifically studying how potential foes have previously waged war. In modern strategy courses this would all be consolidated under ways and means, as would his comments on national defense: "[H]e ought to know all about the methods of defense in actual use, such as the strength and character of the defensive force and the positions of the forts—this last means that he must be well acquainted with the lie of the country—in order that . . . the strategic points may be guarded with special care."[7]

Aristotle's concern with imports and exports would be familiar to any current student enrolled in a strategic studies program, for he emphasizes gaining an appreciation of tracking what and how much is being traded between states—a very modern preoccupation. His prime concern, in this regard, was ensuring that rulers were taxing cargoes leaving and entering ports or crossing borders, a crucial source of revenue. Modern states see this comparison in increasingly mercantilist terms, but the crucial importance of these flows remains the same.

It is when Aristotle discusses legislation that we begin to see hints of Carl von Clausewitz's trinity—the people, the government, and the military.[8] For instance, he addresses the crucial importance of political institutions as a widely accepted legal framework in securing and enhancing the strength of the state.[9] Neither Aristotle nor Rome's ruling elite had a modern understanding of these issues, but they clearly understood their importance. Rome never came close to having perfect institutions—no state in history has ever been so blessed—but when one discusses strategy, what matters is not the perfection of one's institutions, but rather their relative superiority to rivals in terms of outcomes. Rome offered institutions and a legal structure superior to those of any previously found in the ancient world, and for most of the empire's existence its institutional framework was far superior to that of any of its competitors. Unfortunately, Rome, at least until Diocletian's reforms, never truly developed its administrative infrastructure much beyond that required to manage a city-state. But by working with local elites and absorbing their local economic and tax structures into the empire's greater edifice, Rome's organizational structure proved sufficient to rule a huge geographical area for nearly half a millennium.

Aristotle's ideas about what a statesman or policymaker should deeply consider can, with minimal rewording, be used to teach the foundations of strategic thinking in today's military's professional education system. If one took these ideas out of context and put them in front of a professor from any military war college, she would immediately recognize them as the underpinnings of all modern strategic thinking. The Romans had a passion for Greek culture and were devoted readers of Aristotle, as well as the histories of Herodotus and Thucydides, all of which would have been absorbed by every educated Roman. These histories are still taught to senior officers in every war college because, along with Aristotle's writing, they demonstrate a very sophisticated level of strategic thinking.

So, to assume that the Romans were incapable of thinking in strategic terms, one has to believe that somewhere between Aristotle putting his strategic-thinking framework on paper (or papyrus) and the advent of the Roman Empire, educated elites mysteriously lost their capacity to think about statecraft and empire in strategic terms. But this is precisely what the overwhelming numbers of Roman scholars have proposed and accepted since Luttwak published *The Grand Strategy of the Roman Empire*.[10] This historical consensus is elegantly presented in *The Cambridge Ancient History*:

It is probably incorrect to define Roman military policy in terms of long-term strategical objectives, which saw the emergence of various systems designed to achieve "scientific" defensible frontiers. For one thing, the Romans lacked a high command or government office capable of giving coherent direction to overall strategy, which was therefore left to the decision of individual emperors and their advisers. . . . Military decisions were probably ad hoc, as emperors were forced into temporary defensive measures to limit damage and then counterattacked when circumstances and resources allowed. . . . In any case, the Romans lacked the kind of intelligence information necessary to make far-reaching, empire-wide decisions. Indeed, they probably did not have a clear-cut view of frontiers, and came slowly to the idea that they should constitute a permanent barrier and form a delineation of Roman territory.[11]

Take a moment to ponder the meaning of this statement. If it is true, then we must accept that for five hundred years the empire spent as much as four-fifths of its tax revenue on a 450,000-man army; building and maintaining three thousand miles of fortified frontiers (*limes*), supported by tens of thousands of miles of military roads; and conducted hundreds of prolonged military campaigns—all without anyone ever once stopping to give any thought as to how all of this was put together. Security and war were the empire's overriding concerns and the primary business of the state. It is unimaginable that they approached such a monumental effort—sustained over five centuries— as a haphazardly constructed afterthought or in an ad hoc fashion. In a crisis, certain decisions may have been ad hoc—as they are today—but they were certainly made within a specific strategic context, which rulers and their counselors grasped and understood.[12]

Still, despite the obvious logic of the above observations, the overwhelming historical consensus is that Rome did not think in strategic terms, nor was it possible for Romans to do so. Several arguments have been marshaled to make this case, and it is best to take each of these in turn. The first revolves around Roman geographical ignorance and faulty comprehension of the geographical space within the empire and beyond. This debate has already been over-analyzed by modern scholars, but as this topic remains central to any denial of Roman capacity for strategic planning it must be tackled once again, starting with Susan Mattern, who argues: "The Roman view of the geographical world . . . seems at first schematic—that is, simplistic; too simplistic a framework for a complex geopolitical strategy."[13] In this Mattern is following in the footsteps of Benjamin Isaac, who, citing Fergus Millar, wrote that "the

Romans did not have a sufficiently clear or accurate notion of topographical realities to allow them to conceive of the overall military situation in global strategic terms."[14] What Rome did have, as Mattern repeatedly states, were itineraries (*itineraria*) that were used to plan travel from one point to another within the empire. From her perspective, such itineraries were fine for planning a party about to embark on an extended period of travel but useless for military or strategic planning. Isaac amplifies this by stating that it "requires only a glance to determine that such itineraries would be useless to today's military planners."[15] One wonders, then, why the fourth-century author Vegetius would recommend their use for that specific purpose. As he warns in *De Re Militari:*

> First, he should have thoroughly written out as fully as possible itineraries of all the regions in which the war is being waged, so that he can learn thoroughly the intervals between places, not only regarding the number of miles but even the quality of the roads, and inspect carefully the shortcuts, bypaths, mountains, and rivers, faithfully described; indeed the more prudent generals were fortified by having obtained itineraries of the provinces to which necessity used to take them, *which were not only annotated but even drawn.*[16]

By adding "even drawn," Vegetius is almost certainly describing the creation of maps, of the type many historians believe the Romans did not employ in their military operations. Isaac does comment on Vegetius's advice that troop movements should be planned by employing *itineraia picta* but agrees with Mattern that these picture-laden itineraries were of little use in strategic planning.

However, before judging whether itineraries were of any use for strategic planning, it helps to understand what a Roman itinerary looks like and what kinds of information it provided. One of the most famous itineraries, which is still extant, is the Antonine Itinerary (Figure 1.1): a list of place names with notations as to the distance between them. It dates from the third century CE and may have been created for Caracalla's campaigns in the east.[17] Any Roman general with access to this document or anything similar could instantly assess the daily march distances from start to stop, and just as easily calculate the distances along various routes from any point in the empire to any other point. The most famous and best-preserved of these itineraries with pictures is the *Tabula Peutingerianna*—the Peutinger Map (Figure 1.2).[18] This is not just a list of locations and distance, but more like a road map, presenting the information in graphic form. Roads are shown by lines, with the distances between towns and cities notated along each line. In addition

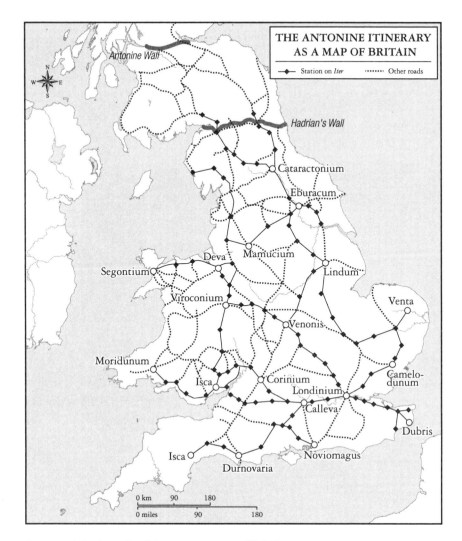

FIGURE 1.1 Antonine Itinerary as a map of Britain

to this kind of detailed itinerary, the Romans employed other sources of geographical data, but only a few of these have survived the centuries. The most famous that has come down to us are Strabo's *Geographica*, Ptolemy's *Geographia* and world map, and the Map of Agrippa—the *Orbis Terrarum*.[19]

Seen through modern eyes, these maps seem to have major problems, and the Roman worldview is certainly not ours. But how Rome saw the world is not the crucial question. Rather, one must ask whether the Romans' worldview, as well as their geographical tools—itineraries and basic maps— was sufficiently accurate to enable them to plan and execute strategy? Susan

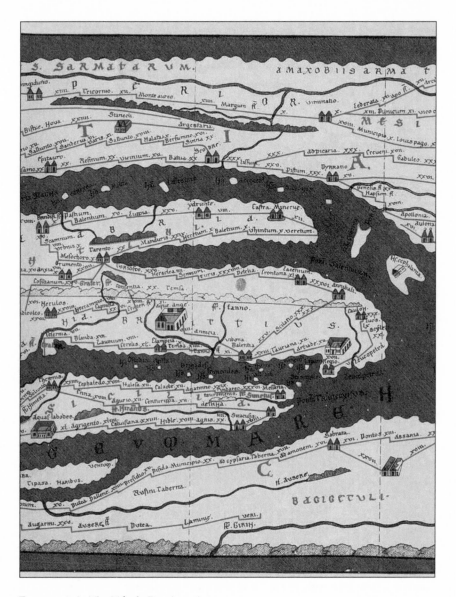

FIGURE 1.2 The Tabula Peutingeriana

Mattern, like most historians, believes it was not: "Modern policy makers would not dream of conducting foreign policy relations or planning a war, much less undertaking one, without accurate scaled maps."[20] This statement is not correct. Maps with the detail and accuracy of the kind most historians declare necessary for the planning of strategy and the conduct of military operations did not really exist until the Austro-Hungarian Empire undertook to map much of Western Europe, a task not completed and published until the eve of World War I.[21] Yet no one claims that when Napoleon was crawling over the inferior maps of his era, sometimes bumping heads with his chief cartographer, General Bacler de l'Able, that he was not engaged in strategic campaign planning.[22] If adequate maps are the basic foundational necessity for strategic planning, then no state or army was capable of plotting strategy before the modern era. But we find Vegetius advising a Roman general:

> If any difficulty arises about the choice of roads, he should procure proper and skillful guides. He should put them under a guard and spare neither promises nor threats to induce them to be faithful. They will acquit themselves well when they know it is impossible to escape and are certain of being rewarded for their fidelity or punished for their perfidy.[23]

Similarly, Frederick the Great, during the Seven Years' War (1756–1763), advised his generals that, when seeking intelligence about an area, they should find a rich citizen with a large family and reward him for information, while at the same time promising to hack his family to death before his eyes if he is less than truthful.[24] Clearly Frederick, commanding approximately fifteen hundred years after Vegetius wrote his instructions, was still having problems getting accurate maps on which to plan campaigns and battles. Still, no one believes that Frederick or the other generals and statesmen of the era were incapable of strategic planning.

The fact is that Roman itineraries provide exactly the type of information required for strategic planning, particularly in its military dimensions. President Bill Clinton once said, during a visit to the aircraft carrier USS *Theodore Roosevelt*, "When word of crisis breaks out in Washington, it's no accident the first question that comes to everyone's lips is: where is the nearest carrier?"[25] Neither Clinton nor the Joint Chiefs had any concern about global geography beyond the distance of the carriers to the crisis area and how long it would take them to make the transit. Henry Kissinger once called aircraft carriers "100,000 tons of diplomacy." Similarly, Rome's legions were the "mobile diplomacy" of the empire. In any crisis, there were only three things an emperor needed to know: where the crisis was, how far from the crisis the nearest available legions were, and how long it would take the legions to travel between these two points. Simply put, no emperor had to know a single geographical fact that was not included in the itineraries of the time. In them, an emperor and his advisers would find detailed information about distances for each leg of the legions' marching route. From that point it was all about assigning commanders, issuing orders for the legions to march, and prepositioning supplies—food and fodder—along the route of the march. This last task was easily accomplished by sending messengers to each stopping point on the itinerary or by the legions sending officers ahead.

Interestingly, while doing some research on the Battle of Yorktown, I came across a map employed by Generals Washington and Rochambeau to move their combined forces from Rhode Island and New York to Yorktown. Like the itinerary-based maps the Romans must have used, the only markings on Washington's maps were the routes of the march and the planned stopping points each evening. All the geographical space along those routes was a matter of supreme indifference to the Allied commanders and their staffs. And, as the Romans must have done, Washington and Rochambeau sent messengers ahead of the armies whose job was to order food that would be collected along each point listed on the map. In short, the tools available to the Romans were those still being employed nearly two millennia later by generals and statesmen who found them sufficient for their strategic needs. The reality of Roman strategic thinking was that they employed a point-to-point analysis to strategy and crisis resolution. Their primary concern was distances and time. When the need arose to move from point A to point B, the fact that the Alps might be in the way was of little concern. What mattered was the number of days it took to cross the space, whether it was occupied by rolling grasslands, deserts, or mountains.

Interestingly, in the war-gaming world, many designers have discovered that the easiest way to think about and simulate the strategic level of any conflict is through using point-to-point designs (itineraries) that look a lot like the Peutinger Map. One of the best war games simulating Roman strategic issues—*Pax Romana*—also employs a point-to-point methodology to address how Rome reacted to problems.

What served the Romans well still underpins how today's generals and statesmen plan and execute military-based strategic endeavors. When planning for crises in any part of the world, almost all military planners start with an analysis of the hubs and nodes that make up the various transport networks. Thus, when planners are told to move military forces halfway across the world, they do not think about maps as most of us would. Rather, they think in terms of networks filled with pathways and nodes where the major variable is the mode of travel—air, land, or sea—and includes basic information, such as how long it takes to go between nodes and the carrying capacity of the vehicles involved. Until the troops are in close contact and fighting, the underlying geographical aspects involved in military operations are barely a consideration. In fact, Systems and Network Centric Warfare, which is based on protecting one's crucial nodes while wrecking those of an enemy, has now become the basis of almost all military planning.[26] Anyone receiving a briefing on current military plans would be struck by the fact that there is no requirement for a geographic map. To strategic planners, all of the geographic features and pretty colors on common maps are nothing but eye candy.

Handed a list of nodes, transit speeds for various modes of travel, and the capacity of each node and pathway to handle traffic, military strategists can deploy the full might of the U.S. military anywhere in the world without ever referencing a geographic map. One can easily see how such information, once set down on paper, begins to look suspiciously like the itineraries the Romans worked with. In short, if a Roman emperor wants to think about future strategy or react to a major crisis in a distant part of the empire, itineraries are the perfect instrument for doing so. Moreover, the Romans, although they never spelled out their approach in manuals, clearly understood the crucial importance of nodes (towns, cities, fortresses, etc.) and paths (the Roman road network, rivers, and the Mediterranean). The evidence, far from indicating that the Romans did not have the geographic tools to think in strategic terms, demonstrates the exact opposite: Rome possessed the precise basic tools that would enable a level of sophisticated strategic thinking comparable to that of the modern era.

Rome's supposed lack of interest in maps or geographical intelligence has been extended by historians to suggest that they had a dearth of information regarding the empire's separate theaters of conflict. This would mean that for nearly a thousand years Roman military commanders conducted military campaigns without any knowledge of the local terrain, possible marching routes, or where their enemies might be—that Rome chose simply to plunge into the unknown and hope for the best. This is absurd. Voluminous evidence in the historical record demonstrates that Roman commanders took a tremendous interest in local geography and were fully capable of planning huge campaigns over vast distances. For instance, in 6 CE, Augustus gave his approval for the destruction of the Germanic Marcomanni confederation under its king, Maroboduus. This was no mean undertaking, as many of the tribe's warriors had at times found employment as Roman auxiliaries and were therefore expertly familiar with Roman methods of war. As Velleius Paterculus, one of Tiberius's staff officers, states: "The body of guards protecting the kingdom of Maroboduus, which by constant drill had been brought almost to the Roman standard of discipline, soon placed him in a position of power that was dreaded even by our empire."[27]

To remove this looming threat, Augustus had his general, Tiberius, the future emperor, mobilize twelve legions and planned a pincer movement from two widely separated provinces. Even conceiving of such a plan, never mind executing the logistics of such a vast enterprise, requires huge amounts of staff work, underpinned by a healthy understanding of the enemy forces, as well as the distances and geography involved. Velleius Paterculus certainly showed a deep knowledge of the threat posed by Maroboduus's huge, highly trained army as well as of the threat created by the geography of the region:

> His army, which he had brought up to the number of seventy thousand foot and four thousand horse. . . . He was also to be feared on this account, that, having *Germany at the left and in front of his settlements, Pannonia on the right, and Noricum in the rear of them*, he was dreaded by all as one who might at any moment descend upon all. Nor did he permit Italy to be free from concern as regards his growing power, *since the summits of the Alps which mark her boundary were not more than two hundred miles distant from his boundary line*. Such was the man and such the region that Tiberius Caesar resolved to attack from opposite directions in the course of the coming year. Sentius Saturninus had instructions to lead his legions through the country of the Catti into Boiohaemum, for that is the name of the region occupied by Maroboduus, cutting a *passage through the Hercynian forest which bounded the region, while from Carnuntum, the nearest point of Noricum in this direction*, he [Tiberius] himself undertook to lead against the Marcomanni the army which was serving in Illyricum.[28]

This great attack was called off when the legions had to be diverted to put down the Pannonian Revolt (6–9 CE). As a consequence of the Varian Disaster—when three legions were annihilated deep in the German forests in 9 CE—another attack into Marcomanni territory was not contemplated again for over 150 years, during the reign of Marcus Aurelius. Before moving on, it is worth noting another expedition deep into Germany, also led by Tiberius. As recounted by Paterculus:

> A Roman army with its standards was led four hundred miles beyond the Rhine as far as the river Elbe, which flows past the territories of the Semnones and the Hermunduri. And with this wonderful combination of *careful planning* and good fortune on the part of the general, and a close watch upon the seasons, the fleet which had skirted the windings of the sea coast *sailed up the Elbe . . . effected a junction with Caesar and the army*, bringing with it a great abundance of supplies of all kinds.[29]

Consider both examples. The first called for one pincer starting from modern Mainz to meet the other arm of the pincer, which started from the great Roman fortress of Carnuntum, well to the east of Vienna. The vast distances involved cover almost the same geographical area as Napoleon's Ulm-Austerlitz campaign and Wagram campaign—some eighteen hundred years later. The second example is even more remarkable, as it called for co-ordinating the actions of two forces out of contact with one another—an army fighting its way across hostile territory and a naval force navigating in waters where no Roman fleet had ever sailed. Nearly sixteen hundred years later, in 1588, despite two years of planning, the Spanish Armada, in a similar enterprise in approximately the same region, failed to link up with the Spanish Army of Flanders to invade England. It was not until General William T. Sherman's army arrived at Savannah, Georgia in 1864 and found a resupply fleet waiting for them that an enterprise of similar scope and hazards was again accomplished by design.[30]

The point is that neither expedition could be planned, never mind executed, without a huge amount of geographical information and comprehension. Further examples of Roman geographic knowledge and its employment in the conduct of military campaigns litter the ancient literature. This makes one thing certain: the Romans had a thorough grasp of the geography within the bounds of their empire, as well as huge swaths of territory immediately beyond their borders. Moreover, as the two examples above demonstrate, the Romans had a clear idea of the capacity and capabilities of the threats within these regions. That does not mean that surprises, such as the Varian Disaster, were impossible. In truth, Rome was often caught unawares, and Roman armies suffered many embarrassments. But for the most part these were the result of misreading an enemy's intent, not a lack of knowledge of their capabilities.[31]

Rome's supposed lack of geographic knowledge has fed one of the more enduring myths of Roman studies: that they had no idea of a fixed frontier on the other side of which security threats lay. Frontiers instead being simply zones or districts within which Rome managed economic and diplomatic affairs with its neighbors. Two of the greatest authorities on the Roman frontiers have declared that the frontiers—*limes*—were an administrative concept unconnected with the military structures that might be found within them.[32] The historian David Cherry, in *The Cambridge Ancient History*, neatly sums up where this burgeoning consensus has led: "[N]one of the frontiers appear to have been wholly defensive in purpose, partly also because the Romans themselves do not seem to have considered the frontiers to be either lines of defense or demarcation. It is now widely agreed instead that the frontiers functioned as zones or borderlands." As far as Cherry is concerned, the Romans themselves never understood that the frontiers behaved militarily or administratively. In this view, there is "little reason to believe that the Roman authorities considered it to be their duty to protect the provincial populations against those who lived beyond the frontiers." Finally, Cherry maintains that even if the imperial government desired to develop a coherent defensive system of defensive barriers and fortifications, "it is unlikely that it could have overcome the delays of communications and transportation that were a necessary consequence of the vast distances which separated the frontiers from the capital, and from each other."[33] But that is exactly what the Romans did: they overcame vast distances and built an integrated system of defensive structures over thousands of miles of frontiers.

Cherry may represent the consensus of historians, but this view flies in the face of the evidence and common sense. As to the questions of whether the Romans considered the frontiers a defensive barrier, it is probably best to let the Romans speak for themselves. As Aristides wrote:

> Beyond the outermost ring of the civilized world, you drew a second line, quite as one does in walling a town. . . . An encamped army like a rampart encloses the civilized world in a ring . . . [defended by] a barrier of men who have never acquired the habit of flight. . . . Such are the parallel harmonies or systems of defense which curve around you, that circle of the fortifications at individual points, and that ring of those who keep watch over the whole world . . . all this one can call a ring and circuit of the walls.[34]

He is joined by Appian, who wrote: "They surround the empire with great armies, and they garrison the whole stretch of land and sea like a single strong-hold."[35] Herodian, writing in the third century CE, added: "When Augustus established his sole rule, he relieved Italians of their duties and stripped them of their arms. In their place he established a defensive system of forts of the empire . . . as if to act as a barricade for the Roman Empire. He also fortified the empire by hedging it round with major obstacles, rivers and trenches and mountains and deserted areas which were difficult to traverse."[36]

While Herodian's comments are more closely related to the situation in the second century CE than they are to the reign of Augustus, he and the others quoted above clearly envision a Roman Empire protected by a strong defensive system manned by Rome's legions. A later author, Zosimus, even condemned the Emperor Constantine for weakening this defensive system to man his mobile field armies—the *comitatenses*—blaming the emperor for adopting measures that gave the barbarians free access to Roman dominions.

As Zosimus saw it, Diocletian, by rebuilding the frontier defenses had secured the empire from barbarian invasion; Constantine, however, by removing soldiers from the frontiers, had destroyed that security: "Thus, he stripped the frontiers of protection and by moving the soldiers to interior cities, made the soldiers effeminate by accustoming them to public spectacles and pleasures."[37] Zosimus, a pagan who tended to blame everything that went wrong with the Roman Empire on its first Christian emperor, is likely not the most reliable writer to interpret the reasons and causes of events, but the point here is that his comments, like the others, demonstrate that the Romans undoubtedly believed they possessed a clearly demarcated, heavily fortified, and well-garrisoned frontier that would defend the empire from enemies beyond it.[38]

Historians looking to deny what the Romans so clearly stated have been forced to make diversionary arguments and increasingly strange assertions. For instance, as the term *limes* appears to have changed definition several times over the empire's five hundred years of existence, Isaac uses these changing definitions to claim that we cannot accept that the military installations found along the *limes* (when they are defined as a line), and throughout the *limes* (when they are defined as a region) necessarily had a military function.[39] Here he is joined by Whittaker, who believes, as a result of having discovered evidence that the Roman fortress of Qasr Bshir in Jordan was employed for civilian administrative purposes, that we have been too quick to describe frontier buildings as defensive installations,[40] even though a photograph of Qasr Bshir still clearly shows battle towers and crenellated walls. One wonders why these historians never asked why a purely administrative center would need such stout and costly defenses; surely the location would be just as efficient as an administrative or trading center without them. The expense of such extensive walls can be justified only if they were meant for security.[41] Following Whittaker, many historians believe that the Roman frontiers should be thought of more as a zone than a line. In this Whittaker is almost certainly correct; where he goes wrong is his claim that the structures within these zones served to conduct mostly, if not entirely, administrative and economic functions, as if such purposes could not coexist with a military role. After all, most medieval castles and fortresses performed administrative and economic functions, but no one doubts their concurrent role as military installations.

So what are these historians missing? For one, how the definition of *limes* changed over the centuries is not important. This is a semantic battle that does little to mask actual events on the ground, where it is impossible not to notice that the Romans invested huge sums in constructing a network of walls, fortresses, forts, naval bases, and towers along the entire length of the Rhine and Danube. Because some of these defensive works were not optimally sited, Isaac would have us believe that we cannot divine the true nature of the whole. But we most certainly can do this through the application of a bit of common sense. Walls are built for only two reasons: to keep someone in or to keep someone out. In Rome's case, these extensive lines of fortifications and supporting infrastructure aimed to stop or delay an invasion force before it could seriously threaten the empire. True, throughout the Roman defensive systems one will, here and there, find a fort that does not appear to have been ideally situated for defensive purposes. All that means is that additional factors must have influenced the location of certain forts and bases. Consider the world today. The United States is littered with well-maintained bases that serve no immediate security need but are located in a powerful politician's district. Rome was not immune to such pressures.

Isaac holds that the great Danube and Rhine rivers were not barriers and that the Romans never thought of them as such. He claims that they were easily crossed by boats and rafts and thus cannot be considered much of an obstacle. He cites Batavian tribesmen trained to swim the Danube with their weapons as an example of why rivers are not truly natural obstacles in a military sense.[42] However, an invading force will need to cross with thousands of troops, pack animals, and wagons.

Pace Isaac, throughout history rivers have presented a natural obstacle, one that works against military movements. That a few exceptional swimmers were trained to cross them scarcely lessens the difficulties that would confront an entire army trying to cross rivers, such as the Rhine and the Danube, that were over a mile wide along most of their course. One should also keep in mind that Roman soldiers were well aware of a crucial point of military doctrine that is still repeatedly drilled into every young military officer: obstacles not covered by troops or firepower are not obstacles. As such, neither the Danube nor the Rhine was ever meant to stand alone against an onrushing horde. That is why Rome reinforced these natural barriers with the most extensive network of fortifications in the ancient world, a network of such grand scope and huge cost that its like was not seen again until the age of Vauban, during the reign of Louis XIV—which, interestingly, saw huge fortifications emplaced in many of the same areas Rome chose to fortify. Within and behind them typically stood fifteen or more of Rome's legions. It was the combination of natural barriers, reinforced with a massive defensive infrastructure manned by the stout legions of Rome, that created a military-centered frontier zone. Too many historians have broken these elements down to their constituent parts and analyzed them separately, leading them to claim, erroneously, that Rome did not have coherent strategic plans. But none of these parts was ever intended to stand or operate alone. Rather, they were designed from the start to be integrated, creating a synergistic effect that maintained the frontiers almost inviolate for the first two hundred years of the empire's existence. It is one thing to have a band of barbarians crossing the Rhine by swimming or in hastily made boats; it is quite another to do so when there was a legion waiting to hack them to death as they came ashore.

Historians appear to understand these facts when they consider movement going in the other direction. In these cases, Roman advances beyond the established frontier zones are always fraught with such difficulties and perils as to make the idea of further conquests too costly to consider. One historian, trying to build this case, quotes an anonymous fourth- or fifth-century source—*De rebus bellicis* (On Military Affairs):

> First of all, it must be recognized that frenzied native tribes, yelping everywhere around, hem the Roman empire in, and that treacherous barbarians, protected by natural defenses, menace every stretch of our frontiers. For these peoples to whom I refer are for the most part either hidden by forests or lifted beyond our reach by mountains or kept from us by the snows; some, nomadic, are protected by deserts and the blazing sun. There are those who, defended by marshes and rivers, cannot even be located easily, and yet they tear peace and quiet to shreds by their unforeseen attacks.[43]

Isaac considers this passage to be of great significance because it was written by a man of military experience and demonstrates that natural defenses, far from being a defensive barrier, acted as an obstacle that prevented the Romans from acting against their enemies. Why he and others suppose that such natural obstacles hinder the movements and actions only of the Romans and not of "native tribes" is difficult to understand.[44]

Major rivers also served other crucial purposes, which made them the natural foundation of any defensive network. For one, they greatly eased logistical and transport problems. The Rhine and Danube were huge highways that alleviated much of the burden of supplying the legions camped alongside them while also providing high-speed avenues of approach when Rome needed to move troops from one sector of the empire to another. Roman legions would have been drawn toward the great European rivers if for no other reason than ease of transport.

Before moving on, it is crucial that two other misapplications of strategic understanding be put to rest. First is the argument that Romans could not have considered the frontiers we have identified as true or permanent frontiers, because they so often sent large military forces beyond them. This imputes to the Romans a siege mentality akin to that of France in 1940, hiding behind its Maginot Line and hoping the Germans would stay on the other side. But this was not the Roman way. For at least the first few centuries of empire, a single imperative appears coded into Rome's strategic DNA: seek out and obliterate troubling populations before they became a threat. The Romans never considered their fortress frontier zones as a final bulwark against the barbarians (Figure 1.3). Instead, the zones doubled as secure bases from which to gather forces and resources to go deep into enemy territory and strike Rome's foes before they could assemble and organize in such numbers as to make a breakthrough into the heart of the empire a real possibility. Of course, as the threats on the other side of the frontiers changed and Rome's capacity became increasingly feeble, Roman incursions became less frequent. Nonetheless, for most of the empire's existence the frontiers were both defensive barriers and staging areas for offensives. Whittaker once called upon historians to give up on the myth that the Roman frontiers were an iron curtain through which nothing passed.[45] In this regard he was correct; but he was thinking in terms of trade, not about how often Rome sent its armies beyond the frontier zones.

The idea has also been put forward and generally accepted that Rome could not possibly have had an all-encompassing theory or, as Susan Mattern calls it, "a coherent empire-wide plan" because they employed dissimilar approaches in different frontier zones. This fragmentation of approaches based on different situations is held up as proof that Rome was incapable of thinking about grand strategy and hence simply defaulted to several local expedients.[46] As modern strategists see it, however, historians have gotten it exactly backward: it would have been the height of strategic folly to employ the same approach throughout the empire when local circumstances dictated different solutions. So, rather than displaying a paucity of strategic thinking, the capacity to employ different strategic methodologies based on circumstances—ends, ways, and means—demonstrates a highly sophisticated strategic appreciation.

One further reason often presented for why the Romans lacked the capacity to think strategically and to create and execute long-term plans is the lack of a general staff or its ancient equivalent. In the modern era, such a staff is responsible for strategic plans and the coordination of major operations. Historians are willing to concede that Roman emperors and even governors employed a *consilium* to advise them on crucial matters of state and justice. According to Dio, the *consilium*'s membership could vary but usually consisted of the consuls, trusted advisers, and fifteen senators, the

FIGURE 1.3 Reconstruction of a Roman fortress, Saalburg, Germany

latter rotated out every six months.[47] And while the power of the *consilium* varied from emperor to emperor, it gradually gained in power and influence as it took on the duties of administering the empire. So what likely started as an informal body of *amici* (friends) became increasingly formalized until by the reign of Constantine it was a separate department of the imperial government—the *sacrum consistorium*. Of course, the *consilium* was by no means a general staff or its ancient equivalent, but its existence demonstrates that there was a body of learned men to advise and assist the emperor. Also, it must be noted that until the Prussians created a planning staff in the nineteenth century, no ruler in history ever had such an entity. Does that mean that Alexander, Gustavus Adolphus, and Napoleon were incapable of strategic thinking? As Everett Wheeler asks, "Should we accept the view that the institution consuming, even on a conservative estimate, 40 to 50 percent of the state's revenues and the most bureaucratized and best-documented aspect of Roman government lacked administrative oversight and planning?"[48] In fact, the Romans maintained a huge military administrative apparatus throughout both the Republic and the empire. How could it have been otherwise? Without such an administrative and planning function, it would be impossible to arm, pay, and feed a far-flung army. Moreover, without some degree of strategic forethought Rome could not fight wars on multiple fronts, as it did many times in its history. As Wheeler points out, "Roman capability in maintaining its army, as well as an emperor's ability to transfer units from one frontier to another and to assemble expeditionary forces for major wars, clearly indicates that general staff work was done, even if the specific mechanisms of higher command and control remain one of the arcana of Roman government."[49]

There is clear evidence that the Romans kept excellent military records throughout the centuries of empire. Tacitus mentions one such document that was read to the Roman Senate soon after Augustus's death in 14 CE:

> This contained a description of the resources of the State, of the number of citizens and allies under arms, of the fleets, subject kingdoms, provinces, taxes, direct and indirect, necessary expenses and customary bounties. All these details Augustus had written with his own hand, and had added a counsel, that the empire should be confined to its present limits, either from fear or out of jealousy.[50]

That such records existed is clear from a later section of Tacitus quoted below. Considering that nearly a hundred years had passed before Tacitus wrote his account of the period, he must have had extensive records to consult as he outlined the dispositions of the empire's military forces for the year 23 CE. It is also notable that Tacitus not only knew where the legions and fleets were but also was keenly aware of their purpose. It certainly appears that someone in 23 CE was thinking in strategic terms and laid out such notions so clearly that Tacitus could reiterate them almost a century later:

> Italy on both seas was guarded by fleets, at Misenum and at Ravenna, and the contiguous coast of Gaul by ships of war captured in the victory of Actium, and sent by Augustus powerfully manned to the town of Forojulium. But chief strength was on the Rhine, as a defense alike against Germans and Gauls, and numbered eight legions. Spain, lately subjugated, was held by three. Mauretania was king Juba's, who had received it as a gift from the Roman people. The rest of Africa was garrisoned by two legions, and Egypt by the same number. Next, beginning with Syria, all within the entire tract of country stretching as far as the Euphrates, was kept in restraint by four legions, and on this frontier were Iberian, Albanian, and other kings, to whom our greatness was a protection against any foreign power. Thrace was held by Rhoemetalces and the children of Cotys; the bank of the Danube by

two legions in Pannonia, two in Moesia, and two also were stationed in Dalmatia, which, from the situation of the country, were in the rear of the other four, and should Italy suddenly require aid, not too distant to be summoned. But the capital was garrisoned by its own special soldiery, three city, nine praetorian cohorts, levied for the most part in Etruria and Umbria, or ancient Latium and the old Roman colonies. There were besides, in commanding positions in the provinces, allied fleets, cavalry and light infantry, of but little inferior strength. But any detailed account of them would be misleading, since they moved from place to place as circumstances required, and had their numbers increased and sometimes diminished.[51]

This passage also lays low another one of Isaac's key claims: that if the Romans had any conception of modern strategic principles, "they kept quiet about it." Tacitus presents clear evidence that Roman were specifically thinking in terms of mobile defense at the strategic level. As he states, the eight legions on the Rhine were given two crucial missions: to defend against the Germans and to handle any trouble that might arise in recently pacified Gaul, while the Dalmatian legions are tasked with supporting the four legions on the Danube and, if required, marching to the aid of Italy. As James Thorne has pointed out, "This is a strategy of mobile defense, if anything is."[52]

David Potter believes that the Romans had lost little of the knowledge imparted by Aristotle centuries before. As Cicero claimed, for a senator to "know the state" he had to know the state of the army, the treasury, and the allies, friends, and tributaries of Rome, along with the attachment of each to Rome.[53] It would be difficult to find a more succinct understanding of the underpinning of all strategic thinking: financial strength that paid for the military forces that were the foundation of Roman power. Cicero also warned, in an observation as true two thousand years later as it was then, that even a state possessed of overwhelming financial and military power could see its advantages thrown away by political imbecility.

Almost four hundred years after Cicero's death the *Notitia Dignitatum* was compiled. This remarkable work, one of the few documents from the Roman chanceries to survive into the modern era, contains a complete accounting of the Western Roman Empire in the 420s and the Eastern Roman Empire in the 400s. It lists all court officials, vicars, and provincial governors, arranged by praetorian prefecture and diocese. Moreover, it lists by name all military commanders (*magistri militum, comites rei militaris,* and *duces*), along with their stations and the regiments under their control.

In short, it is a complete record of the military formations of the empire, along with their locations.[54] Between Cicero's death and the completion of the *Notitia Dignitatum* we have numerous references to censuses and other strategic assessments that would only be made if they were meant to be consulted for strategic purposes. As Wheeler has noted, "If emperors kept detailed records on military strengths and location of troops, did they then fail to ponder their use?"[55]

Finally, let us turn back to David Cherry's overview of Roman strategy, or the lack thereof, to a comment that demands some further analysis: "There is also little reason to believe that the Roman authorities considered it to be their duty to protect the provincial populations against those who lived beyond the frontiers."[56] This viewpoint encapsulates a view that fails to account for either the evidence or common sense. Although no surviving document unequivocally states that the highest purpose of Roman government is to protect the people, one can understand the priorities of Romans through their actions. If they did not care about protecting the civil populations—or, if one is ungenerous, protecting the tax revenues that a secure population provided the empire—there would be absolutely no reason to post thirty legions and a similar number of auxiliaries along the Roman frontiers. Rome undertook this tremendous military effort for the express purpose of securing the provinces and populations of the empire. One must ignore five hundred years of Roman military exertion to believe otherwise.

Coupling the idea that Rome did not truly care about the empire's peoples with the notion that Rome had no conception of the empire's geography negates both the need for a large military establishment as well as any hopes of deploying one in a useful manner. Following this logic means that Rome, for five hundred years, paid for a huge military force without ever being able to articulate a practical justification for its maintenance. Moreover, Rome somehow, by some act of supreme serendipity, managed to post this force along the frontiers, where they were most needed. If the Romans possessed no understanding of geography or capacity for strategic planning, could one assume they were just as likely to have their legions sunning themselves along the Mediterranean coast as to find them posted along desolate frontier zones? But if we accept that Rome's placement of its legions in the absolute best positions to counter the known threats was not purely the result of a magnificent accident, then we must also accept that the Romans were capable of thinking in strategic terms, as well as of planning and executing strategic concepts.

Another idea that has gained currency recently is the notion that the barbarians on the other side of the Roman frontiers were not as dangerous as the ancients made them out to be. If this is true, then for fifty decades Rome wasted vast sums of money securing itself from enemies that rarely raised themselves above the nuisance level. But is it true? That is what we will discover next.

CHAPTER 2 | How Dangerous Were
the Barbarians?

Morning dew lay heavy on the grass when the first of the invading
archers drew back on his bow. For several long seconds the unknown
archer strained while maintaining careful aim. Only when he heard the
roaring battle cry of the massed warriors around him did he relax his fingers
and release his deadly missile. As the shaft flew, dozens of mounted warriors
charged an enemy they had hoped to surprise but instead found drawn up
into a shield wall.

In the tumult, our unnamed archer could be forgiven for failing to note
that his flint-tipped arrow had struck home, sinking deep into the upper
arm of an opponent fifty yards distant. What he surely did not miss were the
horses tumbling into the river as man and beast were brought down by opposing archers. As he drew back another arrow, he could also clearly see the
gold, tin, and copper bands the rich enemy warriors had adorned themselves
with for battle and began to consider how he could position himself to be
among the first to start looting the bodies.

As both sides' arrows flew, the opposing battle lines rushed upon one another, coming together in a crashing impact. The end of the battle was not
far off now, for there is a limit to how long men can stand toe to toe trying to
kill each other. Few could long stand the physical and mental fatigue of close
combat, so battles of the period almost always ended in just a few minutes,
as one side or the other was overcome by fear and exhaustion. But in those
few brutal minutes, hundreds of men died—probably a quarter or more of
those involved.

In the end, the invaders were repulsed. As the defeated war bands fled past him, our archer hazarded a final look at the battlefield; then, forgetting his dreams of glory and riches, he raced off.

As he ran, he could hear the defenders cheering and shouting their victory chant: "Out . . . Out . . . Out!" Although exhausted, the victors' bloodlust was up and they were soon rushing after their routed foes, striking many of them down from behind. The slaughter abated only when increasing numbers of the victorious warriors stopped to loot the dead. For one fleeting moment, our archer considered his chances of retrieving some gold off the dead cavalrymen, but, not liking the odds, he soon took flight again, joining his brethren on the long trek home.

The above reflects one plausible reconstruction of a clash of armies twelve centuries before the birth of Christ at a wooden bridge crossing the Tollense River, a hundred miles north of Berlin near the Baltic Sea.[1] As many as five thousand warriors fought that day, and more than a thousand of them were killed. What they were fighting over has been lost to the mists of time, but some assumptions are easily made. First, the sheer size of the forces makes it nearly impossible to believe that this was a fight between locals or even the massed war bands of the entire region. The archaeological evidence bears this out: strontium, oxygen, and carbon isotopes in the teeth conclusively demonstrate that most of the warriors who died that day came from hundreds of miles off. Furthermore, nitrogen isotopes in the bones indicate a diet heavy in millet, which was a rare foodstuff in northern Europe.[2] Well-preserved bones and artifacts recovered from the area of the battle draw a picture of a relatively sophisticated society capable of maintaining a large warrior class and able to draw military support from a wide swath of Europe.[3] According to the University College Dublin (UCD) archaeologist Barry Molloy, "This is that smoking gun" forcing historians to tear up most of what they thought they knew about the wealth and sophistication of northern Europe proto-civilizations.[4]

Archaeologists note that the Battle of Tollense Valley was fought beside a bridge that for five hundred years had formed a crucial connection along a major trade artery linking the Baltic amber deposits with the Oder River, and then onward to the Bronze Age civilizations around the eastern Mediterranean and Mesopotamia.[5] Amber, used for decoration and jewelry, was prized throughout the ancient world and remains in demand even today.[6] But the Tollense region was also a major source of tin, the base element for making bronze, and only found in a few locations in the ancient world.[7] Hence, sitting at the crux of the amber and tin trades, the bridge across the

Tollense was arguably the single most economically crucial spot in Germany throughout the Bronze Age.

That the German tribesmen were able to recognize the location's vital importance demonstrates a degree of strategic awareness and a capacity for strategic planning, organization, and execution over a large space and through time that most historians believe even advanced ancient societies were incapable of achieving, never mind barbaric Germanic tribesmen. Moreover, it provides archaeological evidence for the near-mythical stories of the Sea Peoples, who came out of the north and, in just five decades of ferocious attacks, collapsed nearly every Bronze Age civilization. These stories of crushing assaults, which likely include that of Homer's Troy, are found throughout Bronze Age sites of the Near East. But for the past few decades, historians have tended to discount the contemporary evidence in favor of a system-collapse approach.[8] A few examples of the dread occasioned by these military adventurers will suffice to demonstrate that a military explanation for the collapse is possible, even likely:

> The unruly Sherden [the ancient Egyptian name for the Sea Peoples] whom no one had ever known how to combat, they came boldly sailing in their warships from the midst of the sea, none being able to withstand them.[9] (From a stela during the reign of Ramesses II)

Cuneiform texts found at the Hittite capital of Hattusas in Ugarit (the Syrian coast) reply to a missive explaining how to combat the Sea Peoples:

> The enemy ships are already here, they have set fire to my towns and have done great damage in the country. Did you not know that all of my troops were stationed in the Hittite country and that all my ships are stationed in Lycia and have not yet returned? So that the country is abandoned to itself. There are seven enemy ships that have come and done very great damage.[10]

In another written in Ugaritic cuneiform we find:

> When your messenger arrived, the army was humiliated and the city was sacked. Our food in the threshing floors was burnt and the vineyards were also destroyed. Our city is sacked. May you know it! May you know it![11]

Despite this and other contemporary evidence, many historians still find it difficult to reconcile their vision of small and loosely connected tribal groupings of central and northern Europe having the capacity to launch a sustained invasion capable of collapsing the warlike states of Anatolia and

Mesopotamia and come close to toppling mighty Egypt. They find it more likely that the Bronze Age collapse was a result of earthquakes, famines, and climate change that struck in a cascading series of events, recovery from which was beyond the capacity of ancient civilizations. In this interpretation, the Sea Peoples were small bands of wandering marauders who took advantage of the calamities and ensuing chaos of their neighbors but were not responsible for their collapse.

This, however, belies the contemporary evidence, which talks about invaders defeating standing armies, destroying ripening fields, and pillaging walled towns. There is, in fact, no extant record of an ancient society being unable to meet the military challenge because it was already beset by other crises.[12] While other factors were stressing late Bronze Age societies, it is going too far when one removes military invasions as a central cause of the collapse. Those societies under attack certainly knew the cause of their undoing:

> No land could resist their arms, from Hatti, Kode, Carchemish, Arzawa, and Alashiya on—being cut off at one time. They desolated its people and its land was like that which had never existed. They were coming forward toward Egypt, while the flame was prepared for them. Their confederation was the Peleset, Tjeker, Shekelesh, Denen, and Weshesh, lands united. They laid their hands upon the lands as far as the circuit of the earth. (Ramesses II victory monument)[13]

Disregarding such evidence of the destruction wrought by invading armies is a historical conceit possible only if historians insist that societies outside of the great civilizations of the age were incapable of organizing and executing sustained military operations.

The Tollense battlefield turns this reasoning on its head. It presents indisputable evidence that northern tribes were capable of previously unsuspected feats of military organization, planning, and execution. It is no small accomplishment to organize, move, and—most crucially—feed thousands of warriors over an extended march, and it is nearly impossible to do so on an ad hoc basis. The only way such a force could live off the land on such a march is if there were vast tracts of settled agriculture along the route. If such an agricultural bounty existed then we must also examine much of our current understating about the levels of organization of northern tribal societies during the era.

The key point here is that more than a thousand years before Augustus brought the Roman Empire into being, the tribes the Greeks and Romans called barbarians were demonstrating a capacity to sustain land and naval attacks over the course of decades. Moreover, these attacks were pressed with a ferocity and intensity capable of extinguishing all but one—Egypt—of the most powerful empires of the Bronze Age. Whatever the cause of these southward invasions of the northern tribes, they presented a huge and immediate threat to the settled civilizations of Mesopotamia and the Mediterranean.

After hundreds of years, the great Mesopotamian and Anatolian Empires had reestablished themselves only to find that the greatest threats to their existence were not one another, but, as Herodotus points out, the horse-mounted Cimmerians and Scythians coming through the Caucasus. Upon their arrival in approximately 650 BCE, they defeated a Median army to take possession of all of northern Mesopotamia.[14] From this stronghold, which they held for twenty-eight years, they raided as far south as Egypt, leaving horrendous damage in their wake. As Herodotus relates: "The whole land was ruined because of their violence and their pride, for, besides exacting from each the tribute which was assessed, they rode about the land carrying off everyone's possessions."[15] This time the invaders were defeated only through trickery when their leaders were invited to a feast and, after they had drunk to excess, murdered. Soon thereafter the great Scythian war bands dispersed and slipped back to the steppes.

Not much later, in approximately 530 BCE, we find the builder of the Persian Empire, Cyrus the Great, soon after conquering Babylon, feeling threatened by a huge Scythian army—the Massagetai—that had settled into the plains north of Babylon. After apparently several years of preparation, Cyrus led his army north. At first things went well, and Cyrus defeated a segment of the Scythian force and even captured the son of their queen, Tomyris, prompting her to write to Cyrus: "You bloodthirsty Cyrus, pride not yourself on this poor success . . . Now hear what I advise, and be sure I advise you for your good. Restore my son to me and get you from the land unharmed. . . . Refuse, and I swear by the sun . . . bloodthirsty as you are, I will give you your fill of blood."[16] Cyrus ignored Tomyris's warnings, and, true to her word, she destroyed the Persian army. When Cyrus's body was discovered among the slain, Tomyris ordered his head cut off and placed it in a bag filled with blood, giving him his fill.

Just a generation after Cyrus's defeat and death, Herodotus details how the Persian King of Kings, Darius I, around 513 BCE, tried to eliminate the Scythian threat by invading their homeland. In pursuit of his highly mobile foe, Darius pushed deep into Ukraine, and in the end, as Herodotus makes clear, the Persian army was extremely lucky to escape destruction.[17] Although Herodotus is silent as to further conflicts between Persia and the various Scythian tribes, the Persian kings considered these nomadic tribes a continuing existential threat. How else does one explain their failure to adapt their armies to the challenge of massed Greek hoplites?

In 490 BCE, outnumbered forces of heavily armored Greek hoplites decisively defeated a Persian force armed and equipped for rapid movement. That pattern was repeated, with minor variations, for over 150 years. At Plataea, during the march of Xenophon's ten thousand, at Granicus, Issus, and finally in the crushing defeat that Alexander inflicted upon Darius III at Gaugamela, the Persians never came up with an answer to the devastating impact of armored hoplites smashing into Persian armies protected by wicker shields. Assuming that the Persians were not fools and that they comprehended the reasons for their multiple defeats, only one thing explains a 150-year failure to adapt. The simple explanation is that, throughout this period, the Persians considered the Scythian threat to be far more dangerous than the Greek or Macedonian. Because combating the Scythians required forces that could move as fast as the steppe nomads, the Persians always placed a premium on maintaining large cavalry forces and quick-marching light infantry formations. Such a mindset made it impossible to adapt the Persian military so that it could cope with heavy hoplite infantry in a set-piece battle. The point, however, is not to judge Persian strategic choices. Rather, we need to acknowledge that even when challenged by armies that would eventually destroy their empire, the Persians remained convinced that the most serious threat they faced was the destructive power of the northern tribes.

This is important because it explains many of the strategic decisions made by the Romans throughout the five hundred years of the Empire.[18] If the tribes north and east of the Danube and Rhine were truly capable only of sporadic raiding with limited forces, then it is impossible to explain why, at the height of its power, Rome thought it necessary to maintain an average of fifteen of its precious legions along these rivers, as well as another three or four to keep watch over restless Picts in Caledonia (Scotland). Manning these frontiers and paying for regular expeditions into barbarian lands always created a huge drain on the Empire's resources, one that could be justified only if the barbarian threat was considered truly existential.

But when one considers the power and might of Rome, it is hard to conceive of the Empire, particularly in its early centuries, before it was riven by internal division and destructive civil wars, being threatened by motley barbarian tribes singularly or in combination. This outlook still predominates among modern historians, who routinely state that Parthia—the only other great organized empire on Rome's borders—was always the greater strategic threat. It is strange, then, that for the first 250 years of its existence, the

Roman Empire contented itself with a mere four to six legions facing the Parthians on the eastern border.

Was this a strategic miscalculation on the part of Rome, or was there something to be terrified of lurking in the mists and forests of the cold north? If it was a miscalculation, then it was one repeated by dozens of successive emperors. Worse, when Rome eventually relaxed its guard in favor of other strategic interests or other momentary priorities, it was the barbarians that swarmed in and destroyed the Western Empire and left the Eastern Empire reeling. One could argue that the barbarian groupings in the fourth and fifth centuries were of an entirely different nature than those of the early years of the Empire. That is fundamentally true, but it does not negate the fact that such dangerous groupings existed even during the Principate, although they were not usually sustained over long periods.

Rome had good reason to fear the northern barbarian tribes: from their earliest days the Gauls were the greatest threat to the city's survival. In 390 BCE a Gallic force led by the chieftain Brennus defeated a hastily assembled Roman army at the Battle of the Allia and entered the city itself.[19] The story of the ensuing sack and Rome's revival may include more myth than reality, but these myths endured as an objective reality for the Romans well into the late Empire. As such, they were always part of the mental framework upon which later strategic approaches were built. The impact on Roman attitudes was so great that the date of the Battle of the Allia—July 18—was viewed until the end of the Empire as accursed.

Other parts of the 390 BCE defeat and sack also did much to set Roman attitudes and future strategic thinking. After the defeat, the Romans fortified themselves within the citadel on Capitoline Hill and prepared for a siege. Unfortunately, there was not sufficient space on the hill for the entire population, and priority was given to the young, particularly those who could bear arms. The elderly were left behind, but to ease their qualms and reconcile them to their fate they were joined by every former Roman consul. As the Gauls moved through the cities, they saw the consuls seated around the forum in their regal gowns of office. For a long time the Gauls were stayed from slaughter by the regal magnificence and stately manner of the consuls. Then, as Livy relates, "M. Papirius roused the passion of a Gaul, who began to stroke his beard, . . . by smiting him on the head with his ivory staff. He was the first to be killed, the others were butchered in their chairs." A general massacre of the aged Romans ensued.

The Romans on the Capitoline, after withstanding a short siege, agreed to pay the Gauls a thousand pounds of gold to depart.[20] When the Romans complained to Brennus that the scales were calibrated to cheat them, "Brennus tossed his sword on the scale, *uttering words intolerable to the Roman ears, namely 'Vae victis,'* or 'Woe to the vanquished!' "[21] Before the Gauls could get away, however, they were met by another Roman army, led by the previously exiled General Camillus, which had force-marched to the city's aid. This time the Romans won a decisive victory, and according to Livy the "slaughter was total: their camp was captured and not even the messenger survived to report the disaster."[22] When the annihilation was complete, Camillus supposedly stated, "Non auro, sed ferro, recuperanda est patria" (not by gold, but by iron, is the nation to be restored).[23]

Livy's and Plutarch's recountings of this tale were written hundreds of years after the event, and there are other, conflicting versions. But it is their accounts that dominated the Roman imagination and from which the Romans absorbed strategic lessons. The first of these lessons was that when dealing with barbarians, one had always to negotiate from a position of strength. The ideal—often neglected in times of crisis—was to ensure it was always the other side that suffered the "woe of the vanquished." Second, and most crucial, Rome's salvation was always to be found in the "iron" of the legions.

In the decade before Julius Caesar's lifetime Rome's survival was again cast in doubt when fierce Germanic tribes—the Cimbri, supported by the Teutones—defeated several smaller Roman forces before annihilating a newly raised eighty-thousand-man army at the Battle of Arauiso. This was Rome's first taste of the *Furor Teutonicus*, as described by Plutarch:

> [T]heir courage and daring made them irresistible, and when they engaged in battle they came on with the swiftness and force of fire, so that no one could withstand their onset, but all who came in their way became their prey and booty, and even many large Roman armies, with their commanders, who had been stationed to protect Transalpine Gaul, were destroyed ingloriously.[24]

This was the greatest military disaster Rome had suffered since Hannibal destroyed their field army at Cannae over a hundred years earlier. But like Hannibal, who failed to follow up his great victory with an immediate march on Rome, the barbarians marched through Gaul and into Spain, rather than diverting south to finish Rome off. The delay gave the Romans time, which they put to good use. First, they elected as consul Gaius Marius, the recent victor of the Jugurthine War, and then gave him unprecedented authority to restructure the army. In what became known as the Marian Reforms, Marius did away with the requirement that a legionnaire had to own property. In a single stroke, the Roman army went from being a well-trained militia raised from the propertied classes to a professional force of long-serving soldiers, dependent upon leaders who could guarantee their pay and grants of land when they retired. Consequently, the armies of Rome in a remarkably short time switched their primary allegiance from the Republic to their generals. It was, of course, this switch that led inexorably to the great civil wars, first between Marius and his former subordinate Sulla, then between Caesar and Pompey, and finally between Octavian (Augustus) and Mark Anthony.

With this new army, Marius won a series of major victories against the barbarians, first destroying the military power of the Teutones at the Battle of Aquae Sextiae, before defeating the Cimbri at the Battle of Vercellae. In this latter, well over 100,000 Cimbri were slaughtered, the bodies left to fertilize the fields; it was later said that the people of Massalia fenced their vineyards with the bones of the fallen, and that the soil where the bodies wasted away grew so rich that it produced great harvests for many years afterward.[25]

Only two generations later, Marius's nephew, Julius Caesar, took nearly a half dozen years and employed as many as eight legions to subdue the barbarian Celtic and Germanic tribes in Gaul. If Plutarch's numbers are to be believed, the conquest of Gaul involved storming eight hundred cities and towns, subduing three hundred nations (tribes), and fighting over three million tribesmen in a series of pitched battles that left more than a million barbarians dead.[26]

If the Romans needed further proof as to the dangers presented by the barbarians, it arrived almost coincident with the advent of the Empire. In 9 CE three Roman legions were annihilated, presumably with all or most of their auxiliary forces, in the Teutoburg Wald, east of the Rhine. I will discuss this event at greater length later in this book, but for now, just ponder the enormousness of what it took to wreck three legions—close to twenty thousand men—in combat: warriors from probably a dozen or more tribes had to be recruited, they all had to arrive at a specific place at a specific time, and huge amounts of food had to be available along their march routes and at the ambush site. Moreover, each group of warriors had to be trained to combat a Roman legion and then integrated into a coherent operational plan. Finally, this supposedly hastily assembled ramshackle force had to defeat three veteran legions. By any measure, this was an immense organizational feat, one that, despite so much evidence to the contrary, many historians believe the barbarian tribes were incapable of, at least until the later centuries of the Empire.

Clearly, the barbarian tribes, milling in varying numbers along the Empire's northern and southern frontiers, were a persistent danger to Rome, one that required constant vigilance. As history demonstrates, even those societies that had just barely emerged from the Neolithic period were capable of sustained military exertions that could, in the Bronze Age, bring down civilizations. They remained remarkably dangerous throughout the Iron Age, having come close to destroying the Roman Republic on more than one occasion. If the barbarian threat was not capable of destroying the Roman Empire during its first two centuries, it was still capable of inflicting horrific damage to Roman arms, as well as to substantial portions of the most exposed provinces. The threat presented by the barbarians grew as the tribes amalgamated into larger groupings in the later centuries of the Empire, but from the beginning the threat from beyond the Rhine and the Danube was always the risk the Empire took most seriously—and for good reason.

CHAPTER 3 | Paying for a Strategy
Funding the Republic

I T TOOK SOME time for Rome to discover that an empire built on the back of its legions could be made to pay for itself. After the first two wars against Carthage nearly bankrupted the state, Rome's financial woes ended upon its final victory over its only real rival in the western Mediterranean. As the Republic's legions advanced their standard across the eastern Mediterranean, Rome first gorged itself on the plunder of captured territories and rich cities. Then, after they had extracted all the riches readily at hand, they levied a charge on the defeated enemy for the cost of the war. As Polybius wrote:

> To sweep the gold and silver, however, into their own coffers was perhaps reasonable; for it was impossible for them to aim at universal empire without crippling the means of the rest of the world and securing the same kind of resources for themselves.[1]

Only after these war indemnities (*stipendia*) were collected did Rome begin the long process of knitting the conquered regions into Rome's economic network.[2]

Carthage, because of its defeat in the Second Punic War, paid into Rome's coffers over 24,000 talents, including a payment of two hundred talents annually for fifty years. In another instance, after Antiochus III's armies were smashed at the Battle of Magnesia, the Seleucid ruler was forced to pay an indemnity of 15,000 talents.[3] From what we know in the literary sources, coupled with rough estimates on the size of the take from plunder, a fair estimate is that in the fifty years after the Battle of Zama that concluded the

Punic Wars, Rome received nearly 46,000 talents from its enemies—1,050 tons of silver per year.[4] Most of this bounty went toward fielding the army and enriching the generals. In the process, the legions became longstanding forces, more professional; and, fatally to the Republic, they began transferring their allegiance from Rome to the generals who enriched them.

It is always difficult for modern readers to grasp the enormous amount of this transfer of wealth from the other Mediterranean states to Roman coffers, which is too often expressed in talents or currencies that have no meaning in the modern world. Consequently, some perspective is needed. Pliny the Elder, in his *Natural History*, gives us two accountings of exactly how much money was in the Roman treasury—the *Aerarium Saturni*—at a specific moment in time. The first, in 157 BCE, between the Second and Third Punic Wars, states that it held 17,410 pounds of gold, 22,070 pounds of silver, and 6,135,400 sesterces in minted coins.[5] Once the calculations are done, this totals out to a little over 18 million denarii—3,002 talents.[6] Pliny, writing in the middle of the first century, states that "at no other period was the state more wealthy."[7] He also notes that Aemilius Paullus, after destroying King Perseus's Macedonian army, pillaging the royal palace, plundering seventy towns, and capturing 150,000 slaves, had paid 300 million sesterces into the treasury just fourteen years earlier.[8] One gets some idea of the costs the state was incurring—mostly to fund the military—from the fact that less than one-fifteenth of the booty from the war with Macedon was still in the treasury just over a decade later. Still, Rome felt wealthy enough in 167 BCE to exempt all of Italy from property taxes, a privilege that lasted until the crises of the third century CE.

The question remains: what could Rome buy with the 18 million denarii (3,002 talents) in the treasury in 156? When one considers that a legionnaire was paid about 112 denarii a year, it would cost close to 600,000 denarii (120 talents) to keep a full-strength legion in the field for a year, if the only cost was paying the soldiers.[9] So the 3,002 talents could have paid for twenty-five legions in 150 BC.[10]

Basic system of coinage	
as (pl. *asses*)	bronze coin, the basic unit; 4 *asses* = 1 *sestertius*, 10 *asses* = 1 *denarius*
sestertius (pl. *sestertii*)	silver coin; 4 *sestertii* = 1 *denarius*
denarius (pl. *denarii*)	silver coin, occasionally minted in gold
aureus (pl: *aurei*)	gold coin; 1 *aureus* = 25 *denarii*

The entire system of making war pay through conquest and expansion ended abruptly when Rome's armies reached the limits of their capacity to sustain operations—the English Channel, the Rhine River, and the edges of the Parthian Empire. Once these limits of empire were reached, Rome should have ceased major military operations and consolidated its gains. This was the moment to end the plundering and tributes and begin integrating the conquered territories into a coherent economic network, which would provide tax revenues indefinitely. What Roman generals did instead was launch a series of civil wars to determine who would own the great prize of the Roman Empire.

Although such disputes had been a hallmark of Roman politics since the clashes of Marius and Sulla, for our purposes we will consider Julius Caesar's march on Rome in 49 BCE as the point at which these internecine wars embroiled the entire Empire. At their conclusion, nothing was as it was before.

Julius Caesar was the first to realize that if one was going to ask legionaries to fight one another, a general had better ensure the loyalty of his legions. A reputation for gaining victories and having the esteem of your troops would go only so far. It was far better to be the highest bidder for their services. The legions had become so addicted to booty and donatives that they would cheerfully slaughter one another for the right monetary incentives. Hence, in a preemptive move, more consequential than crossing the Rubicon, Caesar doubled the pay of the legions to 225 denarii a year per soldier—raising the price to pay and sustain one legion for a year to approximately 300 talents. This pay raise, which remained the base pay for a legionnaire until the reign of Domitian (81–96 AD), not only bought the loyalty of his legions but also began the process of subverting the loyalty of his rival Pompey's legions.

However, it was one thing to declare an extravagant pay raise and quite another to fund it. It is no wonder, then, that one of Caesar's first acts upon entering Rome was to raid the treasury. Finding his way blocked by the tribune Metellus, Caesar ordered him to move aside. When he refused, Caesar threatened him with execution and warned, "And this young man is more disagreeable for me to say than to do."[11] Metellus wisely withdrew, allowing Caesar to help himself to 15,000 gold ingots, 30,000 silver ingots, and 30 million sesterces in coin.[12] This amounted to about 12 million denarii (2,000 talents). Long after the raid, the poet Lucan wrote, "Rome was for the first time poorer than a Caesar."[13] But while the sums seized seem enormous, they were barely enough to pay the troops Caesar had on hand for six months.[14] This more than anything else explains why Caesar, after famously saying, "I go to meet an army without a leader, and I shall return to meet a leader without an army," marched west to confront Pompey's forces in Spain, rather than against Pompey himself in the east.[15] He needed the production from the bountiful Spanish silver mines to pay his troops.[16] In the meantime, Pompey was calling on the princes of the east—many of them placed in power by Pompey at the end of the Mithridatic Wars in 63 BCE—to fund his legions.

The Roman civil war was costly, but so was the peace. At the end of the fighting, Suetonius reports that Caesar paid "each and every foot-soldier of his veteran legions twenty-four thousand sesterces [over twenty years' worth of pay] by way of booty, over and above the two thousand apiece which he had paid them at the beginning of the civil strife."[17] To pay these tremendous sums, Caesar, who was never hesitant to seize funds from any available source—he stole the gold roof of the Capitol and replaced it with gilded bronze—outdid himself to pay for the war and the ensuing peace. According to Suetonius, he undertook an unprecedented level of "bare-faced pillage and sacrilege."[18] It is little wonder that Caesar's veterans so readily allied themselves with the young Octavian—from whom they expected similar largesse—in his wars against Caesar's assassins and later against his ally Mark Anthony.

Before Octavian's and Mark Anthony's falling out, both men discovered that Caesar's largesse and continuous fighting had emptied the treasury. At a time when legions were available to the highest bidder, the triumvirs ordered a proscription that left three hundred senators and two thousand equestrians dead.[19] Unfortunately, selling the confiscated estates of the murdered men did not bring in nearly as much money as hoped—unsurprisingly, because those wealthy enough to purchase the confiscated lands were often among the murdered, and those who still possessed wealth were reluctant to advertise the fact while the cash-strapped Octavian and Mark Anthony were still on the prowl. Discovering that they still did not have sufficient funds to pay all that they had promised, the triumvirs assured the impatient legions that they would be permitted to loot the great cities of the east. The legions were also promised the riches of eighteen Italian cities, which would be theirs as if they had been conquered in war.[20] This, it was hoped, would meet the cash payments promised to the forty-three legions currently on the triumvirs' rolls: 5,000 denarii per legionnaire, more than forty years' pay.

In equally brutal fashion, Caesar's assassins and the triumvirs' opponents— Brutus and Cassius—raised their own war chest in the eastern provinces. These provinces normally paid taxes of 50 million denarii per year (8,000 talents), but this was judged insufficient to pay for the loyalty of the legions. Consequently, Brutus and Cassius demanded payment of ten years' worth of tribute in just two years. Those cities that protested or refused (such as Rhodes and Tarsus) were seized and looted.[21]

At the Battle of Philippi, which was fought in two parts separated by weeks, Brutus and Cassius were forced to pay huge sums to retain the troops' loyalty. According to Appian, "[E]ach soldier [was promised] 1,500 Italic drachmas, to each centurion five times that sum, and to each tribune in proportion."[22] Before the second battle, Brutus offered an even larger payment: "[W]e will give you an additional reward of 5000 drachmas for each soldier, five times as much to each centurion, and twice the latter sum to each tribune."[23] In all, Brutus and Cassius—in a losing cause—paid or offered their soldiers about 150 million denarii, enough to pay their entire army's base salaries for nearly fifteen years. After their victory at Philippi, Octavian and Mark Anthony surely confiscated most of these funds for their personal use. Moreover, they collected a huge indemnity from those provinces and cities that had backed their enemies, demanding a minimum of nine years' taxes paid in two years, while "kings, princes, and free cities should make additional contributions according to their means."[24]

This and other exactions fueled Octavian's continuing war against Sextus Pompey and Mark Anthony's plunge into Parthia, as well as the cost of the civil war between Octavian and Anthony. This last conflict once again bankrupted the state, which needed the long internal peace Octavian's victory generated to recover.

Augustus and the Coming of Peace

For well over a century Rome profited and expanded through war. But it was peace that made Rome, and more certainly the Empire, rich. To see how, we must first consider one of the overlooked practical impacts of the spending on the civil wars. When all was said and done, they had resulted in one of the greatest transfers of wealth in history. Taking a page out of Sulla's playbook, Octavian and Anthony instituted proscriptions in which money and land were taken from murdered Roman elites and redistributed to both the legions and into more productive hands. Moreover, the exactions demanded of client rulers, provinces, cities, temples, and just about anyone with stored wealth could not help but free hundreds of thousands, possibly millions, of talents of trapped wealth.

This is similar to what economic historians witnessed when England's Henry VIII dissolved the monasteries, freeing huge amounts of capital from the "dead hand of the church."[25] It was Henry VIII's freeing of land and capital for more productive use that set the initial conditions for the start of the Industrial Revolution. Similarly, a strong case can be made that the capital freed to pay for Rome's civil wars may have had an even more profound impact, given their enormous geographical scope and the number of persons impacted. Before this, the greatest freeing of capital in the ancient world took place when Alexander conquered the Persian Empire. Starting with an almost empty treasury, Alexander funded his invasion with the silver and gold he found stored in the major cities along his route. In one instance, Diodorus Siculus relates, 2,500 tons of gold were found in a single storehouse, representing the accumulated savings of over two hundred years of Persian rule.[26]

The comment that would give a modern economist pause is that the filled Persian treasuries' stored wealth accumulated from when Cyrus built the Empire two hundred years before. Depending on which source you read, Alexander's total take varies, but historians have centered on 180,000 talents as the final figure—enough to pay all the Principate's legions for fifty years. From an economic perspective, if this money had been allowed to flow through the economy, rather than being hoarded, the Persian Empire would likely have been much richer and far less brittle than Alexander found it. But without any theory of modern economics or any true concept of how to finance wars with debt, most rulers thought it in their best interest to hoard their wealth for emergencies such as war.[27] Of course, the catch was that the Persian ruler required time to deploy these stored riches in the event of war. Alexander's hard-marching Macedonian army never gave Darius III the chance to do so. It was the freeing of these funds that later paid for the wars fought by the Diadochi—Alexander's successors.[28]

The Roman civil wars, starting with Julius Caesar's march on Rome and concluding with Octavian's victory at Actium, had lasted for nearly twenty years and encompassed the entire Mediterranean. During that time, the belligerents' need to quench their inextinguishable thirst for additional funds emptied every treasury, raided every temple, and murdered many men who had large amounts of stored wealth that could be seized. When the wars ended, the economy was awash in cash. Moreover, although no ancient economists were toting up a statistical record for historians to pursue, the Mediterranean economy was likely vibrant and growing throughout the conflict. This is because, until the modern era, great conflicts tended to be exceptionally good for the overall economy of the warring parties.[29] Envisioning such economic outcomes is easy when one considers the expenses that must be paid out to supply and transport huge armies over vast distances. So, while rulers and governments might bankrupt themselves paying for endless wars, the foundational economy typically prospers mightily. The exception, of course, is those cities, farms, and businesses that find themselves directly in the path of an army set on devastation. But even in these cases, agriculturally based economies can typically come back from devastation far faster than a modern economy. One only has to look at Athens's return to wealth and power after its defeat in the Peloponnesian War, or how fast Carthage rebuilt its economy to repeatedly contest Rome's economic supremacy in the western Mediterranean.

But rebuilding after wars does not increase wealth; it only brings a devastated community back to something approaching prewar levels of economic activity.[30] Where armies tread, huge amounts of structural capital— buildings, granaries, irrigation canals—are often destroyed. Rebuilding these capital investments does not leave a region or state better off than it was before; it just returns the region to the status quo. Moreover, in an age of endemic warfare—which is certainly true of the entire Mediterranean region before the Pax Romana—most societies must have been wary of investing too much in expensive infrastructure that was always a target for future marauders and invading armies. Such wariness would have acted as a natural brake on economic development throughout the Mediterranean.

By removing this worry, the Empire's general peace set the conditions for a huge economic expansion throughout the Mediterranean region. For the first time since the dawn of civilization and the creation of the first city-states, one power could enforce a general peace on a large portion of the known world. More crucially, Rome was increasingly able to draw these conquered states into an integrated economic system. The result was that capital investment was no longer being applied to repairing the damage from repeated conflicts but rather, increasingly, to growing the economy. Such investment would have gone toward increasing the amount of arable land under cultivation, building industry, and increasing trade. As more and more of the various sub-regions of the Empire became convinced that peace was going to last, they became increasingly willing to invest in costly infrastructure that greatly enhanced the scope, efficiency, and productivity of the agricultural economy. There were still many subsistence farmers throughout the Empire, but there is increasing evidence of a fast-growing, money-based market economy, centered on an increasing number of cities and towns.[31] There is also substantial archaeological evidence from the first two centuries of empire demonstrating that considerable capital investment was being widely adopted in the agricultural, industrial, and mining sectors by both state and private property owners for the purpose of maximizing returns.[32]

Countering this argument are historians who insist on viewing the Julio-Claudians as ruling during a period of unceasing war. In this view, Augustus's reign is a period as bloody as any other in Roman history.[33] Making much of Tacitus's statement that the Pax Augustus was a "peace stained in blood," and by focusing on the many battles along the frontiers of the Empire—including the Varian disaster—these historians overlook an important point:[34] no matter how violent the frontiers or how many legionaries were still fighting to expand the edges of the Empire, the vital inner core was virtually untouched by war for over two centuries. If there was one great idea driving Roman strategy in this period, it was the imperative to keep threats that were constantly brewing beyond the frontier zones at bay while developing and growing the economy at the Empire's core. Whether this formula can be found in the few remaining ancient narratives we have at our disposal is not as crucial for my analysis as are the actions of the emperors regarding the placement and employment of Rome's legions. This constant military activity was expensive, but the burden—all else being equal—would have lightened over time, the number of legions and auxiliaries staying relatively constant as the economy grew.[35]

But while the frontier zones became increasingly fixed, the opportunities for fiscal relief from the booty of successive conquests lessened, and the expropriation of the riches of other states became less crucial to Rome's finances. Periodically there were still major additions to the Empire, and one can assume that when Trajan returned from his Dacian conquest in 106 CE he carried with him sizable amounts of plunder. But for the most part, the post-Republic conquests added only a pittance in immediate gains from war when compared to the profits made when Rome's legions first marched across the Mediterranean. Moreover, after some determined but ultimately unsuccessful attempts to push the standards far north and east, Rome began to see that, except for mineral-rich Dacia, beyond the Danube, the dense forest regions were too economically backward to be worth the cost of conquest and occupation.

Expansion and conquest did more than increase the amount of farmland and farmers available to tax: it also gave Rome control of vast expanses of exploitable resources such as forests, fisheries, and, most crucially, mines.[36] Rome—mineral-poor for the first centuries of the Republic—took control of Carthage's Spanish mines during the Second Punic War. Pliny tells us that a single mine provided Hannibal with three hundred pounds of silver a day to pay the mercenaries he employed to invade Italy.[37] According to Strabo, a single mine near New Carthage "embrace[d] an area four hundred stadia in circuit; and . . . forty thousand workmen stayed there, who bring into the Roman exchequer a daily revenue of twenty-five thousand drachmae."[38] Pliny gives us a bit more information on his own period. One can safely discount his commentary on gold being extracted "in India by the ants, and in Scythia by the Griffins" in favor of what he witnessed. The mines Pliny saw were apparently producing less on an individual basis than they had decades earlier, but the total take from the region stayed about the same as new mines were put into operation. Thus, for the Empire's first two centuries, the amount of gold taken from the same area remained roughly the same—25,000 drachmae (1,600 talents) annually—which was enough to pay and sustain five legions for a year.[39]

This was the economy that powered the Roman Empire for most of the first two hundred years of its existence. As the Empire matured, so did its economy. Patterns of trade would change, successive crises would alter the political landscape, climate change would strike at the heart of the agricultural foundations of prosperity and change the political context, and finally civil wars and invasions would complete a long process of economic fragmentation. These changes to the Roman economy impacted the strategic choices and the execution of Rome's strategic initiatives and will be addressed as this narrative proceeds.

CHAPTER 4 | The Core of Roman Strategy

ROME HAD A good run. From Octavian's victory at Actium in 31 BCE to the traditional endpoint of the Western half of the Empire in 476 CE, an impressive five hundred years passed. By this measure, the empire lasted fully one-fifth of all of recorded history.[1] The Roman Empire's decline and final collapse, in fact, eclipsed the total length of existence of any other empire. It helps to place this duration in context: five hundred years ago, Machiavelli was busy writing *The Prince*, Martin Luther had just received his degree in theology, Copernicus was putting the finishing touches on a theory that placed the sun at the center of the solar system, and Henry VIII was on the throne of England. Any historian trying to unearth a single consistent, centrally planned, and coordinated strategy over such a lengthy period is on a fool's errand.

The longest-lasting strategy the United States ever came up with was outlined in NSC-68, the foundation of our national policy toward the Soviet Union during the cold war.[2] Since then, we have been subjected to a new national security strategy every two to four years. Although the pace of change during the Roman era was snaillike compared to that of the post–Industrial Revolution era, Rome was not an empire in stasis. While the Empire's visible trappings changed little, there were vast differences between the Empire of Augustus and that of his successors. Over the centuries the Empire's underlying economy, political arrangements, military affairs, and, most important, types of external challenges it faced were changing constantly. In short, every factor influencing the creation of Roman strategy was in a continuous state of flux, making adaptability to changing circumstances as important to Roman strategists as it is to strategists of the modern era.

At the highest level, however, certain strategic imperatives tend to dominate. This is where policy and grand strategy overlap to the point of being indistinguishable. This is particularly true when political and military affairs are dominated by a single person: the emperor. In my current position, I am often asked what the grand strategy of the United States is, and the best I can come up with is that it is a set of ideals that we sometimes attain but just as often fail to meet. For instance, the Preamble to the U.S. Constitution sets forth a national grand strategy as good as any ever expressed in any of the many dozens of strategic plans the government has released since its publication.

> We the People of the United States, in Order to form a more perfect Union, establish Justice, insure domestic Tranquility, provide for the common defense, promote the general Welfare, and secure the Blessings of Liberty to ourselves and our Posterity, do ordain and establish this Constitution for the United States of America.

The Preamble in many ways echoes the Declaration of Independence's self-evident truths—"that all men are created equal; that they are endowed by their Creator with certain unalienable rights; that among these are life, liberty, and the pursuit of happiness"—which is also as good a foundation for a national grand strategy as any other. In fact, with just a bit of editing work, Franklin Roosevelt recast this sentiment into the "four freedoms," a strategic phrasing that carried the country through the Great Depression and World War II: freedom of speech, freedom of worship, freedom from want, and freedom from fear.[3]

Unfortunately, no such document has survived the collapse of the Roman Empire, forcing us to extrapolate a grand strategy from Roman historical writings and most of all from Roman actions. Based on such evidence, Rome's grand strategy was not much different from that of any other empire:

- to maintain the integrity and stability of the Empire;
- to protect the Empire from external enemies; and
- to expand the borders of the Empire when possible and profitable, but always with an eye to expanding the Empire's influence where physical expansion was not possible.

Finally, because Rome was ruled by a single person, his most important concerns were, by definition, rolled into the Empire's grand strategy. And every emperor, starting with Augustus, had the same overarching concerns: prestige and personal security. These two concerns were always entwined, as the greater an emperor's prestige, the more secure he was. Although prestige was never a guarantee against revolts or assassination, it surely helped. Moreover, the longer an emperor remained alive (and on the throne), the more secure he became, as increasing patronage and preferment opportunities allowed him to build a strong base of loyal clients and allies—most crucially in the army. A lengthy reign also gave an emperor time to put into place the conditions for a dynasty that would outlast him.

Throughout the Empire's existence, the surest way to build prestige was through military successes, and the less secure an emperor was, or felt himself to be, the greater his need for military victories. Similarly, military defeats or the failure to engage a perceived military threat increased tremendously the risks to an emperor's safety.

When examining Roman strategy through the ages, one can never neglect this vital imperative, for it explains nearly every action that otherwise does not appear to make strategic sense. To better understand this phenomenon, it helps to examine the echoes of this same driving motivation in our current politics. How often in recent decades have U.S. presidents been accused of letting the tail wag the dog when they give the appearance of ordering military actions to distract the people from scandal or domestic problems? Many view what we now call "wars of choice" as attempts by one president or another to temporarily boost his prestige or to distract the nation from other immediate concerns. Still, the worst thing that can happen to an unpopular president is for him to be turned out of office. The stakes were infinitely higher for a Roman emperor, as well as for his family, advisers, and supporters, who often shared his fate. Consequently, for the emperors of Rome, there was always a clear hierarchy of strategic concerns, at the top of which was survival. Moreover, even if an emperor was resistant to sending out or leading major military expeditions, he was surrounded by a host of advisers continually pushing him toward military actions that would enhance their own chances of survival, even if such conflicts weakened the overall strategic position of the Empire.

Why Rome Halted

In 9 CE Publius Quinctilius Varus, the first governor of the new Roman province of Germania, was departing his summer headquarters near Minden for the legionary fortress of Moguntiacum (today's Mainz) when word came that a small German tribe had revolted. Revolts were nothing new to Varus;

in his previous assignment as governor of Syria, he was tasked with enforcing a harsh tax regime on the locals, and as almost always happened whenever a conquered people first felt the yoke of Rome's fiscal requirements, Judea rose in revolt.[4] Employing the Roman playbook for snuffing out insurrections, Varus rapidly marched with two of his four legions to relieve a legion trapped in Jerusalem.[5] On his approach, the city of Sepphoris was stormed and its population sold into slavery. The visible might of the legions, coupled with examples such as Sepphoris, broke the rebels' will, and Jerusalem was surrendered without a fight, which did not stop Varus from crucifying two thousand suspected insurgents.[6]

Having added another successful example to the Roman playbook, Varus saw no reason to deviate from proven methods. Moving rapidly at the first sign of rebellion in Germania, he set out with the three legions at his disposal—XVII, XVIII, XIX.[7] Unfortunately for Varus, his opponent, Arminius, was Roman educated and trained, and therefore well acquainted with the Roman playbook.

Spread over ten miles and marching as if they had few concerns, the Roman column became uncharacteristically ragged and undisciplined. As the legionaries saw it, after years of campaigning by Tiberius and his brother Drusus, the Germans were a beaten people. Some of them might revolt from time to time, but few considered this any more worrisome than the sporadic revolts in Gaul after Caesar's conquest. Consequently, many legionaries were wandering unarmed among the camp followers when disaster struck.

Rain came early on the second day's march, growing heavier as morning gave way to afternoon. Fighting against the pelting rain and lashing winds, the legionaries trudged forward in mud that brought the baggage train to a crawl. Bundled up against the elements, they became insensible to everything except their misery. Entering a narrow pass between two sections of Teutoburg Wald, the unsuspecting Romans never saw the carefully laid trap and marched into it haplessly.

Beset on all sides by missiles, the legions fell into chaos, emboldening German warriors to edge closer, hurling ever more missiles and overwhelming parts of the Roman line. Gradually but inexorably, battle-hardened centurions restored order to the wavering column as they gathered nearby legionaries to their standards, drew swords, and led counterattacks. After a ferocious fight, the first frenzied German assaults were repulsed.[8] The Romans had bought themselves time, and Varus still had the bulk of three shaken but rapidly recovering veteran legions at hand. As the survivors constructed a fortified camp and burned their cumbersome baggage train, Varus held a council of war, which decided to march west, toward the fortified Roman base at

Xanten. Even after a miserable night, the still-undaunted legions quickly smashed a gap through the German lines and headed west.[9]

Varus, once again, played into Arminius's hands. As the dogged legions marched into the narrow Kalkrieser-Niederweder-Senke pass, Arminius and the bulk of his German force waited behind a wall built along the pass's entire four-mile stretch. Although the Romans were again assailed from all sides, this time they were ready to meet the assault. However, instead of offering a head-to-head clash, the Germans stayed behind the cover of their protective walls, hurling missiles by the thousands. Most of the Romans hunkered down behind their shields while some cohorts, unwilling to remain passive targets, advanced on the German positions. Most of these unsupported assaults were easily repulsed, but others broke through, only to be cut down by the thousands of Germans waiting beyond the walls.[10]

As Roman cohesion began to collapse, Arminius unleashed his massed warriors on the faltering legions. Thousands fell as each side hacked at the other with sword and ax. German losses must have been greater, but they were continuously reinforced throughout the day, while the Romans, still a hundred miles distant from their fortress, despaired of help.

The remains of the Roman column retreated west, probably toward Osnabrück, and camped upon a nearby hill for the night. Lacking the energy to fortify their camp, the legionaries huddled against the elements and a growing tide of barbarians. Their gloom increased when it became known that the cavalry had deserted and Varus had committed suicide.[11] On the fourth day they were again ambushed in a wooded area, and by noon it was all over. After a four-day running fight, the Germans had obliterated three legions. The Roman survivors were tortured before being hanged or burned alive. Their heads were nailed to trees or the skulls taken home as souvenirs.[12] Six years later Germanicus, at the head of a new Roman army seeking vengeance, revisited the battle site. Tacitus recorded the event:

> In the plain between were bleaching bones, scattered or in little heaps, as the men had fallen, fleeing or standing fast. Hard by lay splintered spears and limbs of horses, while human skulls were nailed prominently on the tree-trunks. In the neighboring groves stood the savage altars at which they had slaughtered the tribunes and chief centurions.[13]

In a virtual instant, Roman power east of the Rhine vanished, and two decades of Roman efforts to subdue Germania lay in ruins. Distraught over the collapse of his policy and the irreplaceable loss of three of the Empire's twenty-eight legions, Augustus went into mourning, tore his clothes, and let his hair and beard grow. As he walked through the halls of his residence, ancient sources claim, from time to time he would stop and hit his head against a wall, wailing, "Varus, give me back my legions."[14]

Just before the Varian Disaster, the limits of Rome's rule north of the Alps and extending to the Balkans had been established along the Danube, just short of modern-day Bohemia, which lay in the gap between the headwaters of the Danube and the Rhine. In 6 CE, Augustus, not content with this limit, had every intention of adding this territory, occupied by the Marcomanni and their seventy thousand warriors, to the Empire. He was close to doing so as a dozen legions moving under Tiberius from Carnuntum in the east and Sentius Saturninus coming from the west were close to trapping the Marcomanni army, under their king, Maroboduus, in a giant pincer movement. But before the jaws could be shut, the Illyrian tribes in Tiberius's rear revolted, in what Suetonius called the most serious foreign war since Hannibal's invasion two centuries before.[15] Suetonius also tells us that Tiberius "carried on for three years with fifteen legions and a corresponding force of auxiliaries, amid great difficulties of every kind and the utmost scarcity of supplies," before the revolt was finally crushed.[16] Giving Tiberius over half of the total combat forces of the Empire demonstrates just how serious Augustus and the Roman people considered this rebellion, which if successful would have cut the Empire in two and placed a threatening barbarian army on the Alpine passes into Italy.

The war lasted three bloody years, and the Romans appear to have suffered several brutal reverses, particularly in the first year.[17] Dio makes an interesting observation concerning these reverses: "When Augustus learned of these things, he began to be suspicious of Tiberius, who, as he thought, might speedily have overcome the Dalmatians, but was delaying purposely, in order that he might be under arms as long as possible, with the war as his excuse."[18] Here we see some of the first stirrings of a wariness that would impact Roman strategic execution for the next several centuries. As Augustus had proven after the Battle of Actium, a victorious general with a loyal army at his back could ask for much and be denied little; emperors were therefore wary of allowing commanders to gather too large a force under their command. When they were forced to do so, they worked hard to ensure that the glory of any victory accrued to the emperor and not the commander in the field. In fact, few things were more life-threatening to a Roman commander than a string of glorious successes. It is no wonder that so many of them decided they had to make a grasp for the purple before the emperor had them killed.

The Great Illyrian Revolt was led by the kings of two different tribes, both of them named Bato. Their forces had originally been brought together to assist the Roman war against the Marcomanni, but upon coming together and realizing their military strength, they revolted. Velleius tells us that they had as many as 200,000 men under arms and were led by capable men who "possessed not only a knowledge of Roman discipline but also of the Roman tongue[;] many also had some measure of literary culture, and the exercise of the intellect was not uncommon among them."[19] This is high praise indeed and indicates that, like Arminius, many of these barbarians were as well educated as most Romans and were familiar with the methods of Roman warfare, probably as a result of their long service in Rome's auxiliary forces. In short, it was a formidable force, and according to Velleius, they got off to a good start: Roman citizens were everywhere overpowered, and a large detachment of veterans was exterminated to a man. The wholesale devastation by fire and sword caused a panic in Rome that reportedly left Augustus shaking with fear.[20]

At the start of the war, Tiberius was set on seeking out and annihilating the main armies of the insurgents, but when they proved elusive, he settled in for a grinding war of attrition. By occupying well-placed fortresses and sending out forces to lay waste to the countryside, he gradually ground down the barbarians' forces and will to persist. Augustus, still in a near panic, raised a new army to come to Tiberius's assistance. To man it Augustus even bought slaves from their owners and paid for their maintenance so that they could be enlisted in the army. Tiberius judged this force, commanded by his nephew, Germanicus, to be nearly useless and sent most of it home. He also returned three legions that had marched from the lower Danube (Moesia) back to their home bases to repel Dacians, who were taking advantage of Rome's distraction to probe across the Danube.

There are two points of strategic interest in these actions. First, the incursions of the Dacians, which took place whenever Roman frontiers were denuded of troops until they were conquered by Trajan a hundred years later, demonstrate that the barbarians were typically able to gather accurate intelligence on the state of Roman defenses along and beyond the frontiers. Furthermore, when these defenses appeared weakened, the barbarians were always ready to take the chance of conducting damaging raids into the Empire. In the early first century, they were unable to gather sufficient forces to overrun an entire province, but this danger would only worsen over time.

In any event, the style of war Tiberius adopted eschewed pitched battles and, as such, did not require tremendous masses of troops. Rather, Tiberius employed Rome's two great military advantages over the barbarians: engineering and logistics. By building fortresses at crucial locations and securing his veterans within them, he disrupted the enemy's communications and food supply. On the other hand, Rome's suburb commissary arrangements made sure the scattered cohorts of the legions remained well fed. The barbarians soon found that Roman interdictions made it impossible to coordinate their actions throughout the theater, making their forces easier for the fast-marching Roman detachments to isolate and destroy. But the crucial factor was food, and on this point the barbarians were unable to counter Tiberius. Velleius, who was on Tiberius's staff, soon noted that the barbarian forces were "reduced to the verge of destruction by famine" and quickly became incapable of meeting the Romans even when battle was offered under circumstances where a well-fed army might have defeated the Romans.[21] Starvation eventually left the unity of the tribes in tatters, and after three bloody years the rebellion collapsed.

In the short term, it may appear that neither the Illyrian Revolt nor the Varian Disaster had changed anything. What had taken place in Germany and Pannonia was a replay of events that Rome had already endured many times in its long history. Armies appeared to contest Roman dominion, often inflicting costly early defeats on the Romans, but then Rome mustered its latent power to put overwhelming force in the fields and the will to sustain these forces for years. This was the formula that had crushed every opponent Rome had ever faced. And it was the formula employed in the first century's first decade.

We have already seen the swift and decisive Roman reaction in Illyria. Similar events also took place in Germania in the wake of the Varian Disaster. Having just quelled the revolts in Pannonia, Tiberius was sent north to restore the reputation of Roman arms in Germania. Along with his Germanicus, Tiberius first restored calm to the Rhine frontier and spent the next two years campaigning in Germania. These were vicious and bloody affairs meant to terrorize the tribes clustered along the Rhine. Because these assaults never penetrated far into barbarian territory, they were clearly not aimed at conquest. Rather, they were reminders that, despite Teutoburg Wald, the legions remained invincible, and few tribes were beyond Rome's reach.

In the immediate aftermath of Augustus's death, there were two further campaigns, led by Germanicus. Twice he fought major but inconclusive battles against Arminius. At one point rumors arose in the Roman camps on the Rhine that part of Germanicus's army, commanded by Caecina, had been destroyed and that the victorious Germans were marching west. The garrison was about to destroy a bridge that would have left Caecina's hard-pressed but far from destroyed legions trapped on the far side of the Rhine when the prompt and courageous action of Germanicus's wife, Agrippina, averted a disaster. As Tacitus describes it, "Meanwhile a rumor had spread that our army was cut off, and that a furious German host was marching on Gaul. And had not Agrippina prevented the bridge over the Rhine from being destroyed, some in their cowardice would have dared that base act."[22]

A minute examination of Germanicus's invasions is not necessary.[23] What is crucial is understanding that in two great battles Arminius managed to hold the disparate tribes together long enough to field an army that six Roman legions failed to crush. Germanicus, despite his failure to bring victories in two major campaigns, remained certain that one final attempt would suffice to crush the barbarians west of the Elbe. But Tiberius had had enough. He ordered Germanicus back to Rome: "since the vengeance of Rome had been satisfied, [the Germans] might be left to their internal feuds."[24] Germanicus was reluctant to obey and tried to delay his departure with promises of ultimate military success, but Tiberius was not deceived. For the new emperor, the risks of future campaigns in Germania far exceeded any benefit to the Empire.

It is hard to overstate the long-term strategic impact the combination of Teutoburg Wald and the Illyrian Revolt had on the future of Rome. Roman plans to incorporate Germania at least as far as the Elbe were put on temporary, and eventually permanent, hold. For the next five hundred years Roman territory went only as far as the Rhine, although Roman military and economic power reached far beyond it. In strategic terms, the frontier was a territorial limit that in no way limited Rome's zone of influence. Still, echoes of the Roman decision to halt at the Rhine and Danube are still being felt two millennia later, as Europe continues to cope with Latin-Teutonic and Slavic-Teutonic divides that in the twentieth century were the foundational cause of two world wars.[25]

On Rome's eastern frontier, this one facing the Parthian Empire, initial plans for Rome's eastward expansion collapsed when a Roman army under Crassus was annihilated at the Battle of Carrhae (present-day Harran, Turkey) in 53 BCE. In the years following that disaster, there were a few major attempts to replicate Alexander's conquest, and Julius Caesar was reportedly planning such a campaign when he was assassinated. Augustus, however, opted to settle that frontier on the Euphrates, at least for a time, and undertook some face-saving diplomacy to have the standards lost at Carrhae returned to Rome. This was sufficient return for the imperial propaganda machine to portray the halt of the legions' advance in the east as a victory. In Africa, Roman frontiers, despite some deep (but temporary) penetrations along the Nile to just beyond the first cataract, ended at the point where the desert made further conquest impossible.

The Great Halt

There is much to be said for the idea that the locations of the Roman frontiers were not part of a preconceived strategy. Rather, they were accidents of circumstance determined by where the legions were forced, by either geography or military defeat, to halt their previously inexorable forward momentum. This was not the case at the start of Augustus's reign—before the Romans began to accept that there were limits to the Empire's expansion. For Augustus, the idea that Rome was destined to rule over the entire world was still accepted as the city's destiny, and Virgil's words, published as Augustus was coming to terms with the Parthians, remained state policy and part of an ingrained national consciousness: "Romane, memento (hae tibi erunt artes) pacique imponere morem, parcere subiectis et debellare superbos" (Remember, Roman, you rule nations with your power (these will be your talents) and impose law and order, spare the conquered, and beat down the arrogant).[26]

That Augustus accepted, even internalized, Virgil's commentary is demonstrated by the fact that he added more territory to the Roman Empire than any other emperor. He did so by focusing most of his energies on cleaning up the imperial mess his ambitious Republican predecessors had left him. For instance, Caesar had seized Gaul, but the area between Gaul and Italy was filled with Alpine tribes yet unbowed. Even large portions of Gaul had not yet completely accepted Roman rule. Also, while much of Spain had been controlled by Rome since the Second Punic War, large areas in the north and west remained unpacified. Cleaning up these areas and then pushing forward at the margins of the Empire was the primary occupation of most of the legions during Augustus's long reign.

But by the time of his death, Augustus certainly appears to have accepted that there were limits to what Roman arms could accomplish, going so far as to warn his successors "to be satisfied with their present possessions and under no conditions to wish to increase the empire to any greater dimensions. It would be hard to guard . . . and this would lead to danger of their losing what was already theirs."[27] Whether Augustus actually wrote this is still debated.[28] It is certain, however, that Augustus himself was not content with the borders bequeathed to him.[29] His *Res Gestae* clearly establishes that Augustus considered himself a conqueror and wanted history to remember him as such.[30]

> I extended the territory of all those provinces of the Roman people on whose borders lay peoples not subject to our government. I brought

peace to the Gallic and Spanish provinces as well as to Germany, throughout the area bordering on the Ocean from Cadiz to the mouth of the Elbe. I secured the pacification of the Alps from the district nearest the Adriatic to the Tuscan sea, yet without waging an unjust war on any people. My fleet sailed through the ocean eastwards from the mouth of the Rhine to the territory of the Cimbri, a country which no Roman had visited before either by land or sea, and the Cimbri, Charydes, Semnones and other German peoples of that region sent ambassadors and sought my friendship and that of the Roman people. At my command and under my auspices two armies were led almost at the same time into Ethiopia and Arabia Felix; vast enemy forces of both peoples were cut down in battle and many towns captured. Ethiopia was penetrated as far as the town of Nabata, which adjoins Meroe; in Arabia the army advanced into the territory of the Sabaeans to the town of Mariba. I added Egypt to the empire of the Roman people. Greater Armenia I might have made a province after its king, Artaxes, had been killed, but I preferred, following the model set by our ancestors, to hand over that kingdom to Tigranes, son of King Artavasdes and grandson of King Tigranes; Tiberius Nero, who was then my stepson, carried this out. When the same people later rebelled and went to war, I subdued them through the agency of my son Gaius and handed them over to be ruled by King Ariobarzanes, son of Artabazus, King of the Medes, and after his death to his son Artavasdes. When he was killed, I sent Tigranes, a scion of the royal Armenian house, to that kingdom. I recovered all the provinces beyond the Adriatic Sea towards the east, together with Cyrene, the greater part of them being then occupied by kings. I had previously recovered Sicily and Sardinia which had been seized in the slave war.[31]

In fact, before the events of 6–9 CE, Augustus likely remained committed to conquering the entire world, possibly only because he did not fully grasp the extent of territory beyond Rome's frontiers.[32] As the adopted son of Julius Caesar, it was inevitable that he would judge his own accomplishments in comparison to those of his illustrious predecessor and strive mightily to equal or exceed them, particularly in the first decades of his reign, when his hold on power was less secure. Moreover, Caesar made his greatest conquests in Gaul with only a fraction of Rome's resources at his disposal. Augustus, with the full might of Rome under his singular control, surely considered little as being beyond his grasp.[33] His dreams, of course, were thwarted by Germanic barbarians, but before this, Germania's conquest was likely just a planned first stepping-stone to great glory. Augustus viewed the conquest of conquest of Germany beyond the Elbe as necessary for the Empire's security, as well as a step toward the envelopment of territories beyond. According to J. C. Mann, such plans were not wildly unrealistic: who in the early days of the Republic could have foreseen that Rome would eventually conquer the whole Mediterranean region? The gods had given the Romans so much; it was impossible believe that what remained would be kept from them.[34]

Mann considers the Roman frontier to have been an accident of history, drawn at the limits of Rome's ability to project power any further. In this view, Rome ceased its expansion not as a matter of policy, but because of exhaustion. This strategic appreciation is only half true. Rome certainly suffered setbacks in Germania, but the decision to halt was certainly a strategic policy, as Rome could easily have mustered the resources to continue offensive operations for years or even decades to come. This is demonstrated by the fact that when Augustus sent Germanicus back to the Rhine in 13 CE and gave him command of eight legions—a third of Rome's total military forces and equal to the number of legions needed to conquer Gaul—he likely had the final conquest of Germania in mind. Still, for many historians, the path set out by Edward Gibbon on the first page of his magisterial work *The History of the Decline and Fall of the Roman Empire* remains the dominant historical theme:

> The principal conquests of the Romans were achieved under the republic: and the emperors, for the most part, were satisfied with preserving those dominions which had been acquired by the policy of the senate, the active emulation of the consuls, and the martial enthusiasm of the people. The seven first centuries were filled with a rapid succession of triumphs; *but it was reserved for Augustus to relinquish the ambitious design of subduing the whole earth, and to introduce a spirit of moderation into the public councils.*[35]

In the final analysis, it was not Augustus who called a halt to Roman expansion, but Tiberius. Furthermore, if Tiberius had not already been renowned as one of Rome's greatest generals and acclaimed as the deified Augustus's "chosen" successor, it is unlikely that he could have long resisted the pressure to continue the conquests.

When Tiberius called off Rome's further expansion there was still no sign of a Maginot Line mentality, and the *limes*, such as we find under the Flavians, did not exist. It seems clear that no Roman was yet considering a policy focused on keeping the barbarians out. Instead, one can argue that Rome appeared to be holding to a policy of conquest.[36] This is likely true, up to a point. The Romans, for several reasons, were not yet worried about defending the Rhine. First, they were generally on the offensive. Even when the idea of conquest was given up, conflicts were almost always the result of Roman forces crossing the Rhine looking for a fight. Moreover, despite the accomplishments of Arminius and Maroboduus in creating powerful tribal confederations, these were not lasting political entities. The natural state of the tribes beyond the frontier during the Principate and for most of the next two centuries was characterized by fragmentation. However, even if the barbarians were able to cross the Rhine or Danube in large numbers, Rome was still capable of concentrating huge amounts of combat power along any threatened point of the frontiers. In short, the barbarians would have been playing Rome's game. Finally, the regions adjacent to the Rhine and Danube frontiers were economically backward and not yet fully integrated into the Empire's economic or political system. In other words, they were not rich enough, nor did the inhabitants have the political clout, to force the Romans to spread its legions out along the entire frontier for their immediate protection. There was no reason for extensive fortified lines when few external enemies were capable of reaching deep into the core areas of the Empire. Besides, one never knew when the emperor might have a change of heart and send the legions forward on another campaign of conquest.

One criticism of Rome's manning the entire frontier in force was that it left no strategic reserve worthy of the name. Theodor Mommsen, the founder of modern Roman history, claimed such a mobile striking force in the wake of the Crisis of the Third Century was the most important moment in the development of Roman strategy.[37] An argument could be made for that claim, but probably not the one Mommsen makes, for he views it as a beneficial development. Since Mommsen stated his position, the idea that the Romans employed an intrinsically flawed defensive system until they created large mobile field armies and gave up on the notion of a linear defense in favor of a defense in depth has become generally accepted.[38] It is, however, wrong.

Even with good Roman roads, it took a legion 67 days to march from Rome to Cologne and 127 days to march from Rome to Antioch.[39] Thus, the strategic mobility of the legions was very low when compared to the size of the Empire, making some forward basing of the Empire's reserves necessary, since basing thirty legions in and around Rome would have been as absurd as placing a legionary every twenty meters along the entire frontier. But for the Romans it made sense to deploy all or as much as possible of the army forward, because the legions on the Danube and Rhine frontiers were their own strategic reserve.

One must remember that the first-century barbarian tribes were incapable of massing large formations at multiple points for simultaneous breakthroughs in the Empire, nor could they sustain large forces for extended periods. Consequently, until at least the third century, even the most dangerous barbarian penetration was limited almost entirely to the frontier provinces. Of course, any penetration into Dalmatia or Pannonia was getting dangerously close to Italy and could easily threaten east-west communications. That is why an additional two legions were usually stationed in the region, and emperors were always quick to react to any threat to this vital area. The Romans knew it was absurd to think that a strategic reserve positioned deep in Gaul, Italy, or the Balkans could easily reach a threatened location: they possessed keen knowledge, born of long experience, of the transport and logistical realities regarding this kind of movement.[40] Any such force would have to march for hundreds of miles overland, dragging much of its supply train behind it. Likely it would have to continue drawing massive amounts of supplies along the same routes once it arrived in the theater, as no supplies would be available to move along the Rhine or Danube except for what the units on those frontiers required for their subsistence.

But what if almost all the combat power in the west not absolutely required to maintain internal stability were kept along the river lines? First and foremost, the largest concentrations of these troops, though scattered, would sit athwart the most likely spots for barbarians to cross. As noted above, from these locations they were well placed for rapid incursions across the frontier to destroy dangerous enemy concentrations before they could metastasize into a problem requiring force on the scale needed to crush the Pannonian Revolt. In the event, if these measures failed and there was a barbarian breakthrough, every legion along the impacted river line could easily board barges and move to the trouble spot in a fraction of the time it would take for an inland reserve to arrive. Just as crucially, these legions would already have made plans, likely using contractual arrangements extending over many years, for all their supplies to move to their established locations. Within their frontier fortifications the Romans would have secure logistic bases that could forward supplies along the river lines as easily as the troops moved. When the crisis ended, the legions could just as easily return to their original bases. Only during the Late Empire, when it was often impossible for the Romans to move securely along the frontier rivers, did an inland reserve army make any sense, and even then it was probably not the best strategic option.[41] Moreover, while the legions could and often did march to Antioch, they just as often made use of their command of the Mediterranean to move troops and supplies by sea. One must never lose track of the strategic importance of the

Mediterranean, which reduced transport and communication times within the vital core of the Empire to a fraction of what was required if everything had to move entirely by land, as was true of the Persian Empire.

For the time being, therefore, the most sensible strategic option in the western portions of the Empire, inclusive of the Balkans, was to keep the legions concentrated along expected invasion routes and positioned well forward. It was only after the Civil War in 69 CE that emperors fully comprehended the dangers involved in maintaining concentrated forces that might fall under the sway of a charismatic general with designs on the purple. In the east, where metropolitan-based logistics made taking and holding cities the route to victory, it was even more logical to keep the legions concentrated. Thus, even after 69 CE, the latent threat of Parthian power made successive emperors wary of dispersing their eastern army, particularly after client states along the border were annexed into the Empire.

CHAPTER 5 | The Infrastructure of Empire

THE STRATEGIC INFRASTRUCTURE of the Empire consisted primarily of the road network and fortified structures, which include cities,
towns, and the *limes* along Rome's frontiers. Of course, other infrastructure,
such as canals, irrigation systems, and aqueducts, were all crucial in the
maintenance of the Roman economy, which provided the foundation of all
strategic actions. But this work assumes that these could be built and sustained only in an environment in which Roman military power maintained
a general peace. And the maintenance of peace required, above all else, roads
and forts.

Rome's Nervous System

The Roman road system was built solely for the purpose of speeding the
movement of the legions. Everything else the roads were used for was
simply an added benefit. Most everyone has heard the phrase "all roads lead
to Rome." But to better comprehend how the Romans understood the role
of their road network, it is best to reverse that statement: "all roads lead
away from Rome." Rome was the center of the Empire, from which, at least
through the centuries of the Principate, all power emanated. Rome built its
thousands of miles of roads for the singular purpose of pushing power out
from the Empire's core to its frontiers and then, later, from one part of the
Empire to another.

By the time of Diocletian (284–305), the Roman road network consisted of 56,000 miles of roads, supplemented by over a thousand bridges, an impressive total that was not exceeded until the early twentieth century.[1] One estimate places the cost of building this network at approximately the same as that of maintaining thirty legions for the entire five hundred years of the Empire.[2] As this is only the construction cost and does not include yearly maintenance, it is clear that the cost of the Roman road network greatly exceeded the cost of the army during the span of the Empire. As such, it was a major drain on the Empire's financial resources. Of course, in the same way that the Roman army paid for itself by maintaining the Pax Romana, which underpinned Roman prosperity, the road network, by hugely easing the cost of trade, more than justified its expense.

The primary military purpose of the road network was to speed the movement of the legions from their bases to either a point of crisis or a mobilization point. It has often been theorized that the roads were necessary to ease the movement of supplies, particularly food and fodder. But there is no evidence in the extant records of this ever having taken place.[3] There is a very good reason for this: a well-defined limit exists on how far premodern military formations could move if they had to carry their own food and fodder. In a modern example, the German army in 1914 rapidly exhausted its supplies once it got over a hundred miles from its railheads. This more than any other factor explains the failure of Germany to defeat the French army in the first year of World War I. General William Tecumseh Sherman, in 1864, did lead his army 285 miles in his famous "March to the Sea," but his soldiers mostly lived off the land, and the animals were expected to make only a one-way trip. A Roman army, no matter how liberally supplied with wagons and pack mules, could travel at most about two hundred miles, and then only if the beasts of burden were allowed to perish rather than make the return trip. Any farther and the wagons and mule packs would consist of nothing but grain and fodder for the animals, which would be rapidly consumed. For a Roman army to move over a thousand miles, as it often did, orders would have to be dispatched all along the march route weeks or months ahead of time, requiring local officials to gather supplies at selected points all along the route. Unless the march route could be supplied by sea or river transport, there was no other way to accomplish the task.

The reality of an extended Roman march then was that the beasts of burden carried the soldiers' requirements—tents, utensils, weapons, siege trains, and artillery—but little or no food. But because food was a necessity, the only time roads were intensively used for the logistical support of the armies was for short-distance affairs, moving food from nearby port facilities to bases or from nearby agricultural centers to encampments. When the army needed to move bulk supplies to a distant location, maritime transport was the method of choice, as it was faster and cheaper. Wheat moved by sea could travel at twice the speed of land transport, cover nearly unlimited distance, and do so at about one-fiftieth the cost.[4] The second major strategic purpose of the road network was moving key personnel and information, which was often one and the same. To accomplish this, the Romans maintained the *cursus publicus*—Rome's nervous system. This system was first established by Augustus and maintained until the fall of the Western Empire.[5] At intervals along all of the Empire's major roads, there were stations where animals were maintained, along with wagons and carts. These were made available only to those on public business and high-ranking soldiers. Rome did not maintain anything like the American west's Pony Express, with a corps of dedicated messengers. Rather, if a governor wished to send a note to the emperor, he would have to send someone from his own staff. At these stations the messenger would be able to change modes of transport (get a new horse), but he would not find a team of professional messengers waiting to take the note on the next leg of its travels. The crucial advantage of this system is that the messenger came from the scene of events whence the message was dispatched and could be further interrogated to provide context and additional information as required.

To make sure the *cursus publicus* was not overused, only a few persons within the Empire were permitted to issue permits (*diplomata*) for the use of the system's resources. Such permits would often limit the number of resources a traveler could use. For instance, a messenger who had to get to Rome with vital information—such as if a mass of barbarians had crossed the Danube and were making their way south—might be authorized a new horse at every stop, while a messenger delivering another of Pliny the Younger's incessant requests for guidance might have to make do with a new and rested horse every half dozen posts. One of Pliny's messages dealt directly with the workings of this system:

> I beg you, Sir, to write and tell me whether you wish the [*diploma*] permits, the terms of which have expired, to be recognized as valid, and for how long, and so free me from my indecision. For I am afraid of blundering either one way or the other, either by confirming what ought to lapse, or by putting obstacles in the way of those which are necessary.

To which Trajan replied:

> The permits, of which the terms have expired, ought not to be recognized, and consequently I make it my special duty to send out new permits to all the provinces before the day when they are required.[6]

Most permits were issued by the emperor, who would send fixed quantities of preapproved permits to each governor to make use of them as he saw fit. In the later Empire, a few high-ranking officials—praetorian prefects—were also entitled to do so.

While the speed of information traveling from one end of the Empire to the other appears agonizingly slow to modern readers, who can reach practically anyone in the world instantaneously, for a strategist the speed at which information travels is relative. While Rome ruled, its capacity to move information long distances was unparalleled, giving it a decisive informational advantage over its enemies. Even the Persians, who had made use of a royal communications system since the days of Cyrus and Darius, could not match the speed and efficiency of Rome's network, as the Persians could not make use of sea or river transport, except for short distances along the Tigris and Euphrates rivers. How the Romans thought about this network is captured in an oration given around the middle of the second century by Aelius Aristides:

> And if the governors should have even some slight doubt whether certain claims are valid in connection with either public or private lawsuits and petitions from the governed, they straightway send to him [the emperor] with a request for instructions what to do, and they wait until he prepares a response, like a chorus waiting for its trainer. Therefore, he has no need to wear himself out traveling around the whole empire nor, by appearing personally, now among some, then among others, to make sure of each point when he has the time to tread their soil. *It is easy for him to stay where he is, and manage the entire civilized world by letters, which arrive almost as soon as they are written, as if they were carried by winged envoys.*[7]

No doubt Aristides was overstating the capabilities of Rome's communication system, but the big picture is correct—a Roman emperor could influence events in every corner of the Empire, no matter his location. In fact, the weakening of this capacity likely had a large influence upon Rome's ability to meet successive crises during the later Empire. In this regard, Richard Duncan Jones, in a remarkable piece of detective research, calculated the differences in communication times between the two eras. By examining data on how long, on average, it took for news of a new Emperor to reach Egypt—fifty-seven days during the Principate—and comparing it to the travel times indicated in the double-dated edicts of the Theodosian Code (438 CE), which took, on average, 134 days, he was able to document the collapse of Rome's transport network.[8] A more than doubling of communications times from the core of power to the frontiers had to have had a huge impact on the conduct of strategic policy and military operations.

The Walls of Rome: The Limes

The term *limes* was originally used to describe a boundary, not a frontier, and certainly not a fortified frontier. By the end of the first century, the term was still used to describe the boundaries of the Empire, and only later as a frontier district. It was also often employed in reference to the roads linking Roman military installations along the frontier. Only in the third century does the word become synonymous with a wall or fortified boundary. Although it never carried the same connotations as we give to national borders in the modern world, as the Romans always understood it, there were many reasons to place forts and other structures beyond the boundary.[9] This is a key point: The *limes* might be the boundaries of the Empire's territory, but they were never meant to mark the limits of Roman power or influence. The Roman Empire might end at the Danube, the Rhine, or the Euphrates, but there was never any question of Rome's acting far beyond these boundaries when it had an interest in doing so. In the Roman mind, the Empire's territory might be measurable, but Roman influence was boundless.

Although Rome never lost its expansionist impulse, and while successful foreign wars were typically the surest way to ensure regime longevity, by the time Tiberius ascended to the purple Rome's boundaries were increasingly fixed. In fact, by the first decades of the Principate, Rome was much more concerned with internal security than with expansion. In this regard, it is worth, once again, examining the placement of the legions as presented by Tacitus in 23 CE:

> But chief strength was on the Rhine, as a defense alike against Germans and Gauls, and *numbered eight legions. Spain, lately subjugated, was held by three.* Mauretania was king . . . *Africa was garrisoned by two legions, and Egypt by the same number . . . Syria . . . was kept in restraint by four legions . . .* the bank of the Danube by *two legions in Pannonia, two in Moesia, and two also were stationed in Dalmatia,* which, from the

situation of the country, were in the rear of the other four, and, should Italy suddenly require aid, not too distant to be summoned. *But the capital was garrisoned by its own special soldiery, three city, nine praetorian cohorts.*[10]

Note that Tacitus tells us that the eight legions on the Rhine were not just there to guard the frontier—they also had an internal stability role in the event the recently conquered Gauls became restive. The same is seen in the east, where the primary role of the four legions in Syria is to keep the eastern provinces "in restraint." Guarding the frontier against the Parthians is assigned to client kingdoms, which are kept safe from major attack by their ability to call on the legions for aid. Even the Danube is lightly held by four legions—two on the upper Danube (Pannonia) and two on the lower Danube (Moesia). Notably, the two legions held in reserve, deeper in the Balkans, do not have a primary responsibility of aiding hard-pressed forces on the frontier. Rather, they are held in reserve in case Italy required aid.

It is worth taking a moment to note that Tacitus's recounting of the locations and strategic purpose of each of the Empire's major concentrations of military power is positive proof that the Romans clearly understood the geography of their Empire and could arrange forces in accordance with strategic considerations. But it also reveals that Rome was not yet overly worried about protecting the frontiers. What concerns they did have were subsumed by the strategic necessity of maintaining internal stability and securing the position of the emperor. Given the weakness of Rome's external enemies, it would be odd if we saw large expenditures on permanent frontier defenses that were not yet required.

It is not until the reign of Claudius that we first see Rome building rudimentary permanent defenses along the frontiers. As there likely was no increase in the threat level, an explanation is required. Two are readily at hand. The first is that the legions had now been largely static on the Rhine and the Danube for almost a generation. It is only natural that their encampments would transform over time into more comfortable and secure permanent installations and that connecting roads would be built along with smaller outposts to watch the areas between major camps. The second is a consequence of Claudius requiring more than the two new legions he built—XV Primigenia and XXII Primigenia—to conquer Britain. These troops had to be taken from the Rhine, and removing them greatly weakened the forces along that frontier. Interestingly, we find that the legionary base at Xanten was rebuilt using stone at about this time. Stone, of course, provided a much-enhanced defense for a smaller garrison than the earlier wooden palisade. Moreover, there was an expansion of smaller forts, called watchtowers, all connected along the frontier. On the Danube, Thrace, long occupied and still holding its client status, was annexed, legions were moved from Raetia to the Danube, and new roads such as the Via Claudia were built. In short, Claudius's need for troops to expand the Empire and to give him a military reputation necessitated the installation of Roman *limes*.[11]

From these small beginnings, Rome increasingly emplaced a fortification system that stretched along its entire 4,800-mile frontier system, reaching its apogee in the forty years between 120 and 160 CE. This is the period, starting with Hadrian, when Rome constructed the bulk of its fortified lines along the frontiers.[12] Crucially, as you move from region to region, there is no set pattern to which the *limes*'s engineers were required to adhere, as many factors went into their building. The first and possibly the least important was local resources, as it was much easier to build from local material than to have to import stone or wood from distant portions of the Empire. More important was regional geography. Britain could have a solid stone wall along its entire land frontier because it spanned barely sixty miles from end to end. Similarly, having the ability to incorporate a major river into the defensive system allowed Rome to construct defenses relying on infrastructure other than solid walls from the North Sea to the Alps. Similarly, Rome did not need to defend the vast desert tracks along its African frontiers—here a few good roads and a couple of forts could do the job. The most crucial consideration was always the threat presented by Rome's enemies. Walls and rivers could stop almost any threat the Principate faced in the Western Empire. In the east, however, a more sophisticated enemy capable of massing huge armies was not going to be deterred by a wall or any kind of linear defense (Fig. 5.1). In the east, Rome required strong points arranged in depth. These strong points, placed along key avenues of approach and incorporating the walls of the east's great cities, were designed to attrit a Persian army in a series of wasting sieges that bought time for the Roman field army to mobilize and march.

The purpose of the *limes* has been much disputed in recent decades. As one historian writes: "Some of the activities of the Army in these regions [Northern Europe] continue to baffle scholars. There is no real consensus as to what such monumental linear boundaries as the walls of northern Britain or between the Rhine and the Danube were for or how they functioned."[13] Another historian has identified twenty-one separate reasons for the construction of the *limes* system.[14] They range from "a piece of rhetoric" to a place to reflect on "Rome's failure to conquer the world." Much of this *"limes* denial"

FIGURE 5.1 Reconstructed gate of Roman fort

has already been discussed earlier in this work. Unable to accept that a fort or system of fortifications can serve multiple purposes, too many historians have employed alternative reasons ranging from the probable to the absurd to obscure the primary reason Rome would undertake such a vast expense. But if we were to allow just a bit of common sense to enter the argument, the answer is apparent: For Rome, the *limes* served the same crucial purpose all walls at all times have served—to keep the people on the other side of the wall out.[15] The *limes* were first and foremost a military system designed to aid the legions in the defense of the Empire. One can easily see this in the Roman general Arrian's thoughts on the *limes* in a report from one of his inspection tours:

> At Apsaros, where the five cohorts are stationed, I gave the army its pay and inspected its weapons, the walls, the trench, the sick and food supplies that were there. [At Phasis] the fort itself, in which 400 select troops were quartered, seemed to me, owing to the nature of the site, to be very secure, and to lie in the most convenient spot for the safety of those who sail this way. In addition, a double ditch has been put round the wall, each ditch as broad as the other. The wall used to be of earth, and wooden towers were set up about it; now both it and the towers are made of baked brick. And its foundations are firm, and machines are installed, and in short, it is fully equipped to prevent any barbarians from even approaching it, let alone to protect the garrison there against the dangers of a siege.[16]

But just how effective were the *limes*, and was the system worth the cost? General George S. Patton considered all fortifications a waste of resources and monuments to the stupidity of man, but that was before his Third Army's rapid advance was halted by the broken-down German border defenses, manned mostly by raw recruits. Of course, the expense of fortifications always appears wasteful once they are pierced. But to strategists no walls or fortified zones are meant to be impassable. Thus, Rome never intended the *limes* to be an impenetrable barrier; they had too great an understanding of war to cloud their thinking with fanciful ideas. After all, the Romans were the ancient world's master of siege warfare. They knew only too well that any fortress can be taken by a large enough force of men determined to take it. But walls make everything harder for an enemy. For instance, when the Goths, in the fourth century, abandoned the siege of Adrianople because it was costing them too many men, their leader, Fritigern, declared he would "keep peace with walls."[17] In that regard, Patton was right: if men can overcome oceans and mountains, fortifications can also be overcome. Of course, fortifications that reinforce such natural barriers can be fiendishly difficult to defeat.

For Rome, the *limes* served several strategic purposes depending on their location, including acting as a shield to mass forces behind for a surge into enemy territory, deterring or defeating raids and other small incursions,

FIGURE 5.2 Reconstruction of a Roman fortress

establishing points of contact for trade and diplomacy, delaying a major invasion force, and making it difficult for a booty-laden enemy force to escape Roman territory. But their primary strategic purpose was to permit an economy of force.[18] A lone legion in a fortress could defend against enemy armies that it would take multiple legions to confront in the open (Fig. 5.2). Rome was able to concentrate forces for a true crisis because it could leave only skeleton forces in the *limes* and count on them to contain all but the most serious threats. In this role, the *limes* succeeded spectacularly for over two hundred years, until during the Crisis of the Third Century the defenses were struck at multiple points by large numbers of enemies. Still, in the wake of the crisis, during the reigns of Diocletian and Constantine, the *limes* were largely rebuilt and strengthened. It was not until they were weakened by civil war and neglect that the western *limes* were overrun and the integrated defensive systems wrecked beyond repair.

CHAPTER 6 | An Army for Empire

A FTER ACTIUM AND the death of Mark Anthony, Augustus, now the sole ruler of the Roman world, had had at his disposal sixty battle-hardened legions with which to enforce his will. But that was a problem, for he now had far more legions than required to defend or even to expand the Empire, as well as far more than the Empire could sustain. Unfortunately, he commanded legions that fully comprehended that they—not Augustus and not the Senate—were the ultimate political power. They could either enforce the will of Augustus or break him. Unless the army was reduced and rewarded in a manner they approved, Augustus's first weeks as ruler of the Empire could easily have been his last. But politics, not war, was where Augustus's true genius lay. He had shown up for the wars, for to stay in Rome would have cost him the respect and possibly the obedience of the legions. But the actual conduct of the war had been left to Agrippa, his closest friend and adviser.

To prove that decades of crisis and civil war were finally over, Augustus had to reduce the size of the army. Many in the army wanted this also. They had been conscripted and held in the service to fight the civil wars, and now that the conflicts were at an end, they expected to be discharged, with a suitable reward. Providing these rewards had always been a problem, because the civilian population was always unwilling to see lands confiscated and handed over to soldiers returning to civilian life.

Augustus had other major concerns. For one, the Empire required a professional standing army, loyal to the state and, more crucially, to the emperor personally. During the last decades of the Republic, such long-serving armies had transferred their ultimate loyalty from Rome to their commanding general. After all, it was he who ensured their rewards, particularly when wars ended and their service was no longer required. Sulla had shown the way when he displaced thousands of civilian farmers and handed their lands over to his legions. Pompey, on the other hand, had demonstrated how powerless a general—or a new emperor—could become if he discharged his troops before ensuring their rewards.

Augustus broke the legions' dependence on their generals by fixing the system so that rewards were guaranteed by the state and fixed in accordance with a soldier's length of service. In 6 CE, Augustus placed this program on a firmer legal and financial footing by creating a new tax—the *aerarium militare*—to finance veterans' settlement. According to Dio, Augustus paid the first 150 million sesterces out of his own pocket, thus purchasing another huge amount of legionary loyalty.[1] In a stroke he had invested every legionary with a personal stake not only in the stability of the Roman state, but in Augustus's rule.

Two other problems with standing armies were taken care of together. Armies become quite dangerous to the standing political order the closer they are to the center of power, where they are continually exposed to politics. Moreover, an idle army is a dangerous army. So when Augustus reduced the post–Civil Wars army by more than half, he solved several problems at once. First, given the size of the territory it had to protect, as well as his future expansion plans, Augustus ensured that the legions would almost always be busy. During those rare times when the legions were not committed to combat or military expeditions, they could be worked to exhaustion building the roads and ports that knitted the Empire together. The strategic drawback to this course of action is apparent: by opting for efficiency and the security of the regime, the Empire failed to build a reserve force sufficient to meet crises, which were sure to arise. But one must remember that any reserve force, idle and conscious of its strength, was a mortal threat to an emperor. Also, as we have seen above, Rome used river lines and sea power to develop clever ways of creating reserves out of the frontier legions.

By placing the bulk of the army along the distant frontiers, Augustus, at least for a time, limited the amount of political infection that would have tugged at the legions' loyalties had they remained in Italy. In fact, Italy was almost entirely demilitarized, with only the Praetorian Guard and the urban cohorts allowed to remain in the country. Augustus was apparently rather proud of his settlement, as he listed it in the *Rae Gestae* as his first major accomplishment as emperor.[2] According to Augustus, he had paid 860 million sesterces from his own funds to purchase land for the hundreds of thousands of discharged troops.[3]

Once the demobilization was completed, Augustus was left with twenty-eight legions, drawn from his and Mark Anthony's army. By 5 BCE the length of enlistment was set at twenty years for a regular legionary and sixteen years for a praetorian, although many served far longer. In fact, many of the soldiers who mutinied in Pannonia in 14 CE complained of being required to serve over thirty years.[4] This meant there were approximately 150,000 legionaries in the entire Roman army and, according to Tacitus, approximately the same number of troops in the auxiliary forces, which consisted of non-Roman soldiers.[5] For the next three hundred years, the total number of legions always approximated this figure, with a low of twenty-five in the aftermath of the Varian Disaster. The total number of legions eventually grew to thirty-three under Septimius Severus, and for a short time, during the Crisis of the Third Century, the total number hit thirty-six, but it is extremely doubtful that many of these legions ever approached their full complement of troops.[6] That meant that, on average, approximately 300,000 legionaries and auxiliaries guarded a population of sixty million, covering an area of two million square miles, encircled by 3,100 miles of frontiers.

Each of these legions consisted, on paper, of a little over 5,000 men, substantially organized in the same manner as were the legions Julius Caesar brought into Gaul. The smallest tactical unit, consisting of 80 men, was the century, commanded by a centurion, who was assisted by two or three junior officers. Six such centuries formed a cohort of 490 men, and there were ten cohorts in a legion. The first cohort of each legion was designed differently, having only five centuries, but each of them being double strength. There is ongoing debate as to whether this was true of all legions and whether it was a temporary measure or a permanent arrangement. One would think that each legion had an administrative staff, logistical support, and many specialists (engineers, signalers, musicians, and the like) who would have to be accounted for and organized. It is easy to imagine them all being stuffed into a single cohort, where they would be added to the normal complement of legionaries. Once you add in a small cavalry force of 120 men for scouting and delivering messages, you have 5,120 men. Until the middle of the third century, these legions were all commanded by a legate, appointed by the emperor himself. These *legati Augusti* were almost always senators of high rank (former praetors), and they were assisted by six tribunes. The tribunes were doing their military service as the first steps in public-service careers as either senators or equestrians.

There remains a misconception that the auxiliaries were second-rate units and not particularly valued, at least when compared to the legions. Although they were often paid less, this likely reflects the fact that they were not Roman citizens and were often not held to the same regulations as the legions. Still, there is no doubt that these were professional and highly trained organizations, quite capable of holding their own in the battle line. Moreover, they often provided crucial support units that were not found in the legions, including much of the Roman cavalry, archers, slingers, and even skirmishers.

These units were raised in the provinces and originally maintained strong ethnic identities. The Pannonian Revolt (6 CE) demonstrated the dangers of recruiting auxiliaries from one province and then letting them serve near their homes. When you put too many auxiliary formations within their home province, two things happen: they begin to feel and comprehend the strength of their combined military power, and they begin to absorb the attitudes of the province, which were often anti-Roman. It was much safer to move auxiliaries to locations where they did not speak the language and felt little sympathy toward the inhabitants. Over time, however, local recruiting would change the identity of such units, and by the second century you even find Roman citizens within auxiliary formations.[7]

In the wake of the Varian Disaster the borders of the Roman Empire stabilized. The only major additions in the west were Claudius's conquest of Britannia and Trajan's conquest of Dacia. But after these provinces were incorporated into the Empire, emperors were mostly content to let the frontiers from the North Sea to the Black Sea settle into place. Rome would often send expeditions across the frontier zone to punish or intimidate the tribes, sometimes with no greater purpose than to enhance an emperor's reputation as a warrior. From time to time there would be defeats, but these were almost always local affairs that had only a fleeting impact on the Empire.

In the east, the strategic picture facing the army was very different. Here Rome faced another superpower: Persia's Parthian Empire. Tensions between the two empires always ran high, with political control of Armenia being a constant source of irritation. Except for Armenia, the rest of the Romano-Parthian frontier was remarkably stable. The truth is that the Parthians never presented a real threat to Rome. In fact, it was normally the other way around, for emperors styling themselves as the next Alexander—Trajan and Septimius Severus—would launch expeditions deep into Persian territory, even going so far as to sack the Parthian capital at Ctesiphon and annexing Mesopotamia. But neither Trajan nor Severus was able to capture the fortified city of Hatra, which stood at the nexus of major trade routes near the Tigris River, just southwest of modern Mosul.

In the end, Rome did not long maintain either Trajan's or Severus's conquests, as they proved impossible to defend. The same was true of the Parthians, who were never strong enough to hold on to any gains they made against Rome. The problem for both states is that they were facing the "edge of empire" effect. With a huge effort, either state was capable of invading the other and inflicting damage, but operating so distant from the core of their power, they could not sustain any gains for long. Given the resources available and the capacity of ancient transport systems, both empires had grown to their maximum sustainable size. That, of course, rarely kept one from pushing its claims in the other's sphere whenever they felt strong enough. As we shall see, this situation changed when the Sassanids replaced the Parthians.

Often unchallenged along the frontiers, the armies soon turned to politics. During the Julio-Claudian period, kingmaking was undertaken by the praetorians, starting with Claudius, whom a praetorian supposedly found hiding behind a curtain. As Suetonius relates:

> [I]n great terror at the news of the murder [Nero's], he stole away to a balcony and hid among the curtains which hung before the door. As he cowered there, a common soldier, who was prowling about at random, saw his feet, intending to ask who he was, pulled him out and recognized him; and when Claudius fell at his feet in terror, he hailed him as emperor.[8]

The next day the still-terrified Claudius allowed the praetorians to declare him emperor, but only after he had promised each of them 15,000 sesterces.[9] Even when the praetorians did not directly make an emperor, their approval was necessary to consolidate power. For instance, Nero, upon his accession, was immediately carried to the praetorian camp, where he was hailed as emperor, after offering them a donative.[10] Of course, the power of the praetorians was insignificant when compared to that of the legions. It is doubtful that even the full might of the soft, city-living praetorians could have stood up to a single battle-hardened legion. Although the praetorians were instrumental in disposing of Nero, they had little impact once the legionary armies cast their favorite into the scrum of 69 CE—the Year of the Four Emperors. Tacitus amusingly relates that upon the approach of Vitellius's leading cohorts, the praetorians—supporting Otho's claims to rule—rashly left their fortified position and rushed the approaching legionaries, only to be cut to pieces. At Cremona, what forces Otho had gathered there, including the praetorians, were swept aside by a mere two legions. When Vitellius's legions later faced those of Vespasian, the praetorians appear to have played no part. They did, however, remain a potent force within Rome until they were finally dissolved by Constantine. But emperors by this point ruled by consent of the legions.

Vespasian and Titus, both successful generals, had no problem controlling the soldiery, but their successor Domitian considered it wise to increase their pay from three hundred to four hundred sesterces. For most of the next century the fiction of adoption by the current emperor of his chosen successor kept the legions relatively quiescent. Still, it was the support of the Rhine legions that likely forced Nerva to adopt Trajan, and the legions' loyalty was always a good counterpoise to the power of the praetorians. This came to an end when the praetorian prefect Quintas Aemilius Laetus directed the assassination of Commodus. But the praetorians fatally overplayed their hand when they assassinated Commodus's successor, Pertinax, despite a promised donative of twelve thousand sesterces.[11] The praetorians then put the Empire up for auction.

Within a fortnight, the Rhine and Danubian legions were on the march, commanded by their choice for emperor, Septimius Severus. Julianus rallied the praetorians for a final stand. But as the Romans within the city watched the praetorians prepare for war, they were "overcome by laughter." As Dio relates: "[T]he Pretorians did nothing worthy of their name and of their promise, for they had learned to live delicately; the sailors summoned from the fleet stationed at Misenum did not even know how to drill."[12] They did not even bother to engage with Severus's rapidly approaching legions:

> Severus, on becoming emperor in the manner described, inflicted the death penalty on the Pretorians who had taken part in the slaying of Pertinax; and as for the others, he summoned them, before he came to Rome, and having surrounded them in the open while they were ignorant of the fate in store for them, uttered many bitter reproaches against them for their lawless deed against their emperor, and then relieved them of their arms, took away their horses, and banished them from Rome.[13]

Severus rebuilt the Praetorian Guard from the legions, which would cause further problems for later emperors, since the Guard killed a number of them, including Severus's son Caracalla. Still, the legions remained the final arbiter for those desiring ultimate power. Not for nothing did the dying Severus advise his son: "Be harmonious, enrich the soldiers, and scorn all other men."[14] If only subsequent emperors had listened to him, the next half century would likely have been considerably more peaceable. It was left to Diocletian, in the wake of the Crisis of the Third Century, to form a new force of bodyguards, which greatly reduced the power of the praetorians. Finally, Constantine, in the wake of the Battle of Milvian Bridge, disbanded the Praetorian Guard and scattered its remaining troops to distant legions.

We can mark the reign of Severus as the point where everything changed. To support his campaigns against the Parthians, Severus also increased the size of the army and boosted their pay, a combination that stretched the Empire's financial resources. Moreover, for the first time in 125 years, Rome had been taken and occupied by a Roman army, making it obvious to all that Rome was a military autocracy.[15] This only reinforced the fact that the true center of Roman power was located in whichever of Rome's armies the emperor was residing. The power of the army in the political domain only grew as Rome faced the dual threats of barbarians to the north and the Sassanids to the east, when the Danubian legions were able to make a dizzying succession of soldier-emperors.

Fighting the Roman Army

Josephus famously said of the Roman army:

> [T]hey have never any truce from warlike exercises; nor do they stay till times of war admonish them to use them; for their military exercises differ not at all from the real use of their arms, but every soldier is every day exercised, and that with great diligence, as if it were in time of war, which is the reason why they bear the fatigue of battles so easily; for neither can any disorder remove them from their usual regularity, nor can fear affright them out of it, nor can labor tire them; which firmness of conduct makes them always to overcome those that have not the same firmness; *nor would he be mistaken that should call those their exercises unbloody battles, and their battles bloody exercises.* Nor can their enemies easily surprise them with the suddenness of their incursions; for as soon as they have marched into an enemy's land, they do not begin to fight till they have walled their camp about; nor is the fence they raise rashly made, or uneven; nor do they all abide in it, nor do those that are in it take their places at random.[16]

For the Empire's first two centuries, this professional force awed and overmatched all of its opponents. A legion could be overwhelmed by vastly superior numbers, and if multiple legions were surprised in close terrain, as at Teutoburg Wald, it was possible to destroy them. But when massed and ready for battle, Rome's legions were nearly unbeatable. In fact, for most of the Empire's long history, the greatest threat a legion faced was another legion. To comprehend how they fought, one needs to build a mental image of an ancient battlefield. In the popular imagination, ancient battlefields were loud, swirling melees, where little could be heard over the din of clashing metal and screaming men. Any legionary caught in such a melee would find his field of vision narrowing, often to just a few yards to his front, since his focus was understandably centered upon those few persons nearby who were trying to kill him. This image may be accurate at the very tip of the spear during the climactic moments of a battle, but it certainly does not accurately reflect the entire battlefield through all of its phases. In fact, in the opening phases of a battle, as both sides formed, maneuvered, and advanced, an ancient battlefield was in all likelihood eerily quiet.

While the ranks were forming, there would be an undercurrent of muttering, as veterans spoke a few words to lift the courage of men new to battle. There would also be some shouting as officers placed their units into line. But when all was set, a prolonged quiet settled over the battlefield, and the men mentally steeled themselves for the ordeal ahead. Eventually one or several leaders would give a pre-battle oration. This was often first given by the army commander, but it was rare that he could be heard by more than a fraction of the force, so most men were left to draw strength from the speeches of their local commanders.

Unless caught in an ambush, opposing armies always took time to pray, read omens, and offer sacrifices. Then would come singing, chanting, and the banging of swords on shields, allowing individuals to draw strength from the great mass of the entire force while simultaneously intimidating their opponents. Eventually the noise would end. The armies were ready, waiting only for the commanders to order them forward. Soon enough flags would wave, bugles blow, and drums beat. Among the Romans, centurions would wave their swords, shout the order to advance, and start walking. The cohorts followed, each man tucked behind his own shield and inching toward his right to cover the exposed portion of his body behind his neighbor's shield.

Typically, a Roman legion would advance silently toward a waiting or onrushing enemy. While there are many instances in the record of Romans running into battle screaming and then falling into some disorder, this does not appear to be true of the more disciplined veterans. When an army did charge, it was almost always to close the final hundred yards or less and was often done by both armies simultaneously. Typically, the moment for the final charge was announced by loud trumpet blasts. Upon hearing them, the armies shouted their war cries and launched themselves at their foes. Even at this late stage of an advance, battle-hardened troops could still react to unexpected situations. At the Battle of Pharsalus, for instance, Caesar's veterans charged, but Pompey's legions stood still awaiting the impact. Seeing this, the Caesarian legions "of their own accord repressed their speed, and halted almost midway, so that they would not come up with the enemy when their strength was exhausted."[17]

We know from various sources that when two armies were close to impact, they habitually shouted war cries—in the Roman case, three loud shouts—and beat their weapons upon the shields. Moments later would come the first crashing impact, and then silence. Only on movie screens does this contact turn into thousands of shouting men all fighting individual battles, heedless of maintaining their formations. Even the thunderous noise of crashing shields and clanging steel is most likely a myth, at least when disciplined forces are involved. Hollywood needs noise and swirling confusion, but either was anathema to engaged soldiers, who while fighting had to listen for the sounds of signals and the orders of their immediate commanders.[18] To be separated and then isolated from one's formation and forced to fight alone was a death sentence.

As mentioned, the greatest danger a legion faced in a set-piece battle was another legion. Appian presents a unique description of just this kind of fight when he describes two armies of Roman veterans meeting at the Battle of Forum Gallorum:

> Being veterans, they raised no battle-cry, since they could not expect to terrify each other, *nor in the engagement did they utter a sound, either as victors or vanquished.* As there could be neither flanking nor charging amid marshes and ditches, they met together in close order, and since neither could dislodge the other, they locked together with their swords as in a wrestling match. No blow missed its mark. There were wounds and slaughter but no cries, only groans; and when one fell, he was instantly borne away, and another took his place. They needed neither admonition nor encouragement since experience made each one his own general. When they were overcome by fatigue, they drew apart from each other for a brief space to take breath, as in gymnastic games, and then rushed again to the encounter. Amazement took possession of the new levies who had come up, *as they beheld such deeds done with such precision and in such silence.*[19]

There are several points worth noting here. First, a legion was expected to be able to maneuver, both as it approached the battle and in the midst of it. That means that some of a legion's cohorts could make a frontal attack to pin an enemy mass while others charged a perceived weak spot and still others could maneuver to fall on an enemy's flank or rear.

As related to us by Caesar (and we should assume that the legions of the principate were at least as well trained and professional as Caesar's), these were not armed mobs that commanders lost all ability to control once set upon one another. Rather, a legion was the most maneuverable and adaptable organization ever placed upon an ancient battlefield. When supported by artillery (catapults, ballista), cavalry, and the light forces resident in its auxiliary formations, the legion was a truly formidable fighting machine. Caesar, in his *Commentaries*, gives us a picture of how he acted at the decisive point of the Battle of Alesia. Rather than always being in the fray, commanders in the Roman era typically kept some distance from the main fighting, sending in reinforcements as needed. They were thus free to move to critical areas and if necessary plunge into battle themselves. Thus we find Caesar at Alesia managing a battle rather than participating in it, as would Alexander the Great:

> I went to other parts of the line in person, and urged the men there not to give in under the pressure. I told them that the fruits of all their previous battles depended on that day, and on that very hour. . . . First I sent some cohorts with young [Decimus Junius] Brutus, then others with the legate Gaius Fabius. . . . Finally, when the fighting was getting fiercer, I went in person, taking fresh troops to relieve them. . . . I then hurried to the point where I had sent Labienus, taking four cohorts from the nearest redoubt. I ordered some of the cavalry to follow me, and told others to ride round the outer fortifications and attack the enemy from the rear. . . . Labienus realized that neither ramparts nor trenches were proving capable of checking the Gauls' violent attacks. Fortunately, *he had been able to collect together 11 cohorts, drawn from the nearest redoubts*, and he now *sent messengers* to tell me what he thought must be done. I hurried on so as to arrive in time to take part in the action. . . . The enemy knew who was approaching *by the color of the cloak I always wore in action to mark me out*; and from the higher ground where they stood, they had a view of the lower slopes and so could see the squadrons of cavalry and the cohorts I had ordered to follow me. They therefore joined battle. . . . Suddenly our cavalry could be seen to the rear, and fresh cohorts were moving up closer. The Gauls turned tail, but our cavalry cut off their flight. There was great slaughter.[20]

Also noteworthy is that that these formations were not tightly packed masses of men, as we can see in Arrian's description. There was room to remove the wounded from the front line and time to replace him before an enemy could plunge into the gap. Arrian also points out that even in the chaos and press of combat, tired legions "drew apart from each other for a brief space to take breath, as in gymnastic games." This presents another characteristic of pre-modern warfare: the fighting was rarely continuous. Hand-to-hand combat is both brutal and exhausting. Anyone who has ever wrestled or stepped into a boxing ring knows how tiring such contests are. Fighters who spend months or years conditioning themselves are often barely able to walk or hold their arms up after only a very few minutes. Add in the enervating fear that came from knowing one is engaged in mortal combat, and no human being would long withstand the mental and physical stress.

It would only take several minutes of close combat before the front line needed to be replaced and only a bit longer before an entire cohort was at the point of physical collapse. As they exhausted themselves, cohorts would of necessity pull away from the battle, rest, reform, and then, if they were veterans or had an inspiring leader, after a short or long respite close again with their foe. Keep in mind that after pulling away from combat, units would have to go through much of the same pre-battle ritual that preceded the opening of the engagement. It takes time for men to summon the will to close for mortal combat in the first place. Consider how much more difficult it would be to return to such a fight after surviving the first brutal moments. This is likely what gave the highly disciplined Roman legions, particularly veteran troops, their great advantage over barbarian hordes; the legions would almost always return to the fight, while a less disciplined force would not. Barbarians had to win on the first onslaught or face almost certain defeat. This is not a matter of valor: both sides in any fight are on average possessed of men of similar courage. But when this is extinguished by fatigue, only discipline can force a unit back into the fight. When armies were evenly matched in terms of numbers, skill, and discipline, battles could last many hours and even, in a few instances, several days.[21]

To sum up, the bulk of Roman battles, at least until the Crisis of the Third Century, involved disciplined and well-led troops, were slow to develop, and were eerily silent, and the actual fighting was sporadic and spread over many hours. Because of Roman training and discipline, it was rare to find a force that could match them on the battlefield, at least when the numerical odds were close to even. Moreover, in the event of a Roman army's being defeated, the resilience of the Roman state, even during times of crisis, ensured that new legions were soon available to restore the situation. Given that the Roman Empire was built and maintained on the backs of the legions, anyone attempting to comprehend Roman strategic thinking must understand how the Empire's core instrument of power was organized and wielded.[22]

Despite the volume of evidence dealing with Roman warfare, there is still much we do not know or are uncertain about when it comes to legionary organization. The legions of the Early Empire were similar in strength to those of the Republic, although their internal organization was much different. A full-strength legion had somewhat over five thousand men, organized into ten cohorts, of which the first cohort was approximately twice the strength of the first. The cohort was the legion's primary tactical unit and typically consisted of six centuries of eighty men, each of which was divided into ten squads of eight men. (The first cohort appears to have had only five centuries, but each was of double strength.) On a campaign, these eight men would share a tent or a single room in a garrison. Each legionary was equipped with a bronze helmet, a mail shirt (later replaced by segmented iron plates), a curved rectangular shield (*scutum*), a short sword—the famous *gladius*—and two javelins (*pilum*).

Each legion also had attached cavalry arm of 120 men, chiefly employed as escorts and messengers. In this establishment, there are no signs of the republican *maniples*, although the rank structure maintains much of the old nomenclature. We find that there remains a *pilus prior* and *pilus posterior*, and a *princeps prior* and *princeps posterior*, and a *hastatus prior* and a *hastatus posterior*, all of which echoed the three-line formations of the Republic—the *planni* (*triarii*), *princeps*, and *hastati*.[23]

During the first centuries of the Empire, a legion was commanded by a legate (*legatus legionis*); most of the legates had already held the rank of praetor. Under the legate were six tribunes, one of whom was of senatorial rank, while the remainder were equestrians. The tribunes appear to have been advisers or to have held administrative duties. There is no real evidence that they held military commands within the legion, but historians are unsure whether a tribune was placed in charge of each cohort. There was also a prefect of the camp, who may not have outranked the tribunes in class status but certainly did so in terms of command authority. Typically this job would be assigned to a senior centurion as his last job before retirement. Below the tribunes were the centurions, the long-serving professional soldiers of the legion, each of whom commanded a century. The first century was commanded by the *primus pilus*, who was usually the senior centurion within the legion.[24] Most of a legion's leaders, though not all, received their position through the patronage of the emperor.[25]

Marching and fighting beside the legions were the auxiliary cohorts (infantry) and *alae* (cavalry). These units were drawn from throughout the Empire, particularly from the frontier provinces. Although some cohorts were armed almost as heavily as the legions themselves, they were typically used as light infantry and cavalry. By Augustus's time, most of the auxiliary cohorts and *alae* were standardized at between four hundred and five hundred men, although they grew to a thousand men by the time of the Flavian emperors.[26] Similar to the legions, each cohort was broken into eighty-man centuries, while the *alae* were broken into groupings of thirty-two men each. In the Augustan period, most auxiliary cohorts were led by their own chieftains. Likely as a result of the revolts of 68–69 CE, particularly that of the Batavian cohorts, this command structure was changed by the Flavians so that auxiliary cohorts and *alae* were commanded by Roman equestrians.

For too long, probably owing to Tacitus's attitude toward them, auxiliaries have been considered second-rate troops. Recent interpretations of the evidence, however, indicates that they often fought alongside the legions in a complementary rather than a supplementary role as "well-trained and reliable troops who could fight in the line of battle with the legionnaires, as well as providing the diversity of forces vital to Rome's military success, in the form of cavalry, camel riders, slingers, archers and the skirmishing troops that had been lost to the legions with the manipular system."[27]

CHAPTER 7 | Roman Naval Power

T HE ROMAN NAVY does not get much attention in imperial histories. Nonetheless, Augustus was acutely aware that his fleets made his final victories in the Civil War possible. It was the fleet that had destroyed the power of Sextus Pompey—the last hope of those looking to restore the Republic— and secured Augustus's base of power in the Western Mediterranean.[1] Moreover, it was the fleet's victory at the Battle of Actium that ended Mark Anthony's bid for supreme power and gave Augustus control of an undivided empire. Despite historians' lack of attention to Roman naval power, it was the glue that bound the Empire together. As long as Rome maintained its naval supremacy, it also retained the resilience to recover from any shock. This was demonstrated during the Crisis of the Third Century, where, despite some major naval reverses in the Black and Aegean Seas, the Empire's overall naval dominance secured Rome's hold on the great tax and resource spines of North Africa and Spain. It was only after the Vandals took control of the bulk of Rome's western naval forces that the final demise of the Western Empire became inevitable.

Augustus always recognized the worth of a permanent naval establishment as an element of strategic power; given his military experience, how could it be otherwise? At the end of the Civil War he controlled fleets totaling approximately seven hundred ships, far more than were needed to enforce Rome's will during a general peace. The surplus ships were laid up or burned, while Agrippa organized the remainder into two large imperial fleets (*classis*). Both of these praetorian fleets—the *Classis Misenensis*, stationed at

Misenum (near Naples), and the *Classis Revennas*, at Ravenna—were based in Italy.[2] The size of these fleets is unknown, but since three legions were built from their ranks without apparently disrupting naval activities, one can estimate that each fleet consisted of at least twenty thousand sailors plus a large force of marines, as well as a substantial support establishment ashore.[3] This was probably enough to permanently man seventy-five to a hundred warships in each fleet.

For a brief time there was a third smaller fleet, made up of ships captured from Mark Anthony, stationed at Forum Julii in southeastern France, but by the time Claudius was emperor it had vanished.[4] Over the decades many other fleets and bases were established around the Mediterranean. These included the great provincial fleets, such as those mentioned by Tacitus. One such fleet, the *Classis Germanic*, is first mentioned in 69 CE, when its prefect had to run for his life because the legions suspected him of assisting in the murder of the governor of Germania Inferior, Capito, whom they held in high regard.[5] This fleet likely got its start as a temporary invasion fleet, built by Drusus to support military operations in 12 BCE. It was eventually based at Altenburg, just a couple miles south of the legionary base at Cologne.[6] Although this fleet sometimes operated in the North Atlantic, it was mostly a fluvial fleet assigned to patrol the Rhine. Two other fluvial fleets—the *Classis Pannonica* and the *Classis Moesica*—patrolled the Danube. The Pannonian fleet, based in modern Zemun, patrolled the upper Danube, while the Moesia fleet, based in Noviodunum (modern Isaccea), was responsible for the lower stretches of the river. The dividing line between the two fleets was likely the gorge known as the Iron Gates, which now forms a long stretch of the Serbian-Romanian border.

The *Classis Britannica*, also first mentioned by Tacitus, most likely was initially formed to support Claudius's invasion of Britain, although ever since the conquest of Gaul there had been substantial Roman naval activity in the region. This fleet was based at Boulogne, but sometime after Britain was conquered, probably in the second century, a second headquarters was built at Dover. For the first 250 years of the Empire the *Classis Britannica* was mainly employed in protecting trading ships between Britain and the Continent. During the Crisis of the Third Century the fleet broke free of Roman control and under its leader, Carausius—the self-styled "Emperor of the North"—began conducting independent operations.[7] But by 300 CE both Britain and the fleet were once again firmly under imperial control.[8]

Besides the two main imperial fleets at Misenum and Ravenna, the Mediterranean was dotted with small fleets and naval installations. The largest of these fleets—the *Classis Pontica*, the *Classis Syriaca*, and the *Classis*

Alexandria—controlled the Black Sea (Pontica), the Aegean and eastern Mediterranean Seas (Syriaca), and the southeastern Mediterranean and Red Seas (Alexandria).[9] These fleets and their bases were maintained for nearly three centuries. But still other fleets were created, typically on an ad hoc basis, in support of specific campaigns and allowed to wither when the immediate need for them was gone. Because of their specific purpose—usually to support a new war—these fleets are commonly referred to in the literature as invasion fleets. Some of them were quite large; for instance, Drusus assembled over a thousand ships to support his operations in Germania.

During the Principate, the fleets' key strategic role was to support the army's operations, as there were no remaining threats to Roman naval superiority within the Mediterranean or along the frontiers.[10] That does not mean the fleet was not kept busy. Besides supporting Augustus's expansion of the Empire into the Red Sea and Crimea and to the line of the Danube, the navy kept the trade pathways clear of pirates. It is difficult to overstate the strategic impact of this: Roman naval power made it safe to trade throughout the Empire and beyond. Consequently, Mediterranean trade grew during the first two centuries of the Empire's existence to levels not seen again until the nineteenth century. As mentioned earlier, it was this huge economic surge that supplied the taxable foundation for the maintenance of the Empire at the height of its power and glory.

Naval dominance also played a crucial role in the governance, management, and general security of the Empire, as messages, orders, supplies, trade goods, and even troops could be sent by sea or river to almost any point in the Empire in mere days, compared to overland travel, which could take as long as two months. Only at the remote edges of the Empire (e.g., deep in the African provinces) are travel times measured in weeks rather than days. It is worth comparing this to the mighty Persian Empire at its pre-Alexander peak. A limited number of messages could move by mounted carriers along the Royal Road from Susa, as the core of the Empire, to Sardis, near the edge of the Empire, in approximately nine days. But once they left the Royal Road, travel times increased dramatically. Moreover, everything else moving throughout the Empire had to move by foot or wagon. For an army or a baggage train to march from Susa to Sardis would take ninety days at a minimum. Without east-west rivers to rely on, lacking internal or surrounding seas, Persian rulers were continually fighting against local fragmentation. Moreover, when there was trouble on the edges of the Empire requiring a massive response from the core of power, it could take an exorbitant amount of time to respond. This is hardly surprising: it could take months for the Persian king to learn about a crisis, many more months to gather forces from across the Empire, and then additional months to march to the troublesome region. This strategic geography would continue to plague the Parthians and the Sassanids as they tried to counter Rome's aggressive challenges.

With the Rhine and the Danube as major internal arteries, Rome found it much easier to concentrate forces at any point along the northern frontier. Moreover, secure river traffic made it relatively easy to supply the far-flung legions along the Rhine and the Danube.[11] Even when Rome opted to move its armies overland, as it often did, the support of the fleet was crucial for immediate logistical support, as well as for massing food and other resources in the projected theater of operations. For the most part, the Empire had little need for a war fleet, since there were few if any naval threats on the frontiers and none within the core of the Empire. The only time there was a real need for large numbers of warships was for the invasion fleets that supported Trajan's Dacian campaigns, as well as those needed to support periodic thrusts down the Euphrates to threaten the Parthian capital. Consequently, the core praetorian fleets at Ravenna and Misenum were allowed to deteriorate when much of their combat power was repeatedly sent to reinforce the invasion fleets.

When crisis struck, in the third century, the diminished Roman fleets were found wanting. As seemingly continuous civil wars drew the legions off the frontiers, the still relatively powerful fluvial fleets and their bases were exposed to barbarian attack. Moreover, the unending conflicts created a constant need for silver, manpower, and war materiel, leaving next to nothing to support the fleets. Overextended and overwhelmed, the Empire's fleets were neglected—except as a source of manpower. Soon the diminished fleets were unable to accomplish their military tasks. Unable to patrol the rivers, the impotent fluvial fleets were forced to stand aside as large barbarian forces—sometimes described as "hordes"—broke through the Rhine and Danube barriers. What strength remained of the fleets was concentrated by Gordian III at Ephesus in the early 240s. From here they supported his assault on the Persians, who had overrun Mesopotamia and were driving toward the coast. Because of this concentration of vessels, the Black Sea fleet was so denuded as to be incapable of offering any serious resistance to Goth and Scythian invaders.

In the mid-250s the Goths demanded ships from the Bosporan Kingdom, a Roman client state that controlled Crimea and the eastern shore of the Black Sea. With their newly acquired fleet, the Goths attacked the Roman naval bases at Colchis and Trapezus before moving on in 257 to attack the rich cities of Bithynia; Chalcedon, Nicomedia, Nicaea, Cius, Apamea, and Prusa were all sacked. By 259 the Goths had penetrated the Aegean with five hundred ships before turning back to their homeland with a sizable quantity of plunder. The emperor, Valerian, who focused on the Sassanid threat after the fall of Dura-Europas in 256, was powerless to stop them. After a short respite, another tribe, the Heruli, joined by the Goths and others, appeared in 267–269 CE. According to Zosimus, the total barbarian force numbered over 300,000 and was carried on 6,000 vessels.[12]

Zosimus greatly exaggerated the size of the barbarian fleets and army, but it was surely a sizable force. What is important to note is that it once again broke into the Aegean with little trouble and sacked a number of cities, including Athens. This time Rome managed to collect enough ships from the *Classis Alexandria* and *Classis Syriaca* to defeat the barbarian fleets in a series of running battles; but it was their defeat on land at the Battle of Naissus that broke the back of the barbarian tribal confederations and allowed Rome to focus its energies on reconstituting the Empire.[13]

By the time of Diocletian's accession to emperor and the return to the Empire of some measure of stability, Rome's naval establishment was very much changed. The great imperial fleets were disbanded into numerous squadrons based in specific regions. Without the praetorian fleets at Ravenna and Misenum to give the navy a centralized headquarters, these squadrons soon lost their identity as part of the Roman navy and came under the control of the local senior military commander.[14] Still, the new naval organization proved strong enough for the Empire to retain its naval dominance along the frontier as well as within its Mediterranean core for the next hundred years.

During this time there was at least one more great sea battle when, during the Civil War between Licinius and Constantine, in 323, Licinius tried to hold the Dardanelles with two hundred triremes. Constantine's smaller force of more powerful individual ships won a decisive victory, forcing Licinius's fleet to withdraw from action for the remainder of the conflict. There were also some great victories by the smaller fluvial fleets. In 357 the fleet on the Rhine helped Julian surround and destroy an invading force of Franks. In 386 the Romans concentrated their Danubian squadrons to crush a huge army of Goths attempting to cross on rafts.[15]

By the end of the century everything had taken a turn for the worse. In the north swarms of invaders came by sea to finally overrun the Saxon forts, and the remaining Roman naval squadrons were either destroyed or captured. Worse, in 406 the Rhine froze solid, immobilizing the fleet. The barbarians swarmed across the almost unguarded frontier and pressed deep into Gaul, permanently breaking the Rhine defenses. Among these tribes was a force of Vandals, who, in 409, crossed into Spain. There they acquired some ships and began raiding the North African coast and the Balearic Islands. In 429 they crossed into North Africa and began marching up the coast. After a slow, decade-long march of destruction, they arrived at Carthage. Here they faced a Roman army under Boniface, who decided that his mission in life was to make a bid for supreme power in Rome. Hence, he took his army to Italy and left Carthage—the greatest city in Africa—at the Vandals' mercy. When Carthage fell in 429, the Vandals captured the bulk of Rome's military fleet, much of its grain fleet, as well as a major port. Within that port was a sizable population of men who knew how to build and sail ships. Roman naval power was irrevocably broken in the west and soon replaced by the Vandals' naval supremacy. For the first time in six centuries, there was a non-Roman fleet in the Mediterranean. It was an unmitigated strategic disaster: all the advantages that came with naval supremacy transferred from Rome to its enemies. Roman generals, preoccupied with the threat of Attila's Huns, awoke to the danger too late.

The first part of this book centered on various themes that will help one grasp Roman strategic thinking and execution. Since 1976, when Edward Luttwak first published *The Grand Strategy of the Roman Empire*, there has been so much debate as to whether the Romans were even capable of thinking in strategic terms that it is vital to demonstrate they could do so early on. Had the Romans truly been incapable of comprehending their empire at the strategic level, there would have been no reason to write this book. Luckily, they clearly planned and operated at the strategic level for the entire existence of the Empire. The remaining chapters in this book are meant to clear the air as to the level of the strategic threats Rome faced and to present some details on what Rome had at its disposal to meet these challenges, including economic wherewithal, basic infrastructure, and its military forces.

Part II of this work employs a narrative history of the Empire to illuminate and explore how these themes dictated Roman policies and actions. This part of the book will take us from the start of the Empire through the height of its glory, and then delve into the Empire at its nadir and near dissolution during the Crisis of the Third Century. Part II is where we will discover how Rome adapted and executed its basic strategy over the course of three centuries. As the historical narrative progresses, I will pause at various points to discuss the underpinning strategic dynamics that are driving Rome's story forward and to examine various strategic options that were available to emperors at crucial turning points. From time to time it will also be necessary to revisit some of our opening themes so as to account for changes in the challenges Rome confronted, as well as the power Rome had available to meet them.

PART II | Rome's Strategic
History

From the Principate to the Crisis

of the Third Century

CHAPTER 8 | The Julio-Claudian Empire

Augustus and the Empire's Strategic Position

After Actium, Augustus found himself as the sole ruler of an empire that stretched east to west from the Euphrates River and the eastern shores of the Black Sea to the Atlantic Ocean, and north to south from the English Channel and the North Sea to the Sahara Desert.[1] To defend this Empire he had the combined force of his own legions and those of Anthony, his opponent in the Republic's last civil war. This was far more than required, and it was more than the Roman economy could sustain. Consequently, Augustus spent considerable time, effort, and silver in demobilizing a bit more than half of this force and finding land for the released soldiers to colonize.[2] By dispersing colonies throughout Italy, but more crucially in distant parts of the Empire, Augustus created a reserve of trained soldiers in regions of doubtful loyalty and in areas threatened by external foes. The remaining twenty-eight legions were spread along the frontiers or left in provinces recently conquered but not fully integrated into the Empire's political structure, to be moved to the frontiers once these regions became more settled.

There was never any question of disbanding the remaining legions, because these were the backbone of Augustus's power. In this regard, Augustus had learned much from his adoptive father, Julius Caesar. Until the rise to power of Marius and Sulla in the last generation of the Republic, Roman armies had always disbanded at a war's conclusion. Pompey, however, refused to follow in his patron Sulla's footsteps, and after a successful campaign in the east, he disbanded his legions. He then tried to get the Senate to purchase the farmlands his legionaries had been promised upon enlisting. He was refused, and without his legions at his back, he had no power to enforce his will. Caesar, on the other hand, never dismissed his legions. He was only too aware that it was the legions' personal loyalty to him that made his dictates legal. Still, it was left to Augustus to turn the legions of Rome into a permanent standing army. In doing so, Augustus, without ever stating such, codified a new and crucial mission for the legions—cowing the senate and people of Rome. How effective the army was as an instrument of political power is brought home by a slightly amusing story of a later Roman emperor—Hadrian—in the *Historia Augusta*:

> With these very professors and philosophers, he [Hadrian] often debated by means of pamphlets or poems issued by both sides in turn. And once Favorinus, when he had yielded to Hadrian's criticism of a word which he had used, raised a merry laugh among his friends. For when they reproached him for having done wrong in yielding to Hadrian in the matter of a word used by reputable authors, he replied: "You are urging a wrong course, my friends, *when you do not suffer me to regard as the most learned of men the one who has thirty legions.*"[3]

Augustus from the start of his reign made sure all these legions remained under his direct control. In Strabo's words, Augustus "became established as lord for life of war and peace," a set of powers that was passed on or assumed by his successors.[4]

Augustus, however, did not rely solely upon the legions as the foundation of his political power (Figure 8.1). He had come of age in the civil wars between Caesar and Pompey, where he learned an important lesson, reinforced by his own experience: military loyalty was fickle. To reinforce his position as sole ruler of the Empire, Augustus hid the coercive power of Roman arms behind a façade of reluctance to rule. Consequently, he ceaselessly portrayed himself as a man only too happy to lay down the burdens of rule, if only he could do so without Rome's once again falling into the brutal chaos that marked the last decades of the Republic. He pushed his claim that he would prefer to retire to a carefree civilian life without ever for a moment halting his accumulation of political power, or for a single instant loosening his grip on the legions. How he did this was never so masterfully summarized as by Tacitus:

> When the killing of Brutus and Cassius had disarmed the Republic; when Pompey had been crushed in Sicily, and, with Lepidus thrown aside and Antony slain, even the Julian party was leaderless but for the Caesar [Augustus]; after laying down his triumviral title and *proclaiming himself a simple consul content with tribunician authority to*

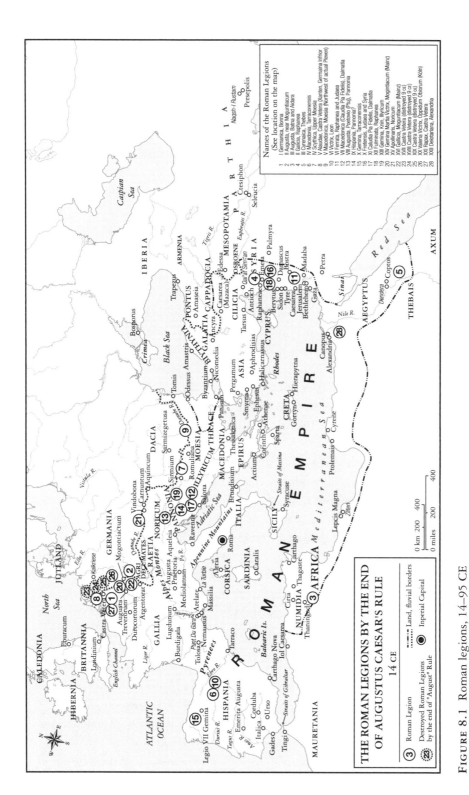

FIGURE 8.1 Roman legions, 14–95 CE

safeguard the commons, he first conciliated the army by gratuities, the populace by cheapened corn, the world by the amenities of peace, then step by step began to make his ascent and to unite in his own person the functions of the senate, the magistracy, and the legislature. Opposition there was none: the boldest spirits had succumbed on stricken fields or by proscription-lists; while the rest of the nobility found a cheerful acceptance of slavery the smoothest road to wealth and office, and, as they had thriven on revolution, stood now for the new order and safety in preference to the old order and adventure. Nor was the state of affairs unpopular in the provinces, where administration by the Senate and People had been discredited by the feuds of the magnates and the greed of the officials, against which there was but frail protection in a legal system forever deranged by force, by favoritism, or (in the last resort) by gold.[5]

In a series of senatorial acts and settlements, in 27 and 23 BCE, Augustus gave up his hold on Rome's two consulships but acquired to himself the right of a permanent *imperium* (total military authority), which had previously been granted on a temporary basis and only outside the sacred boundary of the city—the *pomerium*. His imperium was further augmented by a grant of *maius imperium* (greater power), making Augustus's military authority superior to that of the provincial governors. Augustus, without ever being declared a tribune, a position closed to the patrician class, was voted the tribunician powers—*tribunician potestas*—for life. These powers included the ability to convene the Senate, propose legislation, and veto laws not to his liking. To help him handle the huge administrative burden engendered by such an accumulation of direct power, Augustus enlisted advisers—*consilium principis*— the start of a more-or-less permanent *consilium* to advise the emperor—and brought in many persons of equestrian rank to undertake the routine tasks of running an empire. In effect, they were the start of a professional civil service.

Finally, Augustus and the Senate agreed that he would exercise direct rule over Gaul, Spain, Syria, Cilicia, Egypt, and Cyprus. Later he would expand his personal rule to cover provinces he created—the Germanies, Raetia, Noricum, and Pannonia. It must be noted that these were all provinces bordering on outside threats and generally still requiring legionary forces to maintain internal peace. Hence, Augustus had direct control of the provinces in which the army was stationed. At the time of his death, only the legion in North Africa was not under his direct control. The remaining provinces remained under senatorial control, although Augustus always retained the right to meddle in their affairs whenever he deemed it necessary. To help maintain order within Rome, and to create a more immediate demonstration of his power, Augustus formed the first cohorts of the Praetorian Guard. In the end, even Augustus's apparent retreats from power, such as giving up the consulships, only served to further increase his actual power, as it was he who selected the men who would fill these posts.

This, in brief, was the political power structure Augustus bequeathed to his successors. In many ways it contained within it the seeds of its own destruction, as managing such an intricate system required an emperor to possess Augustus's political genius. Unfortunately, men possessing such talents were always in short supply, and many of those that did possess them found themselves victims of wary and jealous emperors. But for those emperors with sufficient guile and ruthlessness, Augustus left them with a foundation upon which to exercise supreme power, one that lasted for over two hundred years with only marginal changes. Not until the near-collapse of the Empire during the Crisis of the Third Century was the need to remake the institutional and administrative structure of the Empire thought necessary. But even these changes could not fully compensate for the Empire's one great governance weakness: it was trying to run a massive empire upon a political and administrative infrastructure designed to administer a city and its immediate environs.

Still, despite his placing a veil over his control of the legions and the reality of his autocratic rule born out of a sordid civil war, Augustus needed to portray himself as a successful conqueror. It was what Rome expected of its leaders, and if Augustus was to remain unchallenged, he needed to be clothed in military glory. That Augustus recognized the importance of military glory, or at least a track record of having fought with the legions, is demonstrated by how assiduously he worked to ensure that each of his potential dynastic successors had a military track record acceptable to the legions as well as the Roman populace. Thus, his sons and grandsons, despite their illustrious births, also had to be exposed to military life, where their military prowess could be on display through successive victories.[6]

Besides the requirement for glory, there was also a need to keep the army busy, both to justify its existence and in acknowledgment of the fact that an idle army, conscious of its strength, was a constant threat to his continuing in power. So, although the ancient sources are in almost universal agreement about Augustus's reluctance to go to war, his desire for peace, and his disdain for expansionism, the emperor's actions tell a different story. As his *Rae Gestae* reminds us, Augustus, in terms of square miles added to the Empire, was Rome's greatest conqueror, nearly doubling its size, and he had for a while planned further conquests. Augustus, in word and deed, fully internalized Virgil's commentary—"Roman, remember by your strength to rule Earth's peoples."[7] Not much else is needed to comprehend why Augustus assumed the title of imperator (general), allowed himself to be honored with two triumphs, and was acclaimed by the people and the army as imperator at nearly two dozen public events.

After Augustus

Augustus was dead.

He left behind an empire, or, as he told his associates just before his death, "I found Rome of clay, and I leave it you of marble."[8] While Augustus did order a massive building program throughout Rome, Suetonius Dio informs us that "he did not thereby refer literally to the appearance of its buildings, but rather to the strength of the empire."[9] In many ways, the Empire was as strong as it had ever been, but it was for a time brittle. Augustus had ruled for four decades at a time when the overall life expectancy was thirty-five and even those who survived the plethora of childhood diseases rarely saw sixty. For nearly every person within the Roman Empire, Augustus was the only ruler they had ever known. Many feared a return to the civil wars, while others hoped the embers of a dying Republican idea could be flamed into new life.

The sources are at odds over whether Tiberius was present when Augustus died. Some claim he got there in time to spend an entire day in private consultations with him, others that Livia, Augustus's third wife and Tiberius's mother, kept the death a secret until Tiberius had rushed back from Dalmatia to take charge.[10] There has always been some historical controversy as to whether Tiberius desired sole rule of the Empire. His correspondence with the Senate can surely be interpreted in a way that makes him appear conflicted on the issue. But that was just theater. Tiberius wanted to be asked, even begged, to assume the rule of Augustus, and he wanted to avoid being seen as grasping. For any senators who may have thought otherwise, they only had to examine his first actions after Augustus was dead. First, he kept the death a secret until he was sure that Agrippa, the grandson of Augustus, was murdered. Who ordered this murder has been argued by historians for two millennia, with some claiming Augustus ordered it before his death, as he deemed him unworthy to become emperor. Others believe the orders came from Tiberius or Livia. No matter who gave the order, Tiberius, if he chose to, was certainly able to save Agrippa.[11] That he deemed it safer to remove the only person with a hereditary claim to the throne tells us much of what we need to know about Tiberius's desire to be emperor.

If further evidence is required, his first official actions should seal it. For it was Tiberius, acting as imperator, who gave the watchword to the praetorian cohorts, while soldiers conducted him to the forum and curia. Most crucially, he dispatched letters to the armies as if he were already emperor. Finally, he already possessed the *imperium maius* and tribunician powers, which he jealously guarded throughout his jousting with the Senate. In fact, according to Tacitus, the only place he showed any hesitancy about his role as emperor was when speaking in the Senate.[12]

Tiberius clearly absorbed Augustus's most important lesson: if you wish to rule, first command the army's loyalty. He further solidified his control by quickly approving payments set forth in Augustus's will of a thousand sesterces to every man in the praetorian guards, five hundred to each man in the urban cohorts, and three hundred to all legionaries.[13] Still, in dealing with the Senate he continued to protest his reluctance to accept his elevation to emperor until one frustrated senator exclaimed, "Others were slow in doing what they promised, but that he [Tiberius] was slow to promise what he was already doing."[14] In the end, Tiberius allowed himself to be convinced that he should accept becoming the sole emperor of the Roman Empire.

Tiberius immediately faced the greatest challenge to his rule. The Pannonian and German legions revolted. Their complaints—over-long enlistments, unfair punishments, and low pay—had been accumulating for some time, but the respect, verging on awe, in which Augustus was held had kept the legions quiescent. Now, they sensed an opportunity to either intimidate a new emperor or to elevate their own commander, Germanicus, to the throne as a reward for granting their demands. Germanicus, a grandnephew of Augustus and married to Agrippina the Elder, Augustus's granddaughter, was popular among the people of Rome, but he was either unwilling or unready to make a bid for the throne yet. This was probably a result of pure calculation, as Tiberius, who had spent decades fighting Augustus's wars, was well-respected within the legions, and any attempt by Germanicus to become emperor would have meant another civil war, one he was not at all sure to win. Although the source paints a picture of high drama, these revolts were quickly quelled with a minimal nod to the soldiers' demands; they would be exempted from fatigue duties after sixteen years of service, and the donative promised them after Augustus's death was doubled. But two strategic lessons had been learned by anyone paying attention: restive legions could make political demands; and, possibly more dangerous in the long term, they could be bought off.

In the wake of the mutinies, Tiberius permitted Germanicus to invade Germania in a series of campaigns over two successive years. By now Tiberius surely understood that Germania was not worth the cost, but he still allowed the conflict to drag on. While historians have likely underestimated the extent of the settled economy within Germania, it certainly was far behind Gaul at the time of its conquest. It is conceivable that Rome could have permanently subdued all the tribes west of the Elbe, reorganized the conquered territories into a lasting political structure, and grown their respective economies to the point where the tax haul was worth the effort, but this would be the work of many generations. We can see in the next century the difficulties this would have entailed by examining Rome's problems integrating newly conquered Dacia into the Empire's economic structure, despite Dacia's offering considerable mineral resources, including gold, to ease the transition.

So, if the material costs were great and the payoff both slim and delayed, why continue? Mostly because there were benefits to keeping the restive legions busy and in allowing Germanicus an opportunity to gain military glory. But more crucially, strategy is not always just a matter of material considerations. Rome had lost three legions at Teutoburg Wald, and that insult had not been avenged. If Rome could not properly punish the Germans, the threat they posed to the frontiers would be hugely increased and never-ending. But it was not only the Germans who needed to be cowed—the entire Roman world was watching. The Empire was not yet so solid that rebellions and centrifugal political forces could not tear it asunder. Rome could not afford to show any weakness. And in Germania, it had been shown that Rome could be beaten. In fact, Arminius, who still led the post–Teutoburg Wald tribal confederation, was making much of his successes and Roman mutinies. As Tacitus relates, Arminius had a propaganda field day with claims that the Romans in Germania were the cowards of Varus's army "who had been the quickest to run" and had mutinied rather than face the Germans at war. As Rome's entire strategy rested upon the perceived invincibility of the legions, Arminius was striking at the foundation of Roman power. There would be a time when it would be safe to bring operations in Germania to a close, but not while the superiority of Roman arms remained in doubt.

In 15 CE, Germanicus, with eight legions and an equal force of auxiliaries, made some progress in restoring the prestige of the legions when he recovered one of the eagles lost at Teutoburg Wald.[15] The following year, Germanicus militarily crushed Arminius's tribal confederation at the Battle of Idistaviso. The Germans had attacked as the Romans were forming their battle line straight from their order of march. Germanicus met the onrushing barbarians by launching his best cavalry squadrons into the German flank and sending the remainder of his cavalry in a wide march, to strike the Germans in the rear. Struck unexpectedly on the flank, the German advance paused just as a flight of eight eagles flew over the Roman formation toward the Germans. For the Romans, this was an augury of great success, and Germanicus lost no time taking full advantage of the fortuitous omen. Pointing, he began to shout: "Go . . . follow the birds!"[16] At nearly the same moment the infantry charged, the Roman cavalry appeared in the rear of the German army.[17]

The German army broke in all directions, and Arminius himself only managed to escape by a strenuous effort to smash through the unarmored Roman archers. It was rumored at the time that some sympathetic Germans in the Roman auxiliary forces allowed him to pass.[18] The remainder of the German army was not so fortunate, as Tacitus relates: "The rest were cut down in every direction. Many in attempting to swim across the Visurgis were overwhelmed under a storm of missiles or by the force of the current, lastly, by the rush of fugitives and the falling in of the banks." The slaughter went on until nightfall brought an end to the Roman pursuit. For ten miles around the ground was littered with German dead, while the Romans had suffered very few losses. The Romans were particularly amused to discover, in the German camp, chains meant to secure any surviving Romans. With the battle concluded, the Romans hailed the emperor and erected a victory monument.[19] The sight of the Roman trophy enraged the broken German army, which Arminius and his brother, Inguiomerus, had spent the night rallying. By morning the scattered German forces had reassembled and may even have been reinforced. This time, however, they were content to stay behind their hastily built walls and await the Roman attack. The Germans played into Roman hands when they accepted battle on an open plain where the legions were at their most effective. The battle raged for long hours as the enraged barbarians continuously assaulted the Roman line. But despite taking frightful losses they could make no impression upon the legions. In the afternoon the Germans no longer had the strength to resist the legions' advance, as Germanicus begged his men to finish the slaughter. As Tacitus relates: "Till nightfall [the Romans] glutted themselves with the enemy's blood."[20]

After ravaging the territory of the Chatti and Marsi tribes, Germanicus returned his army to their winter camps near the Rhine. Unfortunately, he sent several of his legions by sea, where they were caught in a terrible storm that severely damaged the fleet and drowned thousands of legionaries. Tiberius had had enough. Not only had the costs of pacifying Germania continued to rise with no expected gains, but Germanicus's victories were making him dangerously popular with the army and the Roman people. Tiberius advised Germanicus to return home to enjoy the triumph he had decreed for him, writing: "He had now had enough of success, enough of disaster. He had fought victorious battles on a great scale; he should also remember those losses which the winds and waves had inflicted, and which, though due to no fault of the general, were still grievous and shocking. He, Tiberius, had himself been sent nine times by Augustus into Germania and had done more by policy than by arms. By this means the submission of the Sugambri had been secured, and the Suevi with their king Maroboduus had been forced into peace. The Cherusci too and the other insurgent tribes, since the vengeance of Rome had been satisfied, might be left to their internal feuds."[21]

Tiberius's reading of the situation was correct. With the departure of the common enemy, the tribes fell out, and Arminius soon found himself at war with the Marcomanni king, Maroboduus. That war ended in a stalemate, but Arminius was dead by 21 CE, murdered by other tribal chieftains who believed he was becoming too powerful. Germanicus, after receiving his honors, was sent to the east with a series of important missions from Tiberius, including the absorption of the client state of Cappadocia into the Empire and to inspect the damage a recent earthquake had done to several eastern cities. While in the east he fell out with the newly appointed legate of Syria, Piso. During their dispute, Germanicus fell ill and died. Germanicus's wife, the formidable Agrippina, saw to it that Piso was accused of poisoning her husband. When Piso committed suicide before his trial, rumor had it that he was protecting Tiberius, who had supposedly ordered the murder to ensure the tremendously popular Germanicus did not attempt to overthrow him.[22]

From a strategic perspective, Rome had become a status quo power. Even though there was no public announcement of the fact, the Roman drive to conquer Germania was placed on permanent hold. Roman legions would continue operating across the Rhine for several centuries, for, as the elites of the Empire saw it, Germania may not be a province of the Empire, but it was assuredly within the Empire's zone of influence. Similarly, the Danube was quiescent, as, like the German tribes, they were too fragmented to pose an offensive threat. Moreover, for the time being, Parthia was preoccupied with its own internal problems as well as concerns along its northern frontiers. As such, it posed no imminent threat. As Tiberius, unlike the emperors who came after him, did not need to burnish his credentials as a warrior, having spent decades leading Rome's armies in Augustus's service, he did not have to launch any wars of conquest to prove his martial credentials.

With at least one of Rome's frontiers permanently settled and the others quiet, the Empire was at peace. Tiberius was content to let it remain so. As far as can be determined from the sources the only militarily related troubles to disturb Tiberius's repose was a minor quarrel with Parthia over appointing Armenia's king, a rebellion of Tacfarinas in North Africa, and a tax revolt in Gaul. All were easily disposed of, with only the intervention in Armenia creating a new long-term strategic concern. In 35 CE, Parthia's king, Artabanus, took advantage of recent military victories on its frontiers and the death of Armenia's king to place his son, Arsaces, on the vacant throne. According to Tacitus, the Persian king disdained Tiberius because of his age and his warlike character.[23]

Tiberius ordered his new legate in Syria, Lucius Vitellius, to handle the matter. He had chosen wisely, and although Tacitus reviles his actions later in life, he does allow that, at this time, Vitellius was a man of virtue and competence.[24] As a first move, Vitellius encouraged Mithridates—brother of the king of Iberia—to seize the throne, thereby initiating a full-scale Armenia-Iberian war. When the Persians tried to intervene, Vitellius prepared his four legions for war and marched them to the Euphrates. Artabanus, who was not ready for war with Rome, retreated and accepted Mithridates on the Armenian throne. The resulting loss of prestige led to a revolt among the Persian nobles, who asked Tiberius to send them a member of another royal line, Tiridates, who was currently residing in Rome, to become their king. Vitellius, with several legions, escorted Tiridates to the Euphrates, where he was taken off by Persian nobles and crowned king at Ctesiphon.

Being a creature of Rome, Tiridates' hold on power was precarious from the start, and he barely lasted a year on the throne. But when Artabanus again moved to retake his throne, Vitellius and the legions marched to the Euphrates. Artabanus, still unwilling to risk war with Rome, met with Vitellius in lavish tents erected by Herod the tetrarch. Here, Artabanus agreed to Roman control of Armenia and even did obeisance to the standards of the legions.[25] Rome had won a great prize at little cost, as it now controlled Armenia, which provided a buffer between Parthia and the vulnerable Roman provinces in Anatolia. But as it was also a dagger aimed at the heart of the Persian Empire, it was to be a region of continual strategic contention between the two powers for the next four centuries.

The rest of Tiberius's reign is a series of stories revolving around a growing mutual estrangement between the emperor, the Senate, and the people of Rome. The stories related to his departure from Rome to live on the island of Capri, the growing influence of his praetorian prefect, Sejanus, and his inability to secure the heir of his choice need not detain us. All of this fed the gossip mill that authors such as Suetonius and Tacitus waded through to present the most lurid and sordid of them to posterity. But, while these stories have been used to fill hundreds of books, plays, and movies, their impact on Rome's strategic position was nil.

Similarly, the vivid stories of the lives of Tiberius's successors offer little to inform us of Rome's strategic imperatives, except the continuing requirement for emperors to secure their legitimacy and hold on to power through the accumulation of military glory. To this end, Tiberius's successor, Gaius Caesar Augustus Germanicus, better known to us as Caligula, undertook an expedition to conquer Britain. Historians offer varying explanations for this sudden expedition, but the most probable one is that he became aware of an attempt on his person that was supported by several legionary commanders, particularly Aemilius Lepidus, Caligula's brother-in-law and the great-grandson of Augustus. To overawe the conspirators, he collected a large army in northern Gaul, using the excuse of invading Britain to mask his intent to use the army against the conspirators if it became necessary.[26]

When no widespread revolt occurred, Caligula likely decided that, since the army was already assembled, he could put it to good use enhancing his military reputation. All his ancestors had made their reputations in war, particularly through fighting Germans. Comprehending his growing unpopularity and having just endured a coup scare, military glory must have appeared the surest way of enhancing his reputation and securing his hold on power. Caligula does appear to have operated for a time in Germania, but he had little to show for it, except to display the power of Roman arms to some barbarians. He clearly planned an expedition to Britain, but for unknown reasons the resolve to see it through was not there, and he soon returned to Rome. Both events have come down to us as farces. In Germania Caligula was accused of sending Gauls, their hair dyed red and with a few German phrases under their belts, across the Rhine so that Roman units he personally led could pretend they were German prisoners and capture them. Rather than attack Britain, he had his legions assemble in full battle order on the shore and then ordered them to collect seashells.[27] As both stories are presented by men of the senatorial order who despised Caligula, there is reason to doubt their veracity. On the other hand, Caligula's failure to cover himself in military glory made it easy to portray him as a coward. Within the year he would be assassinated.

For a few hours as the turmoil of the assassination reigned, the Senate, expecting the support of the urban cohorts, tried to restore the Republic. But it had been too long and too much had changed for such a restoration to be a realistic goal. Before long the Praetorian Guard decided to make its voice heard. One of their number, prowling around the palace, discovered Claudius, the brother of Germanicus and Caligula's uncle, hiding behind a curtain, trembling with fear and certain he was about to be murdered. He was carried off to the praetorian camp, where he was elevated to emperor, and immediately bought the Guard's continued loyalty with a payment of fifteen thousand sesterces per man. Seeing which way the wind was blowing, the urban cohorts deserted the Senate and threw their support to Claudius, and Rome had a new ruler.

Suetonius misleadingly claims that Claudius was the first of the Caesars to resort to bribery to secure the loyalty of the troops.[28] This is hardly fair: previous emperors had also made concessions to the legions and the praetorians to gain and maintain power. Claudius's political crime was to make such a blatant one-time payment for military support. It was a terrible precedent for the future, one that would have a significant strategic impact on later politics as well as on the civil stability of the Empire. Still, Claudius had to do what he could to survive, and in paying the praetorians, he was adhering to the personal strategic imperatives of any Roman princeps: "staying alive, controlling the succession, rewarding clients, and gaining glory."[29]

Suetonius reports that Claudius carried out but one campaign, and that of little importance. He had been accorded triumphal regalia by the Senate, even though he had no military accomplishments, so Claudius decided to burnish his military credentials. His chosen target was Britain, and it is interesting to note that Suetonius considered this first major expansion of the Empire of so little significance that the word "Britain" is mentioned only once in his extensive recounting of Claudius's life. This is a phenomenon that plagues anyone trying to study Roman strategy, for the ancient writers often had no interest in events that are in fact crucial to our current understanding of Roman strategic thought and actions. One is therefore left to sort out the strategic reasoning behind Roman actions from what can be extrapolated from those actions.

The sources are silent as to why Claudius wanted to invade Britain unless we are to accept Dio's contention that "a certain Bericus, who had been driven out of the island as a result of an uprising, had persuaded Claudius to send a force thither." Reason suggests the unlikeliness of any Roman emperor mobilizing four legions and a like number of auxiliaries at the behest of a minor tribal chieftain, unless of course there were other reasons for going. Given that no other explanation presents itself, one can safely assume that the quest for military glory and reputation was a primary driver, particularly for an emperor who had spent only a single day with the army: as a hostage in the praetorian camp the day he was made emperor.[30] How else does one explain his quick trip to Britain, arriving just as the legions were about to capture the capital of the Belgae, a powerful southern tribe? He stayed with the army less than two weeks before rushing back to Rome to award himself a triumph. After all, he had done what had eluded the great Julius Caesar: he had not only invaded Britain but actually conquered it, or at least a portion of it. The final subjugation of what became Roman Britain was arguably not completed for over a generation, during the campaigns of Agricola in 77–84 CE.

We don't know much about the initial invasion, except that it was commanded by Aulus Plautius and it appears to have been made by four legions. One of these legions was commanded by the future emperor Vespasian, who appears to have been instrumental in breaking the tribes' first lines of resistance on the River Medway. Plautius pursued the enemy to the Thames, where he inflicted another defeat on the assembled tribes, killing one of their leading chiefs, Togodumnus. By then British resistance was nearing collapse, and several chiefs were voicing approval of the terms Rome was offering. Plautius now sent for Claudius to take over the armies in time to lead the final victorious salute. Given how fast the Praetorian Guard was ready to march and the readiness of the fleet to transport them, one can assume this invitation was planned before the expedition began. Dio portrays this as a moment of great tension, when Rome's legions were halted by strengthening resistance and only the emperor could provide the inspirational leadership that would ensure victory. Dio goes on to credit Claudius with the ultimate victory: "[Claudius] taking over the command . . . crossed the stream, and engaging the barbarians, who had gathered at his approach, he defeated them and captured Camulodunum, the capital of Cynobellinus. Thereupon he won over numerous tribes, in some cases by capitulation, in others by force, and was saluted as imperator several times." This is quite a heroic effort for a man Dio also described as "afflicted by cowardice, which often so overpowered him that he could not reason anything as he ought."[31] It is certainly fiction, as Dio tells us Claudius tarried in Britain only sixteen days, before rushing home to enjoy a triumph and overseeing lavish games and festivals to celebrate his victory.

The invasion of Britain had served its primary strategic purpose in propping up the stature of an emperor whose hold on the crown was, at best, tenuous. As for further strategic gains, they were a long time in coming. Britain, as a source of metals such as tin and lead, was already substantially integrated into the Roman economic system, and that would only have grown over the years. It is impossible to believe that British farmers, who were overwhelmingly subsistence farmers, could have produced enough surplus to have paid the cost of the four legions left to garrison the new conquest. It would therefore be many generations before the British economy could be taxed for more than it cost to protect the new conquest. But in this case, the Romans demonstrated a degree of patience they were unwilling to expend to hold and develop Germania. One also wonders what the strategic impact of the four legions typically maintained in Britain would have been if they had been on the Danube or Rhine during times of crisis.

As it was, Britain consumed huge amounts of military resources for four centuries without adding much to the security of the Empire. When judged against the cost of losing Britain as a long-term trading partner, the conquest of Britain and the cost of protecting it was a money-losing proposition. By the middle of the second century, Britain was likely producing enough tax revenue to support the cost of its defense, including building and maintaining Hadrian's Wall, as well as the four legions defending the province from the Picts and other tribes north of the Wall. But it is unlikely that the surplus, after paying for the island's defense, ever approached the gains possible through commerce. The creation and defense of a province on a distant edge of the Empire, and far from the Empire's commercial and political centers, was a strategic misallocation of resources. In the end, the last Roman troops left in Britain were removed to help cope with the great crisis of 406 CE, when the Rhine defenses were torn asunder. By then, however, they were too little, too late. It would have been far better had they been on the Rhine at the start of that fateful year.

Still, withdrawal was not a bad idea, even at the risk of its being interpreted as weakness, as it surely would have had been if Rome withdrew in the immediate wake of Boudicca's revolt. Still, any cost-benefit analysis makes withdrawal seem the rational choice. As we saw, in the wake of the Varian Disaster, Rome's withdrawal from Germania was not synonymous with abandoning control or influence. It is worth noting, as evidence for Rome's ability to control Britain, that in the century between Caesar's first invasion and Nero's elevation to emperor, Rome successfully managed British affairs through a network of friendly tribal rulers.[32] In fact, about twenty years before Claudius seized the island, Strabo believed that Rome had already gained all that was possible from the island and warned about the dangers of taking it by conquest:

> At present, however, some of the chieftains there, after procuring the friendship of Caesar Augustus by sending embassies and by paying court to him, have not only dedicated offerings in the Capitol, but have also managed to make the *whole of the island virtually Roman property.* Further, they submit so easily to heavy duties, both on the exports from there to Celtica and on the imports from Celtica (these latter are ivory[a] chains and necklaces, and amber-gems and glass vessels and other petty wares of that sort), that there is no need of garrisoning the

island; for one legion, at the least, and some cavalry would be required in order to carry off tribute from them, *and the expense of the army would offset the tribute-money*; in fact, the duties must necessarily be lessened if tribute is imposed, and, at the same time, dangers be encountered, if force is applied.[33]

To withdraw the army was not to withdraw control and power or to lose all the benefits that might be gained through conquest. Moreover, it must be noted, that, except for a sentimental desire to restore the Empire to its historic glory, the eventual loss of Britain had no practical impact on the Empire's strategic situation. In a pattern that repeats itself in the history of all empires, holdings far from the central core of power, as judged by the ease of movement to threatened locations, have always cost more than what is gained by holding them. Nero, or at least his advisers, could not have helped but notice that holding Britain as a province was not worth the price, since he was planning to abandon the province. Suetonius tells us he changed his mind "only because he was ashamed to seem to belittle the glory of his father."[34] When one considers the opprobrium emperors more secure than Nero suffered when they voluntarily abandoned Roman provinces, it is no wonder that he persisted. No emperor, particularly one without conquests of his own, could afford to surrender those of an earlier "more glorious" emperor, whatever the results of a cost-benefit calculation.

Claudius worked hard at securing his son Britannicus's succession to the throne. But his fourth wife, the formidable Agrippina, a direct descendant of Augustus and daughter of Germanicus, had her own candidate in mind—her son, Nero, from a previous marriage. Through her patronage Nero, three years older than Britannicus, was pushed forward into a succession of leadership positions, ahead of Claudius's son. Agrippina also took the sensible precaution of ensuring the Praetorian Guard was on her side by removing its current commander and placing someone loyal to her—Afranius Burrus—in command. Nero's position in the race for supreme power was further secured by his marriage to Claudius's daughter, Octavia. From that moment on, Claudius's days were numbered, as it was crucial to Agrippina's plans that Claudius died before Britannicus was of an age to contest Nero's right to rule. As Britannicus approached his fourteenth birthday, Agrippina decided to employ poison to hurry matters along.[35]

Nero took the throne in what was becoming the customary way: Burrus escorted the young Nero to the praetorian camp, where, after promising what was quickly becoming the customary bribe of fifteen thousand sesterces, he was acclaimed emperor. Next, he was taken to the Senate, likely with a large praetorian escort to help convince wavering senators, to recognize his full imperial powers. Advised by both Burrus and the philosopher and author Seneca, Nero in his first years as emperor appears to have done well. For instance, when the court seers predicted Nero's destruction and advised him to kill anyone who was seen as an immediate threat to his rule, Nero's hand was stayed by Seneca's wise comment: "No matter how many you may slay, you cannot kill your successor."[36] But as the years passed, the calming influence of his advisers, as well as that of Agrippina, waned. When they passed from the scene—Agrippina and Seneca by imperial order—an unrestrained Nero was free to give himself over to his baser passions. There is no need, in a strategic analysis such as this, to detail Nero's foibles and the manifold errors that wrecked his relations with the Senate and alienated him from the people. What is worth noting was that Nero failed to avail himself of the one tried-and-true method of reversing his slide in popularity: achieving military glory.

There were opportunities to do so. The first was Boudicca's revolt in Britain, which began when Boudicca, queen of the Iceni, was scourged and her daughters outraged. Roused by these insults and the loss of lands seized by the Romans, the Iceni warriors "flew to arms."[37] From a strategic perspective, what is noteworthy is that the timing of this revolt coincides with the reorganization of Britain's political structure to integrate it into the Empire as a province. When Rome first conquered a new province, it spent the next few years consolidating its rule. Roman administrators would arrive and start to overlay themselves atop the old tribal structures. Soon afterward would come a flood of tradesmen looking to take advantage of newly opened commercial activities. Some, like Seneca, would use their wealth to cheat the natives, and others would start employing Roman organizational skills and the support of the army to take over much of the new province's commerce. As this process progressed, there would come a point where the newly conquered territory was deemed ripe for official fleecing—Roman taxes—to begin. In the days of the Republic, Rome's conquests were mostly states and cities that had centralized economic and taxing systems going back many hundreds of years. As such, the people were used to paying taxes, which Rome, without much fanfare, diverted from these states' former rulers to itself. This was not true of conquered barbarian territories. With no tradition of paying taxes to a distant unseen treasury, the organization of a province for tax gathering was usually the final insult in a long list of gathering resentments. Boudicca herself was aware of the anger the Britons felt toward Roman taxation and made it a key part of her appeal to the tribes. All that was required at this dangerous period of a newly installed Roman regime was a spark and a leader.

In 9 CE, Arminius had provided both in Germania; in 60 CE, Boudicca did the same in Britain.

Here was a moment for an emperor to show real leadership, as Roman losses in the initial stages of the revolt had been serious, including a full legion—the newly raised Legio IX Hispania—which had been virtually annihilated, with only its commander and some cavalry fleeing to safety.[38] Tacitus tells us that another seventy thousand citizens and allies were executed on the gibbet, by fire, and by crucifixion. As all of the ancient sources are relentlessly hostile to Nero, it is difficult for historians to peer through the rhetorical fog to see where and how Nero impacted imperial strategy during this crisis. But because it was crucial to his survival that he be viewed as a successful military commander and diplomat, he must surely have been active in these roles.[39] Unfortunately, with reports of disaster flooding Rome, all our sources tell us about Nero's actions is that he forsook valor in favor of appearing in Naples for its quinquennial festivities to play the lyre. Nero, who had always valued the accomplishments of Greek civilization, was certain that he could win lasting fame and glory through his artistic accomplishments, which would match anything he could gain on a battlefield. But that was not the Roman way, and his frequent stage appearances exposed him to ridicule. One could say that this universal condemnation would have little impact on Roman strategy, except for one crucial factor: these historical works, including those still extant and many more lost to history, were written in the years immediately following the reigns of these emperors. As such, they were read by future emperors, who could not help but learn what behavior would be applauded as well as what actions would damage an emperor's reputation. Taken collectively, these histories provided a series of how-to manuals on how a Roman emperor should behave. Not every emperor would or could live up to the ideals set forth in the histories, but they could not escape them. When they failed to live up to them, the imperial propaganda arms spared no effort in making it appear as if they did so. When that failed, an emperor's time on earth was coming to an end.

With Nero otherwise occupied, saving Britain as a Roman province fell to the commander on the scene, Gaius Suetonius Paulinus, who wasted no time gathering the remnants of the Roman forces that had escaped the slaughter and adding them to his Legio XIV Gemina. He also called on Legio II Augusta to join him, but its prefect, cowed by the size and ferocity of the revolt, declined to leave his fortress.[40]

With about 10,000 men, Paulinus took a position somewhere along Watling Street and awaited an enemy that hugely outnumbered him. Although Dio's number of 230,000 Britons is not to be believed, it is likely that Paulinus faced as many as eight to ten times his numbers, making it impossible to extend his line the whole length of Boudicca's army. Fearing encirclement, Paulinus separated his army into three divisions and spaced them out between natural barriers on each flank.[41] Boudicca and her huge host, because of their overwhelming numerical superiority, remained sure of victory, regardless of the Roman defensive posture. They were about to learn that there is a vast difference between destroying a newly raised legion and taking on the veterans of the XIV Gemina. The Britons' charge was halted by a fusillade of missiles. When the Romans had exhausted these they launched a countercharge before the Britons could reorganize their shattered front. Boudicca's army broke, but flight was impossible—their own wagons barred their retreat. The slaughter was nearly total, and Dio makes a point of telling us that no one was spared, including the women traveling with the army.

An excuse was soon found to recall Paulinus to Rome, for it was unsafe for an unpopular emperor to leave a victorious general in command of legions increasingly loyal to their commander. Such a commander was likely to get imperial designs of his own. But Paulinus was not disgraced upon his return. Rather, he was rewarded with high honors as Nero tried to wrap himself within the cloak of the general's glorious victory. Paulinus was therefore on hand to command continental-based legions in support of Otho's claims to the throne in 69 CE—the Year of the Four Emperors.

Nero had also avoided an earlier chance to wrap himself in military glory by going to the eastern half of the Empire to command the legions fighting to maintain Rome's influence in Armenia. Here he could have followed the example of Claudius and stayed far from the fighting while garnering the glory of his general's victories. However, he opted to allow the new governor of Cappadocia and Galatia, Gnaeus Domitius Corbulo, to solve what was becoming a perennial problem: Armenia.

In 51 CE the usurper Rhadamistus, an Iberian prince, sat on the Armenian throne, enjoying lukewarm Roman support. But his tenuous hold on power ended when the new Persian king, Vologases I, looking to bolster Parthia's influence in the region, invaded in 52 CE and placed his brother Tridates I on the Armenian throne. Vologases and his army were soon called away to deal with uprisings within Parthia, allowing Rhadamistus to return. He did not last long, as the Armenian people rebelled against his harsh rule, forcing him to return to Iberia, where his father, probably at Rome's behest, had him executed.[42] Tiridates returned, with a Parthian army at his back.

This was the situation when Corbulo assumed command in the east in 54 CE. What Corbulo found waiting for him must have been dispiriting for a soldier who had recently commanded the battle-hardened Rhine legions.

According to Tacitus, "The legions transferred from Syria showed, after the enervation of a long peace, pronounced reluctance to undergo the duties of a Roman camp. It was a well-known fact that his army included veterans who had never served on a picket or a watch, who viewed the rampart and fosse as novel and curious objects, and who owned neither helmets nor breastplates— polished and prosperous warriors, who had served their time in the towns."[43] Corbulo began a long period of brutal training while waiting for one of the German legions with its auxiliaries to join him. Matters were allowed to rest as they were in Armenia until 58 CE, when Corbulo, his forces finally ready, marched.

The years before his invasion had not found Corbulo idle. When he marched out of Cappadocia, with three legions and a similar strength in supporting auxiliaries, armies of local client kingdoms simultaneously marched out of Iberia and Commagene. Unable or unwilling to meet the advancing Roman armies in open battle, that war rapidly turned into a series of destructive raids, as Corbulo captured the major Armenian cities. But after the great cities of Artaxta and Tigranocerta fell, all resistance ended, and Corbulo placed Tigranes, a Roman puppet, on the throne. He was allotted a thousand legionaries, three auxiliary cohorts, and some cavalry for protection as Corbulo returned with the main army to Syria. Because Parthia's King Vologases was occupied with an internal revolt, here things might have rested, except that Tigranes unwisely decided to attack neighboring Adibene, which was under Parthia's protection.

In 62 CE the war recommenced, but this time the Parthians attacked both Armenia and Syria. The Roman troops assigned to protect Tigranes, who was besieged in Tigranocerta, resisted fiercely, while at the same time Corbulo prepared to meet the Persians on the Euphrates. Vologases, surprised to find the Roman army waiting for him, was ready to negotiate an end. But before this was accomplished, Nero sent a new commander, Lucius Caesennius Paetus, to take command in Armenia. He failed to cover himself with glory, and after having two legions forced to pass under the yoke at Rhandeia, he began a long retreat out of Armenia. These embarrassing defeats were kept hidden from Rome, where it was commonly believed that the Roman commander had defeated the Parthians. Thus Nero, looking to take political credit for Paetus's assumed victories, allowed trophies and victory arches to be erected on Capitoline Hill.[44] Only when a Parthian delegation arrived in Rome making unacceptable demands did Nero become aware that he was losing the war in Armenia. Nero called a council to decide between "the hazards of war and an ignominious peace."[45] According to Tacitus, there was no hesitation in deciding for war.[46] Paetus was immediately recalled, and

Corbulo was given extraordinary powers—*imperium maius*—and ordered to correct the situation. Nero met Paetus immediately upon his return to Rome and pardoned him for his loss in terms so insulting Nero likely assumed Paetus would commit suicide over his loss of honor: According to Tacitus, Nero said that "he was pardoning him on the spot, lest a person with such a tendency to panic might fall ill if his suspense were protracted."

Corbulo sent Paetus's two broken legions to Syria to recuperate. He then added the V Macedonica from Pontus and the XV Apollinaris from the Danube, and he picked cohorts from Egypt and Illyria to his two veteran legions on the Euphrates. Corbulo, instead of marching this overwhelming force into Armenia, advanced across the Euphrates into Parthia.[47] As this huge Roman army, under a competent commander, approached Armenia from the south, Vologeses sent envoys to discuss peace. Corbulo, judging that matters had not yet gone so far that war to the bitter end was called for, was ready to entertain a compromise. Corbulo offered to destroy his advanced fortifications on the Parthian side of the Euphrates, while the Parthians agreed to remove their soldiers from Armenia. The Romans also agreed to allow Parthia's candidate, Tridates, to remain on the Armenian throne if he traveled to Rome to receive his crown. The Parthians got the king they wanted on the throne, while Rome got to maintain its hegemonic claims in Armenia by crowning the Parthians' choice.

Nero took full advantage of Corbulo's victory. When in 66 CE Tiridates came to Rome to receive his crown, he was welcomed extravagantly.[48] Nero also took the opportunity to have himself declared imperator and held a triumphal ceremony in his own honor. And just in case the Roman people missed the point, he ordered a celebration for the closing of the doors of the Temple of Janus, as a sign that, because of "his" military accomplishments, Rome was not at war anywhere.[49] While the general peace held for fifty years, the rapprochement with Parthia could never last. By the mid-80s the Parthians were supporting the false Nero in the east and otherwise stirring up trouble for Rome, but they were careful to always keep their activities below the level where Rome would mobilize its legions and march. Much of this renewed Parthian antipathy was surely a reaction to Rome's increasing military stranglehold of the eastern borders, where there appears to have been unceasing construction of fortifications.[50]

Nero, improving on how Claudius clothed himself with the glory of military victory, learned that it could be done without ever leaving the confines of his palace. Nero also bequeathed his successors and their generals another tradition of import when he ordered Corbulo's death. Although Dio informs us that Corbulo had no designs on becoming emperor, for an emperor as insecure as Nero, who had military achievements of his own, a fearsome general, loved in Rome and supported by the legions, was an unbearable risk.[51] While traveling through Greece, Corbulo was ordered to commit suicide. The condemned man, as soon as he understood the order, seized a sword and dealt himself a heavy blow, exclaiming "Thou art worthy!"—a term reserved for the acclamation of a hero. Nero had shown the way for future emperors who felt similarly threatened by a general who was too successful. He had also put every future general on notice that if their successes in the name of Rome were great enough, they might as well revolt and claim the purple, since they had little to lose in the attempt. Moreover, as Sulla, Caesar, and Augustus had proven, the only way for a general to be successful in Rome was to return to the eternal city with an army at his back. These lessons drove the course of events after Nero's assassination, when four men held the title emperor in a single year—69 CE. It was, in fact, the boiling anger of the eastern legions, who considered that their favorite general had been ill treated, that made it possible for Vespasian to claim and hold the throne after Nero's death and a short but intense civil war.

But there was one more major disturbance of the Pax Romana before Nero's reign ended. In 66 a new procurator for Judea, Gessius Florus, arrived in Jerusalem intent on collecting forty talents in tax arrears. When the money was refused, Florus had seventeen talents held within the Jewish temple seized. Long-simmering passions exploded into an open revolt, and by mid-year most of the Roman outposts in Judea had been destroyed and the III Gallica Legion had lost over fifteen hundred men. The first Roman counterattack on Syria was a fiasco; the soldiers barely escaped after having fought their way from the walls of Jerusalem to the sea, at a cost of over five thousand men.[52] Nero, having ordered the death of Corbulo, found himself in need of a military man. In December 66 he settled on the fifty-seven-year-old Vespasian, a man who had made his reputation as a leader and warrior as legate of the II Augusta Legion during the invasion of Britain a quarter of a century before. Vespasian's first act was to send for his eldest son, Titus, to join him in Syria with troops from Egypt. He then spent the next several months in Ptolemais, southern Syria, concentrating and training a force of sixty thousand men, including most of Corbulo's well-trained veterans. When the Roman army finally advanced, it eschewed a rapid thrust to Jerusalem in favor of a methodical reduction of every Jewish stronghold.[53] With only Jerusalem left to conquer, Vespasian halted the offensive. Word came from Spain that Galba was raising a legion and planned to march on Rome, remove Nero, and make himself emperor. Vespasian decided it would be best to wait until the political situation was clearer before completing the subjugation of the Jews.

In the meantime, III Gallica was taken from his army and moved to Moesia (Thrace) to aid in halting an expected thrust by barbarians from across the Danube. The legion, which had distinguished itself fighting for Corbulo, had spearheaded Vespasian's offensive and fought with particular ferocity as it avenged the legionaries killed in the opening days of the revolt. It was now arguably the most battle-tested legion in the Roman army. It also hated Nero for his treatment of Corbulo. Loyal now to Vespasian, the legion was perfectly placed in Moesia to strongly influence events in the next year—the Year of the Four Emperors.

Before the III Gallica entered the sordid politics of the era, it had one more great battle to fight. They had been moved to Moesia for a reason: Roman strategic intelligence had detected preparations among a Sarmatian tribe, the Rhoxolani, for conducting a raid into the Empire. Taking advantage of Rome's distraction in Judea and the political turmoil after Nero's assassination, the Rhoxolani, who had massacred two cohorts the previous winter, mobilized nine thousand cavalry and were on the march. The III Gallica caught them unprepared, laden down with booty, and with their speed diminished by slippery roads and deep mud. Says Tacitus, "They were cut down as if they were in fetters."[54]

Tacitus provides us with some insights into fighting barbarian tribes that belie the popular picture of warfare along the Danube and Rhine at this time:

> For it is a strange fact that the whole courage of the Sarmatians is, so to speak, outside themselves. No people is so cowardly when it comes to fighting on foot, but when they attack the foe on horseback, hardly any line can resist them. On this occasion, *however, the day was wet and the snow melting: they could not use their pikes or the long swords which they wield with both hands, for their horses fell and they were weighted down by their coats of mail. This armor is the defense of their princes and all the nobility: it is made of scales of iron or hard hide, and though impenetrable to blows, nevertheless it makes it difficult for the wearer to get up* when overthrown by the enemy's charge; at the same time, they were continually sinking deep in the soft and heavy snow. The Roman soldier with his breastplate moved readily about, attacking the enemy with his javelin, which he threw, or with his lances; when the situation required, he used his short sword and cut down the helpless Sarmatians at close quarters, for they do not use the shield for defensive purposes.[55]

This passage presents some interesting tidbits of strategic importance. One, these barbarian tribes are not impoverished nomads, barely eking out an existence through slash-and-burn agriculture. Assembling nine thousand heavy cavalry for an extended period later proved to be beyond the means of all but the richest medieval princes and kings. That feat alone points to an economy capable of maintaining a semi-permanent military force far beyond just a few retainers gathered around a powerful tribal leader. That they were able to equip these horses, as well as a substantial number of the soldiers, with chain mail is a further indicator of substantial wealth and a level of industrial organization that barbarian tribes are rarely credited with, at least at this early date. Clearly, proximity to the Roman Empire was already impacting the organization and military capacity of the tribes along the Danube. This Sarmatian force reveals that the great transformation of the barbarian tribes into amalgamated proto-states was already under way. Once completed, it would turn the northern barbarians into a much more formidable enemy.

Note also how Tacitus describes the barbarians' preferred methods of fighting. One could be forgiven for thinking he is describing heavily armed medieval knights charging lines of exposed infantry, attempting to break their opponents through shock. Historians generally point to the Battle of Adrianople (378) as the start of heavy cavalry's dominance over infantry, but clearly the transition was in evidence long before.[56] In any event, Tacitus certainly believes that a Roman legion, caught on an open plain, had something to fear from a barbarian cavalry charge, and this at a time when the legions still ranked as the supreme instrument of warfare.

One crucial strategic development taking place during the reigns of Claudius and Nero that the extant literary sources mostly overlook, but that we must note, is Rome's changing views on the utility of client states. In 46 CE Thrace, a semi-autonomous client state, was officially annexed by Claudius and made a province of the Roman Empire. With its northern border on the Danube and its eastern border resting on the Black Sea, Thrace was a region of vital importance to Roman security. But it had always been a troublesome client, upon which Rome had expended enormous resources, first trying to conquer it and then, after its conquest, spending the next 150 years developing it into a reliable client state. It had not been an easy process, since the Thracians periodically revolted, costing Rome at least one consular army under Gaius Porcius Cato, which was trapped and destroyed in 114 BCE. Later Thrace alternated sides in the civil war between Pompey and Caesar, took the Republican side against the triumvirs, and then finally backed the winner when it aided Augustus in his campaign against Mark Anthony.

Thrace could also be a dangerous foe, for, as Strabo points out, it could field 15,000 cavalry and 200,000 infantry.[57] Herodotus, writing five hundred years before, says of them:

> The Thracians are the biggest nation in the world, next to the Indians; were they under one ruler, or united, they would in my judgment be invincible and the strongest nation on earth; but since there is no way or contrivance to bring this about, they are for this reason weak.[58]

It was the Thracians' internal squabbling that made them relatively easy prey for Rome. During their most troublesome periods as a client state, there were often multiple Thracian kings for Rome to deal with and play off against one another.[59] But Rome brought rapid change to Thracian society, including unification under a single king, at least on Rome's side of the Danube.[60] In 46 CE that king, Rhoemetalces III, was murdered by his wife, which sparked a popular revolt against Rome. It was not well prepared, and the Roman forces on the scene, employing their customary brutality, crushed it without aid. But the revolt had alerted Rome to a new danger. Once integrated into the Roman economic system, Thrace became rich as well as politically unified, making it a significantly more powerful and dangerous military opponent. By enriching their client states, Rome was simultaneously increasing its own peril. Therefore, in 46 CE Thrace was placed under the direct control of a procurator and integrated as a province into the Roman Empire.

What the Romans did with Thrace was happening all along the frontiers of the Empire, for many of the same reasons. For instance, in 40 CE Caligula, likely in the wake of a recent revolt, invited Ptolemy of Mauretania to Rome, where he was promptly executed. Mauretania was promptly annexed and turned it into two provinces: Mauretania Tingitana and Mauretania Caesariensis.[61] Annexations in the east centered at first on those client states neighboring Armenia, and in Judea, where the client-state system was breaking down as increasingly powerful Roman clients fought each other over boundaries. Worse, Rome, despite wishing to avoid involvement in these petty disputes, could not help but be drawn in. Moreover, as these client states became more unified and economically stronger and learned the Roman ways of war, the danger of rebellions or their aligning themselves with Persia increased. Because the old system was no longer working, Rome adopted another one and brought its clients closer to its bosom as provinces. By the end of Vespasian's reign, Commagene had been absorbed into the province of Syria, the province of Cilicia was created, and Cappadocia-Galatia was reconstituted to include Lesser Armenia and Pontus Polemoniacus.[62]

Edward Luttwak identifies this as one of Rome's first great strategic mistakes. As such, it is worth taking some time to examine his argument and proposing some counterpoints. First, let's examine Luttwak's thoughts on the benefits of the client-state system:

> Since clients would take care to prevent attacks against provincial territory. . . . The provision of internal security was of course the most obvious function of the client states, and the most commonly recognized. In addition, however, efficient client states would also shield adjacent provincial territories from low-intensity threats emanating from their own territories or from the far side of the client state periphery. . . . Against high-intensity threats, such as invasions on a provincial or even a regional scale, client states and client tribes could contribute both their own interposed forces and their capacity to absorb the threat, in other words, they could provide geographic depth. . . . Another obvious contribution of client states and client tribes to Roman security was the supply of local forces to augment Roman armies on campaign. Naturally, these troops would fall into the Roman category of auxilia, i.e., cavalry and light infantry, rather than legionary forces of heavy infantry. . . . Auxiliary troops contributed by clients had played an important role in the campaigns of the republic, not least because they could provide military specialties missing from the regular Roman arsenal, such as archers, and especially mounted archers . . The complementarity between auxilia and legionary forces was an important feature of the Roman military establishment; moreover, the forces maintained by the client states were substantial.[63]

Luttwak also makes a case for the Romans letting client states absorb the first blows of a major attack with their forces. This would allow the much richer areas, deeper within the Empire, to escape damage while allowing the Roman army time to deploy. He makes much of the slow strategic deployment of Roman forces as the reason Rome required client states to absorb the first enemy pounding.[64]

It is a wonder, given the blasts of incredulity greeting much of Luttwak's work, that few have questioned this part of his analysis, particularly because almost all of it is faulty. First, few of these states could provide for their own internal security. Quite the opposite was more often true. As outlined above, virtually every Roman client state, at one time or another and often on multiple occasions, went through prolonged periods of internal instability requiring significant deployments of Roman troops to restore order. The Jewish Revolt was just the latest of these internal collapses. Moreover, because many of them were a consequence of dynastic squabbling, there was little hope these internal conflicts would ever end, since there was always someone with a claim to the throne who could take advantage of the always present popular discontent to make a bid for power a viable option. The only way Rome could ensure domestic stability was to remove the dynasts and replace them with the Empire's administrative apparatus.

Another major problem in managing client states manifested over time. Free of other major security concerns, since Rome would always act to ensure against threats coming from outside the Empire, the client states increasingly turned upon one another in quests to add to their own dominions. Each one of these events required Rome's attention and often the employment of troops to enforce Rome's will. For much of the first hundred years of the principate, the legions were busier intervening in squabbles between clients than they were combatting enemies beyond the frontiers. Once again, the simplest solution to putting an end to this constant intermural quarreling was to remove the client-state dynasts and replace them with governors.

Luttwak's contention that the loss of client states cost Rome its auxiliary forces is incorrect: Rome continued to draw on the client states for specialized auxiliaries for centuries. But in military terms, those were the least of the benefits accrued. Many of these client states became the legions' primary recruiting regions, and by the third century legionaries from former clients who had risen through the ranks were generals and even emperors. Also, as each client was absorbed into the Empire, its treasury was confiscated for Roman purposes. This one-time windfall was then renewed every year as the new province was brought into the Roman taxation system. Such taxes often turned client states, which had been cost centers for Rome, into valuable revenue producers, and this revenue only increased as the new province's wealth grew within the security of the Empire.

Finally, Luttwak misinterprets how buffers work in times of geopolitical competition and war. First, the role of a buffer is to provide strategic depth by using its extensive land area to absorb and blunt the impact of an enemy assault before the enemy army reaches the vital core of the Empire. But a newly formed province can do this as easily as a client state, and without any of the above-listed problems endemic to the client-state system. Moreover, a client state typically has only its own internal resources for employment in its defensive preparations, where a province would probably have the full resources of Rome at its disposal. These additional resources made it possible to fortify the frontiers as well as to build extensive fortifications around cities and at choke points on the routes along which an enemy army was likely to advance. Moreover, with some exceptions, the armies of client states were rarely a match for what the Persians could throw at them and were therefore little more than speed bumps on the march to Antioch and the Mediterranean coast. Because Roman provinces had Roman legions stationed within them, the Persians or other invaders would immediately come against the best troops the Romans had. Even if these frontier legions and fortifications proved insufficient to stop the threat, they would buy considerably more time than the client state's forces for the legions to assemble and defend the core provinces against a foe sure to have been greatly weakened during his advance.

In short, contrary to Luttwak's analysis, the transition of Rome's client states into provinces was a huge gain to the Empire's economic well-being and security. The client-state system was a stopgap measure based on security concerns that arose after the Roman civil wars had ended. But the system had outlived its usefulness and was now exposing Rome to additional dangers. As circumstances changed, Rome, as it always did, adapted. In this case, adaption meant absorbing many but not all of its clients into the Empire. Moreover, most of these client states were in the east and had lost their security function because of Corbulo's treaty with the Persians. The results of these new arrangements were self-evident: Rome enjoyed peace for the next century, when the world again began to shift during the reign of Marcus Aurelius (161–180).

CHAPTER 9 | The Year of the Four Emperors
and the Flavians

T HIS CIVIL WAR, fought in 69 CE, is difficult to assess in strategic
terms. For one, the events of that year are convoluted enough to fill complete books and have done so.[1] For another, the year was but a waypoint that
marked the change from the Julio-Claudian dynasty to that of the Flavians.
In and of themselves, the momentous events of that year had virtually no
lasting strategic impact. The legions marched, four men of high standing
declared themselves emperor, and one of them—Vespasian—succeeded in
making his claim stick. After it was all over and the legions had returned
to their posts on the frontiers, the basic political structure of Rome and the
Empire remained seemingly unaffected. Rome's citizens could be forgiven for
not noticing much of a change. The one true change in the Empire's strategic
situation was that the collaboration of the Senate and Praetorian Guard in the
selection and sustaining of emperors came to an end, although this change
was disguised for over a century of peaceful transitions at the top. From 69
CE forward the legions would be the final arbiter as to who ruled, and when
the various field armies were not in agreement, civil war was the result.

But before the civil war of 69 CE ended, Rome also crushed two revolts,
both appearing more dangerous at the moment than with the benefit of historical hindsight. Vespasian had left his son Titus to take Jerusalem and wipe
out the last vestiges of the Jewish Revolt. He also moved his generals north
to crush the Batavian Revolt along the Rhine. Both revolts failed because, despite their initial successes, they did not spark wider uprisings against Rome.

Neither Syria nor Egypt took advantage of Rome's distraction in Judea to try and cast off their chains. Likewise, although the leaders of the Batavian Revolt declared a Gallic Empire free from Roman domination, most of Gaul refused to join in the rebellion. And here is the true underpinning of the Empire's strategic stability: virtually all of the Empire's conquered peoples were happy to be under Roman control. Isolated outbursts were not a danger to the whole because the risk of contagion, at least until the third century, was remarkably low. Thus, Rome was free to concentrate its forces to crush revolts and then disperse them back to their home regions as soon as the fighting ended without running any undue risk of further ruin while the frontier legions were away. This happy situation did not go unchallenged, forcing Rome to adapt its political system after Domitian's assassination (96 CE) and as new enemies in Dacia and Persia required massive military responses, but once these were complete the threats to the Empire were, for another century, rarely very serious and never existential (Figure 9.1).

But before the fruits of the Pax Romana could be fully enjoyed, Rome needed to survive the tumult of 69 CE. Trouble began a year later when Gaius Julius Vindex, governor of Gallia Lugdunensis—the province surrounding modern Lyon—revolted, probably with the support of the powerful governor of Hispania Tarraconensis, Servius Sulpicius Galba. Vindex failed to gather popular support, and his bid for the throne was soon short-circuited by the arrival of the Rhine legions, commanded by Lucius Verginius Rufus. At the Battle of Vesontio, the trained and disciplined Rhine legions massacred the recently raised Gallic levies, leaving Vindex to commit suicide.[2] After the battle, the Rhine legions pleaded with Rufus to claim the throne. But Rufus, demonstrating that he did not possess the same fire to rule that others had in abundance, refused all such entreaties. Dio is convinced that such an energetic man, supported by a "large and zealous military force," could easily have made himself emperor. Instead, he left the legions and traveled to Rome, where he remained an éminence grise in the transition to power and through much of the Flavian era.

Galba, who did have the will to power and was always Nero's most dangerous rival, was initially condemned by the Senate as a traitor. But, for reasons that remain unclear, Nero lost his nerve and removed himself from any role in administering the Empire. The Senate was quick to move into the vacuum, and the praetorians were bribed to desert the regime. Galba's condemnation was reversed, and the Senate declared him emperor. Nero, deserted on all sides, committed suicide, and word was soon sent to Galba that he was welcome in Rome.

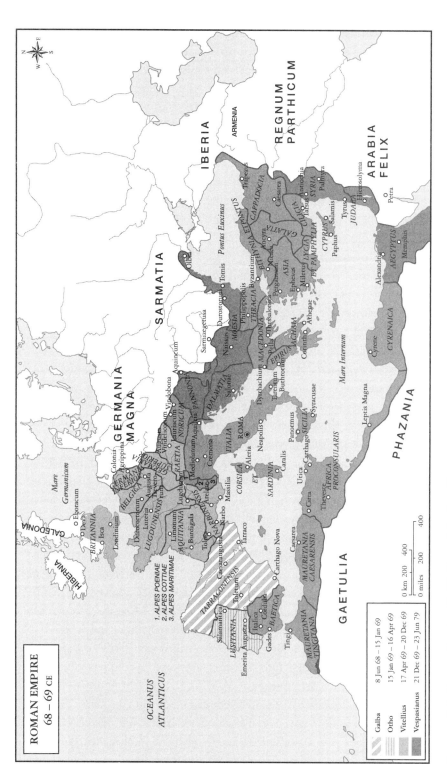

FIGURE 9.1 Roman Empire 69 CE, Year of the Four Emperors

Galba then began to make a series of unforced errors that led to his ultimate ruin. For one, he did nothing to secure the support of the legions, particularly those along the Rhine. With Rufus gone, the commanders of the Rhine legions appeared eager to swear their support to the new emperor, but their loyalty went unrewarded, and Galba soon appointed new commanders, including Aulus Vitellius, to command the legions of the lower Rhine. Marching with only one newly raised legion, supplied by the governor of Lusitania, Galba took precious time to raze any town and city that did not immediately accept his authority. Once in Rome, he continued the Neronian terror, soon turning the city's elites against him. Worse, for reasons unknown, he refused to pay the praetorians their bribe and compounded that error by refusing to show the Rhine legions the respect they thought they deserved and by refusing to send the rewards they were expecting. Galba's quip at the time, "that it was his habit to levy his soldiers, not buy them," endeared him to nobody.[3]

Seeing how events in Rome were playing out, Vitellius, the emperor's own man on the Rhine, secured the allegiance of the disaffected legions and raised the flag of revolt. The elderly Galba put the final nail in his own coffin when he adopted a young senator, Lucius Calpurnius Piso, as his successor, over his strongest supporter, Otho. Otho wasted little time running to the disaffected Praetorians, who, after getting their financial demands met, turned on the emperor who had refused them their accustomed bribes. By the end of the day Galba was dead, having been murdered by the Praetorians in the Forum.

The Senate quickly approved Otho as emperor. Unfortunately, half of the Rhine legions had already departed their camps and were heading for Rome. Otho at first sent emissaries to Vitellius to negotiate, even offering to marry Vitellius's daughter. But the legions were on the march, and the time for talking had passed. At the last minute Otho began gathering troops to meet Vitellius's army on the Po River. Having sent for several Danubian legions, he hoped to hold out long enough to marshal these veterans in northern Italy. His plans were thwarted by an early thaw that allowed the Rhine legions, commanded by Vitellius's generals, Valens and Caecina, to cross the Alps and unite their forces at Cremona. After several minor fights, the two armies met in the Battle of Bedriacum (also called the Battle of Cremona) to decide the issue. At first Otho's forces, anchored by the few cohorts of the Danubian legions to arrive, as well as the arrival of the fourteenth legion (famous for crushing Boudicca's Revolt), made some headway. But the Vitellian legions soon recovered and charged. As Tacitus tells it, the Vitellian "lines were intact; they were superior in strength and in numbers. However, Otho's troops put up a brave resistance despite their disordered ranks, their inferior numbers, and their fatigue."[4] In many places the terrain made it difficult for the formations to come to close quarters. Where they could do so, the fighting was hard: the soldiers of both sides pressed the "weight of their bodies behind their shields; they threw no spears but crashed swords and axes through helmets and breastplates."[5] But in time, numbers and discipline had the desired effect; the Vitellian legions gained the upper hand and proceeded to encircle and destroy much of Otho's army.[6] Tacitus tells us that the pursuit was without pity and the roads were soon blocked with the dead, as, "in civil wars captives are not turned to profit."[7] Only the fourteenth legion fought its way back to its camp, arriving intact to man the camp's defense and to provide refuge for the remnants of the Othonian army.

The Vitellian legions halted before the camp, whereupon Otho's generals negotiated their army's surrender as the soldiers of both sides lamented the evils of having Romans fight each other in a civil war. Upon hearing the extent of his losses, Otho committed suicide; he had lasted barely three months. With his final victory assured, Vitellius himself crossed the Alps and made for Rome. He had only just arrived when news came that the eastern legions had hailed Vespasian as their emperor. Vitellius must have known that Vespasian's rise heralded another military showdown, which makes his next moves all the more baffling. Instead of reconciling the Othonian legions to his cause, he dispersed them to isolated corners of the Empire. The First *Adiutrix* was sent to Spain, and the fourteenth was returned to Britain. Only the thirteenth legion was kept in northern Italy, but it was kept busy with construction projects. The new emperor's worst move, however, was to order the VII, XI, and XII legions back to the Danube. These battle-tested legions had no love for Vitellius and were further alienated by the perception that the Rhine legions were favored over them. Once back on the Danube, they were heavily influenced by the actions of Vespasian's III Gallica. This legion, only recently transferred from Vespasian's army, maintained its prior loyalties and was the first of the Danubian legions to declare for Vespasian.

Once the rest of the Danubian legions had followed III Gallica's lead, Vespasian was left holding a very strong position, one made all the stronger by the fact that he was already wrapping up operations in Judea. All that was left to do was capture Jerusalem and several outlying fortified outposts, including Masada. These operations could be left to his son, Titus, and accomplished with a much smaller force than was currently under Vespasian's command. With the cooperation of the legate in Syria, C. Licinius Mucianus, Vespasian secured the support of the Eastern Empire, including the few remaining client states, as well as the assurance that the Syrian legions would march under his banner. As his legions began their long march toward

Italy, Vespasian was in Egypt, from where he could control Rome's vital grain supply.

On July 1, 69 CE, Vespasian was proclaimed emperor in Alexandria. A couple of days later the Syrian legions hailed his ascent, followed by the Danubian legions in August. Unwilling to wait for Mucianus's legions to arrive, the Danubian commander, Marcus Antonius Primus, gathered the Danubian legions and entered Italy in early October. In doing so, he denuded the Danube frontier, leaving it open to attack from the still-dangerous Sarmatians. Upon arriving in the Balkans, Mucianus was therefore forced to leave a large portion of his army behind while he rushed the remainder to join Primus. The fighting was over before he arrived.

Primus's forces encountered the Vitellian legions at the same spot Otho's army had been defeated, Bedriacum. Before the battle commenced, Vitellius's commander, Caecina, tried to bring the army over to Vespasian. However, when the troops became aware of what was happening, they revolted. After having already beaten a small portion of the Danubian forces that had supported Otho, they could not bear the thought of surrendering to the same foe. "Has the glory of the German troops sunk to this," they cried, "that without a struggle and without a wound they will offer their hands to fetters and surrender their weapons to the foe? What are these legions that are opposed to us? Those we defeated!"[8] Caecina was fettered with chains, leaving the eight Vitellian legions in the field without a recognized leader, since the sickly Valens was not yet with the army. Primus moved quickly to take advantage of the Vitellian demoralization and lack of leadership. An early cavalry skirmish was won by Primus's forces; these then broke two Vitellian legions, which fell back into Cremona. As the bulk of the Danubian forces approached the battlefield, they demanded to be led in an immediate assault of the city, for they wanted its plunder and knew that would be forbidden if the city surrendered with clemency. Primus was about to give in to their demands when word arrived that an additional six Vitellian legions had arrived and were preparing for immediate battle.[9]

As Tacitus points out, "The wise policy for the troops of Vitellius was to revive their strength by food and sleep at Cremona and then to put to flight and crush their opponents, who would be exhausted by cold and lack of food. But being without a leader, destitute of a plan, at about nine o'clock in the evening they flung themselves on the Flavian troops, who were ready and in their stations."[10] The seesaw battle lasted throughout the night, and at one point the Danubian legions seemed about to break through the hard-pressed Vitellian VII Legion when they were stopped by massed artillery, which inflicted severe damage on Primus's XV Legion.

At daybreak the issue remained undecided. During a pause in the main action, Primus harangued each legion in turn, reminding the Danubian legions that they now had the chance to wipe out the disgrace of having been defeated by the very same foes not a few months before; telling them that it was "useless to challenge the Vitellians with threats and words if they could not endure their hands and looks."[11] But it was with III Gallica that he spent the longest time and upon which he pinned all of his hopes. This legion had not been at the first Battle of Bedriacum and had never been defeated in battle. Primus reminded them of their ancient glory, as well as their recent achievements: their victory over the Parthians when Mark Anthony commanded and over the Armenians when Corbulo led them, and their recent destruction of a large Sarmatian army. When he was done, the III Gallica, following a tradition common to the eastern legions, loudly hailed the rising sun, and upon hearing it the rest of the army gave a loud cheer. The Danubian legions advanced to battle.

The Vitellian legions, noting the renewed spirit and well-ordered ranks of their enemy's advance, misinterpreted III Gallica's hailing the sun as a welcome sign to reinforcing legions. Rumors rapidly spread that Mucianus had arrived with the Syrian legions. Not only that, but as night turned into day, it was quite apparent to the Rhine veterans that in the absence of an overall leader, no one had properly ordered their lines to meet the oncoming assault. With the Danubian legions advancing double-quick, there was no time to fill gaps or to align units into a solid formation. Being veterans, they attempted to rally to their standards, but this just opened the gaps between units even wider. The masses of Primus's legions hit the ragged Vitellian line like a thunderclap and smashed it asunder. Then, as in all ancient battles, the real slaughter began. Tacitus tells us that every soldier cursed the killing, thinking it was a horrible deed to murder relatives, kinsmen, and brother legionaries: "They called the deed a crime, but they did it."[12]

There was still some minor fighting left to do, followed by a period of prolonged negotiations, before the Senate declared Vespasian the rightful emperor, but the end was never really in doubt. The main job now was to heal the wounds of civil war, but before that could be done, the Flavians had to reconcile with their former enemies and put down a revolt centered around Batavian auxiliaries on the Rhine.[13] There were some tense moments as the Rhine legions were brought back into the fold, but it was rapidly done, likely because there was no other viable choice for emperor. The Flavians eschewed retribution and punishment in favor of rewards and a slow reorganization that eventually saw several legions disbanded and new ones raised to replace them. The success of the Flavian reconciliation can be judged by the decades of stability that followed the tumultuous year 69.

Crushing the Batavian Revolt was trickier business, not least because it was probably instigated by Vespasian's supporters looking to keep some of Vitellius's Rhine legions pinned down. Once started, it took on a life of its own and spread along the entire reach of the Rhine from the North Sea to modern Switzerland. Still, it failed in two regards. First, despite calling for the creation of the Gallic Empire, few Gauls rushed to the cause. And second, pleas for help from the German tribes across the Rhine went almost entirely unheeded. When the Flavians sent nine veteran legions to restore order, the Batavians could measure their time left as a political force according to the legionary march tables.

In general, Vespasian and the Flavians gained the internal security of the Empire through a policy of moderation and caution. There was no reason to threaten or punish, as the Roman elites—senators and equestrians—rapidly learned their place. There was no movement to return to the days of the Republic, and everyone comprehended that emperors were now chosen by the soldiers. However, if the emperor was keen on stabilizing the Empire, then he still needed to put time and effort into winning over and coopting Rome's elites. After all, it was from these two groups that emperors selected the men who managed the imperial administration, governed the provinces, oversaw major imperial initiatives, and generally kept the Empire's daily business running. They had their own value system and expectations, and every wise emperor from Augustus to at least Severus paid careful attention to their needs and desires.[14] Eager to bring these men into his service, Vespasian, in his *Lex de imperio Vespaisani*, codified a set of rights and privileges that earlier emperors had presented on an individual basis.

During the combined reigns of Vespasian and Titus, this inclusive approach to running the Empire brought significant gains, particularly in terms of improving strategic stability. Domitian, at the start of his reign, kept many persons in place who had proven their worth under his father and brother, ensuring the imperial administrative apparatus continued to function efficiently. This broke down sometime after the start of a localized revolt in Germania led by Lucius Antonius Saturninus, who appears to have held a personal grudge against Domitian. The revolt was soon crushed by Aulus Lappius Maximus Norbanus and the future emperor, Trajan, but not before it impacted the emperor's emotional state.[15] From this point forward, according to Dio, "he quite outdid himself in visiting disgrace and ruin upon the friends of his father and of his brother."[16] There is every reason to believe that the testaments of the ancient authors overstate the case against Domitian, as his willingness to kill senators or other elites did not endear him to that class, which provides most of our extant historical works from the period. But their commentary does give one the flavor of the times and the attitudes of Roman elites. As Dio states, no one felt safe, because Domitian was "putting many of the foremost men out of the way on many different pretexts, some by means of murder and others by banishment. He also removed many from Rome to other places and destroyed them."[17] Future emperors would have to spend considerable effort repairing the rift, with varying degrees of success, until the day they no longer deemed the effort worthwhile.

The biggest, immediate strategic change caused by Saturninus's revolt was Domitian's order that no more than a single legion could be collocated, a lesson in managing the loyalty of the troops that he should have adopted from Augustus. No Roman emperor, particularly one who had not solidified his support, could afford to let a third or more of Rome's legions fall into the hands of ambitious aristocrats. To do so would have invited a return to the chaos of the civil wars that had wracked the state for nearly a hundred years before the battle of Actium (31 BCE), and of which the anarchy following Nero's death (68 CE) provided an unpleasant centennial reminder.[18] As a practical matter, this dispersal of the legions not only made it more difficult for the contagion of revolt to spread but also multipled coordination difficulties in the event of a revolt. Domitian was also the first emperor since Augustus to spend a large amount of his time on campaign and away from Rome. His decision to do so was likely driven by the knowledge that when he became emperor he did not have the military reputation of Vespasian or his brother, Titus. Also, as the events of 69 CE proved, emperors were now made and broken by the legions. As such, it was best to be where one could both keep an eye on them and prove one worthy of their respect. But the lasting impact of his lengthy absences was that the Empire's center of power gradually moved from Rome to wherever the emperor was located. Finally, to ensure the loyalty of the legions, Domitian gave them their first pay raise in decades, raising their salaries from nine hundred to twelve hundred sesterces.

Compared to previous wars and campaigns, Domitian's conflicts were minor affairs, which made it easy for contemporary commentators to portray them as reckless or acts of vanity. His first military campaign against the Chatti, in 82–83, was likely aimed at protecting Romanized Germans in the Agri Decumates—a territory covering the Black Forest and the region between the Rhine, Main, and Danube Rivers in present southwestern Germany.[19] Caught by surprise and struck with overwhelming military force, the Chatti were quickly defeated. Domitian then hurried back to Rome to celebrate and enjoy the political fruits of victory, opening himself to ridicule by the very people he thought would be impressed.[20]

He had more success in Britain, where Tacitus's father-in-law, Gnaeus Julius Agricola, led a prolonged offensive into the northern reaches of the island.[21] Agricola had been at war for nearly seven years, slowly pacifying Wales and then advancing into Scotland. In 84 the Caledonians, unified under a chieftain whom Tacitus identifies as Calgacus, marched to meet the advancing Romans, who were threatening the tribe's just-harvested grain reserves. Before engaging the Romans in battle, Calgacus gave one of history's more rousing speeches, part of which has become a famous view of Roman attitudes about war and conquest:

> But there are no tribes beyond us, nothing indeed but waves and rocks, and the yet more terrible Romans, from whose oppression escape is vainly sought by obedience and submission. Robbers of the world, having by their universal plunder exhausted the land, they rifle the deep. If the enemy be rich, they are rapacious; if he be poor, they lust for dominion; neither the east nor the west has been able to satisfy them. Alone among men they covet with equal eagerness poverty and riches. To robbery, slaughter, plunder, they give the lying name of empire; *they make a solitude and call it peace.*[22]

The last line, of course, is often rephrased as "they make a desert and call it peace."

The two armies met at Mons Graupius and formed for battle. According to Tacitus, both armies were evenly matched at about thirty thousand combatants, but Agricola decided to hold his legions back near the Roman camp as a reserve. He then attacked the Britons with his sixteen auxiliary cohorts—mostly Batavians and Tungrians—aimed at the enemy's center, with his cavalry on both flanks and a smaller cavalry held in reserve in the rear. After a rousing speech, ending with a plea to "put an end to campaigns; crown your fifty years' service with a glorious day," Agricola ordered the advance.[23] Eight thousand auxiliary infantry and three thousand Roman cavalry surged forward.[24] An attempt by the Caledonians to outflank the advancing auxiliaries was routed by Agricola's reserve cavalry, allowing the Roman force to continue its advance. With their center bending and Roman cavalry assailing their flanks and rear, the Caledonians broke.[25]

Although the Caledonian losses were great, at least two-thirds of the army escaped into the nearby woods and marshes, where they continued a stout defense until the Romans withdrew. Soon thereafter Agricola was recalled to Rome. Tacitus tells us that the result of all this was that Britain was never completely conquered, and that this failure was solely a consequence of Domitian's jealousy of Agricola's achievements. The more likely explanation is that the start of a greater conflict with the Dacians required a realignment of the Empire's military forces. With every legion serving on or near the frontiers, if a concentration of forces was needed, then a reset of the frontier forces had to follow. In this case, the simple act of calling off a costly and strongly resisted offensive into territories of marginal value freed multiple legions for service elsewhere. Of course, the long-term strategic impact of the move was that northern Britain was never conquered and would eventually be separated from the Empire by the construction of Hadrian's Wall (Figure 9.2).

Although the disarray of the northern tribes, in the wake of Agricola's campaigns, allowed the building of a fortified line in northern Britain to be postponed, the same was not true along the Rhine frontier. Here, despite some limited victories over the Chatti, the amalgamation of the German tribes, in terms of coordination, if not yet merging into proto-states, was sufficiently threatening for Domitian to order the creation of the *limes Germanicus* (Figure 9.3). Keen to protect his victories, the emperor initiated the construction of a fortified *lime* along recently pacified borders. These *limes* would be extended by Hadrian and his successors until they stretched along the entire length of the German provinces and through Reatia (roughly modern Switzerland and Bavaria), where they eventually connected with the yet-to-be-constructed Danubian defenses. The building of such defensive *limes* signaled that the Empire was moving away from conquest in favor of a primarily defensive strategy, at least along this portion of its extended frontier.

The Rhine may have been pacified, but in 85, and for the next four years, Domitian was occupied by conflicts along the Danubian frontier.[26] The most dangerous of these were the Dacians, led by their active, warlike, and competent king, Decebalus.[27] War erupted when Decebalus, in 85, took advantage of Domitian's distraction by troubles along the Rhine to launch his army across the Danube into Moesia, killing the governor and severely damaging a Roman legion.[28] Reinforcements were sent, but the damage was done, and the Dacians had already made off with substantial booty. The following year Domitian sent his praetorian prefect, Cornelius Fascus, across the Danube with several legions to punish Dacian insolence. The army was ambushed in a mountain pass and severely damaged, Fascus was killed, and at least one legion, almost certainly the V Alaudae, was wiped out.

The Roman counterattack took two years to mobilize and was led by Tettius Julianus. By crossing the Danube above where the Dacian army was camped, Julianus pushed unhindered toward the Dacian capital, the heavily

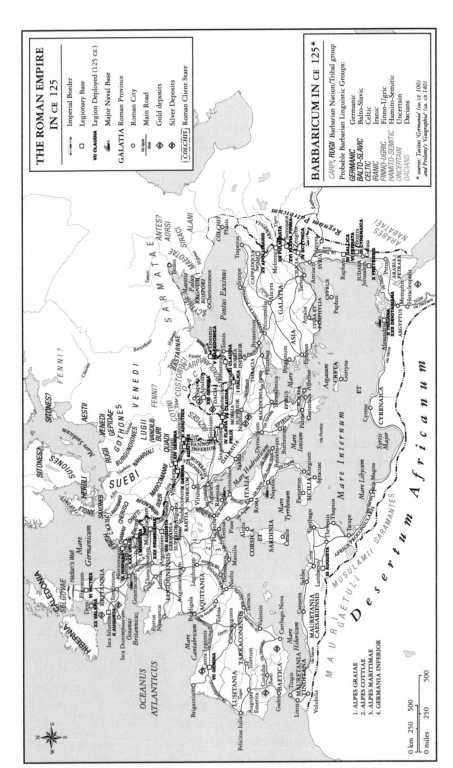

FIGURE 9.2 Roman Empire under Hadrian, 125 CE

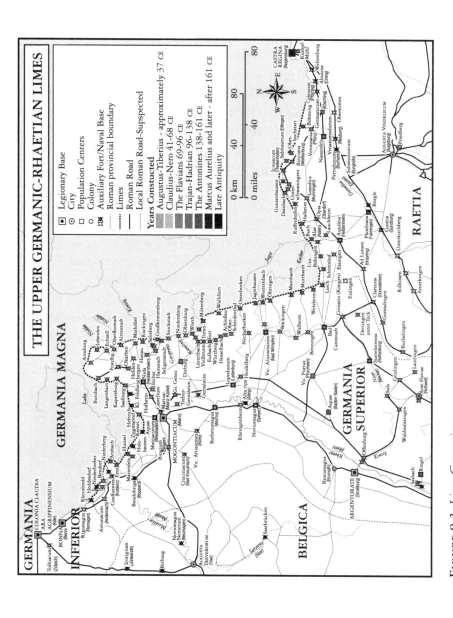

FIGURE 9.3 *Limes Germanicus*

fortified Sarmizegethusa. He first encountered the Dacian army at Tapae, west of the capital, and according to Dio slew great numbers of them.[29] Decebalus, with his capital almost undefended, ordered his remaining forces to "cut down the trees that were on the site and nail armor to the trunks, in order that the Romans might take them for soldiers and so be frightened and withdraw; and this actually happened."[30] It is doubtful the Romans were fooled, but as it was already late in the campaigning season, Julianus ordered the army into winter camp and prepared to finish the Dacians off in the spring.

But while the Romans prepared, Decebalus acted and gained the active support of the trans-Danubian Marcomanni, Quadi, and Iazyges, all former Roman clients who had refused to send troops to support Roman operations.[31] We know nothing about military operations against them in 88 or 89, but it appears that Julianus had to patch up a "shameful" peace with the Dacians so as to deal with this new uprising, only to see it flame up anew in 92. This time, the Marcomanni, Quadi, and Iazyges combined to wipe out a Roman legion, the XXI Rapax. How Rome reacted to this loss of a full legion is lost to us, but it was surely swift and brutal, since by 93 Domitian was in Rome celebrating a triumph over the Sarmatian tribes (Figure 9.4).

The strategic consequences of all this fighting along the Danube were long lasting. Rome may have defeated the Dacians, but it was a near-run thing. Consequently, the legions returned to the south side of the Danube, where they started building the *limes Moesiaen*. Even after Dacia was conquered by

FIGURE 9.4 Trajan's Column

Trajan, these lines appear to have been maintained to at least some extent. They would become Rome's primary defensive barrier along the Danube when Dacia was later abandoned in the third century.

Toward the end Domitian's paranoia, fed by the Saturninus Revolt, sparked successive rounds of executions during his final three years of rule. Tacitus tells us that Agricola, who died in 93, was spared the worst by not having to witness the siege of the Senate house or the killing of many men of consular rank.[32] Eventually, the Senate found its nerve and in 96 had the emperor stabbed to death by one of his domestic staff.

Assessing the Flavian Strategic Situation

Vespasian's accession did not cure all that ailed the Empire. Foremost among the many difficulties that needed fixing was the central government's fiscal condition, which could only be rebuilt and stabilized by a long period of peace and a return to fiscal sanity. Nero's uncontrolled spending had nearly bankrupted the treasury, a condition greatly worsened by the economic destruction of the civil war. To rebuild the treasury and pay the armies, the Flavians instituted several new taxes and improved enforcement of the older levies. Because they undertook these measures before the economy had recovered, the Flavians quickly gained a reputation for having a "lust for money."[33] But economic salvation was not far distant, as Vespasian's rise began a long period of stability, one that extended well past the last of the Flavian era. As noted earlier, such stability was the crucial requirement for rapid and sustained economic growth, as landowners will not make capital investments when there is a risk of their destruction by renewed conflict, and traders are not going to commission the construction of large cargo ships if the seas are not secure. Similarly, when provinces are stable, there is little to no destruction, which means investment capital is employed on new infrastructure and not the replacement of capital stock lost in wars. While there was political instability during the early Empire, this was limited almost entirely to the safety, or lack thereof, of the imperial elites. Although economically damaging, it pales in comparison to the destruction wrought in the civil wars.

This change marked a profound transformation of the ancient world as security and order remade society and economics throughout the Mediterranean. Until the third century, the vital economic core of the Empire was almost always tranquil, and, except for the events of 69 CE, when conflicts did erupt along the frontiers, they were short, localized, and distant from anything critical to the Empire's well-being. This, as we have seen, allowed for a huge post-Actium reduction in military forces, freeing up large amounts of capital for infrastructure investments.[34] Moreover, although the cost of the army was by far the largest government expense, the cost and the taxes required for the army's maintenance were not resented by the populace, as it was widely recognized that the Empire's wealth rested on the prowess of the legions.[35]

Security, as it always was in the premodern world, a spur to population growth, and the Empire's population from Augustus to the Antonines increased by at least a third.[36] This increase alone would have accounted for substantial growth in the overall Roman economy. Unfortunately, population-based growth does not necessarily mean there is an increase in the amount of surplus available for the state's use, for it was possible that all of these new workers were producing at only the subsistence level for themselves and their families, leaving no surplus for the state to seize. But if we can estimate a corresponding one-third increase in gross domestic product (GDP) per capita, because of increased capital investment—likely a low estimate if one examines the complete historical record—then, by the end of the Flavian era, Rome had a huge excess of capital to employ.[37]

This enormous growth of the Roman economy is attested to by shipwreck data, which shows Roman trade hitting its peak in the first century.[38] There was some drop-off in the total number of wrecks as the century waned, but this likely does not represent any reduction in the level of trade. Rather, a stable empire made it less risky to build larger ships, so trade was likely increasing even as the number of ships decreased. We will return to this topic when we discuss the later Roman Empire.

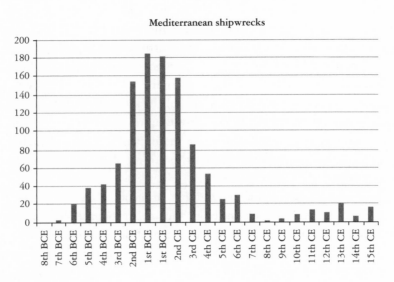

Mediterranean shipwrecks

One can, however, see the same effect in the modern world, where thousands of smaller freighters have been replaced by hundreds of mega-container ships.

Rapid economic growth is also attested by new measurements of lead pollution in ice cores collected in Greenland. The cores clearly demonstrate that the Crisis of the Roman Republic coincided with a sustained period of very low lead emissions. The cores reveal that when the civil wars ended there was a huge increase in lead emissions that lasted throughout the first century CE. Emissions remained high until the 160s, coinciding with the apogee of the Roman Empire under the Pax Romana, only falling off as a consequence of the devastating Antonine Plague in 165–193.[39]

Much of this economic growth was reinvested into more infrastructure projects—roads, bridges, ports, and aqueducts that for two hundred years created a prosperous economic cycle. Much of the funding, as seen in the literary and archaeological record, indicates that significant funds also went toward constructing monumental buildings in Rome and many of the Empire's other cities. This had the effect of speeding up monetary circulation within the urban centers and would have acted as another spur to growth. Finally, economic growth meant there were plenty of funds to start construction on the *limes,* which would continue for much of the next century.[40] From the start, these fortifications were linked to natural defensive features and supported by an extensive network of roads, canals, and harbors. Their strength was enhanced by the creation of exclusion zones around them within which barbarians were forbidden to settle. Tacitus presents one story of a band of Frisians ignoring an exclusion and settling too close to the Rhine fortifications. The provincial governor, Paulinus, ordered them to depart or get approval from Rome. Nero refused their petition, but the Frisians, who had already begun tilling the soil, refused to leave. Writes Tacitus: "As they ignored the order, compulsion was applied by the unexpected dispatch of a body of auxiliary horse, which captured or killed the more obstinate of those who resisted."[41]

In building these fortified defensive zones, Rome was in effect following an adage that was once popular with the American army: "Never put a man where you can put a bullet." This is shorthand for conserving soldiers by expending munitions—substituting capital for manpower. Similarly, Rome was spared the expense and social disruption that would have resulted from enlarging the army, choosing to use fortifications as a substitute for manpower.

It is unfortunate that too many people, including historians who should know better, have taken a quote from the movie *Patton* to heart: "Fixed fortifications are monuments to the stupidity of man. If mountain ranges and oceans can be overcome, then anything built by man can be overcome."[42]

Soon after uttering his quip, Patton had reason to regret it: the old, poorly maintained Siegfried Line and the outdated Metz fortresses stopped his army dead in its tracks for months. What Patton was alluding to was likely what he had just experienced as the Allies pierced the Atlantic Wall. Once the Allies broke through at Normandy, the massive investment in fortifications along the entire length of the English Channel became worthless.

But the barbarians were not the highly mechanized Allied forces in Normandy. Even if they broke through, there were limits to how far a raiding band could penetrate and how long it could stay in unfriendly territory. As discussed above, the *limes*, even in a rudimentary state, were often enough to hold off all but the largest enemy forces. And even if there was a penetration, the *limes* made it possible to economize forces in other areas to concentrate at the point of crisis. Moreover, as the legions moved to reinforce the *limes* adjacent to the penetration, they limited the raiders' escape routes, often forcing them to return the way they had come and into the waiting arms of the legions. Indeed, fortifications are expensive, but they have a multi-millennium track record of success.

These *limes* were not built overnight. Rather, they began under the Flavians as regions cleared of vegetation. Later on tracks and towers were added, but we must wait until at least Hadrian's reign before we see extensive palisades along the tracks and between towers. Much later the wooden towers would be reconstructed in stone, and stone walls would replace oak palisades. These improvements would have been made in tandem with improving barbarian military capabilities, as well as the growing populations and prosperity of the frontier zones. For the Flavians and their immediate successors, the *limes* provided a defensive barrier capable of stopping minor incursions and even halting a major offensive, assuming the Romans had enough intelligence regarding was happening beyond the frontier to allow time for the legions to concentrate. The *limes* also permitted Rome to economize on its forces so that the greatest amount of territory could be protected by the smallest number of troops. And finally, they gave the legions a set of strategic pivot points on which to maneuver in relative safety against any invading force.

As long as the *limes* existed and were properly manned and supported, the Empire was safe. Only when the *limes* were penetrated and abandoned over large stretches was the Roman military edifice placed at risk. Moreover, because any prolonged penetration of the *limes* also compromised the Rhine and/or Danube transport routes, Rome's capacity to rapidly move troops and supplies to threatened sectors of the northern frontier was hugely reduced by any prolonged rupture of the frontier's rivers. It is only after it became impossible to guarantee the security of river transport that we see later emperors building large field armies far from the frontiers, who were now forced to march overland to meet any major incursion. This placed the armies of the later Empire at a severe disadvantage, for no matter how good the road network was, marching troops could never hope to move and concentrate forces at anything approaching the speeds that were possible using river and sea transport. But this is a problem for another day.

For most of the next century, as we shall see, Rome had little to fear from its enemies, and they had much to fear from Rome, which, despite its increasing employments of fortified lines, had not yet abandoned its expansionist impulses. In fact, by allowing extended sectors of the frontiers to be defended with fewer troops, the *limes* made it possible to concentrate forces for emperors such as Trajan and Severus to lead major offensives beyond the Roman frontiers. In many ways, this alternate employment of the *limes* upsets many historians' notions of the *limes'* being an expression of a growing defensive mentality. As the Romans were surely aware, it was the *limes* that made extended offensive operations possible over the next two centuries.

CHAPTER 10 | The Empire at High Tide

AFTER THE MURDER of the last Flavian emperor, Nerva, an aged and temporary custodian of the office, ascended to power. Anyone wishing to describe the Empire whose reins Nerva had taken hold of would be hard pressed to match the eloquence of Edward Gibbon's opening passage in his history of the Empire:

> In the second century of the Christian Era, the empire of Rome comprehended the fairest part of the earth, and the most civilized portion of mankind. The frontiers of that extensive monarchy were guarded by ancient renown and disciplined valor. The gentle but powerful influence of laws and manners had gradually cemented the union of the provinces. Their peaceful inhabitants enjoyed and abused the advantages of wealth and luxury. The image of a free constitution was preserved with decent reverence: the Roman senate appeared to possess the sovereign authority, and devolved on the emperors all the executive powers of government. During a happy period of more than fourscore years, the public administration was conducted by the virtue and abilities of Nerva, Trajan, Hadrian, and the two Antonines. . . . The principal conquests of the Romans were achieved under the republic; and the emperors, for the most part, were satisfied with preserving those dominions which had been acquired by the policy of the senate, the active emulations of the consuls, and the martial enthusiasm of the people.

Despite heading the list of Gibbon's five good emperors, Nerva was, from the start, a mere placeholder.[1] When the Senate proclaimed him emperor, he was already sixty-one years old, weak, and often ill. Moreover, he had no martial reputation and no base of political support; and, most crucially, he failed to gain the loyalty of the legions, who considered his predecessor, Domitian, a warrior and fondly remembered him for their first pay raise in a century. Still, Nerva's first months went well: one of his first acts was to swear to never put a senator to death—a welcome change from his predecessor. His mistake, if it can be called that, was in extending his protection and even friendship to those who had been in Domitian's inner circle. When he proved unable to protect these men from the wrath of those whom Domitian had victimized, Nerva's powerlessness was revealed. It was further demonstrated when, in the middle of 97 CE, the praetorians mutinied. Nerva was locked inside his palace while the praetorians formulated their demands, foremost among them that Nerva hand over Domitian's murderers to their justice. Nerva bravely refused, offering his own neck to the blade instead. But his gesture was for naught: the murderers were soon discovered and executed.

Although unharmed, Nerva comprehended that he had lost the support of the army and as a consequence probably did not have long to live. Childless Nerva's salvation was to adopt as his son and heir the governor of upper Germania, Marcus Ulpius Traianus—Trajan. Trajan was respected in Rome, but more crucially, he commanded the loyalty of the combat-hardened legions along the frontier. Trajan's adoption assured a smooth and peaceful transition of power upon Nerva's death while allowing Nerva to live out the last months of his reign in peace. In his own and history's estimation, he had been a good emperor, once remarking: "I have done nothing that would prevent my laying down the imperial office and returning to private life in safety."[2]

Trajan, born in 53 near Seville, was the first emperor of non-Italian origin, although his family was from northern Italy. He came from a military tradition, and his father had commanded the X Legion in the Jewish Revolts and was a governor of Syria who appears to have held extensive powers beyond his own province. This lineage surely helped Trajan, commander of the German legions, to also lay claim to the loyalty of the eastern legions. He had also been a military tribune in Syria before receiving command of the VII Legio in northern Spain. His legion had marched into Germany to help crush Saturninus's revolt against Domitian. That Trajan was favored by Domitian, who made him a consul in 91 CE, is mostly left out of the contemporary biographies.[3]

Upon his accession to the throne, Trajan did not immediately return to Rome. But in one of his first acts—a point not lost on anyone—he ordered the leaders of the praetorian mutiny against Nerva to join him at his camp, under the pretext that they were to receive a special commission. When they arrived, he had them immediately executed or, in Dio's more sensitive phrasing, he "had them put out of the way."[4] The praetorians, cognizant of the fact that one does not mutiny against an emperor with a dozen legions at his back, remained silent as Trajan exterminated their leaders. Nerva, by adopting Trajan, had proven once again that an emperor needed the army to rule; but Trajan was demonstrating, as had Vespasian, it was the legions that mattered, not the praetorians. It was also the support of the legions that gave Trajan the confidence to forgo an immediate trip to Rome to consolidate power in favor of an inspection tour of the Rhine and Danube frontiers. Visiting the latter was likely a wise precaution, since the Danubian legions appear to have had a particular fondness for Domitian.

Eventually Trajan made his way to Rome, where he was greeted with something approaching rapture by the citizenry, and the praises he received in the Senate would have made a more modest man blush. If the ancient sources are to be believed, Trajan was a man of exceptional virtue and manly vigor. According to Dio, he was "conspicuous for his justice, for his bravery, and for the simplicity of his habits. He was well-served by mental powers of the highest order, neither suffering from the recklessness of youth nor the sluggishness of old age."[5] Just as crucially, at least to the senators who wrote the histories and biographies of the time, "he did not envy or slay anyone."[6] According to multiple sources, his only vice was too great a fondness for food and drink.

He also had a fondness for war. And Dio points out that, during his twenty-year reign, he spent vast sums on works of peace—roads, aqueducts, buildings—but even vaster sums on acts of war.[7] But Dio, who, when writing about earlier emperors, clearly expresses an aversion to costly wars of expansion or conflicts that were waged only to enhance an emperor's reputation, manages to forgive Trajan, saying, "Even if he did delight in war, nevertheless he was satisfied when success had been achieved, a most bitter foe overthrown, and his countrymen exalted. Nor did the result which usually occurs in such circumstances—conceit and arrogance on the part of the soldiers—ever manifest itself during his reign; with such a firm hand did he rule them."[8]

Dio may have approved of Trajan's wars, and the emperor was surely an excellent military commander; but did his wars serve a strategic purpose, or were they just another spasm of glory-seeking within a tradition of imperial expansion not yet extinguished? The question remains hotly debated, but a reasoned response is that the immediate strategic gains from his two major wars of conquest—Dacia and Mesopotamia—more than justified the effort. It was not until well past a century later that there was reason for anyone to question the value of Trajan's Dacian conquest. A hundred years is a very long time in geopolitics, long enough to absolve Trajan of any responsibility for failing to see the difficulties his actions would engender a century hence. This becomes clearer if one examines dates closer to our own time. Should Bismarck—the strategic mind behind the unification of Germany—be held responsible for not foreseeing the rise of Hitler and the perversion of his dream? Can Abraham Lincoln, who likely foresaw the rise of American power in the world, be held responsible for not setting the stage to deal with the Cold War?

Similarly, it is absurd to blame Trajan for not anticipating the massive migratory eruptions out of the east that would one day overwhelm Roman Dacia. Moreover, even if he could forecast parts of a distant future, given Roman military power and wealth during his lifetime, Trajan could have made a strong case that Rome's best strategy was to defend the passes through the Caucasus, which could be done at less expense in blood and treasure than holding the Danube. Even Trajan's Mesopotamian conquests served a strategic purpose at the time, since the Parthians had violated the Neronian settlement of 66 and had to be confronted before they could solidify their gains. Although this expansion of the Empire into Mesopotamia was later viewed as an overextension, even that could be debated. In the first instance, it gave Trajan's successor, Hadrian, a real bargaining chip with the Persians, making it possible to trade Rome's territorial gains for an extended peace. Moreover (although counterfactuals are always dangerous), it is interesting to examine the strategic possibilities if Hadrian had not returned Mesopotamia to Parthia. How much richer would Rome have been if they had held the fertile lands of the Tigris and Euphrates for another century or more? How much stronger would Rome's defenses have been if they had a full century to fortify the Mesopotamian provinces before the intensity and danger of the Persian threat grew after the Sassanids seized power? Similarly, one might also consider how the permanent loss of the Mesopotamian region would have impacted the economy and military power of Persia. The point here is not to ponder various what-if scenarios, but to point out that Trajan's conquests were not strategic folly. At the time, they made strategic sense, and a good argument can be made that if his successors had properly integrated and defended his gains, Rome's strategic position in succeeding centuries might have been considerably stronger. Luttwak claims that Rome did not possess the resource base—which he believes was not much greater than that bequeathed by Augustus—to defend these conquests. But he misses some major points. First, the Empire, because of the extended peace, was, as we have seen, hugely wealthier than it was at Augustus's death and could easily have resourced larger military costs. Moreover, Luttwak takes no account of the major expansion of the Roman resource base that would accrue if the rich Mesopotamian provinces were permanently integrated into the Roman economic system. Unlike Britain, the Mesopotamian Basin was one of the richest regions in the world. More crucially, he is wrong in his belief that Trajan's territorial expansion required a larger military investment. The east, unlike the *limes* in the west, was not a linear system that required manning along its entire length. Rather, it consisted of fortresses and fortress cities along the frontier situated along known avenues of invasion, of which there were few. Rome did not have to expand its forces to hold this territory; it just had to push the forces already in Syria forward to the new frontier.

Trajan at War

Trajan was the first emperor since Titus to take the purple already possessing a reputation as a soldier, and who commanded the respect and loyalty of the legions. This gave him a level of personal security on the throne that no emperor had enjoyed in seventy years. Thus, Trajan could govern in ways barred to his predecessors. For one, he could expand on his base of loyal followers by giving his subordinates—governors, generals, and administrative officials— a freer hand to do this job, and then reward them when they did well. Unlike an emperor such as Claudius, who spent barely a fortnight in Britain before rushing back to Rome to claim a triumph for himself and the title of Britannicus for his son, Trajan had no pressing need to build his reputation upon the toils of others and was therefore free to be generous to those who deserved reward and reputation.

Still, Trajan was a soldier, always more at home in the legionary camps than in Rome. Thus, during his nineteen-year reign he launched three major military campaigns, two of which were into Dacia. Historians have long debated the reasons for these campaigns, but with little solid contemporary evidence available, two default positions dominate. The first is that the Dacian king, Decebalus, minted his own coins, often from gold, alerting Rome to the region's rich ore deposits. The other was that the Roman impulse to garner conquests and glory was not yet extinct. As such, when opportunity beckoned, Trajan was not one to resist the chance to add a rich province to the Empire, as well as eternal renown to his name.

Still, as discussed earlier, there were also very good strategic reasons for sending the legions into Dacia. Primarily, the entire Danube region remained unsettled. Domitian had patched up an embarrassing peace with Decebalus so that he could deal with a new threat along the upper Danube from the Marcomanni, Quadi, and Iazyges. In the initial fighting Rome had lost a full legion, and though the Roman reaction was quick and severe, there is no evidence that these tribes were punished to the point where they were no longer a threat. What was clear is that Rome lacked sufficient resources in the Balkans to undertake even defensive operations against both threats simultaneously. Still, for the time being, the combined threat from the Marcomanni, Quadi, and Iazyges was quiescent, which opened a brief window of opportunity for Rome to deal with the more dangerous enemy: Decebalus and Dacia.

Although the Dacians are usually referred to as barbarians, the name has always been a poor fit. Along with the Getae—a tribe so closely related to the Dacians that the Greeks and Romans often used the names interchangeably—they had held a region that included a slightly enlarged modern Romania for several hundred years before the Romans arrived. The Dacians are first mentioned by Herodotus, who calls them "the noblest as well as the most just of all the Thracian tribes."[9] Herodotus also tells us that they ferociously resisted Darius's formidable Persian army, although they were eventually "enslaved" in 531 BCE. The Dacians, if not fully civilized, were as close to it as any Greek could consider a people who did not speak their language. Not only that, but they were demonstrably capable of mustering sufficient military power to make life difficult for Darius's royal Persian army. For the next six hundred years the Dacians remained in the same region, trading and interacting with the Greeks and other civilizations around the Black Sea, even giving one of their own as the wife of Alexander the Great's father, Philip II.[10]

Dacia may not have possessed the latent power of the Parthian Empire, but it was a highly centralized state with a flourishing economy and the capacity to field a significant, well-trained, and well-equipped fighting force—a force that, when moved to the frontier, was poised to strike quickly toward the mainland routes between the eastern and western halves of the Empire. Rome could hold the Danube against such a threat, but it meant keeping large amounts of forces pinned to the region that would be unable to assist other threatened areas. The surest way to eliminate the threat was an invasion, and with the Empire politically stable and its other frontiers quiet, there might never again be a better time to go to war. Still, such an effort would not be easy, for Decebalus had spent a decade fortifying Dacia, often with the help of Roman engineers, in preparation for just such an attack.

Not much is known about Trajan's first offensive beyond one sentence from his own account and some remnants of Dio's history. We do know that he prepared well and that, in addition to the nine Danubian legions, he ordered two others from the Rhine frontier—Legio X Germania and Legio XI Claudia—to join the massing army. He also created two legions—Legio II Trainan Fortis and Legio XXX Ulipia Victrix—for the campaign. Trajan left Rome early in 101 and was soon leading his legions out of Viminacium and directly toward the Dacian capital of Sarmizegethusa. No doubt foolishly, Decebalus, rather than manning his extensive defenses, advanced to meet the Roman army. A significant battle was fought at Tapae of which we know almost nothing except that losses on both sides were heavy, and Dio tells us that Trajan donated many of his extra garments to be torn into strips and used as bandages for the Roman wounded.[11]

Before Trajan could renew his advance, Decebalus, with the support of allied tribes, attacked Moesia. This attack was repulsed, but we have no evidence of whether Trajan was involved in this fighting.[12] In any event, the threat to Moesia was great enough for Trajan to halt his advance and await developments. The campaign was therefore completed the following spring when Trajan once again advanced upon Sarmizegethusa. The approach march appears to have been relatively easy, and one can assume that Decebalus, having lost two field battles the previous year, was having trouble making good his losses and holding allies to his standard. Dio tells us that Trajan's columns captured several fortified mountains and that they had no trouble doing so.[13] With his fortified line crumbling and the Romans starting to besiege his capital, Decebalus sued for peace. For reasons unknown to history, Trajan accepted, after requiring the demolition of many Dacian forts and the ceding of territory north of the Danube.

Trajan likely knew he was merely agreeing to a truce, and before long he and the Senate were receiving reports that Decebalus, after licking his wounds, was again preparing for war. According to Dio, "Decebalus was reported to him [Trajan] to be acting contrary to the treaty in many ways, was collecting arms, receiving those who deserted, repairing the forts, sending envoys to his neighbors . . . therefore the senate again declared him an enemy, and Trajan once more conducted the war against him in person instead of entrusting it of the others."[14] The Second Dacian War began in the spring of 105.[15] This time progress was slow, as much a result of fierce resistance as what Dio tells us was Trajan's desire to conduct the war with "safe prudence rather than haste."[16]

Trajan's second campaign dragged on for a year, but eventually the Romans fought their way to the walls of the Dacian capital.[17] The Dacians repulsed the first Roman assault, after which the Romans settled in for a proper siege. Once they had smashed the city's water pipes and threatened to burn the city, Dacian defenses collapsed. Decebalus fled but was later betrayed and his head brought to Trajan on a pike. The Romans also discovered where Decebalus had hidden his accumulated treasure in a nearby river.[18] Before returning to Rome, Trajan ordered the Dacian city and its fortress system destroyed.[19] In his wake he left a subdued Dacia, which by 126 CE would be divided into three provinces.

In just one of these provinces, Porolissensis, over five dozen Roman forts have been discovered, demonstrating that the region was rapidly and firmly integrated into the developing *limes* system.[20] This defense in depth along the northern frontier was originally supported by one legion deeper within Dacia, which was later reinforced by a second legion. Because the various Sarmatian tribes were at first defeated and cowed and later integrated through subsidies and trade into the Roman economic system, they would not become a serious military threat to the Empire for another century, when the tectonic population shifts far to the east began disrupting the stability of tribes along the frontiers of the Empire. As such, for the next hundred years the Dacian conquest was instrumental in securing the stability of the entire Balkan region as far south as Greece. Moreover, the land routes between the two halves of the Empire were now secure. As long as these Roman highways running through the Balkans remained unthreatened, they knitted the Empire together into a single seamless fabric, where the wealth and power of either half were available to assist in any crisis faced by the other. It was the loss of this strategic transport network in later centuries that forced each half of the Empire to start looking toward its separate interests.[21]

After a six-year interval of peace that the emperor spent mostly in Rome, Trajan again mustered his forces, this time against the powerful Parthian Empire.[22] The road to war began when the Parthian king, Pacorus II, died in 105. The claimants, Osroes in the western Parthian Empire and Vologases III in the east, began a civil war that dragged on for nearly a decade. In 113 Osroes, in a bid to add Armenia to his domains, installed his nephew, Parthamasiris, on the Armenian throne. This, of course, violated the Neronian settlement, which gave Rome the right to crown the king of Armenia. Similar to the situation at the start of the Dacian wars, the Roman Empire remained politically stable, with no threats visible on the horizon. Trajan, who already had designs on expanding the Empire at Parthia's expense, judged the time right for making a final settlement of the eastern questions. Thus Osroes' action could not have taken place at a better time for an emperor who was already looking for a pretext for war.

As Trajan passed through Athens, he rejected Osroes' pleas for peace; he arrived in Antioch early in 114. Trajan, with eleven legions, left there in the spring for the Cappadocian fortress city of Melitene, then crossed into Armenian territory. Parthian resistance was ineffectual, and Arsamosata fell without a fight. Soon thereafter the Persian crowned king, Parthamasiris, met him at Elegeia, where, before the assembled legions, he removed his crowns and did obeisance. According to Dio, he expected Trajan to return the crown, per the Neronian settlement.[23] Trajan had other ideas, and although he allowed Parthamasiris to depart safely from the Roman camp, he ordered Armenia annexed and converted into a Roman province.

In a single stroke Trajan had blown up the Neronian settlement, clearly indicating he had no desire to find a peaceful accommodation with Parthia. This and his later annexation of Mesopotamia demonstrate a change in Roman grand strategy. Rome was no longer willing to coexist in some semblance of peace with the great power to its east; it was now set on conquering much of the Parthian Empire and demanding the formal submission of what remained. Although Hadrian abandoned Trajan's conquests beyond the Euphrates, this impulse was never fully quashed, and further Roman assaults with an aim toward annexation occurred under Lucius Verus (163–166 CE) and Septimius Severus (197–199 CE).[24] This was only partially reversed in the third century, and only because the Persians, under the more active and able Sassanids, went on the offensive, causing another long-term shift in Roman strategy.

Probably before the campaigning season ended, Trajan marched into Mesopotamia and took the cities of Nisibis and Batnae by September 114.[25] This march was likely necessary to safeguard the passes over the Tarsus Mountains and to secure a strong foothold in Mesopotamia before the Persians could mount a defense, since the annexation of Armenia had made the conquest of Mesopotamia essential. Otherwise the Persians would remain in possession of a resource-rich region from which they could counterattack into Armenia at a time of their choosing. Securing Armenia required Rome to extend its eastern boundaries at least as far as the Tigris River, and probably to some point beyond, deep into Assyria.

After wintering in Antioch, Trajan returned to Mesopotamia to finish his conquest. After ensuring the territory between Antioch and Nisibis was secure, he advanced to the Tigris, where he had boats constructed from timber brought from Nisibis. Trajan then marched upon Babylon, which was taken without trouble, for, as Dio informs us, Parthian power had been destroyed by civil strife and the city was apparently in a state of near-anarchy when Trajan arrived.[26] Although the dating is unsure and hotly debated, Trajan appears to have concluded operations soon after Babylon's fall and returned to Antioch. Here, despite a powerful earthquake that Dio states almost killed the emperor, Trajan planned and prepared for the final step of his campaign: the capture of the Parthian capital, Ctesiphon. At the start of the campaigning season of 116 CE, the emperor was again on the march, this time heading down the Euphrates, which is navigable for supply vessels until it comes parallel to Ctesiphon, which sits on the Tigris, several days' march to the east. The campaign was a success, and all of southern Mesopotamia fell under Roman control, including the capital. Trajan even took time for a voyage during which he reputedly glimpsed the Indian Ocean and lamented that he was no longer a young man and hence would never achieve the greatness of Alexander.[27]

While he was dreaming, what he had already accomplished was breaking down. The Persian army had not put up a stout defense, but it remained intact and dangerous. Worse, many of the cities to the Roman rear—Edessa, Nisibis, Hatra, and Seleucia—revolted, as did much of Armenia. These uprisings were the work of Osroes' brother Mithridates and then, after Mithridates' untimely death, his son Sanatrukes.[28] Worse, just as these disturbances erupted, Trajan learned about a coordinated Jewish revolt in Egypt, Cyrene, and other cities, but, interestingly, not in Judaea.[29] By now Trajan knew that he had tarried too long in the east and had given too much of his time and energy to war rather than administration. For now his provincial legates could handle the Jewish revolt, but he needed to settle the east quickly. Standing fast in Ctesiphon, the emperor dispatched his generals to crush the Mesopotamian revolts. Nisibis was retaken by L. Quietus, who went on to burn Edessa, while Erucius Clarus and Julius Alexander put Seleucia to the torch.[30] When Trajan received word that Vologases, son of Sanatrukes, was leading an army against the Romans in the north, he offered him a portion of Armenia in return for peace.[31] He used the same method to buy off a Parthian general, Parthamastaphes, who was a nephew of the king. In lieu of a battle, Trajan placed Parthamaspates on the throne of Ctesiphon, as a client king to Rome.[32] This face-saving measure allowed Trajan to present Parthamaspates to the Senate and the people of Rome as a vassal of the Empire. To reinforce this message, Trajan had coins stuck celebrating the event that sported the inscription REX PARTHIS DATUS—"A king has been given to the Parthians."

At this point Trajan bowed to strategic reality. He was learning what Julius Caesar had learned during the conquest of Gaul: one cannot subdue a hostile population merely by marching through its territory. What is required is a long period of integration enforced by the legions' capacity to inflict unacceptable levels of violence upon the recalcitrant. In Caesar's case, it took over eight years of campaigning before the Gauls were finally beaten down enough to be brought fully within the Empire's bosom. It is worth noting that Caesar never had to contend, except for a few troublesome incursions of German warbands, with a situation where the Gauls were receiving funding and military support from an outside power, such as the Armenians and Mesopotamians were receiving from the strategic core of the Parthian Empire. But Trajan, with an entire empire to concern himself with, could not afford to spend a decade or more pacifying his new conquests, so he was willing to apply the fig leaf of creating new client states and cut his losses. However, before he departed the region, and probably as another face-saving measure, Trajan turned his attention to the siege of Hatra, the last major city in Mesopotamia still resisting Roman arms. But the city continued to resist fiercely, forcing Trajan to lift the siege and return to Antioch. Leaving their supposed client king in Ctesiphon, Roman troops were withdrawn to the Euphrates, where they could secure northern Mesopotamia. Trajan likely planned to conduct at least one further campaign in the region, but, overcome by illness in 117 CE, he canceled plans for further campaigning and left for Rome, leaving Hadrian in charge of the army. His small flotilla made landfall in Cilicia, where Trajan died.

In the final strategic analysis, it is hard to believe that Trajan's conquests were not driven by a love of glory, as many of the more disapproving ancient sources claim. But, as discussed earlier, adding to the glory of Rome and Roman arms, and to the personal glory of the emperor, was always a requirement of any emperor's strategic calculations. Trajan, a successful military commander before being elevated to the purple, may have been more secure in his position than many previous emperors, but he was not immune to the need to add to his personal luster. Moreover, a love for glory does not indicate a lack of concern for security and defense.[33] Where such concerns overlap—and a case can be made for such an overlap in both the Dacian and Parthian Wars—there was always going to be an irresistible urge to action, particularly for a warrior-emperor such as Trajan.

Hadrian, after a period of high drama at court centered on Trajan's widow, Plotina, succeeded Trajan as his adopted son. Although this adoption is hotly disputed by the ancient sources, Hadrian lost no time informing the Senate of his elevation. Because Rome's largest army supported his claim, there was little a senator or any other possible aspirant could do to challenge his rule.[34] It is hard to conceive of a man more different from Trajan ascending the throne. For although Hadrian had spent the requisite time in the camps expected of any ambitious Roman aristocrat, including two tours in the Danubian legions, he was a man of peace and not given to warlike ventures. Aurelius Victor says of him:

> He was quite considerably learned in literature and was called by many "Greekling." He devoured the pursuits and customs of the Athenians, having mastered not merely rhetoric, but other disciplines, too, the science of singing, of playing the harp, and of medicine, a musician, geometrician, painter, and a sculptor from bronze or marble who approximated Polycletus and Euphranoras.[35]

What is one to make of an emperor who Victor thought would much rather employ the legions in the "building and beautifying of walls" than fight? It surely was never going to make him popular among the Roman elites, who had delighted in Trajan's putting Rome back on its true course of conquest and glory. From his first major act as emperor—abandoning virtually all of Trajan's gains in Mesopotamia—he seemed set on proving he was his own man and no slave to the notions of Trajan or the Roman nobility. In giving up Mesopotamia, he cited Cato's precedent when he told the Roman Senate that "the Macedonians, because they could not be held as subjects, should be declared free and independent."[36] This was certainly an unpopular move, given the herculean effort Rome had expended in making these gains against the hated Parthians. At least four of the leading men of the state, all of consular rank and probably commanders in Trajan's army, strongly resisted this move.[37] Hadrian, claiming that they had conspired to overthrow him, had them all executed, poisoning his relations with the Senate, as well as contemporary historians (all senators), for the remainder of his reign. Dio informs us that baser reasons for these executions were in play: they were all rich men, and, their having been found guilty of treason meant that all of their property would be forfeited to the emperor.[38] Consequently, Hadrian would have to buy back his popularity, which he intended to accomplish the old-fashioned way. Upon entering Rome, he canceled all debts owed to the imperial treasury, which pleased many a senator in debt, and ordered huge, crowd-pleasing spectacles in the arena for his birthday.[39]

Strategically, what are we to make of Hadrian's decision to abandon Trajan's conquests, keeping in mind that the Parthians had already reversed much of what Trajan accomplished as soon as the legions departed? Parthamaspates was soon overthrown in Ctesiphon, and the Romans had to carve out a small kingdom for him, precariously placed between two rival empires. Still, Trajan's achievements demonstrate that the Parthian Empire was tottering and likely would have been catastrophically beaten if Rome persisted. But that would have taken an emperor of a more military mien than Hadrian. It also would have taken a lengthy commitment of time—measured in years—and colossal amounts of money. At this point in the Empire's history, there are no indications Rome was prepared to exert itself in this way. The impulse for glory and conquest had not vanished, but the patience and stamina to see a prolonged, bloody war through to the end had been waning for some time. Moreover, there were limits to the amount of time an emperor could dedicate to one region before things began going wrong elsewhere. In fact, on his way to Rome, Hadrian had to stop and negotiate with the Roxolani, where he ended up ceding territory in Moesia and sparking fears that he was preparing to withdraw from Dacia also. As long as emperors remained reluctant—for good historical reasons—to trust independent generals with forces large enough to complete a conquest that might take years, there were limits to what could be accomplished and kept at the edges of the Empire. Rome had become a state capable of conducting ferocious campaigns over a limited period, but it was no longer capable of fighting protracted wars far from its central core of power.

Hadrian proved to be an energetic and effective ruler. He spent more than half of his reign touring the Empire, travels that reinforced the fact that Rome was no longer the Empire's center of power. His journeys—a grand inspection tour of the Empire—lasted ten years and ranged from Spain in the west to the Black Sea in the east, and south to north from Africa to Britain.

The *Historia Augusta*, which must always be used with caution, has a lengthy discourse dealing with how he dealt with and managed the legions in Germania:

> Though more desirous of peace than of war, he kept the soldiers in training just as if war were imminent, inspired them by proofs of his own powers of endurance, actually led a soldier's life among the maniples [common soldiers], and, after the example of Scipio Aemilianus, Metellus, and his own adoptive father Trajan, cheerfully ate out of doors such camp-fare as bacon, cheese and vinegar. And that the troops might submit more willingly to the increased harshness of his orders, he bestowed gifts on many and honors on a few. For he reestablished the discipline of the camp, which since the time of Octavian had been growing slack through the laxity of his predecessors. . . . He made it a point to be acquainted with the soldiers and to know their numbers.[40]

Dio, by no means a fan of Hadrian, agrees with the authors of the *Historia Augusta* as it pertains to Hadrian's revitalization of the army and adds this crucial observation:

> He so trained and disciplined the whole military force throughout the entire empire that even today the methods then introduced by him are the soldiers' law of campaigning. *This best explains why he lived for the most part at peace with foreign nations; for as they saw his state of preparation and were themselves not only free from aggression but received money besides, they made no uprising. . . .* Seeing all this, the barbarians stood in terror of the Romans, [and] they employed Hadrian as an arbitrator of their differences.[41]

As shown in the emphasized portion above, Hadrian was a firm believer in the Roman adage *Si vis pacem, para bellum*—"If you want peace, prepare for war."[42]

Strategically, as R. A. Birley has noted, Hadrian's frontier policy created artificial demarcation lines that supplemented preexisting forts and signal stations and thus suggested that the period of Roman expansion was at an end.[43] Additionally, Hadrian's movement of some forts and units to better locations, leaving most others undisturbed, had the effect, even if unintended, of tying specific formations to their assigned portions of the frontiers. This gradually reduced the strategic mobility of the legions, who became increasingly reluctant to conduct operations far from where they were putting down roots. As the decades passed, it became much more common to move one or more cohorts (vexillations) rather than entire legions.

Hadrian's settling of the Roman frontiers is nowhere better exemplified than in the wall in Britain that still bears his name. As Hadrian moved the entire Legio VI Germani from Germania Inferior to Britain, along with three thousand auxiliaries from three different legions along the Rhine, it is safe to assume that there was substantial trouble that closely coincided with his visit to Britain. The wall, over eighty miles long, with turrets, mile castles, and ditches on both sides, took over six years to build and separated the quasi-pacified Britons in the south from those Britons who, as the *Historia Augusta* puts it, "could not be kept under Roman sway."[44]

The *Historia Augusta* also points out that throughout his travels, wherever the emperor discovered that "the barbarians are held back not by rivers but by artificial barriers, Hadrian shut them off by means of high stakes planted deep in the ground and fastened together in the manner of a palisade."[45] Here is literary evidence that the *limes* were progressing beyond isolated forts and signal stations and now included wooden walls along the vast stretches of the frontiers that were not protected by natural barriers. This included the construction of stone fortifications and walls in the Pontus area to block the passes through the Caucasus, built by Hadrian's governor Arrian—the author of a biography of Alexander the Great.[46] It is no wonder that during this period the meaning of the word *limes* transitioned from "frontier road" to "frontier barrier." It was also during this period that Hadrian had the great plantations of the African provinces—the tax spine of the Western Empire—cut off from marauders who would periodically explode out of the deserts and mountains to the south. This was done through the building of mile castles, similar to those along Hadrian's Wall, with walls linking them together.[47] This line was supported by the Legio II Augusta, which Hadrian moved 150 miles south to Lambaesis.[48] Here it was still 150 miles north of the fortified line, but it was well positioned to intercept forces that would have been channeled toward the legion by the *limes*.

The only conflict of major proportions during Hadrian's reign was another Jewish revolt, this time centered on Roman Judaea, which had still not recovered from the Roman-Jewish conflict of 66–73 that had been brutally crushed by Vespasian and his son Titus. The immediate spark of the conflict is unknown, but the explanation found in the *Historia Augusta* is that the Jews revolted because the Romans forbade circumcision, an order nowhere else attested, but this can be discounted. More than likely, the revolt had a combination of causes, including Hadrian's suspected plans to assimilate the Jewish Temple into the Roman imperial cult, the continuing heavy hand of Roman administrators who never understood the Jews' unique culture, and economic tensions between Jews and Roman colonists who were given imperial writ over prime agricultural land in the region. What these factors required to ignite an open revolt was a leader, and they found one in Simon bar Kokhba.

The revolt likely erupted in the summer or fall of 132 CE. The Romans were caught by surprise and overwhelmed by the ferocity and extent of the uprising. Despite their careful planning, the Jews were frustrated by the immediate Roman reaction. The conflict soon degenerated into a vicious guerrilla war in which Jews targeted not only Romans but also any Jews who refused to join the rebellion. Unable to cope with the Jewish forces arrayed against him, the Roman governor Tineius Rufus pleaded with Hadrian to send him the Syrian legions. In reply, Dio tells us, "Hadrian sent against them his best generals. First of these was Julius Severus, who was dispatched from Britain, where he was governor, against the Jews."[49] Severus, whose career took him from one hot spot to another, appears to have been Hadrian's fireman. Summoning the Syrian legions and at least one legion, or its equivalent strength in vexillations, Severus undertook a methodical war of extermination. According to Dio, the Romans killed over a half million Jews in battle, with those who perished from famine and disease beyond counting. Fifty fortified towns were leveled, and a further 985 large villages were razed; "thus nearly the whole of Judea was made Desolate."[50] This was a return to the methods the Republic had employed during its great period of expansion. The Romans were relearning that there was much to gain from a policy of sowing terror to control native populations, particularly along its northern frontiers.[51] Soon after the war ended, Hadrian did away with the name of Judaea and, after consolidating Judaea, Galilee, and Samaria, he created the province of Syria Palaestina.

Hadrian may have been one of those rarest of creatures, an intellectual emperor with no taste for war. But despite his pacifist nature, he did more to set the future strategic course of the Empire than almost anyone else. He brought a practical end to Roman expansionism, thus conserving untold resources for future endeavors. In practical terms, he established the borders—even if these remained basically zones of contact—and undertook serious measures to fortify the frontiers. To support his barrier walls and forts, he reorganized the army, improved its training, reequipped it, and returned many formations made lax by the routine of garrison duty to earlier levels of discipline. Fronto, an orator and tutor to the future emperor Marcus Aurelius, mocked Hadrian for constantly training an army that he never let fight. But Arrian, in his small book *Tactica*, praised Hadrian for returning the legions to discipline that was good for them.[52] Arrian, who had led troops in combat, realized as few other Roman literary sources did that few things are as successful in building unit pride and loyalty than hard training conducted often. Further, there were few things more dangerous to the stability of the Empire than bored soldiers who were no longer held to strict disciplinary standards. When later emperors and authors lamented the collapse in legionary standards, they were harking back to Hadrian's legions.

Just before his death Hadrian adopted a popular senator, Antoninus Pius, as his son and successor, on the condition that Antoninus adopt two future emperors, Marcus Aurelius and Lucius Verus. Upon Hadrian's death, Antoninus ascended to the purple with little opposition. Antoninus's rein is difficult to fully grasp, as the narrative sources have virtually nothing to say on the topic, which in itself is a testament to the perceived tranquility of the Empire during his reign. It was during Antoninus Pius's reign that Aristides gave his speech in praise of the Empire. Part of that speech has already been quoted in this work, but it is merely a small part of an oration that presents the Empire as an idyllic world enjoying unimaginable peace and prosperity.

Vast and comprehensive as is the size of it, your empire is much greater for its perfection than for the area which its boundaries encircle. . . . For the eternal duration of this empire the whole civilized world prays all together, emitting, like an aulos after a thorough cleaning, one note with more perfect precision than a chorus; so beautifully is it harmonized by the leader in command.[53]

While the Empire was indeed stable and growing increasingly wealthy under Antoninus's benign leadership, it was by no means peaceful. We know of extensive operations north of Hadrian's Wall that led to the creation of Antoninus's Wall, which stretched between the Firth of Forth and the Firth of Clyde. This wall was made mostly of turf and fronted by a ditch but was only half the length of the more famous wall to the south. That it was abandoned in favor of a reinforced Hadrian's Wall (Fig. 10.1) twenty years later likely demonstrates that northern Britannia was far from subdued, despite Antoninus's legate's winning enough victories for the emperor to claim for the only time in his over twenty years on the throne an acclamation as imperator, adding some military luster to a reputation devoid of military experience. His reluctance to personally campaign in distant lands was transformed into a praiseworthy quality in an emperor by the orator Cornelius Fronto: "Although he committed the conduct of the war to others while remaining in the palace at Rome, yet as with the helmsman at the tiller of a warship, the glory of the whole navigation and voyage belongs to him."[54] Aristides, in his oration, also portrays the emperor's disinclination to leave Rome as something Antoninus should be commended for, and he makes a pointed reference to Hadrian's constant traveling in doing so.

> Therefore, he has no need to wear himself out traveling around the whole empire nor, by appearing personally, now among some, then among others, to make sure of each point when he has the time to tread their soil. It is very easy for him to stay where he is, and manage the entire civilized world by letters, which arrive almost as soon as they are written, as if they were carried by winged messengers. [He] conducts public business in the whole civilized world exactly as if it were one city state.

Other revolts are known, but they were either crushed quickly or did not seriously impact the general peace of the Empire. A revolt in Western Mauretania in 145 proved troublesome, mostly because it was so distant from any permanent legionary base. But the conflict was localized on the far southwestern edge of the Empire, and although it took six years to quell, it was barely

FIGURE 10.1 Hadrian's Wall

noticed by anyone outside the region. Similarly, there is evidence of trouble within Dacia that required a reorganization of the province. This again was handled quickly and efficiently by his legates and generals on the scene.

We also have evidence of military preparations and possibly probing attacks by the Parthians, as well as attacks along the periphery of the Danubian and Rhine frontiers, all of which were repulsed without disturbing the Empire's core. What we are witnessing is the Hadrianiac *limes* and the concurrent revitalization of the legions acting exactly as they were designed. Antoninus may not have been a warlike emperor, but he did nothing to weaken or disturb what Hadrian had put in place. Thus, Antoninus was able to remain in a central location where he could easily be found and had the entire Roman administrative system at his fingertips, so that he was able to coordinate the movement of generals, who could handle situations as they arose. Considering the scale of the threat, the *limes* bequeathed to him were more than sufficient to break any assault without the rest of the Empire taking much notice. Antoninus's great strategic achievement, as Aristides notes, was his checking of the Empire's "continuous, irrational and violent lunges . . . the emperor had settled the empire."[55]

In other words, Antoninus, at least for a time, removed the impulse for conquest and expansion as a driver of Roman imperial strategy. This was done in recognition of the fact that Rome had reached the limits of how far a city-state could expand given the resources and infrastructure of the ancient world without fundamentally remaking the governmental structure administering an empire. After all, until Diocletian's reforms the Empire was still controlled and administered through a system that had changed little since Rome first became a Mediterranean power. If the Empire was going to survive, the system needed major reforms; tinkering around the edges was not going to make enough of a difference to meet the challenges ahead. Unfortunately for Rome, it would take the near-death experience of the Crisis of the Third Century to force the adoption of such radical change. By then it was too late to do more than buy additional time, at least for the Western Empire.

In the meantime, Antoninus did what he could to keep external enemies at bay. Archaeologically, we can still find traces of extensive new fortifications along the Dacian borders. Antoninus also expanded the Germano-Raetian *limes*, advancing them as far as the Necker River and converting the wooden structures emplaced by Hadrian with stone towers and forts. Between these forts, at least in Raetia, extensive walls consisting of sturdy palisades and an extensive ditch were built. It appears that Antoninus also began expanding the recruitment of noncitizens into the legions while also increasing the amount of local recruiting a legion was permitted. This, of course, further increased the inclination for legions to remain permanently rooted in one area. Despite increasing external pressure, the number of legions remained at the Augustan level of twenty-eight, with no major increases in auxiliary formations either. Rome was continuing a policy of substituting defensive infrastructure for additional legions.

Luttwak, employing current strategic terminology, refers to the strategy employed during the period of the Flavians through most of the second century as "preclusive defense" and negatively compares the reliance on static frontier positions to the mobility of the early Principate.[56] As an example of the supposedly increasing brittleness of the Empire's structure, he mentions that Nero was able to deploy three legions to the east without overly stressing the system, but that Trajan's expedition in the east nearly collapsed the Roman system. Luttwak conveniently neglects to mention that Trajan was employing *eleven* legions in his campaigns, not three. For another, he overestimates the impact that Trajan's eastern expeditions had on the Empire as a whole. Trajan's conflicts were certainly expensive, but there are no indications that they came close to stressing the Roman treasury. Certainly Antoninus, upon his accession to the throne, never appeared short of funds. One must note that the legions required pay and food regardless of whether they were on campaign or resting in their fortresses. What counts in terms of expenses is the marginal difference between what the military cost in peacetime and what it cost when at war. In the Roman period, the difference was not great. Moreover, it could be hugely reduced in direct proportion to the amount of resources and plunder that could be taken from enemy lands. For instance, once Decebalus's treasury was found, the Dacian Wars likely paid for themselves. Whatever difference there was would have surely been made up by the sale of Dacian slaves.

In truth, the strategically mobile armies of the early Principate were a reflection of a strategy that was still focused on expanding the Empire and was made possible because enemies that could threaten the economic core of the Empire were few. Of course, barbarian war bands could strike across the Rhine or the Danube almost at will, but there were limits to how far they could go and how long they could stay. Their mission was to collect some booty and race home before Roman cohorts ran them down.

But now consider this same territory in the mid-second century. In Tiberius's time, these border regions, far from the Empire's economic core and not yet integrated into the Roman trading system, were not much richer and in fact were often poorer than the barbarian lands. But as the Pax Romana continued, these regions became increasingly richer. Farming expanded, trading links were created, towns and cities formed, and populations increased. In fact, Rome's economic core spent the entire two centuries of the Principate expanding toward the frontiers. By the middle of the second century, any barbarian raids that penetrated the border were no longer hitting mostly open and unsettled lands. Rather, they were striking at well-heeled subjects of Rome, capable of vocally demanding protection. Such raids were now striking at the economic vitals of a region and therefore directly impacting the Roman resource and tax base.

This new societal structure, arising just behind the frontiers, coupled with the waning impulse for conquest, realigned the Empire's strategic priorities. There was no need for large mobile armies if there were not going to be further conquests. Also, as the newly enriched frontier provinces required more immediate protection than they received during the early years of the Principate, the legions and their auxiliaries had to be spread along the entire frontier. Moreover, to ensure these dispersed forces were not defeated in detail, the frontier required a much more extensive defensive infrastructure. Antoninus reveals, through his actions and governing policies, that he clearly understood these shifting strategic dynamics. Appian, who wrote during Antoninus's years as emperor, demonstrates that most Romans were aware of and likely supported this change of strategic priorities and policies: "They surround the empire with great armies and they garrison the whole stretch of land and sea like a single strong-hold."[57]

Luttwak is also wrong when he declares that the margin upon which the system depended was dangerously thin.[58] When one considers what Antoninus was dealing with, the system was more than adequately manned and resourced. It did not receive its first severe test until the reign of Antoninus's successor, Marcus Aurelius—a harbinger of things to come—but even then it proved resilient and up to the task. This ended in the Severan Age, but that was a consequence of a rapidly changing set of external threats, the return of political instability within the Empire, and Rome's failure to adapt as the situation changed.

Antoninus died in his sleep in 161, just after he had given the watchword "Equanimity" to the tribune of the Praetorian Guard. He was succeeded by Marcus Aurelius, who insisted on making his brother, Verus, co-ruler. Marcus, ten years older and having been promoted to Caesar years before, was always considered to have more *auctoritas* and therefore was considered by all to be the actual ruler—a state of affairs that Verus, who enjoyed the luxuries and pleasures of the court more than the tedium of rule, apparently approved. According to our sources, Marcus was surely the right man at the time. Aurelius Victor believed that the Empire would have collapsed during his reign if it had been in the hands of a lesser man. And Marcus certainly faced many challenges. According to Victor, "There was never rest from arms, and wars were raging through all Oriens, Illyricum, Italy, and Gallia, and there were earthquakes not without the destruction of cities, inundations of rivers, numerous plagues, species of locusts which infested fields, there is almost nothing by which mortals are accustomed to be vexed with the most serious difficulties that is able to be described which did not rage while he was ruling."[59]

Trouble came almost immediately and on multiple fronts. According to the *Historia Augusta*, "War was threatening in Britain, and the Chatti had burst into Germany and Raetia."[60] Marcus handled these two problems as Antoninus would have, sending two of his better generals—Calpurnius Agricola against the Britons and Aufidius Victorinus against the Chatti—to win victories for him. As we hear nothing more of these conflicts, one can assume both generals were successful and accomplished their mission with the forces already in the area.

But it was the Parthians who presented a real problem, one of a higher order of magnitude than dealing with some frontier tribes. Vologaeses III, taking advantage of the confusion that comes with any transition of power, sent his Parthian army into Armenia, deposed its king, and installed his relative—Pacorus.[61] The fact that Vologaeses was able to march so quickly and with an overwhelming force indicates that such a move had long been planned and prepared for. The Cappadocia governor, M. Sedatius Severianus, following the Roman playbook of quashing trouble as soon as it arose with whatever troops were immediately available, marched with a single legion. He walked into a trap near Elegeia, and after a short fight, he committed suicide. The legion was wiped out.[62] Before the campaigning season ended, the Parthians had advanced into Syria, routing the three legions of the governor, Attidius Cornelianus. The situation was bad and getting worse, and it was decided that one of the co-rulers would have to go east to rebuild the army and restore morale. Verus was given titular command, but Marcus made sure he was surrounded by the best generals in the Roman army. This proved an early precursor to the later Empire, where all-powerful generals fought the wars and ran the Empire, while emperors became little more than pampered puppets. As his generals led the armies, Verus divided his time "amid the debauches of Antioch and Daphne and busied himself with gladiatorial bouts and hunting."[63] It was Marcus who mobilized and sent three legions east from the European frontiers—*V Macedonica,* from Moesia, *II Adiutrix* from Pannonia, and the *I Minerva* from Germania Inferior. One can assume that these legions marched with a substantial force of auxiliaries. The *Historia Augusta* also credits Marcus with most of the strategic actions, stating he oversaw the "workings of the state, and, though reluctantly and sorely against his will, but nevertheless with patience, was enduring the debauchery of his brother. In a word, Marcus, though residing at Rome, planned and executed everything necessary to the prosecution of the war."[64]

This is evidence that, despite the legions being settled in permanent fortresses along the frontier, they had not yet lost their strategic mobility. The details of their march to the war zone are not recorded, but the capacity of the Roman transport system to move three legions, their auxiliary forces, and equipment from disparate regions of the Empire to a single threatened point remained its greatest strategic asset. Not only did this system have to transport the initial forces, but it also had to move the thousands of tons of supplies required to feed and equip these forces from all over the Empire to Antioch, where the Roman army was marshaling. It is also noteworthy that the infrastructure of the *limes* system was considered sufficient to hold back any other threats to the frontier until the legions returned to their bases. This is worth thinking about, as the three departing legions along with their auxiliaries comprised approximately twenty percent of Roman combat power along the Rhine and Danube frontiers. Moreover, the departure of the legions would have opened up huge gaps of undefended territory for barbarian warbands to advance into. Although the sources are silent on how Rome adapted, leaving huge gaps in their defense structure was unacceptable. One must assume that nearly every legion along these frontiers had to send vexillations to man the various fortresses, forts, and towers vacated by the departing legions. Now, consider, for a moment, the scale of such movements and the coordination involved in realigning defensive arrangements over 1,500 miles of frontiers and ask how the Romans, who supposedly had no concept of strategy and only a marginal comprehension of the Empire's geography, and were supposedly without a set of administrative staffs to handle military affairs, managed to pull this off. The literary evidence for how Rome could accomplish such a massive and complex undertaking in under a year may not exist, but surely the fact that they accomplished such a feat must count for something.

With at least a portion of the armies marshaled, Rome took the offensive when Statius Priscus, in 163, took the fight into Armenia. With two legions, and after twenty days' hard marching, he took the capital, Artax, by storm, thus allowing Verus to claim the title Armeniacus. The Romans installed a new emperor, not in Artaxa, but in a new capital city specially constructed for the purpose some twenty miles closer to the Roman border. The new king was from the Parthian ruling family, the Arsacids, but he had been raised in Rome, was senator, held consular rank, and was likely the safest Parthian royal Rome could place on the throne. Even while the Romans settled accounts in Armenia, the Parthians, also in 163, deposed the pro-Roman ruler of Osroene, in northwestern Mesopotamia, and installed their own client, forcing the Romans to move south, further down the Euphrates.

The main Roman counterattack came in 165, and was led by a Roman general, C. Avidius Cassius, a general of stern countenance and something of a martinet.[65] The *Historia Augusta* has a lengthy list of lurid examples of his sternness as a disciplinarian, including his policy of cutting off the hands of most deserters, while breaking the legs and hips of others. It even credits him with coming up with a new punishment for criminals en masse: "after erecting a huge post, 180 feet high, and binding condemned criminals on it from top to bottom, he built a fire at its base, and so burned some of them and killed the others by the smoke, pain, and even by the fright."[66]

The Historia Augusta is often unreliable, but if Cassius was even a tenth the disciplinarian he is painted to be, then he may have been precisely the man to take command of the Syrian legions. For the orator Fronto gives us a depressing vision of the legions as they were found when Verus arrived: "The men had spent more time lounging at tables in open-air cafes than with their units." The need to bring the Syrian legions back to full readiness and then to integrate the various legions into a cohesive army likely accounts for the delay in launching the counterattack. In the meantime, it is worth noting that the main Roman defensive system had held up rather well. Armenia had performed well as a buffer state, wearing down Parthian armies before Rome even entered the fray. When the Parthians moved south, they managed to capture a weak client state (one of the few remaining) and little else. For the Romans held all of the well-fortified major cities, which became even more formidable as the routed Roman field force fell back upon the cities, swelling their garrisons. The largest of them, Antioch, was impregnable to the Parthians of the second century and acted as a base of operations for the future. For a time, the Persians were free to occupy spaces on the edge of the Roman fortified zone, but they were incapable of interfering with Cassius, as he amassed a tremendous counterattack force.

When the Roman attack came, it struck with overwhelming force. With Armenia secure, the Romans were able to attack in two major columns. The first advanced into Mesopotamia to capture Edessa and reinstall the Roman client king, Mannus, to the throne of Osroene. Defeated Parthian forces fell back on Nisibis, where they were besieged and at least one Persian army broken. Even as Edessa was taken and Nisibis besieged, a second Roman column, led by Cassius, moved further down the Euphrates, where he defeated a Persian army at Dura-Europos, which received a Roman garrison for the first time. Before the year ended, Cassius marched further into southern Mesopotamia to attack the twin cities of Ctesiphon, on the left bank of the Tigris, and Seleucia on the right. Despite having opened its gates to welcome the Roman army, Cassius permitted Seleuceia to be sacked. The devastation was so great that it was still empty ruins when another Roman army passed two centuries later.[67] Then, concentrating his full force upon Ctesiphon, the Parthian capital was taken, the city sacked, and the royal palace turned to ashes.

Cassius had surpassed Trajan's accomplishments in the east, having not only captured the Parthian capital but also shattered their armies. But his army was tired, running low on supplies, and showing the first signs of having been infected by the plague. Still, the army returned to Antioch in good order. In keeping with tradition, Verus and Marcus both accepted the acclamation of imperator (for the third time each), though neither was anywhere near the site of the fighting. The following year Cassius once again led the Roman army deep into Parthian territory, overrunning Media without much trouble. The ease of this march demonstrates how shattered the Parthian military had been the year before. The reputation of the Parthian ruling dynasty, which had started this war with great fanfare and success, was also damaged. In time, their falling prestige and inability to avenge their military disasters lead to the dynasty's downfall and the rise of the Sassanids.

Besides the shattering of Parthia's field armies, enhancing the long-term security of Armenia, and diminishing the Parthian royal family's prestige, Rome also held onto slight territorial gains by pushing the frontiers out as far as Dura-Europas, which, along with Nisibis and Amedia, were to become the foundation of a new fortress line that would be the demarcation line in future Roman-Parthian conflicts. But for now, Rome's decisive victory bought thirty years of peace, which was considered secure enough that the three legions sent from the Rhine and Danube frontiers were returned to their bases. The prolonged peace and the return of the legions came just in time, for Rome's next challenge was already upon it.

Almost from the start of Marcus's reign, there had been raids into Raetia and the surrounding area. But the *limes*, superior diplomacy by Marcus's representatives in these areas, and subsidy payments (bribes) had generally maintained a quasi-peace. The pressure was mounting, however. No one knows exactly what was happening beyond the Rhine and Danube frontiers, but we can make some educated guesses. First, the Goths were starting to move, whether under pressure from others or looking for better agricultural grounds. Whatever the reason, they were departing the Vistula in increasing numbers and pushing toward the Black Sea. Such a mass migration had a knock-on effect throughout the non-Roman world, as other tribes were displaced and likely had to fight for whatever lands they could get. This pressure could easily have started many tribes heading toward the Roman frontier.[68] Moreover, taking advantage of Rome's neglect, border tribes had grown much more dangerous. Because of their proximity to the Empire, they had grown richer and more powerful. They had also learned to trade and talk with each other. While by no means up to Roman levels of coordination, their capacity to coordinate big muscle movements was at a high point. Moreover, Antoninus's twenty-two years of benign neglect, coupled with Marcus's half-dozen years of distraction in the east, had a profound impact on the barbarian psyche: an entire generation had come of age without seeing firsthand any display of Roman power. The fear of Roman arms was waning.

One could suppose that Rome's years of bending over backward to avoid open warfare, at least until matters were concluded in the east, had emboldened the tribes. Thus, increasingly large groups, reacting to population pressure, felt they could cross the frontiers to settle in unclaimed or unwatched lands with impunity. Roman officials would naturally have tried to regain this territory as soon as the legions, which had been fighting in the east, returned to their bases. And this is likely all the spark that was necessary to start the war. For Rome, it could not have happened at a worse time, for famine and plague stalked the land. We will examine the strategic impact of the Antonine Plague later in this book. For now, we will just note that the plague had been brought west by the returning legions, who had probably contracted it in or near Seleucia in the winter of 165–166. It was the deadliest scourge to strike the Empire up to that time and carried away as many as twelve million people, and in some areas as much as a third of the population died. Unfortunately for Rome, it struck the legions particularly hard, leaving several of them devastated just as a new war was starting. The plague was also the most likely culprit in the death of Marcus's co-ruler, Lucius Verus, in 169, and a recurrence of the pestilence may also have been responsible for Marcus's death in 180.

Marcus was surely aware that trouble was brewing, which likely accounts for his decision to build two new legions in Italy, eventually named II and III Italica. He had also gambled that his legates, employing the strengthened *limes,* could maintain the peace long enough for the eastern conflict to be concluded and the legions to return to their bases. As he awaited their arrival, the troops manning the *limes* would have to hold as best they could. However, neither the legionaries nor their supporting auxiliaries could be everywhere. One can imagine that the lightly held frontiers were often penetrated, sometimes by small raiding parties, at other times by larger groups looking to settle and farm within the Empire. Knowing that they had to avoid a possibly ruinous major conflict, the local legates and commanders would have had to tolerate many of these intrusions, which would have grown larger and penetrated deeper as the barbarians became more emboldened.

Eventually the three legions sent to the east returned, and with these, and his newly raised legions, Marcus considered that he had sufficient forces to put things right. For a time he was delayed by the need to conduct extensive religious festivals in order to purify the city in the hopes of alleviate some of the dread of a renewed war and to relieve the Empire of the twin blights of famine and plague.[69] Once the rites were completed, the two emperors set out together at the head of the forces mobilized in Italy. It was not long before they were met by representatives from several tribes begging for pardons. This demonstrates how far the situation had deteriorated: Marcus was being approached by sizable numbers of barbarians in northern Italy, a sure sign that large sections of Pannonia had been overrun and settled by earlier waves of barbarians, forcing the latecomers to move further south. An occupation of this extent could not have happened in just the few years Marcus had been emperor and likely reflects the effects of over two decades of enforced peacefulness under Antonine. In any case, Verus pushed his brother to accept a negotiated settlement and end the war. Marcus, however, thought that the offers were insincere and that the barbarians would continue to expand their zone of occupation as soon as Marcus dispersed his army.

Dio records that soon thereafter a mighty battle was fought in Italy and a brilliant victory was won. One may wonder how great a battle a mass of unorganized farmers could have put up, but it did serve to bloody the new legions before they were brought against more formidable foes. Soon after crossing the Alps and doing all that was "necessary for the defense of Italy and Illyricum, Verus died from the plague, leaving Marcus as sole ruler of the Roman Empire."[70] Marcus returned with his brother's body to Rome, where he spent the next eight months preparing for a new campaign in the north.

The renewed fighting, which came at a time when the plague was carrying away ten million or more Romans, severely stressed Rome's resources. Because the legions were particularly hard stuck by the pestilence, Marcus employed new methods to keep their numbers up. For instance, for the first time since the Punic Wars, Rome enrolled slaves and gladiators into the legions. Recruiting throughout the Empire was also stepped up, and the *Historia Augusta* informs us that brigands and bandits were enrolled into the army.[71] Marcus also armed various German allies who were willing to fight their tribal kin. This included the addition of new auxiliary formations, as well as individual recruitment of Germans living north of the frontier.

Marcus, after expending vast sums in the east and on other government programs, was also finding it difficult to fund a northern war. Its cost could not be paid for out of plunder, as the areas of conflict were poor agricultural regions, and the cities and towns that were in these regions were already under Roman control. Therefore, the economic burden had to be undertaken by an empire with an empty treasury in the midst of a plague.

Rome would eventually recover from the effects of the pestilence, but that was still many years distant. This makes it worth considering the strategic impact of a widespread plague.[72] Besides the loss of millions of productive farmers, almost all trade within the Empire would have ceased, as ports refused to allow non-local ships entry and towns and cities closed their gates. One can suppose that the famine Rome was experiencing at the time had little to do with a lack of food within the Empire but was instead a consequence of a plague-induced collapse of the transport system. It would not be long before this economic collapse impacted taxes and forced a cutback of all but the most crucial imperial initiatives. To overcome the funding shortfall, Marcus ordered a debasement of the silver content of new coinages. This granted a short-term financial reprieve, since the markets always took some time to adjust prices to the reduction in silver.[73] Marcus Aurelius was likely compelled to this unattractive course because he did not believe he could raise taxes in an economy reeling from the plague. He even took the drastic step of selling off his personal property to raise funds.[74] As the *Historia Augusta* makes clear, this auction brought in spectacular amounts of money. Thus, one can assume that the auction was window dressing for a series of forced (Marcus would say "encouraged") loans from Rome's rich elites, only too happy to pay a huge premium to avoid the alternative methods of being declared a traitor, killed, and having one's property confiscated.

The war opened before Marcus had left Rome, when in late 166 or early 167 a large war band of six thousand Langobardi and Orbi smashed into Pannonia. Marcus's generals reacted rapidly. First, Macrinius Avitus took a strong cavalry force north to limit the invaders' ability to move freely and then hem them into a smaller area where the infantry could cut them to pieces. Once they were hemmed in, another Roman general, Candidus, led one or more legions in the destruction of the raiding party. Nonplussed by their failures, eleven barbarian tribes aligned together for this war chose the Marcomanni king, Ballomarius, to negotiate with the Pannonian legate Ilallius Bassus.[75]

It was not until late summer 169 that Marcus felt free to return to the north, probably basing himself in Sirmium. In 170 he opened the campaigning season with a massive offensive across the Danube. The result was a strategic disaster, for the imperial army, when commanded by the emperor, absorbed virtually the entire Danubian command. It could hardly be otherwise, since the emperor surely could not be expected to personally lead a minor punitive expedition.

Although the events of 170, along with those of most of the years following, are sparsely covered in the sources, the larger picture can be outlined. Marcus struck north in hopes of crushing or severely punishing the Iazyges. But this massive assault hit open air: the Iazyges wisely retreated in front of the massive Roman force. Various sources place this force at the equivalent of twelve legions (not including many vexillations from legions throughout the Empire that are attested to in various archaeological sources), thirty-four *alae* of cavalry, and ninety-six cohorts of auxiliaries, making this one of the largest armies Rome ever assembled.[76] But Marcus's inability to gain a decisive victory, along with the denuding of the frontier, emboldened the tribes to the east and west of the Iazyges to cross into the Empire at several points. A large force of Quadi and Marcomanni, led by the Marcomanni king, Ballomar, crossed the Danube, encountering only a hastily scraped-up Roman force. The Romans fought bravely, but their best formations were with Marcus, and they were soon overrun. The Battle of Carnuntum reportedly cost Rome twenty thousand men, and the barbarians continued unhindered into northern Italy, where they placed Aquileia under siege. The shock of having a major Italian city besieged by barbarians was great enough that it was still remembered in Ammianus's history some two hundred years later, when he was writing about renewed barbarian assaults across the Danube in his time:

> The Quadi, who had long been quiet, were suddenly aroused to an outbreak; they are a nation now not greatly to be feared, but were formerly immensely warlike and powerful, as is shown by their swift and sudden swoops in former times, their siege of Aquileia in company with the Marcomanni, the destruction of Opitergium, and many other bloody deeds performed in rapid campaigns; so that when they broke through the Julian Alps [they were difficult to vanquish].[77]

Besides pointing out the swath of destruction the Quadi and Marcomanni left in their wake, Ammianus makes a key strategic point: once the barbarians had penetrated the frontier defense and alpine barriers, there was very little to hinder them. The frontier was a hard shell protecting a soft interior. There is discussion in the sources of the *Italiae et Alpium*—a line of forts that were supposed to keep the barbarians from crossing the Alps. Almost nothing is known of this defensive plan, probably first put in place in 168, but it is assumed to have included the two new Italian legions and a series of forts guarding the approaches and passes from Raetia to Dalmatia. Whatever this defensive barrier had been in 168, it was almost certainly gone by 170, probably because Marcus took many of the troops who should have manned these installations with him across the Danube.

Besides the penetration of the Alps, the first by a hostile army since 101 BCE, the Balkans also came under assault by the Costoboci. The fighting here was very severe, and at least one Roman legate, the governor of Moesia Superior (his name is not recorded), was killed.[78] He was replaced by the governor of Dacia, Claudius Fronto, who was also killed later in the same year, although not before winning several battles and reversing the tide of war in the Balkans. But before he did so, the barbarians devastated Thrace and Macedonia and penetrated as far as Achaea, where they destroyed the shrine of the Mysteries of Eleusis.

As Rome reclaimed the Balkans, the job of expelling the invaders from Italy continued. This task was entrusted to Marcus's son-in-law Pompeianus, who had as an adviser a future emperor, the procurator P. Helvius Pertinax. Marcus, in the meantime, moved to Carnuntum, where his army was trapped by a new wave of barbarians. Cut off from receiving any overland supplies, the army was held together by supplies delivered by the fleet at regular intervals. The port of Salonae in Dalmatia was probably the hub of this endeavor, as it was fortified the year before by vexillations from the newly formed II and II Italica legions; one wonders if they were kept back in this new fortress, for they were not yet deemed ready to fight in a major battle. This was not the only fortifying going on: throughout the Balkans towns and cities began erecting walls, a practice that would become common throughout the Empire in the wake of the Crisis of the Third Century.[79]

The following year, 171, the Marcomanni started for home, having either been pushed out of Italy or decided that they had as much loot as they could carry.[80] They were pursued by the forces of Pompeianus and Pertinax and cut off by Marcus's legions in Carnuntum. Trapped somewhere close to the Danube, the barbarian army was annihilated and their captured booty returned to the provincials from whom it had been stolen.[81] The battle, of which we know nothing, was large and decisive enough for Marcus to add the title "Germanicus" to his name. Marcus remained in command through 172 and 173, while the Marcomanni licked their wounds north of the Danube. The same must have been true of the Iazyges, whose losses in the Balkan fighting must have been horrific. This left Marcus free to focus his attention, once again, on the Quadi. By the end of 172 the Quadi campaign must have been concluded decisively enough to bring representatives from numerous local tribes to Marcus's headquarters to plea for peace. The formidable Quadi were allowed to end the war on the condition that they forbid the Marcomanni and Iazyges, who held lands to their west and east respectively, from crossing their territory.

In 172, with the Quadi out of the war and the Marcomanni isolated from any support, Marcus took the fight into what is now Bohemia, the Marcomanni stronghold. It was a difficult campaign, costing the life of one of the praetorian prefects, Macrinius Vindex, but the Romans eventually won, not least because the army was now gaining faith in the emperor's military ability and the growing belief that he was divinely favored—a belief that would grow in the next stage of the conflict.[82]

Because of the difficulties Rome was facing from the Marcomanni, some of the Quadi were tempted to reenter the fight, or at the very least take in and shelter Marcomanni fleeing Rome's vengeance. As such, Marcus now turned, once again, on the Quadi. During this campaign a portion of the Roman army was trapped. Writes Dio:

The Quadi had surrounded them at a spot favorable for their purpose and the Romans were fighting valiantly with their shields locked together; then the barbarians ceased fighting, expecting to capture them easily as the result of the heat and their thirst. So they posted guards all about and hemmed them in to prevent their getting water anywhere; for the barbarians were far superior in numbers. The Romans, accordingly, were in a terrible plight from fatigue, wounds, the heat of the sun, and thirst, and so could neither fight nor retreat, but were standing and the line and at their several posts, scorched by the heat, when suddenly many clouds gathered and a mighty rain, not without divine interposition, burst upon them.[83]

In later Christian tradition, the Rain Miracle was brought about because the supposedly Christian Legio XII Fulminata had beseeched Jesus for succor.[84] Dio, however, credited an Egyptian magician, Arnuphis. Neither claim makes much difference to the story; what mattered was that the army now believed Marcus was favored by the gods, a belief that grew when he was also credited with calling down lightning on a particularly troublesome missile engine being used against the Romans.[85]

As Marcus dealt with the Quadi, his preoccupation with the Danube front created an opening for disaffected groups in various parts of the Empire to riots or revolt. Most of these were handled by local legates. But when the Parthians, taking advantage of the eastern legions, weakened by sending vexillations to the Danube, tried to bring Armenia back under its sway, Marcus faced a brewing calamity. The last military crisis in the region had been considered crucial enough to send the co-emperor, Verus, at least as a figurehead. But Verus was dead, and Marcus could not leave the Danube. He therefore granted Avidius Cassius an extraordinary *imperium* over the entire east, powers that had not been granted to any legate or general since Augustus sent his most trusted general, Agrippa, to the east.[86]

While Cassius rallied the eastern legions and checked Parthian ambitions, Marcus once again took his army north of the Danube. With the Marcomanni and Quadi defeated, his target this time was the Iazyges. Unfortunately, we know nothing about Roman military operations, but judging from the harsh peace inflicted upon them, Marcus must have enjoyed a substantial victory. Writes Dio:

They were required to dwell twice as far away from the Ister [Danube] as those tribes [Marcomanni and Quadi]. Indeed, the emperor had wished to exterminate them utterly. For that they were still strong at this time and had done the Romans great harm . . . and that they promptly furnished as their contribution to the alliance eight thousand cavalry, fifty-five hundred of whom he sent to Britain.[87]

It is interesting to examine this peace in relation to what Dio says of Marcus's diplomacy with the other warring tribes a few years before:

> Marcus Antoninus remained in Pannonia in order to give audience to the embassies of the barbarians; for many came to him at this time also. Some of them, under the leadership of Battarius, a boy twelve years old, promised an alliance; these received a gift of money and succeeded in restraining Tarbus, a neighboring chieftain, who had come into Dacia and was demanding money and threatening to make war if he should fail to get it. Others, like the Quadi, asked for peace, which was granted them, both in the hope that they might be detached from the Marcomanni, and also because they gave him many horses and cattle and promised to surrender all the deserters and the captives, besides,—thirteen thousand at first, and later all the others as well. The right to attend the markets, however, was not granted to them, for fear that the Iazyges and the Marcomanni, whom they had sworn not to receive nor to allow to pass through their country, should mingle with them, and passing themselves off for Quadi, should reconnoiter the Roman positions and purchase provisions. Besides these that came to Marcus, many others sent envoys, some by tribes and some by nations, and offered to surrender. Some of them were sent on campaigns elsewhere, as were also the captives and deserters who were fit for service; others received land in Dacia, Pannonia, Moesia, the province of Germany, and in Italy itself.[88]

There is a tremendous amount to unpack here regarding how Rome dealt with barbarian tribes, at least until the Crisis of the Third Century. Some of the tribes were welcomed into an alliance with Rome, while others were only offered terms upon which the Romans would stop killing them. In either case, the Romans expected these tribes to make war on those tribes that were still disturbing the peace (Tarbus and his unnamed tribe in Dacia). This is part of a long-standing Roman military tradition establishing the idea that the most cost-efficient method of fighting the barbarian tribes was to turn them upon one another. The largest and most dangerous tribes (the Quadi, Marcomanni, and Iazyges) were forbidden market rights within the Empire, cutting off a source of much of the tribal elite's wealth during peacetime. Not only that, but these tribes were also forced to turn over thousands of horses—reducing their mobility and ability to farm the heavy German soil—as well as all of their

Roman prisoners and slaves, which struck at the wealth of the entire society. Rome, in short, was terminating the conflict with a final barrage of economic warfare designed to cripple the barbarians' warmaking capacity for decades.

The smaller and more manageable tribes were offered land within the Empire (presumably distant from the Danube frontier), where they would eventually be Romanized and would soon be adding to Rome's tax base. Nearly every tribe appears to have been forced to raise substantial forces of troops that would be formed into Roman auxiliary formations and mostly sent to guard distant points of the Empire. This process was repeated many times, on various scales, for over two hundred years, so it could not have been a haphazard affair. Rather, it was part of a well-thought-out strategic policy to relieve pressure on the borders, weaken troublesome tribes, and strengthen the Empire economically and militarily at the barbarians' expense.

As the war against the Iazyges was concluding, Marcus faced what could have been the most dangerous crisis of his reign: Cassius, with all of the eastern legions at his command, had revolted, and much of the Eastern Empire recognized him as emperor. Appointing him to the eastern imperium had been a wise move. War with Parthia was threatening, there were revolts in Egypt, and other regions were becoming increasingly unsettled. There was much to be done, and no one knew more about the region than Cassius. Just as crucially, he had the respect of the legions and could be counted on to quickly stomp out any resurrection of Parthian power without calling on help from the west, which had little to give. But as we have seen, ever since Rome's first forays into imperialism, when the legions of Sulla, Marius, Pompey, and Caesar were conquering an empire, placing too many legions under the direct control of a general distant from Rome was asking for trouble. The temptation to put those legions to use in a bid for ultimate power was too great for many to resist. This was the great strategic tightrope every emperor had to walk. To secure the Empire, emperors often had to place their trust in generals who were weeks or months distant from imperial control. If they were victorious, they could relieve the Empire of one crisis—as Corbulo had done in the east for Nero and Cassius had just done for Marcus—only to plunge it into another catastrophe as soon as they had accomplished their mission. The conundrum for the general was that, if he was victorious against Rome's enemies, there was a real possibility that a jealous emperor would order his execution, as Nero did to Corbulo. As such, the impulse to revolt and try for the purple often seemed the safest policy. Moreover, the rewards for success were great indeed, as were the penalties for failure, for if Roman history demonstrates one iron law it was that "once a usurper committed to himself to seek the purple, the imperial challenger could not be permitted to live."[89] The modern adage is, of course, "If you take a shot at the king, you must kill him."

Marcus, despite being in poor health, reacted vigorously. His son, Commodus, was summoned from Rome and, despite not being of age, was invested with the *toga virilis* (a sign that he was a grown man) and presented to the army, which always took such things as dynastic succession seriously. The legate of Pannonia Inferior was sent to Rome to ensure that the Senate declared Cassius an outlaw and to also ensure the city did not become restive. Cassius was immediately declared a public enemy by the Senate, but he remained formidable, having at least seven legions at his command and the full resources of Syria and Egypt to draw upon.

Still, Marcus had the support of the rest of the Empire and the vast Danubian army, now battle hardened by over five years of often desperate fighting. It should be noted that Marcus's army still included large numbers of vexillations from the eastern legions, which would have denied Cassius some of his best troops. The news that Rome was about to plunge into civil war also brought many barbarian nations rallying to the Roman cause. What better way was there to prove their newly rediscovered loyalty to an emperor who had beaten them in the field, and also to gain favors and more lenient peace terms from a grateful Rome? Marcus, however, refused all such offers, claiming that barbarians should never be made too aware of internal Roman problems.[90]

The threat ended as suddenly as it had begun. As Marcus was preparing for civil war, he received word that Cassius had been murdered by a centurion, and his head was brought to the emperor.[91] The revolt had lasted less than three months. Its quick end must have left Marcus greatly relieved. He had won his war on the Danube and narrowly averted a ruinous civil war. For the first time since his reign began, the Roman world was at peace along its entire frontier. The loyal Martius Verus, who had kept Cappadocia loyal to Marcus, was sent to take over Syria. His first order of business was to burn all of Cassius's correspondence, as ordered by Marcus. This made it impossible for anyone to know for sure who had written to give their support to the usurper, so Rome was spared a brutal and divisive purge. Marcus later informed the Senate that he did not want the blood of any senator to ever be on his hands. This leniency was greatly appreciated by the Roman elites, but Marcus did execute just enough people to make sure no one considered him weak.

Marcus, however, understood that much of the east had rallied to Cassius and that it would require his presence to secure their loyalty to Rome and to him personally. By July 175 he had begun his first journey to the east, with his son, Commodus, beside him, as well as a large body of troops, just to be on the safe side. His wife, Faustina, also accompanied him, but she died along the way.[92] In 176 Marcus departed Alexandria for Syria but purposely stayed away from Antioch, which had been the originating point of Cassius's revolt. From Smyrna he went to Athens, where he and Commodus were initiated in the Eleusinian Mysteries. Before the winter of 176 the emperor was back in Rome, where he enjoyed a triumph and arranged for his son to be made a consul at the tender age of fifteen. For the next eighteen months he ruled jointly with Commodus.

In the meantime, the tribes so recently defeated along the Danube had risen again, protesting against the peace terms Marcus had imposed upon them. The situation along the Danube had deteriorated to the point that Marcus felt he needed to return to the frontier, with his co-ruler, Commodus, with him. He had left two brothers, the Quintilii, in charge of the frontier, and they had won some victories. Dio refers to them as shrewd, courageous, and experienced.[93] Yet they could not end the wars. Marcus, upon arriving at the frontier, took the ceremonial bloody spear removed from the Temple of Bellona and cast it to the enemy's territory, the last recorded instance of this traditional Roman method of declaring war. At some point in 179, Taruttienus Paternus won a great victory, for which the emperor was acclaimed imperator for the tenth time, while the teenaged Commodus received his third such acclamation.

Marcus was preparing for another year of campaigning when he fell ill and died in March 180. Dio claims he was poisoned by his physicians on Commodus's orders. As he lay dying, he commended his son to the protection of the soldiers, showing that he did not suspect his son, or, at least did not want the soldiers to blame him. When the military tribunes asked for the watchword for the guard, Marcus told him: "Go to the rising sun; I am already setting."[94]

The "rising sun," Commodus, is one of the more interesting figures in Roman history to write about because the sources are so overwhelmingly slanderous of his character. Dio starts a portion of his *Roman History* with the following passage:

> This man [Commodus] was not naturally wicked, but, on the contrary, as guileless as any man that ever lived. His great simplicity, however, together with his cowardice, made him the slave of his companions,

and it was through them that he at first, out of ignorance, missed the better life and then was led on into lustful and cruel habits, which soon became second nature.[95]

The *Historia Augusta* is not nearly as polite:

For even from his earliest years he was base and dishonorable, and cruel and lewd, defiled of mouth, moreover, and debauched. Even then he was an adept in certain arts which are not becoming in an emperor, for he could mold goblets and dance and sing and whistle, and he could play the buffoon and the gladiator to perfection.[96]

Most readers know him as the evil emperor in the movie *Gladiator*. And not for nothing did Dio write of Marcus's death: "Our history now descends from a kingdom of gold to one of iron and rust."[97] Commodus's personal qualities are not, however, the concern of this work, except for the ways in which they impacted Rome's strategic position and decision-making.[98]

But there is reason to mention his personal foibles, for his unstable personality led to a succession of plots against him that only served to make him increasingly paranoid and irrational. His behavior weakened the overall position of the emperor and ruined any possibility of continuing a tradition of a peaceful transition of power, which had served the Empire well since the reign of Nerva. After his death the Empire plunged once again into civil war, and one can easily trace the line of the Empire's dissolution and eventual destruction starting with Commodus's reign. That the Empire lasted another 250 years is due to the rise of superior emperors at crucial moments, who managed to stabilize the Empire for at least a brief periods. But none of them were ever able to establish a new order that could guarantee a peaceful transition of power beyond the next generation.

Rome's post-Commodus longevity is also a testament to the Empire's huge stores of latent and residual power, as measured by its institutions, economic might, and military power, which all, in turn, have to be measured against the relative power of its enemies. Decay, once it set in, may have been irreversible, but as the economist Adam Smith reminds us, "There is a great deal of ruin in a nation."[99] In Rome's case, there was another quarter-millennium of ruin left in it before its final demise.

Of more immediate strategic consequence, Commodus, soon after Marcus's death, made peace with the tribes Rome had been fighting on the Danube frontier for most of the past decade. Historians still debate whether Marcus meant to continue the fighting for another one or two campaigning seasons to incorporate the lands of the Marcomanni and Quadi into the Empire as provinces. The long-term impact of such an expansion is unknowable, as is the possibility of Rome having the will and power to achieve such a goal. All of this, however, is idle speculation, as Commodus's hasty ending of the conflict ruled out any possibility of enlarging the Empire.

Still, indications that Rome was preparing to reside permanently well north of the Danube are found throughout the region's archaeological remains. That the barbarians were exhausted is attested to by the speed with which they agreed to Commodus's terms, terms that were not by any means advantageous to them. The tribes were required to supply Rome's armies with twenty thousand men a year. This was not an insubstantial number and would have added to Roman strength while simultaneously draining the tribes of their best and most volatile warriors each year. The recruits, per Roman policy, would be dispersed to units far from their homelands as a way to break their tribal loyalties and substitute for them loyalty to Rome. The tribes were also at least partially disarmed and forbidden to make war upon one another without Rome's permission. In effect, Rome was creating new client-state arrangements across the Rhine while simultaneously ensuring that the clients would be unable to do much in their own defense, just as dangerous and well-armed tribes advanced toward them from the eastern steppes.[100]

Commodus's other action of long-term import was to further debase the currency. Silver coins were reduced in weight, and the purity of the silver from which they were made was reduced at the same time. Following his father's two currency debasements, this represented a loss of approximately 30 percent of a coin's silver.[101] Though the impact was not immediate, this had two negative consequences. For one thing, it built up inflationary pressure that would finally explode at a time when Rome was much less prepared to deal with it. And, because Marcus, Commodus, and even Nero before them were able to debase the currency and then use the debased currency to fund lavish spending without any serious economic consequences, future emperors came to believe they too were immune to the iron laws of economics.

Despite having made peace with the tribes across the Danube, the area remained restive. There are almost no details in our sources, but there also appears to have been fighting north of Hadrian's Wall, as an ambitious general pushed forces toward the old Antonine Wall. There was also apparently some fighting in Dacia, but little is known of this conflict either. All the *Historia Augusta* has to say about them is, "The provincials in Britain, Dacia, and Germany attempted to cast off his yoke, but all these attempts were put down by his [Commodus's] generals.[102] Dio is a bit more forthcoming, at least about the conflict with Britain:

He also had some wars with the barbarians beyond Dacia, in which Albinus and Niger, who later fought against the emperor Severus, won fame; but the greatest struggle was the one with the Britons. When the tribes in that island, crossing the wall that separated them from the Roman legions, proceeded to do much mischief and cut down a general together with his troops, Commodus became alarmed but sent Ulpius Marcellus against them . . . and he ruthlessly put down the barbarians of Britain.[103]

These conflicts were sufficiently serious to allow Commodus to have himself acclaimed imperator twice more. As we can see, the need for an emperor without any military accomplishments of his own to garland his name and his reign with military victories remained a strategic concern, particularly for an unpopular emperor. The only other serious trouble we are aware of was a legionary mutiny in Britain. This was put down rather easily, but it had a lasting impact on Commodus, who replaced many of the senators commanding Rome's legions with equestrians—men one order down in the social hierarchy. Senatorial power had been waning for a long time, but this move, deeply resented by senators at the time, removed them from the one position from where they could wield influence and hence be a danger to the regime. Eventually senators would be forbidden to command legions, making them superfluous to the state except as administrators, a role they mostly lost as a result of Diocletian's governmental reforms.

Eventually Commodus was murdered by his prefect of the guard, who was in league with Commodus's concubine. They first tried to poison him, and when that failed, a wrestler with whom Commodus often exercised was sent in to strangle him.[104] Herodian leaves us a fitting epitaph: "He was the most nobly born of all the emperors who preceded him and was the handsomest man of his time, both in beauty of features and in physical development. If it were fitting to discuss his manly qualities, he was inferior to no man in skill and in marksmanship, if only he had not disgraced these excellent traits by shameful practices."[105]

CHAPTER 11 | The Severan Interlude

S OON AFTER COMMODUS'S murder, he was replaced by Pertinax, who had no strategic impact on the Empire's course since he ruled for only a little over two months before being murdered by the praetorians, who were irate over his attempts to limit their powers to enrich themselves at the expense of the Roman populace.[1] Dio called what happened next "disgraceful business and one unworthy of Rome," and the event even today has the power to shock: The praetorians put the Empire up for auction. Two main bidders came forward: the city prefect and Pertinax's father-in-law, Sulpicianus, and a former consul and governor, Didius Julianus. As the candidates began bidding, even the praetorians were amazed at the spectacle. Soon the sums being offered were so great that the soldiers questioned whether either man could raise such vast amounts. In the end, they halted the bidding and opted for Julianus, as they feared Sulpicianus might, at a point when he felt secure, seek retribution for the murder of his son-in-law. News of the praetorians' scandalous actions quickly spread throughout the Empire, but with it also came word of a massive popular discontent in Rome. The praetorians, ignoring the will of the people, did all that was possible to secure their benefactor, Julianus, in power, but it was all in vain: the legions, the true and final arbiter of power in the Empire, were on the march.

Three of the Empire's leading generals, Pescennius Niger in Syria, Septimius Severus in Pannonia, and Clodius Albinus in Britain, rebelled. Niger, believing he was the favorite in Rome, declared first but then waited in Antioch. Instead of entering into negotiations with the western army, whose will would be decisive, or marching immediately on Rome, when a rapid advance could have decided the outcome, Niger was content to trifle away precious time. Albinus also declared, but Severus bought his support with the promise he would be made Caesar and hence the heir to the crown. While Niger dallied, Severus, a native of Africa, acted. After buying the support of the army with extravagant promises, he marched south with the complete support of over a dozen legions along the Danube and the Rhine. Severus was perfectly positioned for a quick strike, for he knew of Augustus's warning that an army in Pannonia could be within sight of Rome in ten days.[2]

There was only one thing Severus feared, and that was an assassination. Hence, he surrounded himself day and night with six hundred picked legionaries who supposedly never removed their breastplates until Severus was emperor. Julianus still put his faith in the praetorians, whom he beseeched to train themselves for war and to then march out and confront Severus's army. The praetorians were having none of it. They were fully aware of their inadequacies, and though they may have looked like soldiers and could easily intimidate Roman citizens, in the open field, the veteran legions would cut them to ribbons with barely an hour's pause. Julianus was abandoned and then murdered by the praetorians when reports came that Severus and the legions were in sight of Rome. His final words were, "But what evil have I done? Whom have I killed?"[3]

Severus's first act as emperor was to disarm and disband the praetorians. This was accomplished without bloodshed, through a thoroughly planned and expertly executed ruse, in which the Guard was called to a field to hear the emperor speak to them. Herodian captures the moment:

> Prior orders had been issued to Severus' soldiers to surround the praetorians, now their enemy, at the moment when they were standing with their eyes fixed in expectant attention upon the emperor; they were not, however, to wound or strike any member of the guard. Severus ordered his troops to hold the praetorians in a tight ring of steel . . . the soldiers from Illyricum rushed forward and stripped from the praetorians their short ceremonial swords inlaid with gold and silver; next, they ripped off belts, uniforms, and any military insignia they were wearing, and sent them off naked. The praetorians had to submit to this treatment, since they were betrayed and taken by a trick. Indeed, what else could they do, just a few naked men against so many fully armed soldiers?[4]

In an instant, the power behind the throne for almost two centuries had, for the moment, ceased to exist. Still needing a personal guard, however, Severus selected his best and most loyal soldiers for the role. The Guard would again become active in politics after Severus's death, and it would not be until Constantine destroyed them at the Battle of Milvian Bridge that they were finally disbanded.

Severus could not long enjoy his triumphal entry into Rome, for Niger was finally on the march. Severus, aware of the power and wealth of the East, prepared for a hard war. According to Herodian: "He got ready a large and powerful force with incredible speed, aware that he would need a large army to operate against Niger and the entire continent lying opposite Europe.[5] Once again, we are witnessing both the mobilization of the latent power of Rome and the military's ability to plan, mobilize and execute a military operation that would span months and cross over 1,500 miles. This called for mobilizing a huge fleet (much of Severus's army in Italy departed from the port of Brundisium), coordinating parallel operations for two widely distant armies, and stocking food and other supplies all along the routes of march. It is worth reiterating that this could not have been accomplished if Rome did not possess administrative staffs who understood the pertinent geography and had sufficient professional expertise and experience to plan and undertake an operation that would stress a modern military staff to the utmost. Not only that, once the campaign was completed, these unknown staff officers would have to turn the entire army around and march it back to Gaul to undertake a second trying campaign. It is worth noting that General George Marshall, in World War I, was given the nickname "the wizard" for removing the American army from one fight and moving it to another just fifty miles distant. Similarly, General Patton's staff is still lauded for taking a mere three divisions out of the fighting line, pivoting them ninety degrees, and throwing them into the Ardennes battle a few dozen miles away. But, somehow historians fail to credit Rome with maintaining professional staffs, although someone clearly had to be coordinating these military activities, which were of equal or greater scale, covered a far larger geographical area, and were extended for much longer periods of time than anything Marshall did in WW I or Patton in WW II.[6]

As Severus's forgotten staff officers planned the coming war's details, his private concerns turned to Albinus in Britain, who possessed a formidable army and could easily make the jump to the Continent and into Rome, while Severus was engaged in the east. To keep him quiet, Severus promoted his potential rival to Caesar and began a campaign of letter writing meant to convince Albinus of the high esteem in which Severus held him and reminding him that, while Albinus was in the prime of life, he "himself was old and afflicted with gout, and his sons were still very young," thereby opening the real possibility the Albinus would soon rise to the purple.[7] Only after Niger was defeated did Albinus discover what Severus truly had in store for him. Until then, Severus treated him with every modicum of civility and respect so that the doomed man had no hint of his planned destruction. In his final letter, announcing his victory over Niger, he calls Albinus the "brother of his heart" and asks him to "rule the empire as my brother on the throne."[8] The five messengers entrusted with this letter were instructed to deliver it in public and then to ask for a private audience to discuss intimate matters of the state and the court that Severus wished Albinus to be aware of. When they were alone, they were ordered to slay Albinus with hidden daggers. Albinus, sensing a trap, had the messengers tortured until they revealed the details of the plot. Only then did the credulous Albinus mobilize his forces for war on the continent. It was already too late. Severus had secured the east and joined its power to his own. He was already heading west at the head of a veteran and victorious army.[9]

Before all of this could happen, Niger still had to be defeated. Now alert to the danger, he had fortified the passes through the Taurus mountains, which was the gateway to northern Syria, and also sent a force to hold Byzantium. He also sent an army north, under Aemilianus, which encountered Severus's approaching forces at Cyzicus in 193. Herodian reports that Niger's advance army was shattered by the Illyrian legions without much difficulty, greatly buoying the spirits of Severus's army. Niger's main army continued its advance until he arrived at Nicea, where another "savage struggle" took place.[10] The remnants of Niger's beaten army fell back upon the fortifications within the Taurus Mountains, while Niger himself hurried back to Antioch to raise troops and money.

Approaching the Cilician Gates, Severus found Niger's forces waiting behind their prepared positions. Forcing his way through would not be easy, as the narrow passage made any approach hazardous. The first assault failed, and Niger's soldiers, "fighting back bravely, stood upon the battlements and hurled stones down on the attackers. Thus a few defenders easily held off a great number of attackers."[11] Herodian reports that Severus's troops were losing heart when a mighty storm unleashed torrential rains. Soon, the vast amounts of water rushing down from the mountains swept away Niger's defenses. Severus's troops poured through the gap and reformed for the final push to Antioch.

Niger, as soon as he learned of the disastrous collapse of his defensive barrier, rushed north with his troops. His hastily formed army, recruited from his strongest supporters in Antioch, was enthusiastic. Unfortunately, enthusiasm was not going to count for much when ranged against the sheer murderous competence of the Danubian legions. Both armies met on the Plain of Issus, where Alexander had defeated Darius centuries before (333 BCE). Herodian tells us that the battle was fought with "savage fury," but eventually the enthusiasm of Niger's army waned before the unrelenting onslaught of Severus's professionals.[12]

> After the battle had continued for a long time with terrible slaughter, and the rivers which flowed through the plain were pouring more blood than water into the sea, the rout of the forces of the East began. Driving Niger's battered troops before them, the Illyrians forced some of the fugitives into the sea; pursuing the rest as they rushed to the ridges, they slaughtered the fugitives, as well as a large number of men from the nearby towns and farms who had gathered to watch the battle from a safe vantage point.[13]

Severus's forces had gained a decisive victory, killing over 20,000 of his opponents, while Niger himself was run to ground and beheaded by pursuing cavalry. Severus, believing either that his minions had found a way to dispatch Albinus or that the flattery and titles he had bestowed upon him would keep the British governor quiescent, took his time rearranging eastern affairs. But it was not long before he learned that his plot to murder his rival had been exposed and that Albinus had crossed with much of his army into Gaul.

Before departing for the west, Severus realigned the administration of Syria, breaking it into two separate provinces, and thereby breaking up the concentration of legions that were now under two different legates. Severus knew from practical experience the strategic difficulties that were likely to arise when anyone besides the emperor controlled too large a military force. Dio also informs us that Severus took time to cross the Euphrates and conduct substantial operations in the vicinity of Nisibis, but these did not amount to as much as they could have, as he had to rapidly curtail them to deal with Albinus. Severus did add the client kingdom of Osroene, which had been vacillating between Rome and Parthia again, and made it into a new Roman province that stretched as far as Nisibis. Finally, he gained a good deal of practical experience in the logistic requirements of fighting a war in such an arid environment, which would serve him well in future campaigns. As to why he conducted these unnecessary campaigns, we must return to the strategic imperative of gaining the glory still required to solidify the right to rule. Severus, who had not commanded in person at any of the major battles of the civil war, was still not secure on the throne and was in desperate need of adding to his personal glory. As he had won no personal distinction in the war against Niger, he needed a foreign war, particularly if it could be undertaken with little risk to himself or the army.[14] The quick campaign on the far side of the Euphrates was sufficient to garner him three imperial salutations that could be employed for propaganda value in Rome.

After ensuring that there were sufficient forces to continue the siege of Byzantium, where many of Niger's supporters, despairing of any hope of pardons, were making a final stand, Severus marched his army west. Byzantium, however, held out for three years.[15] When famine finally forced it to surrender, the defenders were put to the sword, the walls demolished, and the city plundered and razed.[16] Byzantium, which would one day become Constantine's capital, Constantinople, was for over a century reduced to a shadow of its former self. And, although the walls were likely rebuilt, Rome was later to pay a heavy price for failing to rebuild the city's fortifications up to their original strength. For, when the Goths captured much of the shipping in the Black Sea, they were able to sail through the Bosporus unhindered to ravage the Balkans. One must, however, wonder how much blame can be attached to Severus for not foreseeing an event that was decades away and not on anyone's view of the strategic horizon. Of course, at some point, the threat did become clear and action should have been taken before the crisis point arrived.

The civil war in the west was held in stasis for more than a year as Albinus consolidated his hold upon Gaul and recruited new forces around the core of the three legions he had brought over from Britain. Unfortunately for his prospects, Albinus failed to secure the support of the Rhine legions, which were being hastily reinforced by the Danubian legions. The fighting had not even begun, and Albinus was already outnumbered four-to-one.[17] Severus also appears to have tarried in Rome for a while, and one suspects he was still securing his hold on power and trying to placate a civil population tired of civil war. Albinus won some early engagements that somewhat buoyed his cause, but if he was to win, he needed a decisive battlefield victory over Severus's main army, and he had to do so quickly, as his adherents were rapidly peeling away.

The two armies finally met at Lugdunum (Lyon) on February 19. Reconstructing this battle is difficult, as the versions presented by Dio, Herodian, and the *Historia Augusta* vary widely. A reasonable account leads one to believe the fighting was prolonged and vicious. For, as Herodian relates, "for a long time each side's chances of victory were equal, for in courage and ruthlessness the soldiers from Britain were in no way inferior to the soldiers from Illyria. When these two magnificent armies were locked in combat, it was no easy matter to put either one to flight."[18] At some point in the battle, one wing of Albinus's army appeared to give way, but it was a ruse to lure

Severus's Danubian legions into a trap. The slaughter was great on both sides, and even the emperor was unhorsed in the middle of the melee. At this point, the emperor had either discarded his cloak and was trying to run away or had removed it to move more easily about and rally his forces. Whichever way it was, seeing the emperor in their midst appears to have rallied the forces on that flank, although that was likely just as much the result of Severus having led his new praetorian Guard into the fight. One might remember that this force was not the barely trained troops that had served previous emperors. Rather, it was now populated by several thousand of the best soldiers in the Illyrian legions.

The front stabilized, and Severus's final reserve, a portion of the infantry, and most of his cavalry were led by Julius Laetus into the fray. Reasons for Laetus's slowness to enter the battle also vary. He either mistakenly heard that Severus had been killed and was now rushing in to win the battle against Albinus and make himself emperor, or, as the front stabilized and it became clear Severus would win, he wanted to make sure the emperor knew he was there for him in his moment of need. Either calculation would have enraged the vengeful emperor, and the mere fact of Laetus's survival seems sufficient proof that no one at the time thought he harbored sinister motives.[19] Albinus was captured, stripped naked, and placed on the ground so Severus could ride his horse over him. While he was still living, he was beheaded, and his head was displayed in Rome. Unlike Marcus Aurelius, who had all of the usurper Cassius's papers burned, Severus used Albinus's captured letters to identify those senators who had supported his cause. When he returned to Rome, nearly thirty senators were executed for treason, further proof of the declining power, influence, and need for the senatorial class. Edward Gibbon rightfully marks this as the end of the ideal of the Roman Republic, stating that the final victory over the senate was "easy and inglorious."[20]

Severus did not tarry long in Rome, and by the end of summer 197, he was again marching east. The *casus belli* was a Parthian attack on Nisibis, the great fortress city on the Euphrates. Severus had taken the city on his last military offensive in the region and had incorporated it and the surrounding region into Rome's defenses. This was followed by the annexations of Adiabene and Osrhoene, which contained the cities of Edessa, Carrhae, and Nisibis, which did away with the fiction of a buffer of client states between Rome and Parthia. Rome then went a step further and annexed territory lying within Rome's current sphere of influence, but that traditionally had been securely part of Parthia's sphere of interest. These last annexations embarrassed the Parthian king, who was already in a weakened position. How weak is made obvious by the fact that the king's brother was marching with Severus, who intended to put him on the Parthian throne if the occasion arose.

From a strategic point of view, Parthia was likely never weaker, and Rome was still near the height of its power. Although much of the eastern army had been depleted by combat in the civil war and then weakened further to provide vexillations for Severus's campaign against Albinus in the west, it easily halted the Parthian offensive. Parthia even failed to take their primary objective, Nisibis, which lay on the Parthian border, as his legate, Julius Laetus, had already saved the city and repelled the Parthian army before Severus arrived with reinforcements. This is a remarkable testament to the resiliency of Rome's military power. Although no one took a tally of the civil war fighting, losses must have been equivalent to a half dozen legions and as much again from the auxiliary forces. Despite these losses, there do not seem to have been any major problems along any of the frontiers except for the brief Parthian foray. It also says something about the Roman military organization and the strength of the *limes* that Rome was willing to risk war with Persia just months after ending their own civil war.

Still, the strategic fabric of the Empire was being slowly eroded. Part of this erosion was visible, such as the neutering of the senate. Much of it, however, was invisible at the time and barely noticed by historians since. The civil war had created deep societal fissures, and Severus's post-conflict purges, conducted across the entire Empire, had solidified these antagonisms. For a civil war is rarely between the contestants and their armies. Elites and even entire populations are almost always forced to take sides. In the wake of most prior civil wars, emperors had followed Caesar's example and shown clemency to their former enemies. Even when there were reprisals, the numbers involved were kept to a bare minimum and most emperors went out of their way to avoid killing senators. It is worth remembering the lengths to which Hadrian went trying to pass the blame for killing just a few members of the senatorial class. But, Severus had cut loose all restraint. As the *Historia Augusta* records: "Countless persons who had sided with Albinus were put to death, among them numerous leading men and many distinguished women, and all their goods were confiscated and went to swell the public treasury."[21] From now on, civil wars were blood feuds where the loser and all of his supporters could expect no mercy. When this was extended into regions, cities, towns, and villages, it became a method for settling old scores and upsetting the established local order. In short, a civil war would, in the future, tear apart the very fabric of society.[22]

By September, Severus was in Nisibis and had collected a fleet of supply vessels to accompany the army as it marched down the Euphrates. The legions' advance was barely contested, as the Parthian king, Vologaeses, abandoned his capital and fled east. The Romans, not for the first time, captured a who's-who of ancient cities, including Babylon and the Parthian capital Ctesiphon. The latter was sacked, and besides yielding a huge number of prisoners destined for the Roman slave markets, Severus also captured the Persian treasury. On January 28, 198, one hundred years after Trajan had become emperor, Severus announced victory and the conquest of Parthia.[23] As he was short of provisions, he opted not to occupy the newly conquered region. Instead, he took his army north, attempting to capture the city of Hatra. When the Romans failed to take the city by storm, they settled in for a siege. According to Dio, it did not go well, as "siege engines were burned, many soldiers perished, and vast numbers were wounded."[24] Severus soon called an end to the siege as well as a second one attempted several months later. But rather than risk another Roman assault, the ruler of Hatra swore to become a Roman client state, making it possible for Severus to fairly claim he had conquered the East. The sieges, besides inflicting severe losses on the legions, had another low point when Severus had the savior of Nisibis, Julius Laetus, executed because he was, according to Dio, "proud and beloved by the soldiers, who used to declare they would not go on campaign unless Laetus led them."[25] We have already seen many examples of just how dangerous it was for an emperor to allow a beloved general to live. But, perhaps, as Herodian alludes, Severus only now discovered the real reason Laetus had held back the reserve at the Battle of Lugdunum.[26]

But what was the overall strategic impact of Severus's war with Parthia? The first and most immediate was that he added the province of Mesopotamia to the Empire and garrisoned it with two of the three legions raised for the war—I and III Parthica.[27] Dio, who did not support this expansion, wrote:

> He [Severus] used to declare that he had added a vast territory to the empire and had made it a bulwark of Syria. On the contrary, it is shown by the facts themselves that this conquest has been a source of constant wars and great expense to us. For it yields very little and uses up vast sums; and now that we have reached out to peoples who are neighbors of the Medes and the Parthians rather than of ourselves, we are always, one might say, fighting the battles of those peoples.[28]

Dio worried that the advance of the Empire to the east only stored up trouble with Persia that was sure to lead to a renewed series of military conflicts, stretching into a limitless future. And, in fact, Mesopotamia, and particularly the cities of Nisibis and Hatra, became the defining issue between Rome and Persia for the next 150 years.[29] Severus's advance may have changed some of the dynamics between the two emperors, but ever since Rome first expanded into the east, Parthians and Romans had never had any trouble finding reasons to fight each other. If Severus had not taken Mesopotamia, it is unlikely that the Roman east would have been the nirvana of perpetual peace that Dio supposes.

Still, Severus's claim that he had created a bulwark protecting Syria is certainly true, and from a strategic point of view it is one of the great triumphs of Roman arms, since for the next 150 years the great cities of Syria, including the second city of the Roman Empire, Antioch, were removed from the front lines and prospered as never before. Dio might complain that Mesopotamia cost much and gave little, but this neglects a very important fact: by improving the security of the Eastern Empire in general, it allowed at least that portion of the Empire to grow spectacularly wealthy. As I have already noted, legions cost the Empire almost as much money when they were idle as when they were fighting a war. The sunk cost of the Roman military was a given whether they were fighting in Mesopotamia or holding the line along the walls of Antioch. But in terms of sparing Rome the destruction of vast swaths of its economic heartland, it was much better to have the legions fighting deep in Mesopotamia than defending the Mediterranean coast.

In an argument I will pick up again later in this work, one of the most detailed surveys of the region shows with near certainty that there were no fortified *limes* along the Mesopotamian frontier, similar to what we find along the northern frontiers, and claims that this this "proves its [a frontier line's] irrelevance as a military concept."[30] This, of course, misses the point. The desert itself was the frontier fortification. Looking for a Roman-built fortified line makes no strategic sense, given the geography and arid conditions of the region. Isaac is setting up a straw man. Rome did not need walls where it had deserts. What it needed was a method of controlling the road systems that allowed traders and armies to cross the desert, and these roads needed to converge upon sources of water. At these points there were cities, which Rome employed as fortified bases to control all movement throughout Mesopotamia, as did every empire over a period of several thousand years. Any Persian army that wanted to approach Antioch over the expanse of a trackless and waterless desert was welcome to try. Along the northern frontiers an enemy could cross into the Empire at nearly any point. In the east, however, there were only a few practical avenues of approach that would allow an enemy to advance deep into an empire. Even the casual strategist could see that the Eastern Empire was best secured by concentrating the legions in or near fortified cities, where water was plentiful, that sat along trading routes upon which supplies could be brought. Nothing could be gained by dispersing the legions along impenetrable deserts.

Could Severus have done better? It has been pointed out that the emperor failed to secure direct control of the Tur Abdin, a mountainous plateau that dominates the northern approaches to Mesopotamia. His neglect left the new Roman province vulnerable to attack from the north. Moreover, by not extending the province to the Tigris, the Romans had left the best invasion route into Armenia in enemy hands.[31] Compared to the overall benefits of holding Mesopotamia, Severus's oversights do not amount to much in strategic terms. Given that the Parthians had been punching bags for Roman arms for decades—some would say centuries—we may be able to forgive Severus such tactical flaws. He was, after all, in the wake of the failed sieges of Hatra, dealing with an army verging on mutiny, and it is hard to fault him for failing to foresee the rise of the far more capable Sassanids a quarter of a century in the future. Before casting any such blame, we must acknowledge that the future is only dimly lit to even the most far-seeing and brilliant strategist. Severus, although not a brilliant strategist, was a capable one. Given the conditions of the time and the situation he faced, he achieved much.

The next ten years of Severus's reign were mostly quiet. The only item of strategic import was when, in early 203, he launched a campaign against the Garamantes, who lived south of Tripolitania. After this campaign he remade the frontier, pushing new fortified posts deep into the Sahara and expanding the African provinces into the desert.[32] These adjustments reduced raids from the nomadic tribes living on the fringes of the Sahara and allowed the remaining fertile lands in the southern parts of the African provinces to be securely cultivated. Other than that, we have no information on major operations or changes in Rome's strategic situation for the better part of a decade. This alone testifies to the overall success of Rome's strategic policy, as all that was required to maintain a general peace was some tinkering around the margins of the frontier.

Even Severus's final expedition, in Britain, falls into the tinkering category, for it served no purpose except to get his sons away from Rome's corrupting influences and give them some practical military experience. In response to some minor increases in raiding by the Caledonian tribes north of Hadrian's Wall, Severus in 208 undertook one last expedition. He was sixty-three and apparently in failing health. Of his two sons, Caracalla and Geta, only the former went north of the wall with the emperor, leaving Geta behind in York.[33] By the end of 209 the Caledonians formally submitted to Rome, and there are indications that construction had begun on a permanent legionary base far to the north of Hadrian's Wall.[34] This is evidence that Severus intended to add the rest of Britain to the Empire, and it is interesting to ponder the consequences of success. At the very least, it would have freed two and possibly three legions for other duties. Such a permanent reinforcement of Rome's continental forces could have made a substantial difference in the tumultuous third century. Even if the legions had stayed in Britain, since they would not have to worry about the Picts to the north, they could have better secured southern Britain from Saxons and other raiding tribes, as well as provided a reserve in times of trouble on the Continent.

A revolt by the Maeatae—a lowland tribe that claimed the area where the fortress was being built—halted construction and forced another campaign in 210. This campaign was mostly conducted by Caracalla, because Severus was too ill to lead the army. The orders from Severus to the legions were easily comprehensible. Writes Dio:

> He [Severus] summoned the soldiers and ordered them to invade the rebels' country, killing everybody they met; and he quoted these words: "Let no one escape sheer destruction, No one our hands, not even the babe in the womb of the mother, if it be male; let it nevertheless not escape sheer destruction."[35]

While the campaign was being waged, Severus died. In his final months, aware that Caracalla hated his younger brother, he did his best to keep him safe from beyond the grave by promoting Geta to the rank of Augustus, as he had done with Caracalla a few years previously.[36] So, for a short period the Empire had three simultaneous Augusti. Severus was also aware that Caracalla, tired of waiting for his father to die, was planning to hasten his demise. Yet he did nothing to punish his son. Dio believes he should have had Caracalla executed for plotting against him and blames him for allowing "his love for his offspring to outweigh his love for his country," for he knew well that he had betrayed Geta, who would soon be murdered on Caracalla's order.[37]

Severus's final admonition to his sons was, "Be harmonious, enrich the soldiers and scorn all other men."[38] This neatly places the Roman military at the core of all strategic thinking and policy. Severus himself had done much to endear himself to the army by raising their pay from three hundred to five hundred denarii, their first raise in over a century. A case can be made that the raise was long overdue, although that only makes sense if there had been a 60 percent inflation in those hundred years. But there is scant evidence for that level of inflation. Despite Severus's further debasement of the currency, it does not seem to have affected prices, at least in any way that meaningfully impacted the legions.[39] Still, under noninflationary conditions, this pay raise, when added to the expansion in the number of legions, placed a substantial added burden on the fiscus. These increased costs could only be met by further debasements, which would eventually become one of the catalysts of a destructive inflationary spiral.

In the meantime, what was Rome getting for its denarii? After the Battle of Actium, Augustus cut the number of legions to twenty-eight. This was further reduced to twenty-five after the Germans wiped out three legions at Teutoburg Wald. Caligula had increased the number to twenty-seven, and after the civil wars of 69 CE, Vespasian maintained twenty-nine legions. Two of these legions disappeared under unknown circumstances but were replaced by Marcus Aurelius in his wars against the German tribes in 165 CE. Here things stood for almost four decades until Severus added his three Parthica legions. By Severus's death, the paper strength of the legions was approximately 165,000 men, with another 150,000 assembled in 250 auxiliary cohorts. Throw in 10,000 praetorians and 40,000 more men manning the fleets, and the total Roman military force approached 400,000 men.[40] In practical terms, this is not much larger than the military force of Augustus and his immediate successors. Moreover, the burden was being carried by a substantially larger population and an economy that had grown immensely during the prior two hundred years of the Pax Romana. Population and economic growth are discussed elsewhere in this book, and there is no need to repeat those details. The key strategic point is that the Empire could afford a larger force than it was maintaining, assuming the will to build such a force existed.

Changes were required to face a changing threat, but without the impulse of an immediate crisis, the impetus for change was not present. Rome would have to confront the challenges of the third-century war with the military it had, not the one it needed. This force still maintained the legions at its core. Were they right to do so? Historians have noted that the army by the time of Severus was already a fossil. Its organization had changed little over a number of centuries, and its tactical doctrines would have been familiar to any general of the late Republic. Moreover. its size and mission had been set in stone from the time of Augustus. At the core of Roman power remained the legions as sanctified by the Servian constitution in the sixth century BCE. "It had evolved into the dominant fighting organization against the Samnites, Etruscans, and Gauls in the fourth century, defeated the Carthaginians and Macedonians in the third and second centuries, developed again in the first century BC into an effective formation against Celtic tribes, and then ossified."[41] The only substantial changes in legionary organization over the centuries were the continual additions of artillery—ballistas and catapults—trading mobility for firepower on the battlefield. Roman success required an enemy so stupid as to continually throw themselves at the strongest part of the Roman lines as fodder for legions to devour. But for several hundred years, this was exactly the case. There was no need for the Romans to adapt their military system when they were mostly blessed with enemies all too willing to cater to Rome's battlefield requirements. Still, by the middle of the second century it was becoming obvious that at least the barbarians were learning, although the Parthians were slower to catch on. This is why it took so long for Marcus Aurelius to defeat the German tribes arrayed north of the Danube: they would do whatever they could to avoid meeting the Romans in a stand-up battle. Only when the Romans reverted to "creating deserts" did the tide turn.

It is easy to conclude from all of this that by the end of the second century CE the only truly ideal enemy for a Roman army in the field might have been another Roman army, and as the battles between Severus and Niger and Albinus suggest, such armies were ideally suited to slaughter each other.[42] The obvious conclusion was that the Romans were unable to adapt their military forces to meet new challenges. If that is the case, and we assume the Romans were at least as smart as we are and could see the same problem that we can, an obvious question arises: why?

We can find the answer in the earlier historical example of the Greeks versus the Persians. Over the two hundred years of Greco-Persian enmity, there was one battlefield constant: the Persians were repeatedly beaten by Greek heavy infantry (hoplites). The list starts with Marathon, when the armored Athenian hoplites smashed through the wicker-shielded Persian lines. Then, a decade later, Persian lines were again crushed by the hoplite charge at Plataea. Over 150 years later, Alexander repeated the performance three times at Granicus, Issus, and Gaugamela. One can easily wonder if the Persians' failure to learn and adapt reflects an element of stupidity. But to find the truth, one has to look deeper into their history and military situation. Burned into the Persian psyche were the immensely destructive Scythian raids dating from the time when Cyrus the Great founded the Empire. These raids penetrated hundreds of miles into Persian territory, leaving an apocalyptic swath of destruction in their wake. The only way they could be countered was by armies that were light and fast enough to catch and corner them. In this context, heavy infantry was useless. The Persians, until it was too late, never viewed the Greeks as nearly as dangerous as another great Scythian raid and were therefore reluctant to adapt their military for the lesser threat in ways that would have left them exposed to what they believed was an existential peril.

Rome faced a similar problem. Until almost the end of the Western Empire, the greatest threat any Roman emperor faced was a usurper who had command of his own legions. Moreover, even though the barbarians often operated in small, highly mobile war bands, they did periodically come together in a force sufficiently formidable as to require the concentrated power of several legions to defeat them. Despite being able to see the need for a more mobile and nimble force to run barbarian incursions to ground, as well as to limit the space that multiple bands could spread into, there were real limits to how far any emperor could go down this path. If an emperor converted too many heavy legions into light forces, he courted disaster, for he could not hope to defeat a usurper. He also would have to run the risk of having his light force defeated in an open battle by a concentrated force of barbarians. Finally, Rome still had to consider an increasingly threatening and more militarily competent Persia, which could easily annihilate any Roman army designed to run down barbarians. Under these circumstances, the best any emperor could do was find the extra resources to add more costly cavalry to the army without reducing the overall strength and combat power of the legions. This meant that any adaptations possible would have to come from adding or converting auxiliary formations, since the legions were still required to meet high-end threats.

Interestingly, this is a problem the United States is facing today. We can see that Islamic insurgencies are going to be a military threat to the global order for decades to come. Current strategists also know that the bulk of the American military is not optimized for this kind of fight. But at the same time, the United States must also consider China and Russia in its assessment of what kind of force structure it requires. The possibility of a superpower war is certainly much lower than that of a future conflict with extremists, although recent events in Ukraine are unsettling many post–Cold War geopolitical assumptions. But if the United States once again decides to fight an insurgency with a military structure designed for a high-end conflict against a great-state peer competitor, it will be able to avoid losing, even if it does not crush the insurgency. Such a case might be embarrassing for a superpower and may for a time demoralize the force, but the nation will survive, and the global order will be generally preserved. But if the United States ever gets into a shooting war with China or Russia with a military optimized to fight insurgents, the battlefield results and strategic impact will be cataclysmically bad. The obvious solution is to pay the cost for a force capable of both. But even if the nation could afford the cost of a dual military, there is zero political will to pay for it. Similarly, Roman emperors and generals could see the choices before them, but the solution was far beyond the Empire's resources.

Those resources were about to be stretched even further. Severus had died, leaving his two sons as joint emperors, a situation the older son, Caracalla would not long tolerate. After quickly making peace with the Caledonians, the brothers, with the rest of the imperial court, made their way back to Italy. Relations between the new co-emperors were so bad that they split the palace and added walls to various corridors so as not to have to see each other. The tension could not last, and during the feast of Saturnalia, Caracalla had loyal centurions stab Geta to death in his mother's arms as he pleaded for mercy. The deed done, Caracalla made his way to the praetorian camp to ensure their support. The price was, according to the *Historia Augusta*, extravagant: "He promised each soldier 2,500 denarii and increased their ration allowance by one-half. He ordered the praetorians to go immediately and take the money from the temple depositories and the treasuries."[43] Reportedly the Roman treasury, filled by Severus's eighteen years of parsimony, was emptied in a single day. But that was not the end of the costs of becoming emperor. II Parthica Legio was stationed just outside of Rome as a counterweight to the praetorians. They too needed to be bought off, but that meant every legion would expect whatever was given to II Parthica. According to Dio, the new emperor outdid himself with lavish promises, exclaiming, "Rejoice, fellow-soldiers, for now I am in a position to do you favors."[44] He then told the soldiers he was one of them and that all of Rome's treasuries belonged to them.

To pay for this extravagance, Caracalla confiscated estates, a move greatly aided by the purge of as many as twenty thousand suspected Geta supporters, and debased the currency further, probably to the point where only 50 percent of a silver coin was actual silver. Despite this debasement, there were still no signs of rapid inflation, as most people accepted the worth of the new coins as if the silver content had not changed. There was a breaking point in the economy where inflation would take off at an unrestrained rate, but Rome was not there yet. When these measures were not enough to refill the treasury, Caracalla extended Roman citizenship to virtually everyone living within the Empire. In the decree announcing his benevolence to the world, he claimed that he wanted all Romans to rejoice in his salvation from the murderous Geta. Few were fooled, for as citizens every person within the Empire was now liable for inheritance taxes and a host of other costly payments to Rome from which they had previously been exempt. As Dio states, "This was the reason why he made all the people in his Empire Roman citizens; nominally he was honoring them, but his real purpose was to increase his revenues by this means, inasmuch as aliens did not have to pay most of these taxes."[45]

All of the ancient accounts are unanimous in their portrayal of Caracalla as a horrendous and vile emperor. But the voluminous stories of his personal failings need not concern us, for they had no strategic impact upon the Empire except to hasten Caracalla's departure from Rome to the army's camps. There the isolated and unloved emperor found acceptance and respect, for the soldiers liked that he ate with them and shared many of the hardships of the camp and campaigns; they most certainly applauded his munificence. In 213 Caracalla led a campaign in the Agri Decumates (generally Raetia) and along the Rhine. He appears to have had some success, as one might expect, when the legions launched an unexpected assault on farming communities. Still, he did rebuild forts and outposts, buying Rome twenty years of peace in the region. The one truly notable item of this campaign is that it is the first time the sources mention the Alemanni, a confederation of tribes that were to plague the Empire in years to come.

Caracalla then conducted a grand tour of the Empire, reaching the Danube in 214. The record here is patchy, but it was likely at this point that Pannonia was split into two provinces, breaking up the Pannonian governor's command of the three legions stationed there, as I Adiutrix was moved to Pannonia Inferior.[46] From there Caracalla made his way to Antioch by way of Nicomedia. What he did while in Syria is unrecorded, but given the accumulation of forces and war materiel present in the region the following year, he must have ordered preparations for an invasion of Parthia. By December 215 he was in Alexandria, where he was given a warm greeting. But Alexandria was always the most fractious of the Empire's cities, and relations between the emperor and the population soon soured. According to Dio, crowds were mocking him and publicly naming him as the murderer of Geta. Enraged, Caracalla released his guard and accompanying troops in an orgy of plunder and murder. How many were killed is unknown, but certainly the number reached the many thousands. When Caracalla wrote to the Senate about the incident, he told them that the number of dead did not matter, since they all deserved their fate.[47]

Caracalla was soon back in Antioch completing arrangements for an invasion of Parthia. He could not have picked a more auspicious moment to attack, as Vologaeses was dead and his two sons were locked in a civil war to replace him. One of them, Vologaeses V, held lower Mesopotamia and was based in Parthia's traditional capital, Ctesiphon. The other, Artabanus V, held the heartland of the Empire, beyond the Tigris. At first Caracalla sided with Artabanus, even proposing to marry his daughter. But this was likely a ruse: when the planned marriage miscarried, Caracalla's army was already marching. Artabanus was caught by surprise and thus allowed the legions to march almost totally unopposed through a huge swath of the territory east of the Tigris. Dio tells us that "the Parthians did not even join battle with him; and accordingly I have found nothing of especial interest to record."[48]

One point of interesting strategic note is found in Herodian, where he presents clear evidence that the Romans and Persians clearly understood the weaknesses and strengths of each other's military systems as well as the potential economic strength of their respective empires. He relates the following, which was supposedly part of a letter from Caracalla to Artabanus explaining why the unification of the Roman and Persian Empires by marriage made strategic sense:

> If they [the Roman and Persian Empires] were united by marriage, one empire without a rival would result when they were no longer divided by a river. The rest of the barbarian nations now not subject to their authority could easily be reduced, as they were governed by tribes and confederacies. Furthermore, the Roman infantry were invincible in close-quarter combat with spears, and the Parthians had a large force of highly skilled horse-archers. The two forces, he said, complemented each other; by waging war together, they could easily unite the entire inhabited world under a single crown. Since the Parthians produced spices and excellent textiles and the Romans metals and manufactured articles, these products would no longer be scarce and smuggled by merchants; rather, when there was one world under one supreme authority, both peoples would enjoy these goods and share them in common.[49]

Caracalla's assault on Parthia appears to have been more of a giant raid than a serious attempt at annexation, for he and the legions, "weary by now of looting and killing," returned to Mesopotamia.[50] Buoyed by success, however, Caracalla was reportedly preparing for another invasion of Parthia, meant to destroy Rome's great rival, when he was murdered.

He was replaced by the praetorian prefect Macrinus. Whether Macrinus plotted against Caracalla because he feared for his own life or because he wished only to be elevated to emperor remains an unresolved historical debate. But after three days, when no other candidates had come forward, Macrinus stepped into the void. As he rapidly secured the support of the large army gathered in Syria, the Senate and Roman people were forced to recognize his rule. But from the beginning Macrinus faced severe problems. For one, the extended Severan family was not pleased that they were being pushed aside and immediately began plotting his overthrow. Doing so, however, required the army or a significant portion of it to abandon Macrinus.

Here the Severans had some advantages, including the fact that the army resented the loss of Caracalla, since he had bestowed many favors upon them. Besides, the Severans had always closely associated themselves with the army, and the soldiers believed any new ruler from that dynasty would likely continue to handsomely reward them. The balance, such as it was, was shifted in the Severans' direction when Macrinus made a crucial mistake: under tremendous fiscal pressure, he reduced the pay and privileges of new recruits. Although the veterans were untouched by this change, they immediately perceived a threat to their own futures. After all, what the emperor could do to new recruits he could just as easily do to them.

Everything rested upon how Macrinus countered a new threat from Armenia, for Artabanus had not been idle. Throughout the winter he had amassed a great army, and by 217 he was demanding the Romans depart from the Mesopotamian provinces that Severus had so recently added to the Empire. With no options open except to fight, Macrinus led the Roman army—probably approximating eight full legions and all of their auxiliaries—out to meet the advancing Persians. The two armies met at Nisibis, where, after saluting the sun, the Persians, with a deafening cheer, charged the Roman line, firing their arrows and whipping on their horses. The legions stood solid in the center of the Roman line, their cavalry and the Moroccan javelin throwers on each flank. Light and mobile auxiliaries filled the open spaces in the line, ready to move to any threatened point. Herodian reports that Persian arrows and the long spears of the mail-clad camel riders inflicted heavy losses upon the Romans, but when the Romans could engage at close quarters, they easily bested the Persians. One way they were able to do this was by feigning retreat and then throwing down caltrops as they pulled back. Covered in the sand, these small balls with protruding metal spikes were invisible to the charging Persians and would cripple their animals. Once the riders had fallen to the ground, the Romans would re-form and close in for the kill.[51]

Herodian tells us that the battle went on for three days, with each side retiring to its camp at dusk. On the third day the Persians, making use of their superior numbers, tried to surround the Roman army, but the Romans thinned and then extended their lines to counter the threat. The fighting was vicious: bodies covered the plain, and both sides were nearing exhaustion. Typically, this was when the Romans would have the upper hand. Persian armies were notoriously hard to hold together, and the Romans were amazed they had stayed in the fight as long as they did. Dio records that Artabanus was ready to make an accommodation, since his troops had been mustered for longer than usual and were eager to return home. But perhaps more crucially, they were suffering from a scarcity of food: the Romans had devastated Parthian stores and locked their own away in local forts.[52]

But Macrinus lost his nerve and offered to negotiate. As Dio tells us, "For Macrinus, both because of his natural cowardice . . . and because of the soldiers' lack of discipline, did not dare to fight the war out, but instead expended enormous sums in the form of gifts as well as money."[53] Artabanus was bought off for two hundred million sesterces, fully an eighth of Rome's annual budget. That was the tipping point. Soon thereafter III Parthica, stationed at Raphanea, beside the Severan stronghold of Emesa, declared Varius Avitus Bassianus—better known to history as Elagabalus—emperor. He was only fourteen years old and bore a striking resemblance to the young Caracalla. He was actually the nephew of the dead emperor, but his mother hinted at him being Caracalla's son, playing on the army's fond memories of the soldier-emperor. Several legions went over to Elagabalus, and the rebel force marched on Antioch, where Macrinus was gathering his forces. A battle was fought to the north of the city, but while the outcome was still in doubt Macrinus fled the field. As any ancient army was wont to do when its leader was killed or ran off, they surrendered to the rebels.

Elagabalus ascended to the throne in May 218. He began his rule in the by-now customary manner and purged all of those who had been loyal to the old regime, as well as other enemies, real or perceived. A particularly favorite target were persons whose wealth needed to be confiscated to prop up the state treasury. He did not forget the soldiers, who had their pay and privileges restored and were promised an immediate donative of two thousand sesterces each, in lieu of sacking Antioch. By 219 Elagabalus was in Rome, where he immediately shocked the sensibilities of the populace, the Senate, the praetorians, and the army. One can spend many pages detailing Elagabalus's bizarre behavior, but we will leave it to a quick comment. An emperor who brought his personal gods with him to replace Rome's deities and made a habit of visiting brothels to sell himself as a female prostitute was not long for this world.[54] That he lasted as long as he did is likely a result of his youth and the fact that the two women in his life—his mother, Julia Soaemis, and his grandmother, Julia Maesa (the sister-in-law of Severus and aunt of Caracalla and Geta)—actually ran the Empire.

At some point Julia Soeamis's sister, Julia Mamaea, comprehended that Elagabalus's behavior was intolerable and moved to secure her own position and safety. Julia Mamaea managed to have her son, Alexander—Elagabalus's cousin—declared Caesar, making him the heir to the throne. Late in 221 Elagabalus tried to have his cousin killed, but no one would carry out the order. The following year, with the support of the III Parthica—the legion that had accompanied the emperor to Rome—Mamaea staged a coup. Alexander went into hiding, which infuriated the soldiers of III Parthica and the praetorians, who thought he might have been murdered. When Elagabalus made his way to the praetorian camp to proclaim his innocence, he became enraged by the overt support the praetorians were showing Alexander's cause and ordered them punished. Elagabalus had overplayed his hand, for there could be but one outcome for an emperor who threatened the praetorians without an armed legion or two at his back.

> First they [the praetorians] attacked the accomplices in his plan of murdering Alexander, killing some by tearing out the vital organs and others by piercing the anus, so that their deaths were as evil as their lives. Next, they fell upon Elagabalus himself and slew him in a latrine in which he had taken refuge. Then his body was dragged through the streets, and the soldiers further insulted it by thrusting it into a sewer. But since the sewer chanced to be too small to admit the corpse, they attached a weight to it to keep it from floating, and hurled it from the Aemilian Bridge into the Tiber, in order that it might never be buried.[55]

Alexander was now emperor, and in a bid to better link himself to the Severan dynasty, which still had the army's respect, he appended Severus to his name. Alexander Severus may have been a name meant to awe, but the fact remained that he was only thirteen and temperamentally unfit to rule. Into this leadership void stepped the strong Severan women, Julia Maesa and Julia Mamaea. Throughout his reign, Alexander was completely subservient to them. This proved his final undoing: when the army finally revolted, among their listed reasons was that he was "a mother's boy" and contemptible for allowing the Empire to be managed by "a woman's authority and a woman's judgment."[56]

Still, Alexander is given high praise from our sources, who judged him against his predecessors Severus, Caracalla, and Elagabalus. These three emperors, who had no compunction about killing senators who displeased them and seizing their wealth, were never going to be popular with the ancient historians, who were all of the senatorial class. But Alexander treated the senators with respect, and Herodian, in listing his better qualities, tells us that "he entered the fourteenth year of his reign without bloodshed, and no one could say that the emperor had been responsible for anyone's murder." For Rome's senators, any emperor who refrained from having them murdered was going to be praiseworthy. But the senators were also pleased he selected sixteen of their number as a special council to advise him. Herodian goes so far as to claim that nothing was done unless these sixteen gave their unanimous consent.[57] We are under no obligation to believe this; one should not pretend that a façade of respect entailed any transfer of real power.

Despite the praise heaped upon him by the sources, there is no disguising Alexander's ultimate failure as the ruler of the Roman world. During his reign, the challenges Rome faced metastasized. Steering Rome through them required a farsighted emperor who was strong, vital, and, most crucially, respected by the soldiers. Instead, Rome was saddled with a lethargic youth incapable of seeing much beyond the palace walls. And as for the soldiers, the hardest men in the Empire were never going to take seriously a boy they thought of as weak and dominated by women. His problems began at home, where he never had the respect of the praetorians, who at one point early in his reign fought a three-day battle with the citizens of Rome, who were no longer willing to tolerate the praetorians' arrogance. Remarkably, the praetorians were losing until they resorted to the drastic action of burning down large sections of the city and threatening more of the same if the population did not desist. At another point Alexander's leading adviser, the jurist Ulpian, whom he had placed in charge of the praetorians, angered his charges. When he ran to the emperor for protection, the praetorians murdered him in front of the emperor and his mother, who pleaded helplessly that he be spared.

Imperial weakness at the center inevitably spread to other parts of the Empire, particularly the frontiers, where the soldiery was increasingly restive. Information as to what was happening in the wider Empire is scarce, and Dio passes over the problems with a single glib sentence: "Many uprisings were begun by many persons, some of which caused great alarm, but they were all put down."[58] But the historian does give at least one hint of how far the rot had gone, telling us that the legions in Mesopotamia were given over to such wanton behavior that they had murdered their commander, Flavius Heracleo, when he tried to instill a modicum of discipline.[59] This dissolution of at least a portion of the legions could not have happened at a worse time, for the Persians were once again on the march. According to Dio, the legions were refusing to fight, and many soldiers deserted and went over to the enemy.[60]

The soldiers had gotten used to being brothers in arms with an emperor who joined them on campaign and in their camps. But for much of Alexander's reign, he was much too young for the hard life of the camps, and his mother would not have been welcomed even if she was inclined to visit the legions in their forward bases. Therefore Alexander let the army, the pillar of all power within the Empire, slip from his immediate control. He and the Severan women neglected Severus's injunction to enrich the army at the expense of all other concerns. When the frontiers were stable, such neglect might not have prompted a crisis for many years. But in 230 the peaceful interval that had prevailed for Alexander's first decade of rule came to an end. He was about to be tested on the frontiers for the first time. He would be found wanting.

In 208 Ardashir had risen to power among the Sassanians in the ancient core of the Parthian Empire, Persis. In 224, at the Battle of Horomozdgan, Ardashir defeated and killed the Parthian king, Artabanus. In 227, after three more years of hard fighting, the last of the great Parthian houses submitted to Ardashir's rule, and he was able to resurrect the title "king of kings." Rome had dithered while a military superpower, united and enflamed by religion—Zoroastrianism—was born and consolidated its power. For the next four hundred years, until the Arabs carried Islam throughout the region, the Sassanids would be a constant and powerful threat to Rome.

By late 229 Ardashir, after securing his eastern border from the Kushan Empire, turned west. The first news that the Persians were on the march was when they attacked Hatra. By 230 the Sassanids were driving deep into Mesopotamia, and the legions on the spot proved unequal to the task of stopping them. A discomfited Alexander first offered terms of peace. Only when these were rebuffed did he start massing forces for a war in the east.[61] Traveling through the Danubian provinces, dispensing donatives, and giving speeches, he collected vexillations from each legion. Herodian tells us that he collected a huge force of troops in the Balkans, and one must assume the eastern legions were also being concentrated near Antioch. Upon his arrival in Antioch, he once again offered peace, but Ardashir refused to meet with the Roman representatives. Instead, he sent four hundred Persian nobles to Alexander with a demand that the Romans abandon all of Syria.[62] Alexander replied by stripping them of their fine clothing and excellent mounts, then dispersed them to work as slaves in the fields.

Before the Roman army could march, there appear to have been a few mutinies in various legions which were quickly put down. Once everything was in order, Alexander, in 231, was finally ready to start his campaign. He broke the Roman army into three parts to conduct an overly complex scheme of maneuver. One column was sent north into Armenia, the second column marched southeast toward the confluence of the Tigris and Euphrates, and the third, under his personal command, marched due east to face Ardashir's army. Alexander was either poorly advised or too headstrong to listen to wise counsel. There is an old military adage that one should not separate his force in the face of an enemy army. There are of course many exceptions to every military adage and principle, but this was not the time for one. Ardashir was in Mesopotamia with the overwhelming bulk of Persian military power. If he was defeated, everything else Rome looked to gain in Armenia or the southeast would have fallen into Roman hands by default. Moreover, a decisive defeat of the main Persian army before a new dynasty could fully secure itself on the throne would have either have collapsed Sassanid rule or left the Sassanids locked in internal fights for power for a decade or more. In either circumstance, the Persian threat would have been vanquished for many years to come, leaving Rome massive amounts of additional resources and time to deal with the threats about to explode upon its Rhine and Danube frontiers.

The best description of the campaign comes from Herodian, and it is a somewhat confusing account. The northern campaign, after a harrowing march through the mountains, appears to have met little resistance in Armenia, where it burned and pillaged the countryside all along its march route. It was Alexander's main army in the center that failed, and this in turn doomed the southern column. For reasons not adequately explained, Alexander was reluctant to bring his army against Ardashir's forces. Herodian believes that Alexander, who had no experience in war, was afraid for his life or was being restrained by his mother in an excess of maternal love.[63] In either case, the failure of the central and most powerful force to advance against the enemy freed Ardashir to concentrate most of his army against the isolated southern force. Herodian claims that the outnumbered Romans were unable to stem the Persian horde and that Rome suffered a staggering disaster.[64]

At least a part of the southern column appears to have made its way back to Antioch, so it was clearly not wiped out, although there is little doubt that the column was severely mauled. By now Alexander had had enough, and the entire army was recalled to Antioch. Herodian believes that Ardashir did not follow up on his victories because he too had taken serious losses. It is more likely that his feudal-based army had reached its time limits and was breaking up, or he understood that it had been easy to beat a Roman army that had kindly split itself into pieces. But going against the concentrated Roman army, supported by the fortress city of Antioch, with a Persian force at the end of its logistical tether, was a far different matter. Rome's army, if not defeated, knew it had not won, and it blamed the emperor's temerity for the inconclusive result. Relations between the army and the emperor were at a low enough point that Alexander overcame his mother's famed miserliness to issue a large donative to calm the soldiers.[65] With the army bought off and the Persians dispersed, Alexander planned his departure from the east.

But while he was still in Antioch, Alexander received more evil tidings: "The governors in Illyria reported that the Germans [Alemanni] had crossed the Rhine and the Danube rivers, were plundering the Roman Empire, and with a huge force were overrunning the garrison camps. . . . They reported also that the provinces of Illyricum bordering on and close to Italy were in danger."[66] Herodian reports that the news distressed Alexander. If so, he had an unusual way of showing it. Rather than going directly to the crisis point, in 233 he first went to Rome to award himself a triumph and claim the Senate's acclamation. He did, however, send the legionaries gathered from the Rhine and Danubian frontiers marching home, where they found their homes destroyed and their families killed or enslaved by the barbarians.

When Alexander finally arrived on the northern frontier in 234, he discovered the army in a foul mood. They had marched home dispirited by their poor showing in the east, for which they held the emperor to blame. Finding their homes and families ruined had further enraged them. For Alexander there was only one feasible option if he expected to hold the army's loyalty. He had to do what was expected of every Roman emperor confronted with such a crisis: lead the frontier legions in a pitiless war to demonstrate the power of Rome and avenge the legions' losses. But according to Herodian, he took another route: "He [Alexander] thought it wise, however, to send an embassy to the Germans to discuss the possibilities of a peaceful settlement. He promised to give them everything they asked and to hand over a large amount of money. . . . Consequently, Alexander undertook to buy a truce rather than risk the hazards of war."[67]

The patience of the legions was exhausted. A junior equestrian officer, C. Julius Verus Maximinus, better known as Maximinus Thrax, rose to the occasion. After gaining the support of the legions concentrated around Mainz, he had himself proclaimed emperor. His first act was to order the execution of a terrified Alexander and his mother.

Events now unfolded rapidly. Maximinus, an upstart, needed to hold the army's support, which could only be done if it was allowed to avenge itself upon the barbarians. Maximinus, therefore, spent the next three years at war. His campaigns are poorly documented, but it appears that he spent at least the first two years fighting along the Rhine frontier and then, in 238, fighting on the far side of the Danube. It has long been believed that these campaigns always took place only a short distance beyond the frontiers. But in 2008 the signs of a Roman battle were found far beyond them, in Saxony, near the town of Kalefeld. Coins found on the site prove that this battle was fought while Maximinus was emperor. The extant evidence reveals that the Roman army was returning from operations on the North German Plain. Upon reaching the Harzhorn Pass, they found it blocked by a large number of Germans and had to fight their way through. From the number of ballista bolts found on the battlefield, it is clear that it was Roman military technology that allowed them to force the pass and march to the safety of the frontier.

At no point did Maximinus ever return to Rome, although enemies were gathering there. To keep the army's support, Maximinus had promised the soldiers a huge donative and a doubling of their pay. Such largesse was costly, and there were few ways the new emperor could obtain the funds for it. Certainly he could not find them within the farms and villages of Germania. Soon he was ordering drastic measures, such as confiscations of property, which alienated him from the rich Roman elites—it was they, after all, who possessed most of the wealth Maximinus was helping himself to. He also lowered the subsidies paid to the Roman populace to help them pay for imported grain. In a twinkling, the common plebs hated the new emperor as much as the Senate did. Both the Senate and the people of Rome were further infuriated by the fact that the emperor did not seem bothered by their animosity. So when an elderly aristocrat, Gordian, and his son, Gordian II, both residing in North Africa, raised the standard of revolt, they quickly garnered support in Rome. The two Gordians had, however, neglected the first rule of a leading a successful usurpation: have as many legions backing your cause as possible. Theirs was a popular revolt; neither Gordian had a legion at his command. They were soon murdered by the governor of Numidia, Capelianus, who was one of the few legates loyal to Maximinus, and who also happened to have a legion—III Augusta—at his disposal. The Gordians had reigned for twenty days.

In backing the Gordians, the Senate had made a very stupid mistake, and as they could not expect any mercy from the fearsome Maximinus, they were forced to double down on it. After appointing a group of twenty august senators to lead the defense of the realm, they voted Maximinus an enemy of the state and declared two of their number, Pupienus and Balbinus, co-emperors. When supporters of the two dead Gordians protested that no one from their family was named as an emperor, the senate added the thirteen-year-old nephew of Gordian II—Gordian III—to the list. The Roman Empire now had four declared rulers at the same time. Only one of them, however, had over a dozen battle-hardened legions at his immediate command. Moreover, the revolt was a solution to Maximinus's biggest problem—his inability to pay his soldiers what he had promised. But there was money in Rome, and he now had a long list of senators who had revolted, making their lives and, more crucially, their property forfeit.

As soon as he heard about the revolt, Maximinus was on the march, departing for Italy with several legions before he even learned that the Gordians were dead. But he now made a crucial error. Upon arriving at Aquileia—one of the few fortified cities in Italy—he decided to lay siege. Aquileia was the first major city any barbarian force would encounter after entering Italy, so naturally its fortifications were strong and well maintained. This was the reason Marcus Aurelius had used the city as his base at the start of his campaigns against the Marcomanni. Maximinus had taken his eye off the prize, Rome, which was now virtually undefended and in turmoil. The generals were always reluctant, of course, to leave an enemy-controlled fortified base in their rear during active operations. But it is doubtful that the garrison could have caused much trouble had it ventured out. Moreover, there was no supply line the base could have stuck: once the legions were in Rome, they would draw their supplies from the city, the countryside, and the port of Ostia. The correct solution was to bypass Aquileia and get to Rome and take control.

Maximinus, however, allowed the siege to drag on until a disgruntled army turned on him. He and his son were murdered by the soldiers of II Parthica in the late spring of 238. Rather remarkably, the army did not proclaim a new emperor. Instead, they settled back and awaited developments. Word soon came that the praetorians, who were fearful for their own position and safety, had settled matters. Pupienus and Balbinus were murdered, and Gordian III became the sole emperor. This was fine with the generals who had fought alongside Maximinus, including two future emperors, Valerian and Decius, who now entered Rome and awarded themselves positions of power from which they could control the young Gordian III. The praetorians, who had once again become a highly polished palace guard without any real fighting skills, acquiesced to the military takeover, as did the Senate. They had little choice, for the Danubian legions were still in Italy, awaiting their promised rewards.

It had been an eventful year, one that had set a single-year record for the number of emperors—six, or seven if Maximinus's son is considered a co-emperor with his father. The turmoil was a harbinger of what was to come, since the death of Maximinus Thrax is considered by most historians to be the start of the military anarchy that was to do so much to worsen the other crises that now beset the Empire. It is worth halting the chronologically based narrative at this point to spend some time examining the new and dangerous challenges Rome was now confronting.

CHAPTER 12 | New Threats

The Sassanid Empire

For Rome, the Sassanids were a threat on a scale the Parthians never were, not only because of their greater military capacity, but also because of their ambition. The Parthians had expended much of their energy defending their positions in Armenia and Mesopotamia. When they did go on the offensive, it was typically to make gains on the margins of the Roman Empire. On a few occasions, when they thought Rome's emperor was weak or distracted, they would risk launching their armies on deep raids of Roman territory. When they did, cities and fortresses might fall, and the lands the Parthians passed through would be devastated, with great loss of life. But even if the Roman military was slow to react, the raiders never stayed long, for there were always limits to how long what amounted to a feudal army could be kept in the field. Eventually the Parthians would leave, dragging their ill-gotten gains back to their homeland. There was never any serious Parthian program of conquest aiming to replace the Romans in the eastern half of their Empire.

This was not the case with the Sassanids, who, according to Dio and Herodian, claimed a right to rule over every region conquered by Cyrus the Great and his Achaemenid successors in the centuries before Alexander the Great dismantled the first Persian Empire.[1] According to Herodian,

> The entire continent opposite Europe, separated from it by the Aegean Sea and the Propontic Gulf [Sea of Marmara], and the region called Asia he wished to recover for the Persian empire. Believing these regions to be his by inheritance, he declared that all the countries in that

area, including Ionia and Caria, had been ruled by Persian governors, beginning with Cyrus, who first made the Median empire Persian, and ending with Darius, the last of the Persian monarchs, whose kingdom was seized by Alexander the Great. He asserted that it was therefore proper for him to recover for the Persians the kingdom which they had formerly possessed.[2]

After the death of Artabanus the Parthian nobility was quickly brought to heel, and many of the great families were brought into the imperial court, while Ardashir appointed members of his own family to all of the kingships within the Empire. Unlike Parthian rulers, these kings were never allowed to become powerful warlords capable of straying from central control. With the throne secure, Ardashir considered his position strong enough to engage with the powers on his borders. He appears to have moved first against the Kushan, who controlled a vast empire straddling both sides of the Hindu Kush. The Sassanids were unable to collapse the Kushan state, but it appears that they conquered Bactria (Afghanistan) and may have exterminated Kushan power north of the Kush. Still, throughout the third century and well into the fourth, the Sassanids could never ignore Kushan. Kushan power was never as great or as threatening as Rome's, but it could be ignored only at some peril. Moreover, though we know almost nothing of other trouble along the Sassanid frontiers, the level of violence must have been great, since most of the tribes migrating toward Rome would first have encountered and tested the strength of the Sassanids.[3]

In 232 Ardashir felt ready to turn west and face Alexander Severus's Roman Empire. Most of what followed has already been related in this book's main narrative. But one big strategic change must be noted here. For over two hundred years the Parthians had been on the strategic defensive, with Roman armies routinely marching deep into the Empire to sack Parthian cities, including their capital at Ctesiphon. From the rise of the Sassanids until Justinian rose to power in Constantinople, the Romans were almost always on the strategic defensive. There would be periodic Roman offensives, but these often met with disaster, and even when there was some measure of Roman success, it was offset by the dissipation of resources that could have been better employed elsewhere. As we shall see, Rome had the strategic answer to the Sassanid threat: fortresses along the main avenues of attack, backed by fortified cities in the interior and Roman legions that could concentrate to defend key points. But having the solution is one thing; adhering to a winning strategy while under pressure to do something more proactive is quite another.

Rome appears never to have understood that the Sassanids presented a fundamentally different level of threat than the Parthians, or that the old methods of dealing with the Persians—invade, sack, pillage—were no longer going to hold the line. In the Sassanids Rome faced an enemy capable of employing more powerful forces, for longer periods, to seize the strategic initiative, which, from at least the reign of Trajan, had lain with the Romans. What saved Roman power in the long run was that the Sassanids, despite claiming to want to reestablish the Achaemenid Empire, never truly had any such plans. How else does one explain the speed with which they abandoned the great city of Antioch after capturing it twice in the third century? Either the Parthians were more interested in booty and carrying off slaves or they realized they could never hold territory so distant from the core of their power and within the second heartland of Roman power. To understand why, one has only to note that the Sassanid army had to carry its supplies across hundreds of miles of desert, while the Romans could use sea transport to mass and supply their forces. Moreover, the Sassanid army was still not a professional force comparable to the Roman army. The Sassanids had centralized their power far more than the previous Parthian rulers, but their army was still more feudal than the long-serving legions. Consequently, there were still limits to how long their forces could stay in the field, since the army was prone to breaking up once it had secured all the loot available for easy taking.

But, in 235 Ardashir captured the cities of Nisibis and Carrhae, and later, in 241, he captured and destroyed the city of Hatra. These combined captures gave the Sassanids control of the terminus of each major approach route to the heart of the Roman Empire and overthrew the defensive frontier established by Septimius Severus. The speed at which these cities fell also demonstrated that the Sassanids had regained the old Persian skills in siege warfare, something the Parthians rarely did very well.

Climate

Although the specific impacts of climate during the formation and decline of the Roman Empire are hotly debated by historians and specialists in the field, few doubt that climate had a substantial impact on the Empire, and hence on its developing strategies.[4] Several strategically relevant points must be made about climate change during the Roman period. The first is the sheer size of the Roman Empire, which, stretched over three continents, meant that the impact of climate change was never even. Consequently, even if one knows the broad changes in climatic factors, such as temperature and rainfall, these aspects of the problem are not going to tell you much about their impact in North Africa as opposed to Britain. For instance, a slight temperature rise might increase the amount of arid territory in North Africa while increasing rainfall in northern Europe. Moreover, given the Empire's size, there were always multiple micro-climates that varied considerably from one another and could change in unpredictable ways.

It is also worth noting that the Holocene Period, in which we now live, began at the end of the last Ice Age, approximately 11,500 years ago. Since the second half of that period, which coincides with the birth of civilization, the global temperature has been remarkably stable, never moving more than a few degrees in any direction. Still, within this range there has been tremendous volatility, with temperatures even a few degrees lower creating a mini–Ice Age capable of causing profound societal turmoil.[5] On the other hand, an increase of a few degrees has historically been equated with the Roman Climatic Optimum and the Medieval Warm Period, when societies around the globe flourished.[6] So, although every specific impact of climate change during the rise and fall of Rome cannot be identified, the overall picture is evident. During what is known as the Roman Climatic Optimum, stretching from 100 BCE to about 200 CE, temperatures were two or three degrees warmer than at present. During these three centuries Rome thrived as the economy and trade boomed and even the lot of the Empire's poor improved markedly. But after 250 CE came a few hundred years of cooling that correlate with Rome's collapse in the west and the advent of the Dark Ages.[7] Within both of these climatic periods, there was still variability: there were years, even decades, of cooling during the Roman Climatic Optimum, as well as the opposite, decades of slight warming interspersed with the centuries-long cooling trend.

Before deciding how Roman strategy could adjust to a post-250 climate crisis, it is crucial to comprehend, that unlike today, when climate variations are continuously tracked by satellite and an array of sensitive terrestrial instrumentation, the changing climate was nearly invisible to the Romans. As the changes took place over multiple lifetimes that included sporadic multi-year reversals, it would have been impossible to identify either a cooling or a warming trend and then attribute it to a natural phenomenon that was likely to stretch out for centuries. What the Romans could see was the direct impact of the weather, but they would have viewed as the work of capricious gods. Droughts and floods were something to be endured, not planned for.

Moreover, although the Pax Romana allowed increased food production, much of this was absorbed by a growing population that left many regions with only a narrow margin of agricultural surplus every year. Thus, even small perturbations in the climate could push some regions to the edge. And even if they could adapt sufficiently to feed themselves, the lack of any surplus denied Rome the taxable resources that underpinned Roman power. Over time societies would adapt to the new conditions, no matter the severity. But they would do so at a lower standard of living, for Roman technology was not advanced enough to help societies adapt in ways that would make any measurable difference in sustaining the agricultural base Rome had enjoyed during the interval of the Climatic Optimum. As agricultural production dwindled, so did Rome's capacity to absorb shocks and maintain power on the margins of the Empire.

All the available data agree that the rise of Rome coincided with a uniquely stable environment. Even with the generally low level of solar activity until 600 CE—activity that correlates closely to natural climate change—the period from 100 BCE to 200 CE stands out as an exceptional stable few centuries. Moreover, it appears that even global tectonics were conspiring with the sun to present Rome with a unique environment for increasing its power, as this period was also remarkable for a lack of volcanic activity. Literary evidence indicates that even the volatile fault that stretches across Anatolia, the Aegean, and deep into the Mediterranean was unusually silent for much of this time.

But starting in 200 CE and accelerating in the middle of the third century, climate becomes increasingly unstable, as compared to the prior three centuries of the Climatic Optimum. Overall, proxy data demonstrates a shift toward a broadly cooler, drier climate, particularly in northern Europe, throughout the tumultuous third century. Even volcanic and earthquake activity picked up through the period, although both eased in the fourth century. But the major volcanic eruptions that are clustered in the middle of the third century were likely triggers for rapid, multi-year climate changes that would have reinforced any ongoing solar forcing. Such rapid changes, even if they persisted for only short periods, would have wreaked havoc with food production across much of the Roman Empire, coinciding precisely with the most difficult crises the Empire had ever faced up till then.[8] While evidence for the precise causes of the great migrations of peoples from the vast Asian steppes is lacking, it is almost inconceivable that climate change's impact on pasture lands was not one of the primary drivers.[9]

Clearly much work remains to be done to match climatic changes with actual events on the ground. But just as clearly, a changing climate set in motion a series of shocks and events that Rome found increasingly difficult to overcome. Moreover, there was no way for Rome to foresee and plan for the consequences of a changing climate. How could an emperor bring together his *consilium* to discuss ways to prepare for a predicted lack of rainfall deep within the Eurasian land mass that would impel the Huns to head west, when they had no idea that such a chain of events was even possible? Thus, for much of the second half of the Empire's existence, strategy became a series of reactions and adaptions to macro-events fundamentally catalyzed by climate change.

Disease

For the Romans, disease was a part of life. With no idea what germs were, no sure way to preserve food for extended periods, and clean water always at a premium, repeated exposure to disease kept average life spans low. This in turn stunted the growth and development of much of the population. But this had always been part of the human condition and was therefore deemed unremarkable. Disease was what it had always been, a persistent backdrop to all other activities.[10] What was remarkable was novel pestilences and plagues that struck with virtually no warning and spread rapidly through a population. In some cases the pestilence could be localized and deaths kept in the thousands. But in others, thankfully rare, a plague would break out and kill millions through huge swaths of territory.[11]

What was required for a devastating plague was a bridging mechanism that could bring a deadly pathogen from one germ pool into another whose population had never been exposed to that particular germ or virus before. In the modern era, this is remarkably simple: the world is interconnected as never before, and a new pathogen can cross continents in hours. In the ancient world this speed of transmission was rare, since the great population pools within which pathogens developed were widely separated. Any carrier of a plague had a good chance of dying long before he could make it to another population center. But if a new pathogen did find its way into the Empire, it could move with astonishing speed, because the integration of the Empire's economy provided the pathways upon which any germ could hitch a ride. And if moving by sea, it could travel almost a hundred miles a day.[12]

By far the worst epidemic to strike Rome was what is commonly called the Antonine Plague, which struck in 165 CE. It originated somewhere deep in Eurasia, likely China, and moved into the Parthian Empire, where Romans fighting in Mesopotamia caught it and brought it back to the eastern cities. When these soldiers returned to their bases along the Danube, they carried the plague with them into the heart of the Western Empire. The epidemic, most likely smallpox or some ancestral antecedent of it, raged for fifteen years and lingered in some regions for yet another decade. The human cost was horrific, and estimates of the death rate in the Empire range from a low of 10 percent to a high of a quarter of the population. The sources are all in agreement that the legions were particularly hard hit by the plague: "in Rome and throughout Italy and the provinces most people, and almost all soldiers in the army were afflicted by weakness."[13] This alone is sufficient to account for the astounding recruitment measures Marcus Aurelius is recorded to have undertaken to fill the legions facing the Marcomanni along the Danube frontier.

Galen, the most famous doctor in the Roman world, apparently left Rome to escape the plague, but he was recalled by Marcus in 168 to tend to him and the royal household in Aquileia. He recorded his experience:

> On my arrival in Aquileia the plague attacked more destructively than ever before, so the emperors fled immediately to Rome with a small force of men. For the rest of us, survival became very difficult for a long time. Most, indeed, died, the effects of the plague being exacerbated by the fact that all this was occurring in the middle of winter.[14]

It is noteworthy that this level of virulence persisted four years after the plague had first established itself. Just how deadly the plague was is also attested to in Jerome's *Chronicle* of 168: "There was such a great plague throughout the whole world that the Roman army was reduced almost to extinction."[15] Our sources can always be counted on to tell us how events impacted the army, since the army was one of the senatorial class's primary concerns. But the economic impact, not usually an area of interest for ancient writers, also faced catastrophe. We know, for instance, that there was a huge collapse in tree felling throughout northern Europe during and immediately after the plague. This corresponded to a significant curtailment in construction projects and the use of charcoal. The impact on mining may have been even more serious. According to an interesting study of Greenlandic ice cores, there was a dramatic fall in European lead pollution at the time of the plague. The authors of this study concluded that "the Antonine plague marked the turning point between high levels of lead-silver production during the Roman Empire period, and much lower levels observed from the mid-second century until the mid-eighth century. The plague disrupted mining through high mortality in, and flight from, mining regions, and reduced demand through population loss."[16]

It is possible that historians have made too much of the plague, as archeologists have done a sizable amount of rural survey work that demonstrates that the Empire's population density grew steadily to a fourth-century peak.

How then do we account for the difference between our narrative sources and the archeological evidence? There are likely several explanations that acted in tandem. The first is that the plague was so fast-moving and deadly that the shock of so many persons dying in so short a time period left an indelible impression for our sources to pass on. There is a very good possibility that this plague mostly afflicted those concentrated in ports, cities, and troop barracks, and may have spared most remote rural areas. Of course, these same cities that took the hardest hits are where our sources are most likely resident. Finally, Roman society was stalked by death, and as much as half the population may have died by age fifteen. Given the food surplus that went hand-in-hand with any pre-modern plague, a society trapped by Malthus's arithmetic would have recovered very quickly. Rome, having recovered from the effects of the Antonine Plague, was soon struck by a second pestilence, the Plague of Cyprian.[17] This time the plague struck when Rome was ill prepared to cope, smack in the middle of the third century. It is first attested in Alexandria, the great transport terminal and entrepôt for Indian and Chinese goods, in 249. It was in Rome by 251.[18] The contemporary record, as one might expect at a time when the fabric of the Empire was being torn apart by invasion and civil war, is sparse. One of the better sources is Cyprian, bishop of Carthage, who describes it in stark terms:

> These are adduced as proof of faith: that, as the strength of the body is dissolved, the bowels dissipate in a flow; that a fire that begins in the inmost depths burns up into wounds in the throat; that the intestines are shaken with continuous vomiting; that the eyes are set on fire from the force of the blood; that the infection of the deadly putrefaction cuts off the feet or other extremities of some; and that as weakness prevails through the failures and losses of the bodies, the gait is crippled or the hearing is blocked or the vision is blinded.[19]

When added to all of the other shocks being inflicted upon the Empire during this period, clearly this new plague could easily have provided the tipping point that would bring down the Empire. The saving grace appears to be that the barbarians invading the Empire were sickened by the plagues as badly as and possibly worse than the Romans. As related in the *Historia Augusta*:

> The favor of heaven furthered Claudius' success. For a great multitude, the survivors of the barbarian tribes, who had gathered in Haemimontum [Thrace], were so stricken with famine and pestilence that Claudius now scorned to conquer them further. . . . And so at

length that most cruel of wars was brought to an end, and the Roman nation was freed from its terrors.[20]

Similarly:

> During this same period the Scythians attempted to plunder in Crete and Cyprus as well, but everywhere their armies were likewise stricken with pestilence and so were defeated.[21]

As this book is being written, the world is experiencing a modern plague—COVID-19. This pandemic has killed millions and sickened probably hundreds of millions more. It has also closed huge swaths of the global economy and disrupted the lives of almost every living human being. Consider how terrible the COVID-19 impacts have been in just the developed world, where almost everyone has access to first-class medical treatment and governments are capable of spending trillions of dollars to alleviate the impact of economic closures. One can probably just barely imagine from this experience the impact of a disease many times more virulent than COVID-19 in a society with no serious treatment methods, no hope of a vaccine, no excess production and food capacity, and no money fountains (central banks) to keep priming the economy. Add to this the fact that barbarians and Sassanid armies were breaching the frontiers and driving deep into the Empire, along with multiple civil wars, and one can begin to understand the full impact the plague had on the Empire's fortunes, as well as the strategic dilemmas confronting the emperors who ruled during this period.

The Barbarians

Tacitus's *Germania*, written at the end of the first century, lists dozens of tribes beyond the Rhine and Danube frontiers. But by the middle of the third century, most of these have disappeared from the record.[22] In their place stands a much smaller number of tribal amalgamations, whose names dominate the sources until the fall of the Western Empire and beyond. Along the lower Rhine and across the Agri Decumates we find the Alamanni; a bit after their appearance the Franks are recorded along the upper Rhine; and along much of the Danube are the Goths, still broken into two large federations, the Tervingi and Greuthungi. Other groups that begin moving toward the Roman frontiers and swarming into the Empire in the early fifth century can already be detected right behind these larger amalgamations, including Saxons, Jutes, Angles, Vandals, Burgundians, Alans, and finally, pushing all before them, the Huns.

These confederations were more closely bonded economically and politically than the tribes had ever been. One should not, however, oversell this.
The old tribes, such as the Cherusci and the Chatti, continued to exist and
even had their own kings. In fact, at the Battle of Strasbourg (357), the emperor, Julian, faced seven kings and ten princes of the Alemanni. But these
kings and princes were following the orders of a high king, Chnodomarius,
who had mustered them for battle. In the past, a truly charismatic individual, such as Arminius—the victor at the Battle of Teutoburg Wald—
could bring the tribes together for at least a short period, but other examples
are rare. But starting in the third century high kings among the Alemanni
and other tribal groups, particularly the Goths, became the rule rather than
the exception.[23] The title of high king was not a hereditary one, and the
Roman sources never deigned to explain how the system worked. We can,
however, assume that we see the very beginnings of a feudal system, where a
high king expected lesser kings and princes to muster their armed followers
on demand, as well as provide him with some type of financial or in-kind
tribute.

What brought this political transformation about? Most crucially, there
was an economic revolution all along the frontier that gradually spread eastward. When Julius Caesar first led his legions into Germania, the tribes were
generally nomadic, as they had no way to maintain the fertility of the soil.
That meant that family groupings would have to pick up and move every few
years in a version of slash and burn agriculture. For the frontier tribes, one
of the great benefits of living alongside the Roman Empire was the regular
transfusion of knowledge, including farming techniques. By the end of the
first century German farmers were settling in one place for their entire lives,
as villages grew much larger and persisted in one location for generations.
By the fourth century, this knowledge had moved deep inland, and there is
substantial archaeological evidence of large Gothic settlements north of the
Black Sea.

Settled agriculture always results in a population explosion, and there is
evidence of immense population growth throughout the Empire's frontier
regions in the two centuries of the Principate. Increased food production is
also the handmaiden of increasing wealth and worker specialization. So it is
little wonder that we find mines capable of producing millions of pounds of
raw iron deep in Poland and that burial sites continually amaze archeologists
with the amount of gold and silver buried with elite personages, as well as
the beautiful craftsmanship demonstrated by jewelry makers. Wealth would
also have increased and become more centralized because of trading with

Rome, as well as the subsidies Rome often paid tribal leaders in return for peace and support.

This economic revolution naturally led to a corresponding social revolution. One can easily imagine how much the prestige and power of a tribal leader increased when he had large amounts of Roman gold and silver to distribute among his followers, particularly if he was able to gain such subsidies regularly. The formula was simple: more food and worker specialization meant that the tribes could afford a full-time warrior class. As the increasing wealth was centralized, some tribal leaders were able to amass numbers of these specialized warriors. This permanent warrior class could then be employed to increase their leader's sway among weaker tribes. This turned into—if one can use the term for a driver of violence and conquest—a virtuous circle, as every military victory increased the prestige and wealth of the victor and drew more chieftains and their warriors into his orbit. Once again, this is not a feudal system yet, but it is rapidly heading down that road.

These tribal amalgamations were something new in the strategic firmament. Individually, none of them could threaten the power of Rome, but they also could not be easily defeated. In the first centuries of the Empire, a well-organized assault upon a single tribe could cause substantial destruction, and Rome's expeditionary force could return to its frontier bases secure in the knowledge that the barbarians had been cowed, likely for years to come. By the end of the second century, however, this had changed, and one has only to look at how hard-fought were the campaigns of Marcus Aurelius to get a feel for how profound such changes were. Barbarians, as was discussed earlier, could never be taken for granted, but even after the great reverse at Teutoburg Wald, Germanicus could still march to the Elbe River confident that his force would not meet its match. Marcus Aurelius, on the other hand, fought for years with practically no gains. Similarly, Maximinus Thrax, whose rise to the purple marked the beginning of the third century's military anarchy, began his reign with a plunge into Germania. Herodian tells us that he claimed victory, but also that the Roman casualties were severe. He appears to have made no impression on the Alemanni, who were almost constantly on the attack in the following decades.

Still, the frontier defenses and the legions were sufficient to hold off even an amalgamation of tribes, something that would not be true if the Empire's resources were stretched by multiple threats. For instance, a Sassanid attack that coincided with massive barbarian incursions would stress the Empire to the point where disaster loomed. If a civil war was added to the mix, disintegration could not be far behind. Such coordination between the Sassanids and the barbarians was never possible, and it is exceedingly unlikely that the various barbarian amalgamations ever coordinated their activities. Still, the barbarians, from long association with Rome, were attuned to what was going on within the Empire. They knew when the legions were denuding the frontiers for a war in the east, or when the Romans were distracted by civil war. They could feel the vigilance along the frontiers lessen, and they knew when it was time to roll the iron dice of war.

Time was also on the barbarians' side. Their numbers were growing, as was their wealth. Both were driving a militarization of Germanic society, which was always going to find an outlet testing itself against the Romans. Rome was able to recover from its near-death experience in the third century, but so did its enemies. There is little evidence that the barbarians across the frontiers of Rome were even much damaged during this century. Moreover, larger and more warlike groups of Goths, Alans, Vandals, and finally Huns were approaching. This mass would push against the frontiers of the Empire until, at the start of the fifth century, they broke like a torrent upon a cracking dam.

A Concluding Thought

A casual observer glancing at a map and tallying Rome's resources at the start of the third century would be hard pressed to spot any weaknesses that may have grown since the early days of the Principate. If anything, the Empire appeared stronger and wealthier than it ever was. Mesopotamia had recently been added as a province at the expense of the Parthians; the population was recovering from the plague and may already have exceeded the numbers it boasted during Augustus's reign. All of this was protected by the fearsome legions and a sound frontier defensive system. But Rome's strategic approach, as well as its defenses, was built to face the challenges and threats of past centuries. Roman strategy was looking backward, and in a pattern repeated by strategists for the next two eons, they were fully prepared to fight the last war. Still, Rome had the resources to adapt on the fly. What stopped them from doing so was the internal rot of their political system. At a time when Rome needed to marshal all of its resources to confront enemies on the far side of the frontier, it was beset by civil war and political anarchy, both of which wreaked havoc on the Roman economic system. Periodically a military strongman, such as Diocletian or Constantine, would establish himself at the top, halting and for a time reversing the rot. But the center could never hold, and within a generation or two Rome was once again at war with itself. This systemic political decay accelerated the Empire's political and economic fragmentation and was the final strategic change Rome faced in its last century. It was the failure to meet this challenge that made it impossible to successfully confront all of the others. In the end, Rome's demise was not brought about by an accumulation of external shocks. Those could have been weathered. It was Rome's continuous suicide attempts, as the elites that sat atop the Roman political, military, and economic systems placed their personal ambitions above the needs of the state, that caused the collapse of the Roman Empire.

CHAPTER 13 | The Crisis of the Third Century

ANYONE TRYING TO discern a coherent line of Roman strategic thinking during the great and repeated crises of the third century is likely on a fool's errand.[1] For fifty years, after the death of Severus Alexander, the Empire was wracked by barbarian invasions, civil wars, famine, disease, and, finally, ruinous conflicts with Persia. Beset by the depredations of powerful new tribal amalgamations—Franks, Alemanni, and Goths—the legions along the northern frontiers were hard pressed to hold the line, a military situation made much worse by having to find the troops and resources to counter powerful Sassanid attacks in the east. Disruptions along the entire frontier were not beyond Rome's capacity to fend off and reverse, if not for the internal political collapse in which at least fifty-one individuals claimed the throne in as many years. In these circumstances, strategy was no longer a matter of foresight and planning, but rather a constant series of adaptions as each new threat presented itself. That Rome survived can be attributed to several factors. First, and most crucially, there were limits to how far barbarian forces could penetrate the Empire, as their goals were never to destroy the Empire but rather to enter it and partake of Roman bounty in the frontier provinces. At this point there were no indications that the barbarians had the capacity to sustain an offensive far beyond the frontiers. That would come. Consequently, the richer provinces went untouched throughout the century. It was from these regions, which Chris Wickham has termed the "tax spine" of the Empire, that Rome found the resources to mount a counterattack and finance a recovery. Second, even the Sassanids, for all of their fearsome power, apparently never wanted to conquer and hold territory. Although they captured Antioch twice during this period, there is no evidence that they ever took measures to put a political and administrative structure in place that would have begun the process of integrating the Levant into the Sassanid Empire. And finally, the Romans adapted their military method just enough to cope with the new challenges confronting them. By any measure, it had been a close run, but the Empire possessed just enough latent power to survive the storm. When it was over, we find the Romans adopting new methods of imperial control as well as reorganizing their military to meet the emerging threats that nearly ruined the Empire between 235 and 285.[2]

One is tempted to skip past these tumultuous years and come out the other side to start discussing strategy again. But, although the Romans are by necessity practicing a policy of rapid adaption throughout these fifty years, there are still moments of high-level strategic thinking as desperate emperors worked to retrieve seemingly hopeless situations. For students of strategy, a close look at certain segments of the crisis years may give them crucial ideas for contextualizing similar problems in our own near future, given that many nations and leaders seem to have adopted a seat-of-the-pants approach to strategy in the wake of rapid change and renewed great-state competition. In fact, in a recent presentation from a retired four-star general given at the Marine Corps War College, the general advised students to take a close look at the Crisis of the Third Century, and particularly Aurelian's reign, for inspiration that could come in handy in the years ahead. He particularly wanted them to study how Aurelian thought about the truly enormous challenges he faced upon his accession and then how he executed a series of limited operations that built upon two single strategic ideas: reuniting the Empire and regaining control of the frontiers. In the end, Aurelian truly earned the cognomen "Restorer of the World." How he did so explains how the stormy years of Rome's first truly great crisis were weathered well enough to ensure nearly two hundred more years of continued existence.

But before arriving at Aurelian's moment in history, there is a story of decay and Roman strategic foundering to examine. That brings us back to Maximinus, for even while he was still emperor there were already hints that things were beginning to unravel. In 236 there had been Gothic attacks on the Black Sea ports of Olbia and Tyras, and in the same year Ardashir moved once again to the offensive, capturing Nisibis, Carrhae, and perhaps Singara. Finally, the Goths broke into Lower Moesia and pillaged the city of Istrus, while the Carpi, a Dacian tribe, crossed the Danube to the west. The local governor, Menophilus, short of troops, was forced to buy off the Carpi's allies—Goths and Sarmatians—just to hold the Carpi in check, and that barely. Most dangerously, the Roman response in the east was slow in coming, as Maximinus first had to settle the northern frontiers; then, after his murder, Rome required even more time to complete yet another political realignment. When this was done, the thirteen-year-old Gordian III remained emperor, but he was surrounded by the Empire's warlords—hard-bitten generals mostly from the equestrian or lower classes. These uncompromising men for the most part had not come up through the Roman political and administrative system, but rather had earned their right to rule by fighting Rome's wars.

They were led by the new praetorian perfect, C. Furius Sabinius Timesitheus, who gathered enough power to be able to force the emperor to marry his daughter. The first order of business was to secure the Eastern Empire, where the fortress cities that guarded the edge of the frontier were either already in Ardashir's control or under siege. Despite the danger, Roman armies did not begin their march eastward until 242, when they would face a new Sassanid ruler, Ardahir's son Sapor I. The reason for the three-year delay is unknown; in the past it rarely took much over a year to concentrate the western legions in the east. One can assume that Gordian III and Timesitheus were having trouble gathering enough troops, since an unsettled Rhine and Danubian frontier limited what forces could be safely drawn away from the north. The threat was considered great enough for Timesitheus to divert the Roman army, marching east, off its line of march to push back the Carpi and Goths to the far side of the Danube. Still more time was then needed to restore the frontier defenses.

At this point Gordian III and Timesitheus made a serious error: they cut off the subsidies and other payments the Sarmatians and Goths had been promised by Menophilus. Local tribal leaders counted on these regular subsidies to remain in power: they distributed the majority of these funds to their most powerful supporters, who in turn paid them out to their supporters. Once these subsidies were cut, only two things could happen, both of them bad for Rome. First, tribal leaders would lose the influence required to effectively rally their warriors to resist the great tribal migrations bursting forth from the Eurasian steppes. The second possibility is that tribal leaders with nothing more to gain from Rome would either take the lead in raiding into the Empire or throw in their lot with migrating tribes ready to do so. Cutting subsidies was a good strategic option when Rome was not facing other threats: the withdrawal of funds on a targeted basis would cause a great deal of instability along specific sections of the frontiers, making the impacted tribes easier to overcome in one of Rome's periodic expeditions across the northern frontiers. But because Rome needed every spare soldier to fight in the east, it was not an optimal time to start upsetting the northern tribes.

There is no way, given Rome's hundreds of years' experience dealing with the Germans and using subsidies as the Empire's primary diplomatic tool, that the generals surrounding Gordian III did not know the consequences of these cuts. One suspects that the cuts were forced by severe financial problems, which are attested to by continuing recoinages and a further debasement of Roman currency. If not, then they were being foolishly optimistic about their ability to win a war in the east and return the army to the Rhine before the northern deluge swamped all before it.

By the summer of 243 the Roman army was massed around Antioch and ready to conduct operations. Edessa also soon fell, and after a major battle at Resaina, Nisibis and Singara were regained.[3] There were, however, further delays, forced by Timesitheus's untimely death and the time it took to appoint a new praetorian perfect, Julius Philip. But by early winter 244 the Romans were once again on the march. At first everything seemed to go well. Rome's legions crossed the Euphrates at Zeugma and went on to capture Carrhae. At some point Sapor I had gathered enough forces to launch a counterattack. The Romans were defeated in the fighting at Misiche, and Gordian III may have been wounded.[4] After this, our sources are so confused that we may never know what took place. What is certain is that Gordian died (or more likely was assassinated), that the army was in dire straits, and that Philip was elevated from praetorian prefect to emperor. Since then Philip has borne much of the blame for Gordian III's death—*cui bono*.[5]

Philip acted fast to end a war Rome was surely not winning, probably hoping to avoid being tarred with the defeat. If so, he failed, as his hasty truce with Sapor was in Rome considered a humiliation. It is easy to see why, for he gave the Persians a free hand in Armenia and reportedly paid a ransom of 500,000 silver dinars for the army's safe passage back to Syria. Agreeing to such a truce is proof that the Roman army was in serious trouble. Still, the fact that Sapor so readily agreed to it must be counted as evidence that the Sassanid army was also on the point of breaking up. But it was Philip who was on the strictest timeline, as he had to rush to Rome to secure his hold on power throughout the Empire before usurpers arose. As events would show, Philip was right to worry about competitors for the purple.

He could not stay in Rome long, for some of the German tribes, led by the Carpi, were raiding deep into the Balkans. By 245 Philip was campaigning on the Danube, but he does not appear to have had sufficient military success to claim any titles. He was forced to return to Rome in 247 to oversee lavish celebrations for the one thousandth anniversary of the city's founding in 248. The expenses of this lavish event were added to the ransom paid to Sapor, the large donatives required to pacify the army, and the general cost of maintaining the Empire's defenses. In total, financial needs were far outstripping imperial revenues. The need to conserve resources and cut spending likely drove Philip's decision to cut off the remaining subsidies going to the Goths, which had remained in place after Gordian III ended subsidies to other tribes in the regions. Cutting these funds was another unforced error, because the Danubian defenses in lower Moesia had not yet been fully restored in the wake of the Carpi's incursions. Just as troubling, the Danubian legions, feeling their power, declared Claudius Marinus Pacatianus emperor, while in the east the legions declared Iotapianus emperor. The fact that usurpers could arise within armies commanded by his close family members, including his brother in Syria, panicked Philip, who went before the Senate and offered to step down. He was saved by a senator named Decius, who Zosimus tells us was gifted with every virtue. Decius advised patience, saying that none of these troubles would last long. One wonders at the source of Decius's insight, but he was correct: within weeks both usurpers were murdered by their troops.

No sooner was the threat of usurpation removed than new troubles arose. In 248 large numbers of Goths, along with their Carpi allies and other tribes, invaded the Empire. Philip, unwilling to risk joining an army that may still have been in revolt, sent Decius to take command. We do not know exactly what actions Decius took, but, within six months he had returned discipline to the legions and halted, for a time, the barbarian incursions. The Danubian legions were so taken with their new commander that they declared him emperor. Philp had no choice now but to collect an army and march against the new and dangerous usurper. The armies, as was typical, put the job of defending the frontiers on pause until the matter of succession was decided. Near Verona, in the summer of 249, Decius won an easy victory, reminding all concerned that a hastily recruited and barely trained army, no matter its size, was no match for the scarred, battle-hardened veterans of the frontier legions.

> The supporters of Decius, though they knew that the enemy had greatly the advantage in numbers, still retained their confidence, trusting to the general skill and prudence of Decius in affairs. And when the two armies engaged, although the one was superior in number, yet the other so excelled it in discipline and conduct, that a great number of Philip's partisans were slain and he himself amongst them, together with his son, on whom he had conferred the title of *Caesar*. Decius thus acquired the empire.[6]

Decius went on to Rome, where he conducted ceremonies to purify the city and return Romans to their earlier piety. As part of this program, he reinstated the office of censor, and even asked Valerian, a future emperor, to take the position. Valerian wisely refused any position as dangerous as supervising Roman morality and spending. Decius, who wanted Rome to return to the old gods, started, perhaps unintentionally, a new round of Christian persecutions. By the end of his reign these were easing off, but the Christian writers who dominate our sources have colored our perceptions of Decius to the present day. Consequently, the return of the plague, commonly called the Plague of Cyprian, is laid at his doorstep as punishment for turning on the Christian community, as is Decius's eventual destruction.

In 250 Decius was once again with the Danubian legions. The civil war, in what was to become a repeating reaction to turmoil within the Empire, had emboldened many of the barbarian tribes along the Danube to again test the frontiers. The Carpi attacked Dacia, Moesia Superior, and the western portions of Moesia Inferior, while the Goths moved against the central portions of Moesia Inferior. This time, the Goths were led by a king, Cniva, with some military talent and the charisma to hold the Gothic tribal units together even when adversity struck. Cniva did not, however, get off to an auspicious start, for his forces were repelled by the local governor and future emperor, Trebonianus Gallus, at Novae. Undeterred, he bypassed Novae and pressed deeper into the Balkans to besiege the city of Nicopolis. In the meantime Decius marched along the Danube, defeating the Carpi bands he encountered and forcing their return north of the Danube. That accomplished, the emperor turned the army to pursue the Cniva, who were marching toward the city of Philippopolis, already under siege by another Gothic force. At Beroea, Cniva turned on the Roman army, catching it resting, its guard down. The Romans were severely handled by the Goths, forcing Decius to retreat to the Danube fortifications around Oescus. Much of Moesia was now abandoned to Cniva's Goths, who returned to the siege of Philippopolis; its governor, Lucius Priscus, after declaring himself emperor, surrendered the city.[7]

Cniva had done what he set out to do. Knowing that he did not have enough troops or resources to hold what he had gained against the might of the Roman Empire, which would be slowly assembled to crush him, Cniva returned north with his massive booty. By now Decius's army was rehabilitated and likely reinforced. As Decius marched east along the Danube, he intercepted the Goths at Abrittus, probably in the summer of 251.[8] Cniva deployed his forces in three lines, at least one of which was concealed by a swamp. The initial Roman attack made good progress as the barbarians fell back upon their main line. It is doubtful that Decius would have wanted his army to enter the swamp, where it would forfeit all the advantages the Romans possessed on an open field. But the evidence shows unequivocally that he was fighting in the front lines, making it impossible for him to command his army beyond those within shouting distance. Besides, an ancient army that scented victory and saw a foe running before them was notoriously difficult to keep in hand. So the Romans plunged into the swamp and were destroyed. As for Decius, we have the word of Zonaras: he, his son, and a multitude of Romans fell into the swamp and perished there, with the result that their bodies, interred in the slime, were never found.[9] Rome had often lost battles, but this result stunned the Empire: for the first time in the Empire's history, a Roman emperor had been killed in battle with barbarians.

Rome was again without an emperor, and the army immediately selected C. Vibus Trebonianus Gallus for imperial honors. Our sources are mostly hostile to Gallus and blame him for betraying Decius.[10] What is more likely is the Gallus maintained better control of his portion of the army than Decius did and refused to let it enter the swamp. This would have been more than enough for his detractors to claim betrayal. But it is difficult to believe that the army would have made Gallus emperor if they suspected betrayal. It is much more likely that they would elect an emperor who had saved their lives and maintained enough power to force Cniva to treat with them to make his escape, rather than overrun a mere remnant.

As it was, as many as three legions may have been destroyed, opening the region to continued barbarian attacks for another two decades, and Ammianus later referred to Abrittus as one of the greatest defeats Rome ever suffered.[11] The extent of the losses will never be known, but all appearances indicate that Rome still had an army in the field, a reinforced line of frontier fortifications, and an enemy trapped in a swamp. Cniva may have been able to take on the reduced Roman army in a swamp, but fighting legionaries on ground of their choosing was rarely a winning proposition. He could always make a run for it, but that meant leaving behind his prisoners and rich booty, which would have robbed him of the prestige he needed to rule his fragmented coalition. But Gallus, like Philip when dealing with Sapor, was on a clock, as he also needed to get back to Rome to secure his hold on the Empire. So a deal was struck allowing Cniva to return north of the Danube with all of his captives and loot as well as an annual subsidy. It is a measure of Gallus's haste to negotiate a deal that he allowed Cniva to take the entire imperial treasury with him.[12]

Gallus made his way to Rome, where he was declared emperor. To reinforce his political position, he adopted Decius's remaining son, Hostilianus, and made him co-Augustus. But within months the plague carried Hostilianus off, and Gallus replaced him with his son, Volusianus, as co-Augustus. As Gallus worked to establish his hold on power, the plague continued unabated. It would eventually kill millions and do much to undermine the Roman economy before burning itself out. Adding to Gallus's woes was catastrophic news from the east, where Sapor, claiming Rome had broken his treaty with Philip, annexed Armenia and was preparing for a renewed war with Rome. The Romans were also preparing for war, and Volusianus was dispatched to the eastern command. In 252 Sapor struck before he arrived, launching his army up the Euphrates, bypassing most of the Roman fortresses, such as Dura, and heading directly for the Roman army at Barbalissus. This is another battle we know nothing about, except that it was a catastrophe for Rome, with a force of sixty thousand either annihilated or so dispersed as to be incapable of effective combat.

Sapor went on to conquer Antioch, as well as much of Syria and Mesopotamia. Writing decades after the fall of Antioch, Ammianus captured the moment:

> For once upon a time at Antioch, amid deep silence, an actor of mimes, who with his wife had been presented in stage-plays, was presenting some scenes from everyday life. And while all the people were amazed at the charm of the performance, the wife suddenly cried: "Is it a dream, or are the Persians here?" Whereupon all the people turned their heads about and then fled in all directions, to avoid the arrows that were showered upon them from the citadel. Thus, the city was set on fire, and many people who were carelessly wandering about, as in time of peace, were butchered; neighboring places were burned and devastated, and the enemy, laden with plunder, returned home without the loss of a single man.[13]

Losing Antioch stunned the Empire, but Gallus was unable to react, for another usurper had arisen. This time it was the governor of Moesia, M. Aemilius Aemilianus, who had led his men against the Goths and won a local victory, whereupon his men acclaimed him as emperor. Aemilian, forgetting the Danube defense, immediately marched on Rome. To meet him, Gallus called upon P. Licinius Valerian to bring his transalpine legions to his aid. Before Valerian could arrive, Gallus, in July 253, met the usurper at Interana, north of Rome, where Gallus's soldiers murdered him and went over to the enemy. But Aemilian's reign was a short one, as Valerian was already marching into Italy. The two armies met near Spoletium, and this time it was Aemilian's turn to be murdered by his troops, who now promised their loyalty to Valerian.[14]

While Gallus, Aemilian, and Valerian were contesting control of the Empire, a new threat arose in the east. A large band of barbarians, probably Goths, had seized boats along the north coast of the Black Sea and pushed through the Bosporus to conduct raids all along the coast of Asia Minor, even burning the great temple of Artemis in Ephesus. After nearly three centuries of the Pax Romana, the cities along the Aegean coast were no longer fortified, making them incapable of self-defense. This defenselessness was compounded by the fact that the Roman army was a frontier force and there were no reserve legions maintained within the Empire. This was all right when the frontiers were well defended and forces could be moved along the river lines; but this was no longer the case, as the frontiers had been stripped to fight the civil wars. The barbarians quickly discovered that the Empire was like an eggshell, with a hard exterior but a soft and gooey inside. And in the third century, that hard shell was usually brittle. The only thing that protected these undefended regions was the barbarians' lack of mobility and their inability to sustain themselves on lengthy campaigns. Much of this mobility problem was solved by being able to move at sea. Like the Sea People whose story was in the opening chapter of this book, the barbarians found that the ability to move rapidly from one undefended point to another was a huge military advantage. This revealed another great weakness in Rome's strategic planning. Since the Battle of Actium, over a quarter of a millennium before, Rome had not faced any naval threat beyond some sporadic piratical activity. Rome still maintained its two major naval bases at Misenum and Ravenna, but these fleets had withered and for the most part just patrolled trade routes. The great, highly trained battle fleets of the Republic were nothing but a historical memory. So when barbarian raiders took to the sea—by stealing Roman trading vessels—there was no fleet to contest them for naval supremacy.[15] In 429 the lack of a fleet to stop the Vandals from crossing from Spain to Africa would push a tottering empire into the abyss. For now the barbarians were looking for loot and not conquest, so their depredations should be viewed as a warning. It was a warning that went unheeded, likely because, with all the threats Rome faced, paying to reconstitute a powerful fleet that was only of sporadic use was judged unaffordable.

Valerian, at sixty years of age, was already an old man, but he was still vigorous. He also had a grown son, Gallienus, whom he made co-Augustus and who was also capable of holding a separate command. The two emperors spent their first year in office in Rome securing their right to rule, as well as accustoming Rome's elites to the idea of a new dynasty that would rule Rome for decades to come. When they felt secure enough, both emperors headed north. Gallienus made his headquarters at either Viminacium or Sirmium, while Valerian eventually continued overland to Antioch with whatever forces could be spared in the west, arriving in late 254.

It is worthy of note that Valerian's army is no longer the army of the Severans. That army had been shattered by decades of defeats and civil wars. Instead of the proud legions of the Principate, we now have small fragments of legions haphazardly thrown together into campaigning armies. For each new crisis and resulting campaign, emperors and generals would scrape together whatever forces were immediately available and march to battle. Over the next couple of centuries, this process would become increasingly regularized.[16] This was unlikely, at this point, to have limited the army's fighting power, since each fragment was still part of a training system that produced soldiers and units that marched and fought according to an established doctrine. In effect, that made the cohorts or vexillations interchangeable. For an example of how this worked in practice, one can examine Julius Caesar's campaigns when his army was unexpectedly attacked by a large force of Nervii:

> A great part of these arrangements [for recovering large work parties] was prevented by the shortness of time and the sudden approach and charge of the enemy. Under these difficulties two things proved of advantage; the skill and experience of the soldiers . . . and that Caesar had forbidden his several legates to depart from the works and their respective legions, before the camp was fortified. . . . Such was the shortness of the time, and so determined was the mind of the enemy on fighting, that time was wanting not only for affixing the military insignia, but even for putting on the helmets and drawing off the covers from the shields. To whatever part any one by chance came from the works (in which he had been employed), and *whatever standards he saw first, at these he stood, lest in seeking his own company he should lose the time for fighting.*[17]

The crucial point in the above is that the legionaries, having been trained in a common doctrine, were able to fall in under any standard and take their place in the line. Similarly, a cohort or vexillation could join with any similar unit and the combined forces behave on the battlefield as a united legion without much loss of effectiveness.

Still, what maintained Rome's overall military effectiveness and explains its resiliency in the face of so many hard blows was infrastructure. Rome still had its imperial road system to move troops and supplies from one threatened sector to the next. Its fleets still controlled traffic along the

Rhine and Danube, allowing for rapid movement throughout the northern frontiers. Moreover, although the *limes* fortifications could be penetrated and damaged, they still stood. Where they stood unmolested or unthreatened, they still allowed Rome to trade forts for men. Throughout the crisis period Rome drew resources from low-threat regions to fight in regions under attack. Once a threat had been defeated and repulsed, these frontier defenses were rapidly rebuilt, allowing the army to mobilize against a future assault. Finally, the fighting so far was still localized. Large and rich areas of the Empire were untouched and continued to provide resources to prop up the provinces under attack and make good battlefield losses. The Empire was under stress, but it still possessed huge reserves of power. What was lacking was the right man to fully mobilize those resources and restore order before the cascade of failures became irreversible. Valerian was not destined to be that man.

Upon arriving in Antioch, Valerian found that the threat had gone. Sapor had taken another huge haul of treasure and captives back east with him. So many prisoners were taken that he was able to employ them in building and populating new cities, which later became the industrial core of a much richer Sassanid Empire. Sapor was making war pay for itself in ways that would enhance Sassanid military power for centuries to come. As for Valerian, he spent the next year restoring as much of Syria's infrastructure as possible, including rebuilding the frontier fortresses. But by the late summer of 256, he was in Cologne with his son. Here they may have shown their comity by launching an ineffectual campaign against the Alemanni before both men returned to Rome in early 257. They could not stay long, for new troubles on the frontiers soon arose. Hoping to either forestall or counter a new Sassanid assault, Valerian headed for Antioch. While he was there, though, a large Gothic force, coming once again by sea, ravaged the province of Pontus and began pushing into Cappadocia. Upon hearing of Valerian's approach, the barbarians, either satiated by the loot and slaves they had already gained or fearful of engaging the eastern army, returned to their boats and made their escape. Valerian's army was not so lucky. According to Zosimus, "The plague then attacked his troops, and destroyed most of them." Valerian led his stricken army back toward Antioch but was forced to divert east to counter another Persian assault.

The rival armies met somewhere between Edessa and Carrhae in the spring of 260. There was likely a battle of which we know nothing. But it must have gone poorly, for the plague decimated the Romans, and Valerian soon asked to negotiate a treaty. The final result is recorded on the inscriptions of the *Res Gestae Divi Saporis* (The Acts of the Divine Sapor):

Valerian Caesar came against me . . . from the land of Mesopotamia with an army of 70,000 men. . . . And beyond Carrhae and Edessa there was a great battle with Valerian Caesar, and Valerian Caesar was captured by my own hand, and the rest, the praetorian prefects and the senators and the officers who were the leaders of this army, were all captured and led into Persia.

An entire Roman army had been extinguished, and for the second time in a decade a Roman emperor had been killed or taken by the enemy.[18] A staggering Rome had little left to oppose Sapor, and he continued his assault on Cilicia. But then a combination of factors brought his campaign to an end. One not usually mentioned is how unlikely it was for Sapor to have captured a Roman army, even one decimated by illness, while his army remained unscathed. Because even Sapor's own *Res Gestae* states that a "great battle" was fought, it is likely that even in victory the Persian host was severely mauled. This is what explains why two local officials, Macrianus and Callistus, were able to rally what troops remained in Syria and, with some help from Odaenathus of Palmyra, check the Persian advance. Sapor was also probably reaching the limits of how long a feudal-type Persian force could be held together. Sapor finally called off the offensive and returned to Persia with additional treasures and slaves that would be put to work building cities deep within the Sassanid Empire.[19]

Gallienus, upon hearing of his father's defeat and capture, promoted his son, Saloninus, to Augustus and left him in Cologne under the guidance of the praetorian prefect Silvanus. Considering that the Empire was now coming apart, it was a useless gesture. In Syria, Macrianus declared that he was now emperor and promoted his two sons, Macrianus and Quietus, as co-emperors, while Odaenathus gave himself the title of Lord of Palmyra and began ruling over a large swath of territory around that city. In the Balkans, the governors of Sirmium and Moesia, respectively Ingenuus and Regalianus, also declared themselves emperor, but their pretensions were rapidly crushed by Gallienus's cavalry commander, Aureolus. Of course, the tribes north of the Danube took note of this disarray and were, as always, ready to pounce. In late 260 and 261 various tribes penetrated the Danube, some of them reaching deep into the Balkans. There are reports of a barbarian assault on Thessalonica in late 261, and of local forces manning the defenses at the pass at Thermopylae.

While this was going on, a force of Iuthungi, part of the Alemanni confederation, pushed across the Alps into Italy, where Gallienus fought them near Milan. He won the battle, but there must have been a large force of

Iuthungi that escaped the fighting or was not engaged. One can suppose that he was claiming a great victory for having destroyed the rear guard. While the rest of the barbarians were heading back to the frontiers with their loot and captives, they were intercepted and massacred by a Roman army put together from forces in Raetia and Germania Inferior. The Roman commander, Postumus, ordered the booty distributed to the victorious army. But in Cologne, Saloninus, advised by the perfect Silvanus, countermanded Postumus's instructions. If refusing the army silver was dangerous, taking away silver that was promised to them was suicidal. The army stormed Cologne, killed both Saloninus and Silvanus, took their promised treasure, and then declared Postumus emperor. By the end of 260 Postumus controlled all of the Rhine frontier, Gaul (except for Narbonensis), and Britain.

The Empire now fractured into three parts. Postumus held the northwest, while much of the east was divided by the Macriani family and Odaenathus of Palmyra. That left Gallienus Italy, most of Spain, Egypt, and North Africa—the economic heart of the Empire—as well as most of Anatolia and the Balkans. He also had a new and powerful army recruited mostly in the Balkans and along the Danubian frontier. This army was commanded by hard men who had spent their lives at war. There were no longer senatorial legates in the legions, since there was no longer a willingness to accept amateurs in military commands just to further their political careers. Gallienus was, in fact, culminating a process begun decades before and remaking the Roman administrative system in a way that placed competent equestrians, mostly of proven military ability, in crucial jobs and left little room for persons of the senatorial class. This new army disposed of a large amount of cavalry, which appears to have operated very closely with the heavy infantry as a combined arms force. Arguably, this army—the *comitatus*—which was attached directly to the emperor, was the start of the field armies that would make their appearance as fully developed entities during the reigns of Diocletian and Constantine. It was separate from the Praetorian Guard, which was still mostly stationed in Rome, and also acted independently of the frontier legions. Furthermore, it was a force optimally designed to move fast and hit hard.

That Roman emperors felt they could make this change reflects several important points. First, the legions were not what they used to be. If they had been, Gallienus would not have had to place his resources in maintaining legions loyal to himself. For him to have committed so much to a cavalry-heavy organization indicates either that he thought such a force could either move fast enough to counter a usurper before he could gather sufficient strength to be a real threat, or that the legions were so weak that a mixed force of infantry and cavalry could overwhelm a force consisting mostly of the legions. The development of the *comitatus* also reflects the changing nature of the threat. Given the increasing number of multiple simultaneous penetrations of the frontier, emperors needed a force that could move rapidly throughout the theater to run down or intercept fast-moving groups of barbarians, but was also strong enough to match these invaders once they had massed for battle. It also suggests an assessment that this force can stand up to the legions in open battle. Otherwise it was mere folly, as there was seemingly no end of persons willing to risk all for the purple; by some counts, over four dozen made the attempt in less than fifty years.

Almost unbelievably, things started to turn around for Gallienus in 261. Surprisingly, Postumus threw away the usurper's playbook, which called for an immediate march on Rome to secure power at the imperial center. Instead, he appeared satisfied to rule the northwest portion of the Empire in hopes of being left alone. Postumus's contentment gave Gallienus breathing room to deal with his other problems, one of which was that the Macriani army was marching west, intent on securing the Empire the old-fashioned way— by taking Rome. Gallienus sent his new mobile army, still commanded by Aureolus, to meet them. As he had done to the armies of Ingenuus and Regalianus, Aureolus made short work of the Macriani, who were both put to death. Gallienus could have sent Aureolus east to restore order and imperial authority in Syria and beyond, but this would have left the Western Empire with weakened frontiers and no supporting field army. Instead, Gallienus made an ally of Odaenathus, bestowing upon him the title *corrector totius orientis* (Corrector of the Whole East). This title came with a writ that gave Odaenathus command of all imperial governors and forces in the east. It is noteworthy that Odaenathus was not a Roman general but a local potentate. If he had been raised within the Roman military system, such a transfer or sharing of power would not be unusual; after all, Augustus had given such power in the east to Agrippa. But to give power over imperial forces to what amounted to a local political official was unheard of. However, it does demonstrate Gallienus's flexibility: he was willing to hand over extraordinary power to a local ruler who swore allegiance to himself while remaining at war with Postumus, who was doing precisely what Odaenathus was but had refused to swear allegiance to the emperor in Rome. Odaenathus, pleased with his new title and increased power, immediately turned on his former allies, Callistus and Quietus, who were murdered by their own men at Emesa just as the Palmyran army approached. Animated by his success, and with Sapor's army having retreated into Persia and then likely disbanded, in 262 Odaenathus pushed his offensive toward the east. All of the border cities and fortresses were soon recovered, and it is possible that he penetrated as far as Ctesiphon.[20] These successes brought a bit of a respite to an empire that had been pushed to the wall. Gallienus took advantage of the time to rebuild the Danubian defenses, paying particular attention to fortifying Aquileia—the gateway to Italy. It was the calm before the storm.

In 265 Gallienus felt strong enough to try and wrest back control of what has become known as the Gallic Empire. After some initial success, Gallienus was seriously wounded during the siege of an unknown city. He soon called off his invasion, leaving Postumus as the de facto ruler of his Gallic Empire, although Spain was edging closer to returning to Rome's imperial rule. While the army was distracted in Gaul, the Goths along the Black Sea raided deep into Asia Minor until halted by Odaenathus, who allowed them to escape with all of their plunder, suggesting either weakness or a reluctance to risk battle when other threats were still looming. Worse was to come. In 267 the various Gothic tribes and their allies along the Danube and the Black Sea coordinated a joint raid upon the Empire. Goths from north of the Black Sea forced their way into the Bosporus and the Hellespont with as many as five hundred ships. Raiding throughout the Aegean, they poured into a nearly defenseless region, sacking Athens, Corinth, Argos, and Sparta. At least some of these Goths made it as far as Macedonia, while others besieged Potidaea and Thessalonica. At the same time, the Goths north of the Danube swarmed into Thrace and laid siege once again to Philippopolis.

The *comitatus* would eventually arrive, but for reasons we shall soon see, it would not do so for over a year. Until then the locals were on their own. Thanks to a recent discovery of fragments of a work by Dexippus, who is the foundational source for most of our later histories of the period, we have a glimpse of how locals were able to eventually organize an effective defense.[21] In a Gothic attack around 262, five years earlier than the current invasion, three locals—Philostratus, Marianus, and Dexippus himself—were selected as generals to take a locally raised force north to meet the Goths at Thermopylae. The Greek governing council—probably the Panhellion— made these selections and raised the necessary troops independently of established imperial structures. Moreover, as other Dexippus fragments attest, these local governments and military forces created unified command structures that were capable of cooperating with imperial authorities when they arrived in the area. Hence, during the great Gothic invasion of 268, despite seeing some of the greatest cities in Greece destroyed, the Greeks were able to organize sufficient manpower and resources to build a wall across the Isthmus of Corinth as well as dispatch several thousand locally raised troops to harry the invading force. These forces eventually joined the counterattacking imperial field army—the *comitatus*—in 269 at the Battle of Naissus, which broke Gothic power for over two generations.

But rather than stay in the Balkans and finish off the raiders, Gallienus handed the responsibility for the army over to Lucius Aurelius Marcianus and then took a large portion of the field army back to Italy. The Empire, which had suffered so many near-fatal blows in just a few years, now underwent another calamity. Aureolus, who until this time had been Gallienus's best and most loyal general, raised the standard of revolt in Milan. He did not, however, claim the title of emperor, probably hoping that one of the other powerful marshals who commanded various segments of the imperial army would do so for him. Thus, even as the Goths were laying waste to much of the Balkans, the army turned away to face yet another usurper. Even as Gallienus marched west, word came that Odaenathus had been murdered. For now, his widow, Zenobia, claimed to rule for her son, Vaballathus, but the stability that Odaenathus had assured was no longer certain, nor was Zenobia's willingness to continue to swear allegiance to the emperor and Rome.

Still, for now the east remained in Rome's orbit and was comparatively peaceful. Another bright spot, from Gallienus's point of view, was news that a revolt had begun within the Gallic Empire. At a minimum, Gallienus hoped to take advantage of the chaos to deal first with Aureolus and then take his army into Gaul. He never got the chance: he was murdered by his own marshals while besieging Aureolus in Milan.

By this time the true power in the Empire lay with the great marshals of the various field armies. It was these officers who now made and broke emperors, and they now chose one of their own, the cavalry general M. Aurelius Claudius, as emperor. The marshals may have come to despise Gallienus, but he was popular with the rank and file. To appease them, Claudius forced the Senate, who still despised the former emperor for removing many of their privileges, to have Gallienus deified. He was relieved of the embarrassment of dealing with Aureolus when he too was murdered. This freed Claudius to turn on a large group of Germanic raiders who had entered northern Italy, destroying them near Lake Garda.[22]

Claudius, following the well-worn script, next went to Rome to secure his hold on power by promoting family, friends, and loyal colleagues to the posts that controlled the day-to-day business of the Empire. Selecting his next move was not quite as simple. Zenobia had successfully established herself in power in the east but had not yet declared independence from Rome. That meant the east could wait. Still, Claudius ordered one of his marshals, Heraclianus, to move eastward to explore the possibility of shaking Zenobia's hold on some of her domains. What forces he had at his disposal or what Heraclianus accomplished, besides enraging Zenobia, is not attested to in the sources. Claudius, turning his attention to the Gallic Empire, must have been happy with his prospects in the quarter. The Gallic Empire was thrown into chaos by one of Postumus's officials, Ulpius Cornelius Laelianus, declaring himself emperor of Germania Superior. Postumus easily defeated him near Mainz but then unwisely refused to allow his victorious soldiers to sack the city. Feeling cheated of their plunder, the army murdered Postumus and acclaimed Marcus Aurelius Marius as their new emperor; but he in turn was soon defeated by Postumus's praetorian prefect, Victorinus, who then declared himself the Gallic emperor. Spain took advantage of all the turmoil to escape the Gallic orbit and swore loyalty to Claudius, exposing the Gallic Empire's southwestern border to invasion. Almost simultaneously, Claudius sent a small army, commanded by Placidianus, into southern France. Placidianus, whose force was not large enough to take on the Gallic army, halted at Grenoble, establishing a strong base for future incursions. Despite these setbacks, Victorinus stabilized Gaul and secured his hold on power of the lands remaining to him. Still, in the following year, the city of Autun, probably at Placidianus's bidding, revolted and declared for Claudius. The revolt did not spread, and Placidianus was too weak to go to the city's aid. Moreover, Claudius had by this time almost certainly marched east with the bulk of the *comitatus*. Autun, abandoned, endured a long siege but was finally taken and sacked.[23]

Watching events unfold, Claudius had two choices: invade the Gallic Empire and restore Roman authority, or return to the Balkans and finish the campaign begun by Gallienus. Invading Syria without securing the Balkans was not feasible, so he would have to bide his time and see what Heraclianus could achieve in weakening Zenobia before seriously entertaining any advance deep into the eastern provinces. Moreover, as Victorinus was showing no more ambition to grow his empire than Postumus had, retaking the Gallic Empire could be put off for another day. Consequently, in 269 Claudius marched east against the Goths to finish what Gallienus had started.[24]

Upon his arrival he found the Danubian Goths besieging Marcianopolis, while the Gothic force that Gallienus had defeated at the Nessos River had regrouped and were plaguing Macedonia. Marcianus, who had been left in charge by Gallienus, had done what he could, but with the main field army in Italy, his options were limited, since the Goths were being continuously reinforced from across the Danube. When Claudius returned with the *comitatus*, he deftly maneuvered to force the Danubian Gothic bands together for a climactic battle at Naissus. According to Zosimus, "Great numbers were slain in this battle on both sides, but the Romans, by a pretended flight, drew the barbarians into an ambuscade and killed more than fifty thousand of them."[25] Claudius improved upon his great battlefield victory by pursuing the Gothic survivors into the mountains, where they were overcome by starvation and disease. The Goths, rampaging through Macedonia, now boarded their ships and took flight, ravaging coastal cities and some Aegean islands as they made their way back to the Black Sea. Still, Claudius's success had a lasting effect. The Bosporus and Dardanelles Straits would be more securely held in the future, limiting the capacity of the Goths and later tribes north of the Black Sea to break through and wreak havoc in the Aegean or along the Baltic coast. More crucially, the Gothic defeat at Naissus broke the military power of the tribes north of the Danube, who were mostly quiet for the next two generations. When the Senate acclaimed Claudius as Gothicus Maximus—"Conqueror of the Goths"—it was well earned.

The Goths, having been taught a hard lesson south of the Danube, began to expand westward into Dacia, much of which was lost to the Empire even if not yet formally ceded. After the Battle of Naissus, Claudius in 270 moved the army to Sirmium while he took stock. He could send the army in Dacia, but that province was no longer worth the massive effort it would take to hold it. The province, while part of the Empire since Trajan's conquest, had never been completely integrated into it, in the same way Gaul had. Rather, it appears to have always been seen as an exploitative arrangement, where Rome invested little but took as much out of its mines as possible. As these mines either gave out or otherwise became economically unfeasible, the strategic reasons for holding Dacia evaporated, as it was far too late to make an expensive effort to move the *limes* forward to the Carpathian passes. Now that the countryside was infested with Goths, Claudius probably considered it best to just let them be in return for a peaceful Danubian frontier. His next strategic option was to take the field army to join Placidianus at his advanced base at Grenoble. But Postumus's successor, Victorinus, still had the loyalty of the Gallic army, making any imperial invasion an uncertain contest. Besides, even if the Goths were temporarily quiescent, removing the field army from the Danube risked letting the Alemanni break through into Pannonia and Italy.

But, by the middle of 270 Claudius had new concerns in the east. Zenobia, incensed by the arrival of Heraclianus on the fringes of her zone of control, must have immediately realized that Syria was too small a power base to resist an all-out imperial offensive. Alone, Syria could never supply the recruits or revenues she needed to maintain her power in the face of a determined assault. If we exclude any possibility of a costly push deep into the Sassanid Empire, she had two options: march into Cappadocia or send her army into Egypt. The first would have put her forces adjacent to Claudius and his battle-hardened *comitatus*, and it would also have forced her to commit a sizable portion of her strength to ward off further depredations by the Black Sea Goths. Egypt, on the other hand, yielded large tax revenues and was still one of Rome's two breadbaskets, along with North Africa. Moreover, it was weakly held, and its effective prefect, Tenagino Probus, had been called to deal with the Gothic breakthrough in the Aegean. Moreover, there was a substantial pro-Palmyrene fifth column in Egypt, led by a Roman officer, Timagenes, ready to rise up and support a Zenobian intervention.[26] So Zenobia sent her army, commanded by her general, Zabdas, into Egypt by way of Roman Arabia.[27]

When the Palmyrene army entered Egypt, Timagenes joined his mobilized Palmyrene sympathizers with Zabdas and overpowered the Roman garrison. Probus, the prefect for Egypt, called off his hunt for Gothic pirates and hurried back to Egypt. He managed to rally enough Roman forces to seize and hold Alexandria and the delta. But Alexandria was lost to the Empire when Zabdas regrouped and counterattacked the small Roman force. Probus retreated south to the Roman garrison at Babylon, which was situated on the southern portion of the delta and occupied a strong hilltop position. But Timagenes, being familiar with the area, led a small force into the Roman rear, winning the battle and securing control of Egypt for Zenobia.[28] The Palmyrenes were victorious, and Probus committed suicide, leaving Egypt firmly under Palmyrene control.

From the beginning of the Roman Empire, emperors had kept a close eye on Egypt. Augustus and his immediate successors had even decreed that no senator could ever be in command there, and a senator needed special permission from the emperor even to visit. Egypt, which always produced a surplus of wheat, was too critical to Rome's survival to risk placing it in the hands of a usurper. Augustus had learned this lesson when Mark Anthony had used food as a weapon in their civil war. It was a lesson that was never forgotten. Zenobia's action forced Claudius's hand. He would take the field army east. But in 270 the plague caught up to the Roman army, killing many, including Claudius.

Claudius's brother, Quintillus, who was in Aquileia, immediately assumed the purple. Unfortunately for his prospects, the Danubian legions, the strongest massed army in the Empire, made their own choice: L. Domitius Aurelianus, better known to history as Aurelian. That army was already marching west to enforce their selection when Quintillus, after seventeen days as emperor, was murdered or committed suicide. Postponing a reckoning in the east or with the Gallic Empire, Aurelian planned to head directly for

Rome. He never got there, because a further collapse of the northern frontier once again allowed the Iuthungi, followed by the Vandals, into Italy.[29] Both were rapidly defeated, but in 271 a much larger force of Iuthungi crossed over the Alps. Defeating this force required three battles, all fought in northern Italy. The first, near Placentia, did not go well for Aurelian but was likely closer to a draw than the defeat portrayed by some sources.[30] Aurelian was able to draw off enough forces to defeat the barbarians in two successive battles at Fanum and Ticinum. The last of these was decisive enough to ensure that nothing is heard of the Iuthungi for several decades.

After ruthlessly crushing two short-lived military revolts, Aurelian made his way to Rome. He was greeted with riots in the streets, as the mint workers were in revolt, for reasons unexplained in our sources. The Roman mob that had once fought the praetorians to a standstill during the reign of Alexander Severus was no easier to defeat this time. The riots were finally put down, but not before many thousands of Romans lay dead in the street. Aurelian now took the opportunity to repair some of the state's finances.

By 270 the silver content of the silver coinage had reached its nadir, with some coins well under 2 percent silver.[31] With war and a planned building campaign to pay for, Aurelian decided to use the riots as cover for the slaughter of some of the richest men in Rome, whose estates could then be confiscated. Ammianus later tells us that Valentinian, when short of funds, tried to excuse his theft "by offering the example of the emperor Aurelian, declaring that as, when the treasury was exhausted after Gallienus and the lamentable disasters to the state, he fell upon the rich like a torrent."[32]

Before departing Rome, Aurelian initiated the construction of a great wall around the city. When completed it was twelve miles in circumference, ten feet wide, and had massive battle towers every hundred feet. Even today the parts of the wall that remain standing inspire awe. Some historians have pointed out that the walls were too massive to be properly manned and therefore could not withstand a siege, others that it was meant as a symbol of both the emperor's power and that he trusted the people of Rome not to revolt. All such speculation misses the point. Walls have since time immemorial been built for one reason: to enhance the security of those within them. There was no other reason to undertake such tremendous expense. Moreover, there were very few fortifications built in an era that could be properly manned by their permanent garrisons. In the event of trouble, the walls would also be manned by the citizens of Rome, as well as by portions of the field army that would have fallen back into the city. We do not have to invent reasons for the Aurelian walls. They were there to protect Rome from invaders (Figure 13.1). In fact, throughout the Crisis of the Third Century, we find cities and towns throughout the Empire, which had not required walls for over two hundred years, building them as fast as possible. During the immediate crisis, this all made sense. But in later decades this refortification of the Empire and the consequent fragmentation of regional defense and local economies had a serious negative impact on Rome's capacity to organize a centrally planned defense.

With Italy secured, Aurelian was free to turn on either the Gallic Empire or Zenobia. This time, the choice was easy. Victorinus had been murdered and replaced by Gaius Exuvius Tetricus, who showed no indication of trying to expand his empire. Zenobia, however, now held Egypt, making her a mortal threat requiring elimination. As he started east, there was another assault of

FIGURE 13.1 The Aurelian Walls

undefined tribes in the Balkans that was easily dealt with by the field army as it passed through. To gather resources for the great war he foresaw, in 272 Aurelian took the huge step of formally abandoning the Dacian provinces. It was a rational move, one that reflected Aurelian's and the Empire's priorities. With resources constantly stretched to the breaking point, Aurelian could not waste money or troops defending the indefensible. Here he was adhering to an old military maxim: if you try to hold everything, you will end up holding nothing. Still, no emperor since Hadrian had voluntarily given up land once it had been declared a province of Rome. Since the Roman psyche still internalized the belief that Rome was meant to rule the world, giving up Dacia was not without serious political risk. To mask what he had done, Aurelian carved a new province of "Dacia" out of Upper Moesia and allowed the imperial propaganda machine to pretend that nothing had changed.

Taking down Zenobia turned out to be an easier proposition than Aurelian likely assumed it would be. First and most crucially, he needed to regain Egypt. This was of such importance that it was conducted as a separate operation, independent of his overland advance. For this task, one of his generals and a future emperor, Probus, was sent with the fleet, such as it was, to Egypt.[33] By May 272 Probus was in Egypt, and a month later Egypt was back in the imperial fold. The fact that Zenobia's Egyptian prefect, Statilius Aemilianus, continued in his role demonstrates that he surrendered the province without a struggle.

Meanwhile, Aurelian continued his march across Asia Minor, where Palmyrene control evaporated upon his approach. He did not meet any resistance until he had reached the city of Tyana, just north of Cilician Gates in Cappadocia, which had closed to him. When Tyana closed its gates to him, an enraged Aurelian exclaimed, "In this town I will not even leave a dog alive."[34] His army, scenting easy plunder, prepared to take the city by storm, but it was surrendered or betrayed before the assault began. With the city in his hands, Aurelian decided to spare it from sack, claiming he had a dream telling him to do so. The army loudly protested, reminding Aurelian that he promised not to leave a dog alive in the city. As Postumus had discovered, denying a Roman army its plunder was a very dangerous proposition, but Aurelian was not intimidated, replying, "I did, indeed, declare that I would not leave a dog alive in this city; well, then, kill all the dogs."[35] The army appears to have appreciated his humor and did not push their claims; there would be other chances for plunder, and it can be assumed a donative was promised. Sparing the city was an excellent diplomatic move, as the cities of Cilicia, formerly a Zenobian stronghold, all threw their gates open to him as the army approached.

Aurelian found Zenobia's army drawn up on the Orontes Plain outside of Antioch, determined to make a stand on ground of their choosing. Here, the heavily mailed Palmyrene cavalry—the *cataphracti*—would be able to run over Aurelian's cavalry before turning on the flanks and rear of the almost defenseless infantry. Aurelian therefore decided to use his lighter cavalry to set a trap, and in a risky maneuver he ordered it to retreat ahead of the Palmyrene cavalry charge until the hot June sun exhausted the heavier cavalry. The Palmyrenes charged as expected, and the Romans ran. Several miles later the heavily armored Palmyrene horses were thoroughly blown and incapable of keeping up the pursuit. The Romans then turned and massacred a large portion of the exhausted Palmyrene cavalry—the core of its military power.[36]

The bulk of the Palmyrene infantry retreated, leaving Antioch to Aurelian. He was detained in the always-fractious city for a while but put the time to good use by calling in reinforcements from throughout the Empire. When he decided to leave Antioch, his army was briefly held up by a Palmyrene force at Daphne. According to Zosimus, the Romans adopted the famous testudo formation of closely interlocked shields to approach and then break the delaying force. Marching on to Emesa, he found the entire Palmyrene army, reportedly seventy thousand strong, waiting for him.[37] We do not know much about this battle, but it appears to have gone badly for Aurelian at first. But just as they had before Antioch, the reformed Palmyrene cavalry overextended itself, even as their infantry formations were becoming increasingly disordered. This opened a window for Aurelian's highly disciplined veterans to counterattack, supported by locals armed with special clubs designed to smash mail and other heavy armor. Once again the battle turned into a slaughter as the remnants of Zenobia's army retreated into Emesa.[38] Before the summer ended, Palmyra was in Aurelian's hands, and Zenobia was his prisoner.

Aurelian and the army began the long overland march to the west, for there was still the Gallic army to deal with. While his army was resting near Byzantium, it became apparent that the leniency he had shown in the east was misplaced. First, Alexandria rebelled, but this was quickly and ruthlessly put down by the Roman forces still in Egypt. Worse, however, news arrived that Palmyra had rebelled. A furious Aurelian turned the army around and marched to the city. This time the army, as angry as their emperor and still without the gains of plunder expected on such a campaign, must have demanded that the city be sacked. Aurelian would have been in no mood to deny them. Palmyra was besieged, sacked, and garrisoned. It would never again rise to its former prosperity.[39]

In 274 Aurelian at last moved against Tetricus's Gallic Empire. Here again diplomacy, as in Egypt and Asia Minor, played a major role, ensuring that

Aurelian's march was unopposed until it reached Chalons—the Catalaunian Plain. There Tetricus, knowing he had little chance of victory, according to some sources, negotiated his personal surrender while placing his army in such a poor position that it was sure to be massacred. This is certainly an imperial fabrication and likely originated as part of imperial propaganda meant to show the unsteady leadership of the Gallic Empire.[40] That the Gallic army was slaughtered in the "Catalaunian catastrophe" is, however, a fact.[41] That Aurelian, as clear-eyed a strategic thinker as Rome ever produced, desired such an outcome is also a later invention. Aurelian would have much preferred for Tetricus's legions to survive to swear loyalty to him and return to man the frontiers. Instead, Gaul's only defensive force was nearly annihilated at a time when Aurelian would soon have to return the field army to Italy and the Danubian theater.

With no army to send to the Rhine frontier, Aurelian was forced to spend the next half year in Gaul overseeing the creation of new security arrangements. Garrisons needed to be recruited, trained, and sent to man frontier forts and outposts. It is also certain that a lot of work was required on the *limes* defenses, since even if the Gallic Empire had tried to maintain them, they were probably not strong enough to be held by the raw recruits Aurelian was forced to send to the front. Aurelian also began to fortify towns throughout the interior of Gaul or allowed it to continue.[42] He was no longer placing his complete faith in the *limes,* unsupported by a field army, to hold off a determined assault. By fortifying towns and cities, he could limit the devastation raiders could cause while ensuring that the returning *comitatus* would have secure bases to maneuver upon and draw supplies from. These fortifications proved their worth, as for in the next quarter century the Alemanni and Franks would tear Aurelian's hastily patched defenses to shreds. In the autumn Aurelian returned to Rome to celebrate his triumphs. There he grandly proclaimed himself as the "Restorer of the World," but it was up to his successors to make his boast a reality.

With Rome's military authority, at least for the moment, restored across the Empire. Aurelian undertook to reestablish Roman finances on a surer footing. The result was a disaster. Rome's economic plight was already in critical condition when Aurelian assumed the purple. Barbarian invasions, civil wars, and the fragmentation of the Empire had all conspired to greatly reduce revenues going to the central government; at the same time, the expense of meeting all the various challenges skyrocketed. The only way quick way to make ends meet was to debase the currency. Amazingly, this debasement never sparked any Empire-wide inflation, even though the amount of silver in a coin, 98 percent during Augustus's reign, dropped below 2 percent during Aurelian's. With no apparent penalty for debasement, emperors were fine with continuing it. The probable explanation for this is that Rome never changed the notional exchange rate of twenty-five silver coins for one gold aureus. That meant a Roman with twenty-five coins containing only 2 percent silver and one with twenty-five coins containing 50 percent silver could both go to a money changer and exchange them for a single gold coin. Assuming this is true, the effective value of Rome's silver coinage never changed. People had faith in its value because they had always had such faith. Roman coins had no more real value than a dollar bill. Like the dollar, it had a fiduciary value and was worth what the central government said it was worth. Rome's silver coins were a fixed medium of exchange that people trusted to retain value. And like the dollar, if people lost their faith, the coins would become instantly worthless.

Aurelian's reforms, which increased the amount of silver in newly minted coins to 5 percent, wrecked that faith. Because he had the mints issue new coins with "XXI" stamped on them—to show the new 1:20 ratio of silver— he made everyone question the value of every coin already in circulation. The only way to make this work would have been to take every old coin out of circulation and replace it with a new coin—an impossible task. Without enough new coins to make an impact, the loss of faith in the old coins sparked an immediate and massive surge in inflation. If you wanted bread and only had old coins, sellers were demanding a lot more of them be turned over to cover their risk in accepting coins that might be valueless. Aurelian compounded his first mistake by issuing a new high-purity gold coin and eliminating the formal link between silver coins and gold. This broke what was the equivalent of a gold standard, where people could count on exchanging a fixed number of silver coins of any purity for a gold coin, and sent people's faith in the silver coins plummeting. The one sure solution to this problem was for Roman tax collectors to accept payments in old coins at the same rate as they did the XXI-stamped new coins. That would have made it clear to everyone that the old and new coins still held the same value in relation to one another. The sources are silent on this matter, but one can assume that the tax collectors would also insist on the new XXI-stamped coins rather than risk being stuck with rapidly depreciating old coins that the imperial treasury might even turn away.

Without a currency that was a reliable store of value, the Roman economy, for at least the next few decades, was underpinned by a system based on payment in kind, which Diocletian was forced to work into his reforms. This would have sounded the death knell for most of the Empire's long-distance trade and rapidly increased the economic fragmentation of the Empire, as local regions were forced to rely on locally produced goods that could be bartered for. Given the wreckage caused by Aurelian's reforms, why did he enact them? First—and this is crucial—no economic theorists resided within the Roman Empire. People could see the economy working, but they had no idea how or why it worked. One could of course argue that, nearly two thousand years later, economists are just as clueless about the workings of the real economy. But from a Roman perspective, if the system could tolerate coins debased to 2 percent, how could it be wrong to start flooding the market with coins containing even more silver? When Aurelian acted, there was no one to explain Gresham's Law—good money drives out bad—to him, and so he had no way to fathom that he was making a mistake. Even after the deed was done and the Roman economy wrecked, no one could explain what he did wrong. If 2 percent was good, then 5 percent just had to be better. As far as Aurelian was concerned, what could go wrong?

Aurelian's primary motive for the reform probably had little to do with economic reform and was much more likely to have been based upon a desire to place his likeness on coins more valuable than any coin issued by his rivals or immediate predecessors. Roman coinage had always been part of the imperial propaganda system; it was a message to the Empire telling everyone who was in charge. His clear intent was to eventually replace every coin circulating within the Empire with one bearing his likeness. But in the end, Aurelian's desire to show that there was now one united Roman Empire, ruled by one emperor, with one accepted currency, caused him to blow up the financial system that underpinned the entire economy. In doing so, he probably did more harm to his subjects than he did good through all of his other actions.[43]

Aurelian did not live long enough to witness the extent of economic damage his reforms wrought; by 275 he was once again on the march. First he went to Gaul, where he repulsed another barbarian invasion. But by mid- or late summer he was back along the Danube heading for Byzantium. In early fall, at Perinthus in Thrace, he was murdered by a conspiracy organized by a member of his staff who had angered Aurelian and feared punishment.[44] That this murder was likely not organized by a cabal of senior officers is attested to by the fact that no one was positioned to immediately claim the purple. It therefore took six weeks to find a replacement—M. Claudius Tacitus.

Tacitus was not, however, long for this world. After leaving Rome, he went to Asia Minor, where the Black Sea Goths were raiding through Pontus into Cilicia. After these invaders were destroyed, he was heading back to Europe when he was murdered by a guard hoping to avoid punishment for killing an unpopular governor of Syria, a relative of Tacitus.[45]

He was rapidly replaced by his praetorian prefect and half brother, Florian. Florian, in turn, was immediately challenged by Probus, the man who had retaken Egypt for Aurelian and was now in command of all of the eastern provinces. Florian, in command of the field army and with the resources of the entire Empire at his disposal, should have won an easy victory.[46] Probus's position, in military terms, was not even as strong as Zenobia's. As Florian advanced, Probus fell back, hoping for a miracle. He was granted one. While camped near Tarsus, Florian's army was ravaged by the plague. As far as his troops were concerned, Florian had lost the favor of the gods. They insisted he step down or share power with Probus. The offer was duly made and accepted by Probus, who had his rival killed immediately after arriving in his opponent's camp.

Probus, born in Sirmium, was the next in a long line of Danubian-born generals who had spent their entire adult lives at war and now dominated the Empire. He was now sole emperor, but he was going to pay a price for a problem he did not create. The first was a consequence of Aurelian's destruction of the Rhine legions, which made up the bulk of the defunct Gallic Empire's field army. The second was the impact of having the *comitatus* far from the Danube frontier for too long. Before the year was out, the Franks and Alemanni had smashed through the weakly defended *limes* and were ravaging Gaul and Roman Germania. The forts along the Rhine were destroyed, as were the remaining military settlements. Even the great fortress cities of Cologne and Trier were captured and looted. Saxons joined in the attack and destroyed most of Flanders. And in northern France, towns and cities discovered that hastily constructed walls were of little value against the invaders: Metz and Reims were sacked and Paris burned.[47]

With large portions of Gaul and Raetia overrun, the security of Italy was soon in doubt. To set things right, Probus immediately headed west with the bulk of the field army. As he advanced, he spent several months defeating the Goths that remained in Asia Minor, correcting deficiencies in the Danubian defenses, and getting temporarily involved in fighting the Goths and Sarmatians. Before he could move on to the Rhine, he was also plagued by what was becoming a chronic problem: revolts. There was fighting in the southern reaches of Egypt of which we know nothing, except the locals seemed to have partnered with nomadic tribes outside the Empire to attack the Roman city of Coptos. And in Asia Minor, the city of Cremna revolted for unknown reasons, requiring a major siege operation to retake the city.[48] One cannot help but see in the revolts the impact of Aurelian's currency reforms as they continued to destroy the fabric of local economies. To these events can be added the widespread wreckage being caused by the *Bagaudae*—revolting peasant bands—throughout Gaul and later Spain, as well as other social disturbances throughout the Empire.[49]

Despite these distractions, by the middle of 277 Probus was ready to start his Gallic campaign, which was to last through most of the next year. At this point we have no idea of the exact events or even a chronology of what he accomplished: the sources regarding the next half decade are silent. We will have to make do with a list of his accomplishments, which include fighting a series of battles against the Alemanni and restoring the Rhine frontier. The *Historia Augusta* makes much of his retaking over sixty major towns and cities, which gives one an idea of just how widespread the Alemanni invasion had been. To make sure these cities were protected in the future, Probus greatly accelerated the program begun during Aurelian's reign to fortify Gaul's cities.

It is worth taking a moment here to consider the long-term impact of all this fighting. Rome's fabulous economic growth during the Principate was built on a foundation of prolonged peace. Cities and towns were able to invest large amounts of capital in agricultural infrastructure with the assurance that it would last generations. In other words, there would be a long-term payoff for the capital expended. One can assume two things about this great Alemanni raid: much of this infrastructure was destroyed or damaged, and the locals would be very reluctant to rebuild it, since the threat of its being destroyed again was ever-present. As this must have been the case for all parts of the Empire exposed to regular barbarian raids, there would have been a widespread reversion to more primitive methods of farming, with a corresponding loss in productivity and tax revenues. Add to this the destruction of trade wrought by the Aurelian currency reforms and the ongoing impacts of plague, war, and economic fragmentation and it is impossible to miss the reasons economic growth halted. Consequently, the Empire that comes out on the other end of these crises is substantially poorer than it was during the Severan era. Finally, building walls is an expensive and manpower-intensive exercise. The limited local capital available was going toward defensive works and paying for locally raised garrisons rather than on repairing and growing the economy.

As part of Probus's defensive building program, the Romans started work on a coastal defense system aimed at protecting the English Channel—the "Saxon Shore." This was a job that had been handled for almost three hundred years by the Roman fleet—the *Classis Britannia*—which was no longer up to the job. One thing that could have postponed barbarian inroads along the English Channel and into Britain would have been to retake those areas of Germania and Gaul recently overrun by the Franks. Probus, however, appears to have left this job to subordinates, who were never given sufficient forces or resources to get the job done. Probus also appears to have made many deals with various barbarian chieftains to trade land within the Empire in return for peace. As always, the Romans did their best to move these barbarians to parts of the Empire far from their homelands, sometimes with remarkably poor results. In one case, a large group of Franks was moved to Asia Minor. Once there they revolted, gathered ships, and proceeded to raid across the Mediterranean, sacking cities and towns in Greece, Sicily, and North Africa. They were repulsed by the locals at Carthage before sailing out into the Atlantic and heading home.[50] The *Historia Augusta* informs us that there were many other problems with barbarians newly settled within the Empire:

> [when Probus settled within the Empire] Gepedes, Greuthung and Vandals, they all broke faith, and when Probus was busied with wars against the pretenders *they roved over well nigh the entire world on foot or in ships and did no little damage to the glory of Rome.*[51]

Probus was also, at this time, accepting barbarian chiefs into Roman imperial service, men who were allowed to take their personal retinue of warriors with them. Barbarians had for centuries been recruited into the Roman army. But in the past they had been led and trained by long-serving imperial officers. Now they were serving under their own leaders and probably fighting in the manner to which they were accustomed, rather than following the methods of imperial warfare and discipline. To paraphrase Adam Smith, "There is a lot of ruin in an army." What Probus was doing was not going to wreck the imperial army's fighting efficiency anytime soon, but the increasing barbarization of the army would one day leave Rome with a force that would be unrecognizable to the early Caesars.

By 278 Probus was forced to leave Gaul to campaign in Raetia against Burgundians and Vandals who had moved into a position to threaten Italy. According to the *Historia Augusta*, "He left Raetia in so peaceful a state there remained therein not even a suspicion of fear."[52] If this is true, it means he left an economic desert that would no longer be paying into the Roman treasury. Probus then continued to the Danube frontier, where he reportedly accepted the surrender of many local tribes. It is impossible to build a picture of events from these scarce narrative sources, but it is safe to assume that Probus was employing the old tricks of Roman diplomacy, subsidies, rewards, and a display of power while he rebuilt the Danubian *limes*.[53] By 281 Probus had gone back to Rome by way of Antioch; once there, he began to plan and coordinate an invasion of Persia. There was likely no better time to avenge the defeats of Valerian, as the Sassanid Empire was being wracked by a civil war of its own. In 282 Probus had gotten as far as Sirmium when he received news that the praetorian prefect, Carus, had revolted and declared himself emperor. He did not have time to react, for he was murdered almost as soon as he heard the news.

Carus was the first emperor in many a year not born in the Danubian regions. As such, even though he surely had a military background, he may have felt a need to add glory to his reputation, which, of course, was still part of a long Roman tradition. If so, what better way to do so than by leading a popular war of revenge against the hated Persians with an army already assembled by his predecessor, who had also kindly left behind a plan just waiting to be executed? Carus put himself at the head of the army and headed east. The Sassanids were unprepared to meet him. Sapor had died in 272, and his son, Ohrmazd, lived only another year. After that the Empire broke down into civil war between rival cousins at the same time it was being wracked by civil wars that would extend through the 280s. For this brief window of time, Rome had little to fear from its powerful rival.

Carus took full advantage of the opportunity, marching to Ctesiphon without meeting any resistance. It appears that the Romans thoroughly sacked the city's suburbs but failed to breach its walls. Carus was then either struck by lightning or murdered by his officers. Whatever story is true, Carus was dead and the army was left leaderless: only his youngest son, Numerian, was with him, but he was still a child. The army was probably led back to Syria by Carus's brother-in-law and the praetorian prefect, Aper. Somewhere along the march route Numerian too was murdered, one can assume on Aper's orders but probably with the support of several senior officers. Aper kept Numerian's death a secret as he attempted to gather enough supporters to make his own claim to the purple. The army, however, did not want Numerian's murderer leading them and chose instead Gaius Aurelius Valerius Diocles, a relatively junior officer in the imperial guard. His first order of business was to summon the army to a nearby hill, where he publicly swore that he played no part in Numerian's murder. He then called for Aper to be brought forward, proclaimed his guilt to the army, and stabbed him to death before the entire public assembly. The hard men of the legions likely admired the firmness and swiftness with which Diocles administered justice. As for Diocles, the only man who could accuse him of complicity in Numerian's murder was bleeding to death at his feet. It was an auspicious beginning to the start of Diocletian's twenty-four-year reign.

Diocletian's next order of business was to reunite the Empire, and to do that he needed to defeat Carus's oldest son, Carinus, in the field. He would do so with the army that Aurelian had assembled and trained and that Carus had led into Mesopotamia. It was a well-trained and battle-hardened force, having served together in the same army for years. Carinus had at his disposal the equally proficient western field army. But this force was having some internal problems. As Carinus marched east, he was forced to take time to crush a revolt by his praetorian prefect, Marcus Aurelius Julianus. Unfortunately, this was just the tip of a deeper command problem: many of the western army's senior leaders were unsatisfied with the emperor, as they would be with any emperor who made a sport of sleeping with their wives. When the two armies met, in the spring of 285, near the river Margus, Diocletian won a relatively easy battle, likely helped by the governor of Dalmatia, Flavius Constantius, and the fact that his portion of the western army changed sides just before the battle. Then, at the start of the battle, Carinus's praetorian prefect, Tiberius Claudius Aurelius Aristobulus, betrayed him as well, leaving the emperor to be killed by his own men.

Diocletian was now the sole ruler of the Roman world. But he recognized that managing an empire that was threatened on multiple fronts was beyond the capacity of any single individual. Without any sons, he was forced to take an unprecedented step of elevating a colleague of no familial relation, even through the fiction of adoption, Marcus Aurelius Maximianus—Maximian—to the rank of Caesar. To make sure everyone knew who was in charge, the relationship between the two emperors was portrayed in religious terms. Diocletian assumed the title of Jupiter, while Maximian became Hercules. They were both gods and therefore divine, but Hercules, as the junior god, was plainly there to help Jupiter with his tasks. This religious sanctification, whether intended at the time or not, served to place the two emperors on a higher plane than rivals who had only military support. This "divine right of kings" would be a foundation of royal power until at least the French Revolution.

Soon after his elevation, Maximian was sent to Gaul to put down some local uprisings of the Begaudae led by a local noble, Amandus. Maximian's initial military successes were undermined by one of his subordinates, Carausius, who commanded the Gallic coast, which included the fleet in the English Channel. His primary role was to stamp out Saxon and Frankish piracy. At this he was spectacularly successful and soon amassed a small fortune, but he did so by unusual means. He would allow the raiders to strike the coast at will, waiting until they were on their return trip and laden with booty to attack them. He would then seize their plunder for his own private treasury. If emperors had learned one thing from the preceding fifty years, it was that persons with independent commands, large financial resources, and a willingness to act outside the normal conventions were always trouble. When

Maximian learned what Carausius was up to, he ordered his subordinate's execution. Upon learning what fate was in store for him, Carausius fled to Britain, raised the standard of revolt, and declared himself emperor. Before 286 was over, Carausius had led northern Gaul and Britain out of the Empire.

Up to this point Roman emperors had always put the threat of revolt at the top of their list of concerns. Barbarians could be smashing through the *limes* and plunging deep into the Empire, but if someone in any part of the Empire revolted, virtually everything else halted as the legions were redirected to the point of internal political crisis. Only when the usurper had been defeated or there was a new emperor would the army return to its routine business of defending the frontiers. Maximian did not follow the playbook. Instead, he stayed on the Rhine frontier dealing with security threats along it. In 287 there was a series of raids that broke across the Rhine, one of which may have attacked Trier while Maximian was celebrating his consulship for the year.[54] His personal conduct of multiple campaigns against coalitions of Alemanni, Franks, and Burgundians fully occupied Maximian's attention, allowing Carausius to secure his position.

Before this, in 286, Maximian realized that if he was to secure the frontiers, put down revolts, and also restore imperial control to the interior of Gaul, he would require more power than was associated with being Caesar. He therefore elevated himself to the rank of Augustus, which Diocletian belatedly approved. One can read this in multiple ways. An uncharitable view would believe Diocletian was forced to accept a fait accompli rather than risk another civil war to reverse Maximian's action. More charitably, Diocletian also recognized the need for Maximian's elevation and fully approved the measure. In practical terms, nothing truly changed; Maximian was still the junior partner and behaved accordingly. In 288 the two Augusti met and agreed on a joint campaign, with Maximian attacking along and probably across the Rhine and Diocletian marching north into Raetia. The campaign was successful enough to allow Maximian to then attack Carausius at Rouen. He won a victory and took a few cities along and near the coast. But his victory was not decisive, and Carausius, who had over two years to prepare for Maximian's assault, counterattacked in the summer of 290, retaking the cities of Rouen, Boulogne, and Amiens. Details are not in evidence, but Diocletian deemed the crisis serious enough that he raced back from the Eastern Empire in the dead of winter to meet Maximian in Milan.

Judging from the number of senatorial meetings and public displays, the two Augusti made it clear that Diocletian was there to shore up public support for his co-emperor while at the same time agreeing on a new plan of operations.[55] Gaul was clearly too disturbed for one person to manage.

Maximian could not both defeat Carausius and hold the frontier. It was therefore decided that Flavius Constantius would take over the fight against Carausius while Maximian would concentrate on rebuilding the *limes* and the administration of Gaul. Constantius was of Dacian descent and may have been serving as praetorian prefect at the time. For at least the last couple of years, he had been holding the northern *limes* against Frankish and Alemanni incursions. He may also have had enough success in one of his expeditions across the Rhine to lay waste to everything from northern Germany to the Danube.[56] By now he was also probably married to Maximian's daughter, Theodora, and was already viewed as Maximian's successor. He would later become the senior of the two Caesars in the tetrarchy, which must have been debated for the first time during the Milan planning meetings. Although we have no source to inform us of what was discussed in the meetings between the two emperors, the future reorganization of the entire administrative structure of the empire must have been a key topic, as the Augusti were not to meet again until the twentieth anniversary of their rise as co-rulers.

What happened over the next two years is almost entirely lost to us. But on March 1, 293, two new Caesars were appointed. Maximian appointed Constantius, while Diocletian promoted C. Galerius Maximianus, who married his daughter Valeria. As his first act as Caesar, Constantius launched an expertly coordinated massive assault on Carausius's Gallic strongholds while at the same time defeating the pretender's Frankish allies in Batavia. Carausius was thoroughly routed, and his power was so undermined that he was murdered by one of his officers, Allectus. It was another three years before Constantius was able to build a fleet strong enough to allow him to attack Britain, one previous fleet having been destroyed in a storm. But in 296 Constantius landed several divisions at various points along the coast, making quick work of Allectus's army. Before Constantius himself could even get to the island to oversee further operations, Allectus was murdered. The Empire was again whole.

Before examining the impact of momentous political and administrative changes of 293, we must examine how Diocletian spent the years during which Maximian was trying to retake Gaul and Britain. After concluding a rapid campaign against the Sarmatians in 285, Diocletian spent 286 in the east, where he seems to have taken advantage of the continuing Sassanid civil war to enhance imperial control and strengthen the border defenses. There is evidence at this time of fort construction all along the Persian border, in Egypt, as well as all along the Danubian *limes*. Diocletian, taking advantage of Persia's internal turmoil, also secured a settlement with Persia over Armenia that was more favorable to Roman interests. Armenia, which had been wholly controlled by Persia since the destruction of Valerian's army by Sapor I, was divided. The Persians retained the eastern portion, ruled by Narses, Sapor I's youngest son. Rome claimed the western portion, placing an Arsacid and Roman client, Tiridates, on the throne. Rome also took the opportunity to push back the Persian boundary beyond the Euphrates. Nisibis remained in Persian hands until the end of the 290s, but Edessa was once again made a Roman stronghold, and Diocletian built an arms factory within its walls.[57] All of this was storing up trouble; after all, Persia was unlikely to be prostrate forever. In fact, by 293 Narses, the youngest son of Sapor I, had defeated his rivals, secured the throne, and begun preparing for war with Rome.

Again, Diocletian, having made peace with Persia, considered the east secure enough to return to the always-troubling Danubian provinces. He conducted campaigns in Raetia, repelled Sarmatian incursions, and met with his co-emperor, Maximian. But by the summer of 290 he was back in the east campaigning against the Saraceni, who, since the destruction of Palmyran military power by Aurelian, were an increasingly potent threat to the security of southern Syria.[58]

Diocletian had once again gone west and was in Pannonia when Narses, in 296, invaded Osroene and western Armenia. As he raced east, his new Caesar, Galerius, took charge. According to Eutropius, Rome got off to a bad start:

> Galerius Maximian, in acting against Narseus [Narses], fought, on the first occasion, a battle far from successful, meeting him between Callinicus and Carrae, and engaging in the combat rather with rashness than want of courage; for he contended with a small army against a very numerous enemy. Being in consequence defeated and going to join Diocletian.[59]

There are two ways to interpret this passage. Either the Roman army in the east was once again routed, or Galerius, with a small, hastily assembled force, blunted the Sassanid main attack, giving time for the full army to mass near Antioch and gather reinforcements from the west. Given what happened next, the latter is the more likely. First of all, the Persian advance halted and did not go beyond what was previously claimed by Sapor I. This pause allowed Galerius to go to the Danube to reinforce the field army there and then bring it east. It was this army that would fight the Persians, since Diocletian soon had to take a substantial portion of the Syrian army to Alexandria to crush a revolt by another usurper. Clearly, instability on the eastern frontier was offering opportunities for those who were hoping a return to the pre-Diocletian political anarchy would present opportunities for them to roll the dice and make a bid for the purple. It is worth noting how efficiently the tetrarchy was now operating in the military sphere. When Narses attacked, in 296, it coincided with Constantius's assault on the usurpers in Britain, while at the same time Maximian was coordinating campaigns along the Rhine and Diocletian was securing Pannonia against the Sarmatians. By 297 Britain had been reconquered, the Rhine was temporarily quiet, there were no recorded assaults along the Danube, an Egyptian usurper had been crushed, and Galerius was ready to move against the Sassanid army. This is quite a testament to both the resilience of Rome's military power and the command arrangements established in 293.

Early in 298 Galerius took the offensive, invading northern Mesopotamia through Armenia. At least two battles were fought, and in the second of them, near Satala, Galerius's legions fought their way into the Persian camp, capturing the Persian treasury and large numbers of the royal family, including Narses's wife, Arsane.[60] Galerius then chased the routed Sassanid army out of Armenia and across the Tigris, going on to recover Nisibis before the year ended. With its army wrecked, its treasury lost, and most of the royal family prisoners, the Sassanids were forced to accept a harsh peace, negotiated by the imperial secretary (*magister memoriae*), Sicorius Probus. The Sassanids gave up five provinces, all of which included major avenues of approach into Armenia or Rome's eastern provinces.[61] Rome quickly fortified the cities within these provinces and integrated them into the eastern frontier's defensive system, now moved considerably further from Antioch than at any time since Severus's rule. For the next forty years, the Roman and Persian Empires were at peace.[62]

Strategic Assessment

Historians can differ on when the worst of the Crisis of the Third Century ended, but the year 298 has to be a leading contender. Rome was unified under a tetrarchy dominated by the emperor, Diocletian; threats to the Danube and Rhine frontiers were now a chronic condition and no longer so acute as to threaten to collapse the state; and, most crucially, Rome was set to enjoy a multi-decade peace with its rival superpower.[63]

The Crisis of the Third Century had brought the Empire to its knees, but by its end the Empire was regaining a surer footing. Yet this hides some important changes in Rome's strategic situation. Rome had been a dominant power for 250 years. Barbarians could win victories and from time to time raid across the frontiers; but during the Principate it was almost always the Romans who were on the offensive, launching regular expeditions across the frontiers to break up concentrations of barbarian power before they became too dangerous. Rome was also almost continually on the offensive in the east. One could be forgiven for believing that the route from Antioch to Ctesiphon was maintained mostly as a Roman training ground. The changes impacting Rome's strategic situation in this century were outlined earlier in this work, but they boil down to just a few crucial elements: dangerous barbarian coalitions, a much more militarily efficient and lethal Persian Empire, and considerably fewer resources. And throughout it all, the Romans were dealing with a collapsing political system that propagated a series of crippling civil wars. It is worth noting that these civil wars were not as ruinous as those of the next century, because so few of them came to blows: in many cases one or the other army killed its leader before battle was joined. Throughout the entire crisis period only one emperor, Philip, fell under the swords of an opposing Roman army. Still, the constant civil wars were a distraction, for the Roman imperative to give a usurper priority over all other security concerns ensured that the armies would often be marching away from the frontiers just when they were most needed.

Rome was trying to meet these challenges with a military remarkably similar in size and doctrine to the forces that served Augustus at the Empire's start.[64] Despite some growth under Severus, who added two legions, the Roman army was much too small to meet challenges on multiple fronts, particularly if the *limes* were penetrated in any force. Each major campaign, therefore, required the assembly of field armies drawn from garrisons in quiet sectors and commanded by senators who did not know their business. Moreover, Rome had gone from being the aggressor in almost every conflict to reacting to each enemy move. In short, it had ceded the military initiative to its enemies.

We have already discussed how all of this was compounded by the increasingly harsh financial straits in which emperors found themselves. With modern techniques of debt financing still more than a millennium in the future, extra money could only be had through added taxes and stricter collections, both of which negatively impacted the overall economy and societal stability. As the century unfolded, the economic crisis, driven by wars, plagues, and botched recoinages, worsened until finally the Roman economy imploded. Trade, as we have already seen in the record of found sunken vessels, collapsed. This in turn drove ever-greater amounts of economic fragmentation, as regions fell back upon local production for almost all goods. Of course, this economic fragmentation struck different locations with varying degrees of severity. But to assume that North Africa escaped the economic catastrophe because it was remote from the conflict zones is a mistake. North Africa's most valuable trade goods often went to northern Europe. When that market dried up, North Africa paid a heavy price.[65] It has been argued that the currency debasement, which wrecked Roman trade and provided a catalyst for inflation, was "only of marginal importance, as farmers or landlords had direct access to the products of agriculture."[66] This is a bit disingenuous, for this reliance on local production was what was driving the economic fragmentation of the Empire and would have an increasingly profound impact as the decades passed. Moreover, it ignores the power of the cities, with their larger populations, their greater financial resources, and their first call on imperial military power to compel farmers to hand over their produce. Finally, Drinkwater claims that, in respect to wage earners, such as lesser bureaucrats and soldiers, the Empire's inflation was by modern standards inconsiderable.[67] Comparing ancient inflation to modern standards of hyperinflation, such as that seen in post–World War I Germany or, more recently, in Venezuela, is absurd. Still, most analysts who have studied the third century's economic crises place the annual inflation at between 3 and 5.5 percent per annum, possibly reaching 10 percent by the time Diocletian felt compelled to issue his Edict on Maximum Prices in 301. If we split the difference and agree on an average inflation rate of 4 percent, that means prices were doubling every eighteen years. This would, of course, be a crushing blow to any wage earner, as there was no wage inflation capable of matching the rate of price increases.[68]

Still, as discussed, even after the economic collapse of the third century, the Empire retained a tremendous amount of latent power, particularly when we measure it against its rivals and enemies. Even after successive major defeats, Rome remained able to muster, train, and field successive armies until such time as Rome's enemies were forced to withdraw from the struggle for long periods of recuperation.

Constant fighting also made it impossible for emperors to stay at home, as many had done during the Principate. Wars were too important to be left to subordinates, and successful generals remained as dangerous to imperial rule as ever. But being with the army had its drawbacks. First, in the event of defeat, there was no one else to blame for failure. For another, emperors who were constantly visible to the soldiers lost much of their mystique. This combination exposed them to new levels of criticism and made them easy targets when things went poorly. Moreover, as the number of crisis points expanded, emperors discovered they could not be everywhere. Provincials were therefore often forced to rely on local officials and commanders for their security. Postumus, Odaenathus, and Zenobia were not emperors, but they were present in the region, and they commanded effective armies. Reversing this breaking up of the Empire took years and a major military effort. But it was also a harbinger of the future. When the next crisis struck, the fault lines were already set and would worsen as the huge fractures of the third century were repeated in microcosm throughout the Empire, particularly in the west. The beginnings of this political fragmentation can be seen in the walled towns and villas of the third century, as well as in the increasing reliance on local production to fulfill regional needs. In the past, people relied on centrally controlled imperial legions for their security. In the future, the imperial field armies would remain a crucial part of any strategic defensive scheme, but local defenses manned by local forces would become increasingly important.

The political upheaval of the third century was not limited to those areas stricken by repeated conflicts. Rome, for hundreds of years the Empire's central city, lost much of its political importance. And by the time Diocletian assumed the purple, emperors felt little need to even visit the city, never mind reside there. Power moved to wherever the emperor was located, and that was increasingly in the great fortress cities near the frontiers—Antioch, Mainz, Cologne, and Sirmium. Moreover, the need for military leaders of true ability and long service gradually pushed senators to the margins and eventually denied them any chance of military commands, which had been the stepping-stone to higher administrative appointments. Commands now went to men of proven ability, and some generals and later emperors were only one or two generations removed from their peasant ancestors. Increasingly, the top jobs of administering the Empire went to military officers of proven ability and not to the professional politicians of the Senate. As the role of Rome's senators was reduced, so too was the power of Rome as the imperial city. Gradually Rome became more of a symbol of the Empire than a source of power or wealth.

Although not discussed much in this work, the third century was also a time of tremendous religious upheaval, as Christianity spread throughout the Empire. Many who still held on to the old beliefs blamed the successive crises on the anger of Rome's pantheon of gods over so many Romans turning from them to worship the new Christian god. At the same time, the Christians blamed the unrelenting catastrophes on the pagans' refusal to give up the old gods, as well as the basic sinful nature of the Empire. In the third century the pagans still had the upper hand, and several emperors ordered persecutions of the Christian communities. These were likely never as far-reaching as the Christian authors of the time present them, but they and religious conflict in general were another source of discontent feeding the general malaise. By

260, however, the persecutions had mostly run their course, and Gallienus's policies opened a new era of tolerance. Just a few decades later the major sources of religious strife would shift from pagan-Christian fractiousness to conflicts between different Christian communities and sects.

Aurelian certainly did much to restore the Empire. By conquering Zenobia's eastern strongholds, destroying the Gallic Empire, and temporarily seeing off the Goths, he indeed earned the title "Restorer of the World." But Aurelian did not bring the decades of crisis to an end: the underlying conditions that sent the eastern and western portions of the Empire on their separate ways persisted. Persia remained a dangerous superpower, sure to pounce as soon as its domestic quarrels were settled. Also, the threats from across the Rhine and Danube remained unabated and may have become more dangerous. Worryingly, these continuing threats would be confronted by an empire possessing considerably fewer economic resources than when the century began.

Drinkwater has argued that even during the worst of the Crisis of the Third Century, the Empire was never threatened with total collapse. He supports this belief by claiming that the threats that precipitated the crisis were not that dangerous: "despite Roman fears, Sassanid Persia had no real intention of reclaiming former Achaemenid possessions in the eastern Mediterranean region; and the Germans, though troublesome, would have been incapable of permanently occupying territory against determined imperial opposition, even if they had wanted to do so."[69] This seems a remarkable assertion, given that the Empire had divided itself into three parts and there was no assurance they would ever reunite again. Without Aurelian's military gains, the Empire, based in Rome, would have been a rump of its former self, yielding far fewer resources than the combined Empire could mobilize. A continuance of this separation for another decade would have led to an incalculable future. It did not require the Persians to permanently occupy previous Achaemenid possessions, nor the barbarians occupying lands beyond the frontiers, to destroy the territorial fabric of the Empire. Just the threat of either was demonstrably sufficient to do so as the locals turned to their own warlords for protection.

While Aurelian did not fundamentally change the Empire's political or administrative structure to meet growing threats, one could argue that the need to fight a series of constant wars never gave him sufficient breathing space to do so. He did, however, leave one thing of inestimable value: a reformed military apparatus. Extending Gallienus's reforms, Aurelian built an unmatchable field army that could be broken into parts as various crises demanded attention or rapidly recombined to meet a major threat. It was this field army that Diocletian used to defeat the Persians and gain four decades of peace. It was a part of this army that formed the backbone of the force Constantius employed to defeat usurpers based in Britain and to restore the Rhine frontiers. It was this field army that allowed Diocletian the breathing space to restructure the Empire.

Still, it was Diocletian's first major reform—the tetrarchy—that ensured the military system he inherited would reach its full potential, since its structure allowed the two Augusti to separate themselves from the fighting of wars. Only when the Empire was faced with more than two major threats at the same time would the Augusti have to lead an army, and even then they could choose the fight where victory was almost assured. By allowing the two Caesars to take over the military aspects of ruling, the two Augusti could distance themselves from reverses, which had so weakened the stature and political power of prior emperors. At the same time, by being removed from the immediate concerns of military command, which would have absorbed their full attention, the two Augusti were positioned to mobilize and allocate the full resources of the Empire to various other conflicts and challenges.

Rome came out of the Crisis of the Third Century a different empire; its political and administrative structure was changed, its army bore little resemblance to the armies of the Principate, its civic fabric was close to being shredded, and its economy was much more localized. Moreover, the threats Rome faced were much greater than those it confronted during the Principate. The barbarians were more concentrated, richer, and better armed; and, most crucially, they had learned how to fight Roman armies. In the east the Sassanids were a vastly more powerful and aggressive force than the Parthians had ever been. But what made confronting these challenges increasingly difficult was first the political division of the Empire, and, later, the practical division of the Empire's resources. Increasingly, in the Empire's later years, we are faced with an Eastern and Western Empire, which rarely went to the assistance of the other and were often at each other's throats.

So much, in fact, changed that we may as well be talking about two distinct Roman narratives. The first, which made up Part II of this book, covered Rome at the height of its power, as well as how Rome adapted to meet new and more dangerous challenge. Part III continues the story of empire but focuses on the consequences of Rome's strategic adaptions, and why they were not enough to stave off the ultimate collapse of the western half of the empire.

PART III | The Late Empire
New Beginnings and an End

CHAPTER 14 | Diocletian, Constantine, and a
New Empire

E VEN AUGUSTUS COULD not manage the affairs of the entire Empire
alone, particularly in times of crisis. In the early years of the Empire he
could rely on Agrippa to enforce his will, and when Agrippa passed there was
Tiberius. By the third century one-man rule was clearly unable to deal with the
multiple simultaneous threats facing the Empire. A succession of emperors
had tried various solutions, with little lasting success. It was Diocletian's
genius to recognize the political truth and attempt to institutionalize a new
ruling system—the tetrarchy. This system, based on two Augusti—one for
the east and one for the west—each served by a Caesar, aimed to ensure that
the man at the point of any crisis had the power to act and that he would be
obeyed.[1] Just as crucially, it was meant to regularize the succession and thus
end the debilitating civil wars of the past: when an Augusti died or retired,
his Caesar would replace him and a new Caesar, acceptable to all, would be
invested. The system worked as long as Diocletian was alive, for his stature
and demonstrated ruthlessness was sufficient to keep everyone in line. But
when he passed from the scene, his arrangements proved no match for human
nature and dynastic ambition.

From the start, Diocletian recognized the system's weakness and tried to
alleviate it through a series of marriage arrangements: Constantius married
Maximian's daughter, while Galerius married Diocletian's daughter, and both
Caesars were adopted by their respective senior Augusti. Later, Maximian's
son, Maxentius, married Galerius's daughter, and Constantius never forgot

about Constantine, his son from an earlier marriage to Helena. Because neither Diocletian nor Galerius had sons, Maxentius and Constantine certainly considered themselves to be next in line as Caesars, followed by becoming Augusti when the first generation of the tetrarchy passed on. When their expectations, particularly those of Constantine, were not met, they proved only too willing to blow up Diocletian's arrangements in favor of seeking a battlefield decision.[2]

While historians have made much of Diocletian's political arrangements, their lack of staying power makes them virtually a strategic nullity. Diocletian could have appointed all three of the other members of the tetrarchy simply to military commands and achieved the same results. His one true achievement was making sure that his system managed to keep the ambitions of his colleagues in check during his lifetime. But because that collegiality broke down immediately after his death, one can hardly call it a lasting impact. Still, from the start of Diocletian's reign until the fall of the Western Empire, there were very few years in which the Empire was not divided between multiple rulers, and most of those years are accounted for by Constantine's sole rule.[3] The problem, of course, was that these co-rulership schemes almost always degenerated into renewed bouts of civil war.

Diocletian's other major reform was to reconfigure the provinces. By far the most crucial changes were a doubling of the number of provinces to approximately a hundred, and then the grouping of adjoining provinces into one of a dozen dioceses, which were then all tied to Diocletian's new fiscal and administrative arrangements. Each of the new dioceses—six in the west (Britanniae, Galliae, Viennensis, Hispaniae, Africa, and Italia), three in Illyricum (Pannoniae, Moesiae, and Thracia), and three in the east (Asiana, Pontica, and Oriens)—was placed under an equestrian official, called the *vicarius* of the praetorian prefects.[4] In most cases, the *vicarii* had no control of the military forces stationed within the entire dioceses. The command of the military forces within a diocese fell to a *comes rei militaris*, who reported to the *magister militum*, who commanded the armies of each of the Augusti. The *comes* controlled the *duces*, who held military command within the various provinces. This left the *vicarii* to manage the civilian administration of their dioceses, including tax collections and paying the soldiers. The *vicarii*, except for the proconsuls in the east (facing the Persians) and in North Africa (supervising Rome's food supply), supervised the governors. As the centers for tax collection, the various dioceses soon became the later Empire's great fiscal centers.[5]

Diocletian also unquestionably increased the size of both the army and the fleet, although there is no reason to entertain Lactantius's commentary about each member of the tetrarchy recruiting a force equal to any single emperor, which would entail a quadrupling of Rome's military forces. What is more certain is that he added to the number of legions while also subdividing them, a process begun much earlier when generals began taking vexillations rather than entire legions on campaign. As the number of legions increased, they also became smaller. This would have increased flexibility, but likely at the cost of shock, which was always a function of mass. It would also have greatly depleted the staying power of the legions on defense. The *comitatus* was retained, and there were certainly several of these mobile field armies at any one time.

A new office of *duces* (future dukes) began to appear along the frontier amid the Crisis of the Third Century. These *duces* were military commanders who initially fell under the command of the provincial governors. Later in the century there is a record of some *duces* commanding smaller field armies, usually vexillations taken from the *comitatus* to fight in other threatened theaters. Diocletian expanded the military authority of the *duces* as part of his program to separate military and civil hierarchies within many provinces. By separating the civil authority from the military power in each province, Diocletian limited the possibility of any single commander becoming powerful enough to revolt: a *dux* might have the soldiers, but the governor would have money. Unless both parties were ready to revolt and one agreed to remain subordinate to the other—an unlikely event—it would be difficult for any rebellion to gain traction. None of this happened overnight, and there are instances of governors still possessing military commands well into Constantine's reign.[6] At the start of the fifth century, the *Notitia Dignitatum* records two *duces* in Britain, twelve along the length of the Rhine and Danube, eight in the east, and seven in Africa.

Diocletian also placed considerable emphasis on rebuilding and strengthening the *limes*, especially along the eastern frontier, where the fortress cities, such as Nisibis, were greatly strengthened and new forts along known avenues of approach multiplied. Much has been made of this apparent attempt to renew the *limes'* function as a preclusive barrier capable of repelling all but the most determined assaults.[7] This, as we have seen, fundamentally misinterprets the reasons for Rome's frontier fortifications. The *limes* could certainly deal with the management of low-level threats and could deter barbarian chiefs without a large force from attacking even when Rome was distracted by other events. But by the end of the third century, no Roman military leader could have failed to note that the barbarian tribal coalitions were powerful enough to penetrate the *limes* at any point of their choosing. If this is the case, then what was Diocletian's intent? By strengthening the *limes*, the emperor was only partially returning to the strategic status quo, allowing Rome to benefit from the same factors that made the *limes* important in the first place. For one thing, frontier fortifications greatly increased security along long stretches of the Rhine and Danube, allowing the riverine fleets to move uncontested along their length. This, as it had done during the Principate, vastly improved operational and strategic mobility, since reinforcements and supplies could move quickly to any trouble spot. For another, the *limes* returned security to most of the frontier provinces, as they were now capable of holding back all but the largest raids. Moreover, more stable frontiers made trade across the frontier zones possible again and also allowed a more controlled migration into the Empire. Finally—and this is where Diocletian's defensive system differed from that of the Principate—there were at least two and more likely several field armies stationed behind the *limes*. These armies could move to engage larger incursions without having to draw troops away from the frontiers, which would encourage further raiding. And, in the event of a truly serious threat, these armies could combine their combat power, again without necessarily having to draw troops from the frontier. Strategic success relied on finding the balance. How strong could you make the *limes* before you were using up troops needed to man the field armies, and how strong could you make the field armies before the frontiers became dangerously denuded of troops? Finally, as always, the great imponderable was another outbreak of civil war. If the field armies turned on one another, all such balancing calculations would be for naught.

It is worth noting that, with the field armies in place, Diocletian was no longer putting his faith in Luttwak's preclusive strategy, which called for stopping all threats at or as close to the frontier as possible. The new system, of course, remained preclusive in the face of low-level threats. But in the face of a large-scale assault, the job of the forces in the frontier zone was to warn, delay, and channel the threat toward the fast-advancing field army. Moreover, because these field armies operated as close to the frontier as possible, they could still draw supplies from bases along Europe's two great rivers.

What is missing from Diocletian's system is the integration of offensive maneuver. In the past, Rome had not been content to rely solely upon the *limes* to meet whatever threat arose. Rather, when Rome received intelligence of dangerous concentrations of barbarians across the frontier, large punitive expeditions would plunge deep into barbarian territory to short-circuit threats before they could metastasize. Diocletian was returning stability, which was crucial to the Empire's recovery, but he was still ceding the initiative to Rome's enemies.

To pay for enlarging the military and rebuilding the *limes*, Diocletian spent considerable time and energy reforming the Empire's tax system.[8] The demographic collapse, a result of the prior century's wars, famines, and plagues, was destructive enough to Rome's finances, but Rome had also seen a huge amount of farmland turn fallow as a result of the wars, a problem that was multiplied by depopulation. The consequence was a major loss in revenue from Rome's two most crucial revenue streams, the poll tax and the land tax. In many cases, the cost of maintaining the armies forced Rome to abandon taxes based on currency collection in favor of taxes in kind, which provided wheat and other necessities directly to the army.

Under Diocletian, internal stability also stabilized the army. For the first time since the Severan dynasty, the size of the army was fixed and known. Because military expenses absorbed most of the state budget, it was now possible to predict almost precisely how much revenue was required every year. Add this predictability to Diocletian's enhanced administrative system, and for the first time Rome was able to carefully budget its expenses. At the same time, the reorganization of the Empire's provinces, the new power of local administrators, and the transition from tax farming to a system where taxes were collected by imperial administrators increased the amount of revenue going to the imperial treasury, but also made the annual tax take much more predictable. For perhaps the first time in its history, Rome was able to calculate both revenues and expenses and create a workable state budget. This new tax system and a realignment of the tax burdens was all accomplished through a new imperial census and land survey of the entire Empire. It was also aided by Diocletian's removal of almost all of the numerous tax exemptions that had been emplaced over the centuries.

Because most of the tax proceeds were paying for the army's upkeep, Diocletian also regularized the substitution of gold and silver for in-kind contributions, making taxes fairer and more proportionate to agricultural yield as well as to the number of taxpayers. Moreover, because the new system accepted most taxes as in-kind payments and made these substitutes a considerable part of every soldier's pay, both the army and the imperial administration were shielded from the consequences of currency depreciation and price rises.[9] While such methods appeared to be an answer to Rome's financial chaos, in the long run the demonetization of the economy continued to inflict damage on interregional trade, accelerating the de facto economic fragmentation of the Empire. Moreover, soldiers who were no longer drawing their pay in coinage from a central authority would inevitably start to see themselves as regional forces dedicated to the defense of a region (and its food supplies) rather than of the Empire as a whole. Still, there is a real limit to how much of the soldiers' wages could be paid in kind. Soldiers expected to be paid in coin, and when it was not received in acceptable amounts, they tended to become dangerous.

This is what made the persistent Aurelian inflation so dangerous in the short term. When initial attempts at recoinage and establishing new values for existing coins failed, Diocletian in 301 issued the Edict of Maximum Prices. The edict listed maximum prices of food commodities as well as a long list of manufactures. It also set the pay for most laborers as well as transport and freight prices. As with every government price-fixing attempt in history, the edict was doomed to failure, as producers withheld food and other goods from the market. In a very short time a vibrant black market was thriving despite the edict's decree of the death penalty for anyone who violated it. In time the edict was allowed to fade away unenforced as prices continued to rise.

Monetary stability and the end of inflation had to wait until the end of the civil war that brought Constantine to power in 324. By allowing the price of gold to rise while issuing large amounts of new gold coins, as had his successors, Constantine stabilized the economy by moving it from a silver base to one of gold. Constantine's new gold coin—the solidus, weighing 1/72 of a pound—became the basis of a new and more stable monetary system, exactly as the silver denarius had done during the Principate. This switch was greatly assisted by the discovery of rich new sources of gold in the Caucasus. This new influx of bullion, once processed into high-quality *solidi*, first financed Constantine's imperial ambitions and then funded his successors for decades. Moreover, this huge influx of bullion, which proved much more resistant to inflation than silver, drove significant economic growth throughout the Eastern Empire.[10] Thus, by the end of the fourth century the Eastern Empire was far wealthier than it had been at the end of the Crisis of the Third Century. The centralized control and distribution of new gold resources knitted the Eastern Empire's economy together, keeping local elites—a newly risen administrative autocracy—integrated and loyal to the imperial power that was driving the economic engine. This economic and political consolidation accelerated even as the Western elites were increasingly distancing themselves from the imperial center.[11] Interestingly, very little of this gold made its way into the Western Empire, providing further evidence that the Empire was divided not only politically but economically.

While this change stabilized the monetary system for the government, the rich, and the imperial elites, it was a disaster for the mass of the population and the long-term health of the economy. Without access to gold, and with the economy bifurcating between those who could purchase goods in gold and those still trying to make do with silver and copper, the latter soon found their money even more worthless than before as inflation galloped along in the first decades of the fourth century. Economic fragmentation continued apace, which always left political fragmentation lurking in the shadows, waiting for an opportunity.[12]

Before turning to the end of Diocletian's rule, we must examine the strategic impact of his edict to restart the persecution of the Christians. While the event has served to tarnish Diocletian's place in history—most surviving histories of the period and later were written by Christian authors—it lasted only eighteen months. And although his successor, Galerius, started the persecutions anew, they were not as widespread as later Christian authors would have us believe, since many local administrators did the bare minimum required to appease the central power. In fact, Constantius, in the areas he controlled, ignored the edict completely, a position that probably did much to guide the young Constantine. His superior Augustus, Maximian, was also not an enthusiastic supporter of the persecutions. These early differences in how Christianity was tolerated or accepted are where we have to look for the persecutions' strategic impact. In the east, the persecutions often continued apace, driving Christianity underground and accelerating the various schisms already forming within the new religion. In the west, however, Christianity was flourishing and was much more apostolic and unified in its outlook and beliefs. It is out of this milieu that the Empire gets its first Christian emperor, Constantine, which, in turn, led to Christianity becoming the dominant state religion within a remarkably short time.

By 304 Diocletian had restored Roman power to a height not seen since the reign of Severus. Having done so, he decided it was time to move aside while he still had the power and unbounded prestige to choose his successors. In 305 he asked Maximian to meet him in Rome to celebrate their twentieth year together as co-Augusti, despite Maximian's having been in the position for only nineteen years. During their meetings, Diocletian either convinced or ordered Maximian to step down from the Augusti and enter civilian life.

On May 1, 305, Constantius and Maximian were back in Milan, while Diocletian had joined Galerius at Nicomedia. As planned, the two Caesars stepped up to the rank of Augusti, with Galerius taking over the east and Constantius the west. Diocletian, likely at the behest of Galerius, had already selected the two new Caesars. One was Flavius Valerius Severus, a close military ally of Galerius, and the other was Galerius's nephew, Maximinus Daia. Diocletian was clearly trying to demonstrate that the rank of Caesar was going to be chosen by merit and not birth. But in doing so he infuriated both

Constantius and Maximian, who both expected to have their sons declared Caesars and then Augusti.

Consequently, all of Diocletian's work was already unraveling as he made his way to his retirement palace in Split (in modern Croatia). First, the Empire was split into four praetorian prefectures, each consisting of three provinces and each controlled by one of the tetrarchs. This had not been deemed necessary while Diocletian ruled, since no one disputed that he was the senior Augustus and had ultimate control of the entire Empire. In the new arrangement, Galerius ruled the three Balkan dioceses, Maximinus ruled from the Dardanelles to Egypt, and Severus controlled Italy, Africa, and Spain, leaving Constantius with Gaul and Britain. Of strategic note here is that Egypt is for the first time officially recognized as being controlled by the east. Ever since Augustus's reign, Egypt, because of its large grain surplus, had been recognized as a province of special concern to Rome, which always had first call on its grain surplus. While Rome could still bid for Egypt's grain, this change in control is a clear acknowledgment that other cities, particularly in the east, now rivaled Rome's claim as the leading city of the Empire.

Soon after these political arrangements were made, Constantius demanded that Galerius send his son, Constantine, who had been working with Galerius in the Balkans, to join him in the west.[13] Before the end of 305, Constantine had joined his father on campaign in northern Britain. When Constantius died in 306, the army, which had a much higher regard for hereditary rights than did Diocletian, declared Constantine emperor. Galerius, who viewed himself as the leading Augustus after Diocletian's retirement, had to acquiesce to Constantine's elevation, since Maxentius, supported by his father, who came out of retirement, also declared himself Augustus. According to Zosimus, "Maxentius . . . could not endure the sight of Constantine's good fortune, who was the son of a harlot, while himself, who was the son of so great an emperor, remained at home in indolence, and his father's empire was enjoyed by others."[14] When Severus attempted to crush Maxentius's revolt, he found that his army remained loyal to Maximian, who had commanded them for two decades. He was placed under house arrest and later murdered. With Severus removed, Galerius was forced to accept the rise of both Maxentius and Constantine, but he only did so as Caesars.[15] Constantine returned to Gaul, where, after leading a campaign across the Rhine to confirm his status as a military commander, he enhanced his position further by marrying Maximian's daughter, Flavia Maxima Fausta, thereby making his co-Caesar, Maxentius, his brother-in-law.

Despite these arrangements, war was looming when Diocletian was asked to come out of retirement and settle affairs. On November 11, 308, with both Diocletian and Maximian present, Galerius proclaimed one of his allies, Valerius Licinianus Licinius, as Augustus in place of Severus; Constantine was recognized as Caesar and, along with Maximinus, assumed the title "Son of the Augusti."[16] Diocletian then returned to his palace at Split, where he spent the remainder of his life growing cabbages. For the tetrarchy, however, there was no such peace. Like all of Rome's emperors, they had a strategic imperative to prove they were worthy to rule, and that could still only be accomplished in battle.

Constantine, as early as 307, crushed a large band of Franks across the Lower Rhine and afterward had their kings fed to the beasts in the amphitheater at Trier. In 308 he launched a punishing invasion of his own across the Rhine. During that same year Galerius was engaged in his own reputational mending by slaughtering the Carpi and their allies along the northern side of the Danube. Licinius would take over these duties in the following year. In 308, and throughout the following year, Maxentius was battling in Africa against the governor of Numidia, L. Domitius Alexander, who had raised the standard of revolt.[17] For as long as Galerius lived, these political arrangements held, just barely. But in 311 Galerius died, as did Diocletian, ending the brief period of stability.

In 310 Maximian, taking advantage of Constantine's being once again called away to battle the Franks, revolted, telling the troops that Constantine had died in battle. But when Constantine appeared before the walls of Marseilles, where Maximian was holed up, the defenders surrendered and Maximian committed suicide, on the strong suggestion of Constantine. The original four members of the tetrarchy were now dead. In their place stood four new emperors who held little trust for one another. In the east, Licinius and Maximinus Daia were already locked in a power struggle, while Constantine and Maxentius kept a wary eye on one another in the west. In 312 Constantine aligned himself with Licinius against Maximinus and Maxentius. He could hardly have done otherwise: if he left Licinius unsupported he would be crushed between the other two armies, leaving him alone to fight the combined power of both.

In 313 Maximinus moved out of Antioch with seventy thousand men. Licinius, caught off guard by the speed of his rival's preparations and advance, was still in Milan when Maximinus arrived opposite Byzantium. The reason for Maximinus's speed was soon discovered, since, owing to faulty preparations, his army had suffered considerable attrition during its rapid march, with a concomitant fall in the army's morale. A fast-reacting Licinius was able to gather strength as he marched across the Balkans, gathering forces as he advanced. When the armies met at Tzirallum (modern Corlu), Licinius was still outnumbered by more than two to one. But, as in many battles of the ancient world, discipline and experience decided the day. According to Lactantius, the battle was a one-sided slaughter:

> So the two armies drew nigh; the trumpets gave the signal; the military ensigns advanced; the troops of Licinius charged. But the enemies, panic-struck, could neither draw their swords nor yet throw their javelins. . . . Then were the troops of Daia [Maximinus] slaughtered, none making resistance; and such numerous legions, and forces so mighty, were mowed down by an inferior enemy.[18]

Maximinus retreated toward Syria but was relentlessly pursued by Licinius, and, once besieged in Tarsus, committed suicide. Licinius, without opposition, then assumed sole control of the Roman east.

Even before all of this took place, Constantine in 312 struck like a thunderbolt in the west. With an army reportedly numbering ninety thousand infantry and eight thousand cavalry, much of it raised from barbarian tribes, Constantine crossed the Alps.[19] Gibbon reminds us that at least half of this great army would have to be left to guard the frontiers, and at this stage of the Empire's history, a mobile force numbering about forty thousand is close to the maximum that can be sustained for a prolonged period.[20] They would face almost four times their number, maintained by the superior supply system in Italy. But as with Licinius at Tzirallum, quality counted for more than numbers. Gibbon's florid prose captures the difference:

> But the armies of Rome, placed at a secure distance from danger, were enervated by indulgence and luxury. Habituated to the baths and theatres of Rome, they took the field with reluctance, and were chiefly composed of veterans who had almost forgotten, or of new levies who had never acquired, the use of arms and the practice of war. The hardy legions of Gaul had long defended the frontiers of the empire against the barbarians of the North; and in the performance of that laborious service, their valor was exercised and their discipline confirmed. There appeared the same difference between the leaders as between the armies. Caprice or flattery had tempted Maxentius with the hopes of conquest; but these aspiring hopes soon gave way to the habits of pleasure and the consciousness of his inexperience. The intrepid mind of Constantine had been trained from his earliest youth to war, to action, and to military command.

Maxentius, through faulty intelligence, had placed a large force guarding the pass near Susa (Segusium) and was therefore taken by surprise when the Rhine legions descended from the pass at Mont Cenis. Moving rapidly, Constantine cut off and destroyed the force at Susa and took the city by storm. Speed was crucial: Constantine was only too familiar with the many invasions of Italy that had failed because they had lost momentum by engaging in long sieges. Just days after the victory at Susa, Constantine's army was at Turin, where it defeated another of Maxentius's separated field forces. In a battle narrative reminiscent of Aurelian's battles against Zenobia, Constantine's forces outmaneuvered, enveloped, and then finally defeated a large force of mailed heavy cavalry, which they beat down with spiked clubs. The people of Turin, not wishing to undergo the ravages of being sacked, closed their gates to Maxentius's routed force but opened them to Constantine.

Constantine immediately marched east to engage a third Maxentian army in the Po Valley. This army, commanded by the praetorian prefect, Ruricius Pompeianus, advanced west to meet the invader outside of Verona, which Constantine had been forced to invest. Again, we turn to Gibbon for a description of events:

> The emperor, attentive to the motions, and informed of the approach of so formidable an enemy, left a part of his legions to continue the operations of the siege, whilst, at the head of those troops on whose valor and fidelity he more particularly depended, he advanced in person to engage the general of Maxentius. The army of Gaul was drawn up in two lines, according to the usual practice of war; but their experienced leader, perceiving that the numbers of the Italians far exceeded his own, suddenly changed his disposition, and, reducing the second, extended the front of his first line to a just proportion with that of the enemy. Such evolutions, which only veteran troops can execute without confusion in a moment of danger, commonly prove decisive; but as this engagement began towards the close of the day and was contested with great obstinacy during the whole night, there was less room for the conduct of the generals than for the courage of the soldiers. The return of light displayed the victory of Constantine, and a field of carnage covered with many thousands of the vanquished Italians. Their general, Pompeianus, was found among the slain; Verona immediately surrendered at discretion, and the garrison was made prisoners of war.[21]

With Verona and Milan in his hands, Constantine now controlled all of northern Italy, and the road to Rome was open. It had been a remarkable military feat, comparable to Napoleon's campaigns in the same region in 1796 and 1800.[22] One must also note that in very recent Roman history, three generals of better-than-average ability and arguably possessing greater advantages than Constantine—Maximinus Thrax, Severus, and Galerius—had all failed in their recent attempts to conquer Rome. The difference is found in the speed with which Constantine conducted operations, which left his enemies in a state of dazed confusion.

Still, even after his defeats in the north, Maxentius remained a formidable foe. He had a large army protected by Rome's Aurelian Walls and supported by recently stocked granaries. He also had the full support of the praetorians, who rightfully feared their own destruction if Constantine was victorious. The odds are very good that he could have withstood a siege, which, in the absence of any knowledge of germ science was always the great killer of invading armies, once they had settled-in to conduct a siege. But, probably because he could not trust in the support of the city's populace, which had recently shown their contempt at the Roman Circus, followed by an attempt to storm the imperial palace, he decided to meet Constantine in open battle. He did so believing that he had the support of the gods, as he had consulted the Sibylline Oracles and took comfort in their prediction that "whoever designed any harm to the Romans should die a miserable death."[23] Of course, oracles only survive because their pronouncements are masterpieces of ambiguity. In this case, the one bringing "harm to the Romans" could just as easily be interpreted as Maxentius himself. Unknown to Maxentius, Constantine was also trusting his fate to faith; in this case, the Christian god. On the day of battle, the shields of Constantine's army all bore the Christian Chi-Rho symbol—☧—a Christogram that stands for the name Jesus Christ. According to Lactantius, the night before the battle Constantine was commanded in a dream to "delineate the heavenly sign on the shields of his soldiers."[24] Another version of this tale, presented by Eusebius in his *Life of Constantine*, claims that Constantine was advancing with his army when he saw a cross of light above the sun and with it the Greek words typically translated as "By this conquer." Later Eusebius describes the labarum, the military standard used by Constantine in his later conflict against Licinius, showing the Chi-Rho symbol.

Buoyed by the Sibylline prediction, Maxentius had a temporary bridge thrown across the Tiber River, after earlier having the sturdy permanent bridge destroyed to slow Constantine's advance. He must have had strong faith in his ultimate triumph to have decided to fight with a river at his back against an army that had known nothing but victory against his forces. His dispositions, however, turned out to be a big mistake, as his forces, when arrayed on the far side of the Tiber with their rear lines on the banks of the river, left the army no room to maneuver or anywhere to re-form in the event of a reverse.

The Battle of the Milvian Bridge commenced at dawn on October 28, 312. In terms of its impact on the course of world events, it was more decisive even than the Battle of Actium over three centuries before. Supposedly, the battle began when Constantine personally led one of two cavalry charges upon the cavalry guarding his rival's flanks. This attack quickly overthrew Maxentius's horse and decided the day. Typically, victorious cavalry depart the battlefield in wild pursuit of a beaten foe. One has only to look at the training Hannibal gave to his cavalry before the Battle of Cannae, and Scipio before the Battle of Zama, to see how difficult it was to restrain this impulse. But this time the Tiber stopped the pursuit, allowing the cavalry to rapidly re-form and strike the unprotected flanks of the infantry. At that same moment, Constantine's infantry stormed forward, routing Maxentius's army. The single improvised bridge could not bear the weight of the retreating troops and collapsed, likely taking Maxentius with it. Thousands of other desperate troops rushed into the fast-flowing river and were swept away, while thousands more were slaughtered on the banks by an implacable foe.

Constantine was now the sole ruler of the Western Empire, as well as its first Christian emperor. In 313 Constantine met with Licinius in Milan and agreed to divide the Empire, a deal sealed by Licinius's marriage to Constantine's sister, Flavia Julia Constantia. This meeting is more famous, though, for the Edict of Milan, in which both emperors agreed to grant tolerance to Christianity and all religions within the Empire. Christians were also given the right to reclaim all the property they had lost during Diocletian's persecutions. Licinius had to depart the conference early to deal with Maximinus's attack, discussed earlier. Despite their agreement, and not for the first time, the Empire proved too small to hold the ambitions of two co-rulers.

Constantine's relationship with Licinius rapidly broke down after Licinius refused to turn over the ringleaders of a plot on Constantine's life who had run taken refuge in the East. The stage was once again set for war. The first battle took place at Cibalae in Pannonia. It must have been an unplanned affair: Constantine had barely 20,000 troops to meet Licinius's 35,000. To offset his disadvantage in numbers, Constantine posted his army in a narrow defile.

As Licinius approached, Constantine ordered a charge. According to Zosimus, "This engagement was one of the most furious that was ever fought; for when each side had expended their darts, they fought for a long time with spears and javelins. Only after the action had continued from morning to night did the right wing, where Constantine commanded prevail."[25] With his left wing collapsing, Licinius judiciously ordered a retreat, but for most of his army it was too late. His cavalry appears to have ridden off to Sirmium, where Licinius collected his treasury and family before moving east to collect a new army. His infantry was left to be enveloped and slaughtered, and as many as twenty thousand of them were killed. As he retreated, Licinius elevated one of his generals, Valens, to the rank of Caesar, a move that, for unspecified reasons, enraged Constantine. One suspects that he saw himself as the senior Augustus and believed it was his right to name Caesars.

With Valens's aid, Licinius formed another army in the vicinity of Adrianople. It is likely that because Valens was an Illyrian he was able to gather a significant number of veterans from along the Danube. Constantine, after securing Sirmium, sent a small force of about five thousand men ahead to make contact with Licinius while holding the bulk of his army in the Balkans to await developments. After securing his rear and gathering additional forces, Constantine advanced to Philippi, where he met peace envoys dispatched by Licinius. Confident that he had Licinius nearly beaten, Constantine spurned the offered peace. In January 317 the two armies met at Mardia (modern Harmanli, Bulgaria) in a conflict known as the Battle of Campus Ardiensis. The battle was a long and bloody affair, and as dusk approached the outcome remained in doubt. According to Zosimus, this is when the five thousand soldiers sent to watch Licinius made their appearance on the battlefield.[26] Approaching unseen from behind a line of hills, this force fell on Licinius's rear and turned the tide. Still, Licinius's veterans were able to draw off during the night and retreat to the northwest. Constantine assumed that his foe was fleeing east to cross back into his bases in Syria and ordered an immediate pursuit. This time his aggressiveness cost him: as he marched east, he left Licinius's army sitting in his rear along his lines of communication and supply. Licinius was in a good position geographically, but he was fighting with an army shaken by two defeats. So he again sent peace envoys to Constantine, who was now prepared to listen, but not until Valens was deposed.

With Valens pushed aside, a peace agreement was soon hammered out. Reflecting their respective military positions, the peace was very much in Constantine's favor. Licinius ceded all his European territories except for Thrace to Constantine and either agreed to execute Valens or did so on his own accord to prove his submission. The two Augusti also agreed to appoint new Caesars, and Constantine's sons, Crispus and Constantine II, along with Licinius's young son, Licinius II, were all soon elevated to the purple. Finally, Licinius was forced to recognize Constantine as his senior and follow all of his imperial orders. The treaty gave Constantine control of the dioceses of Pannoniae and Moesiae, consisting of eighteen imperial provinces and substantial military infrastructure that included numerous military bases, minting centers, and three fortified imperial residences—Sirmium, Serdica, and Thessalonica. At the war's end, Constantine governed eight of the Empire's twelve dioceses, leaving Licinius with only Thracia, Asiana, Pontica, and Oriens.[27]

The peace lasted for six years, but it was always a tenuous arrangement, only maintained for as long as Licinius was willing to take orders from Constantine. But diverging dynastic ambitions and religious positions slowly eroded the peace. The final break was a result of Licinius's repudiation of the Edict of Milan. In December 323 Constantine ordered a public beating or a heavy fine for any imperial officials forcing Christians to participate in pagan sacrifices. Licinius pointedly refused to comply and instead increased his persecution of Christians within his domain. Consequently, both emperors spent the winter of 324 girding for war. Even at the time, the renewed conflict was seen by participants and observers as war driven by religion, with Constantine now firmly a Christian and Licinius making a final stand for the continuation of Rome's pagan traditions.

Constantine, in Sirmium, ordered his son Crispus to join him. Crispus, by now in his mid-twenties, had developed his own reputation as a general in campaigns against the Franks in 319 (when he was still a teenager) and the Alemanni in 323. He arrived in Sirmium with a large force of Gallic troops, all veterans of several campaigns and devoted to the house of Constantine. Constantine opted for a two-pronged campaign in which he would advance with the army into Thrace, while Crispus led a naval assault on the Hellespont that, if successful, would cut Licinius's army off from its base in Syria.

In June 324 Constantine led his army east, and by July he was before Adrianople (modern Edirne), where he found Licinius's larger but mostly raw army in a strongly fortified position. After several days of assembling his army and daring Licinius to advance upon him, Constantine struck on a new idea. He created a diversion by employing a large number of soldiers to cut down trees and pretend to be building a bridge across the Hebrus River, behind which much of Licinius's army was sheltering. After the Licinian forces focused their attention on the fake crossing site, Constantine hid eight hundred of his best cavalry and five thousand infantry and archers in a thick forest at the far end of his line. The next morning, July 3, he personally led them across a fordable section of the river and fell upon the surprised flank of Licinius's army. As the Licinian force degenerated into a chaotic mass, Constantine's heavy infantry forded the river and drove forward. During the battle Constantine directed the special guard placed on the Labarum to move the sacred Christian talisman to any area where his soldiers seemed to be faltering. This seemed to embolden his troops and frighten the Licinian forces. Late in the day, the last resistance was broken by a cavalry charge led by Constantine in which he suffered a wound to his thigh. Licinius retreated with the remnants of his routed army, leaving as many as thirty thousand of his men dead on the battlefield.[28]

Licinius reformed his army at Byzantium and prepared to endure a siege. But when his fleet was annihilated by a combination of Crispus's attacks and a wind that smashed many Licinian ships against unforgiving rocks, Byzantium became untenable. Licinius escaped across the Bosporus and began to raise a new army near Chalcedon. Constantine followed in early September, landing on the Black Sea coast at what was called the Sacred Promontory, and then marched west. Once again Licinius had managed to assemble a large force, including reinforcements brought up from Syria and even a large band of Gothic mercenaries. Upon learning of Constantine's approach, he took up a position at Chrysopolis (modern Üsküdar, a suburb of Istanbul) and waited. It does not take long for a good general to examine an enemy force and determine how much fight it has in it, and Constantine was as good a general as ever served Rome. Looking over Licinius's army, he must have felt nothing but disdain, as his battle plan was nothing more than to order an immediate frontal assault upon an army larger than his own. In one overpowering charge Constantine's army broke Licinius's line, after which commenced the massacre of what was now a mass of nearly helpless refugees. Depending on the account, the Licinian forces lost between 25,000 and 100,000 men. Licinius, with just a tattered remnant, escaped to Nicomedia. There his wife, Constantia, daughter of Constantius I, interceded with her father on his behalf. Licinius surrendered in return for his life's being spared. Constantine sent him to live in Thessalonica but had him executed the following year. Within two years Constantine would also order his wife, Fausta, and Crispus executed, either on suspicion of an affair or as a result of a dispute over the political control of the Empire in which the two had stood together against him.[29] Whatever the real reason for the executions, Constantine soon regretted his precipitate actions and allowed his children with Fausta to remain in the line of succession.

Constantine was now the sole ruler of the Roman Empire, but the end of the civil wars did not bring an end to disputes and controversies. Foremost among these were the numerous disputes between the various Christian groups. Whole forests have been consumed to produce learned works on how Constantine attempted to settle these conflicts, starting with the Council of Nicaea, which was the first council to claim jurisdiction over the entire Christian community. It also set the precedent that emperors had a right, even an obligation, to involve themselves in the church's business and for them to take outsized interest in spiritual affairs. From this point forward the civil government and the church became increasingly intertwined, to the point that, toward the end of the Western Empire, church officials had assumed many of the duties and much of the power of the civil administration. These religious debates are far beyond the scope of this work and will only be addressed when and if they have a major strategic impact on the Empire's fortunes.[30]

One of Constantine's first great acts was to create the city of Constantinople atop and alongside Byzantium. At the time he most likely did not mean this city to be seen as a new Rome or even as a political rival to Rome. He therefore went out of his way to make sure no one could claim he intended for Constantinople to replace Rome as the seat of imperial power. For instance, because Constantinople was to be a city greater than the other imperial residences dotting the Empire, it would need its own Senate. But when Constantine enrolled the city's new senators, he made it clear they were not the equal of Rome's senatorial class. That would only happen decades later, when his son, Constantius II, elevated the dignity of the eastern senators. Still, he fully intended the city to be a testament to his greatness and collected art from across the Empire to adorn the city. Furthermore, little expense was spared in a building program aimed at making the city an architectural rival of Rome. But all of this was meant to demonstrate the greatness of Constantine and not to establish a new primary capital for the Empire.

No matter Constantine's intent, the establishment of Constantinople as the Empire's second city had long-term strategic consequences. Once its great walls were strengthened by Theodosius II, the city was as close to impregnable as was possible in the ancient world. These walls would defend the city for another thousand years until they were blasted apart by Ottoman cannons in 1453. Throughout most of that thousand-year period the Theodosian Walls stood as a bulwark, protecting the Eastern Empire from the northern invaders that collapsed the Western Empire a century after Constantine's reign. As the city grew and prospered, it did become a direct rival of Rome and the home of a separate eastern emperor when the Empire was once again divided.

Constantine further broke with the governance model that had held through the Antonine era by continuing to reform the Empire's administration. In most regards he was not creating anything new, but systematizing and improving upon what Diocletian had created. His one major change was to reopen many imperial jobs to the senatorial class that had been closed to them by a succession of imperial orders in the third century. In reality, what he was doing was fusing the senatorial and equestrian classes into a new imperial order, one in which birth could help one get a remunerative and powerful position within the imperial bureaucracy but talent counted for much more. The key point is that Constantine maintained much of the structure that Diocletian emplaced in terms of provinces and dioceses. He also accepted the permanence of the four great prefectures that had become more formalized during the tetrarchy. Diocletian had assigned each of the four tetrarchs a praetorian prefect, and Constantine maintained these positions. Constantine's great change was to remove his praetorian prefects from their military commands. They were still responsible for the training and care of the soldiers, but they did not command in the field. These praetorian prefects were instead put in charge of the massive imperial bureaucracy that dominated every corner of the Empire. In the Antonine age, many regions, towns, and cities had maintained their own local governments and political traditions. But Caracalla's granting of citizenship to most of the Empire's free persons made it virtually impossible for this to continue. The Diocletian-Constantinian political and administrative reforms only formalized and made permanent a process begun a century before. From now on the governance of every town, city, and province became Roman in character, as an administrative sameness and continuity blanketed the Empire.

Throughout Constantine's reign and that of his successors, the power of a ubiquitous and ever-increasing imperial bureaucracy continued to grow as the Empire's government was systematized across every province. As with the story of the development of Christianity within the Empire, a recounting of decades of administrative history is beyond the scope of this work and will only be addressed as it impacts the Empire's strategic calculus. For now, it is enough to say that the imperial bureaucracy provided the emperor with a myriad of new opportunities to make his will enforceable throughout the Empire. But as these new, administratively created provinces and dioceses became responsible for the enforcement of laws, the collection of taxes, and the payment of salaries to imperial officials and soldiers within their borders, they increased the potential for fragmentation in times of crisis, since a province or the dioceses contained within its borders had everything required to govern itself if cut off from the Empire.

By 328 Constantine either thought he had settled most of the religious disputes or was ready to put them on hold to focus on other imperial business. It had been two years since he had last been in Rome, and even longer since he had been in Gaul, which had been the foundation of his power during the Civil Wars. By September of that year he was in Trier, where he made his twelve-year-old son Constantine II Caesar. He would eventually promote

CHAPTER 15 | The Late Imperial Army
and Strategy

T HE ARMY THAT reestablished the Pax Romana and that Constantine
hoped to employ against Persia did not spring up fully formed at
the start of the fourth century. Nor was it a creation of either Diocletian
or Constantine, although both did much to institutionalize and further develop adaptations already in progress. Also worth noting is that the army
that maintained order throughout the Principate never collapsed. Rather,
it adapted and transformed itself to meet new and unprecedented threats.
This work has already exposed many of the long-standing myths of this
transformation, including the fact that Gallienus did not remove men of
senatorial rank from the army in favor of low-status professionals. A few
senators served in Gallienus's army and were still serving when Diocletian
and Constantine once again expanded promotion channels for rich senators,
who more often chose to rise within the ranks of the imperial administration
instead. Gallienus did of course limit the senatorial participation in the army,
but this was a continuation of a process that was already informally under
way. The reason was simple: as threats to Rome's frontiers multiplied and
became increasingly dangerous, the Empire's survival required long-serving
professionals of superior ability in top army commands, regardless of their
social standing.

   As we have also seen, Diocletian was not guilty of destroying the army's
quality in favor of increasing its size. His most pressing military need was
to strengthen the defenses of crucial—mostly frontier—provinces, and he

did so by increasing the permanent military presence in these regions. By the time of his death, there were approximately twenty-eight legions, seventy vexillations (cavalry), fifty-four *alae* (auxiliary cavalry), and fifty-four cohorts (auxiliary infantry) in the east, while the Danube region was held by seventeen legions and an unknown number of vexillations, *alae*, and cohorts. Britain still maintained two or three legions, supported by five *alae*, seventeen cohorts, and three vexillations; Spain had one legion and five cohorts. Germany had approximately ten legions.[1] These dispositions show the same anxiety as did those early in the third century. The east had additional forces, as befitted the increased threat the Sassanids represented, while the Danube, now threatened by the Goths and required greater forces than the Rhine owing to its proximity to the Italian border. Only in Africa, with eight legions and a similar increase in other forces, can we see a new imperial concern, demonstrated by military dispositions. Because the threats coming out of the desert were not much greater than they had been a century before, this troop increase is likely due more to the new administrative structure than to any crucial military requirement.

Diocletian undoubtedly increased the size of the army, but not by nearly as much as has been sometimes claimed, for the Roman economy at the end of the third century could not have borne the strain. Clearly, the number of legions increased greatly, more than doubling the Severan totals. Still, there is to date no data that the legions were reduced to only a thousand soldiers, as they were during Constantine's reign. But just because a legion had a strength on paper of over five thousand men does not mean that all or even many of these organizations were maintained at anything near their full strength.

The more important question centers on the ability of these units to fight. Since Gibbon's time there has been a strand of historical thought claiming that much of the old discipline was lost during the third century. This belief, however, is not supported by the evidence, since throughout that century Roman armies continuously inflicted serious damage on the Empire's enemies, as well as each other. Rome did, of course, suffer several severe setbacks on multiple fronts during this same period. But what has always distinguished Roman arms since the days of the early Republic was their resilience in the wake of disaster. From the early days of the Republic, when Appius Claudius the Blind convinced the Senate to spurn Pyrrhus's offers of peace while an undefeated enemy army was still in the field, all through the disasters at Cannae, Carrhae, and, in the early Empire, at Teutoburg Wald, Rome had always honored its dead and then rebuilt its armies to continue the struggle. The third century was no different. To paraphrase the American

Revolutionary War general Nathaniel Greene, Rome fought, it got beaten, it rose, and fought again, all without an apparent diminution of its ability to conduct campaigns or win future battles. Nor is there any evidence that the legions and other units along the frontiers, the *limitanei*, had become any more than a useless militia, leaving the real combat to the more professional field armies.

That the *limes* became porous in the third century reflected the fact that the frontier legions and garrisons were continually stripped of forces to sustain the strength of the field armies. Thus, their ineffectiveness had little to do with a reduction in the quality of forces along the frontier. In fact, given the multitude of threats along the frontiers, one could make a strong case that they displayed a high level of professionalism. The great transition of the field army into a predominantly cavalry force was not a creation of Constantine, but rather the natural conclusion of a process begun long before. Moreover, it is likely overstated, since infantry continued to make up a large portion of the field army. Accounts of Roman battles in the fourth century and beyond often leave the same impression one gets from reading about medieval battles, where only the exploits of the cavalry elites are worthy of mention.

To sum up, the late Roman army was not the creation of either Diocletian or Constantine. Rather, it was the result of a long process of change. Constantine, upon becoming sole emperor of the Roman world, reestablished Rome's military based upon reforms and changes that had already been present when the civil wars began in 305. His major initiatives were to accept that the legions were never again going to be maintained at anything approaching their full complements and to institutionalize their new strength at approximately one thousand soldiers.[2] By the end of the civil wars the entire military establishment, including the navy, remained close to what it was during the Principate—about 450,000 troops, of which no more than 30,000 to 35,000 could have been cavalry. It would be hard to maintain more than that given the high cost of maintaining a cavalry and the lack of broad, fertile plains where the horses could graze. So, despite the enlargement of the cavalry, the staying power of the field army—almost always grouped around the emperor or his Caesars and now called the *comitatenses*—remained the infantry.

Despite this continuing emphasis on the field armies as the Empire's premier force, the frontier forces—the *limitanei*—were not groupings of armed and barely trained farmers. Rather, they were highly professional and well-trained garrisons who remained the first line of defense against any invading force. Both Diocletian and Constantine expended vast sums strengthening these forces and their defensive infrastructure. Zosimus informs us that by the end of Diocletian's reign, "the frontiers of the Roman empire were everywhere studded with cities and forts and towers . . . and the whole army was stationed along them."[3] As we saw earlier, Zosimus blames Constantine for wrecking this arrangement:[4]

> Constantine destroyed that security by removing the greater part of the soldiers from those barriers of the frontiers, and placing them in towns that had no need of defenders. . . . To speak in plain terms, he was the first cause of the affairs of the empire declining to their present miserable state.[5]

This single passage has done more to tar Constantine with the weakening of Rome's defenses and their eventual collapse than any other commentary or event. But Zosimus, a pagan who hated Constantine, is lying. Constantine surely removed troops from the frontiers to reinforce his field army for the civil wars, and it was this weakening of the frontiers that necessitated his later campaigns against the Alemanni and the Goths. But as soon as these wars ended, Constantine began a program to strengthen frontier garrisons by increasing the density of fortifications throughout the *limes,* as well as reinforcing their garrisons. Moreover, he constructed a series of new forts at major intersections and other important points behind the immediate frontier fortifications, all of which served to contain and channel any barbarian breakthrough.

Constantine bore this expense because he understood the crucial strategic importance of keeping the Danube and Rhine Rivers protected. As they had done since the reign of Augustus, they were the arteries that made rapid transport of armies and logistics from one theater to another possible. Also, agriculture-based societies recover from war-inflicted disasters faster than the industrial societies of the modern era. With just a supply of seed farms can begin growing crops in the very next season after they were destroyed. But before this could start, the land needed to be repopulated by settlers and returning refugees, who would come only if their security was assured. Moreover, even those who did return are unlikely to make new investments in mills, irrigation networks, storage facilities, and other crucial infrastructure without some assurance that it will not be regularly destroyed by raiders. Returning farmers are not going to be reassured by the *comitatenses,* which would not arrive for weeks or months after a devastating barbarian raid had already marched through. They required positive proof that the military was nearby and ready to stop any incursion, large or small. If Constantine wanted the frontier zones and even the provinces to their rear to return to prosperity and start paying taxes, then he had a strong strategic interest in making the frontiers as secure as possible. There are volumes of archaeological evidence attesting to substantial economic growth throughout Gaul and the Balkans in the fourth century, so it is safe to say Constantine's rebuilding of the *limes* had the desired strategic impact.

These new fortifications do point to a new strategic outlook. Starting sometime after Marcus Aurelius's campaigns, Roman forts became thicker, had only a single gate, and were built with towers capable of holding artillery and that protruded out from the walls, allowing effective flanking firing on any attackers. All of these changes greatly strengthened the defensive capabilities of Roman frontier forces and seem to demonstrate that Rome was finally accepting that it was on the strategic defensive.[6] In the fourth and fifth centuries local Roman commanders rarely ventured beyond the frontier zones to break up dangerous barbarian concentrations or just to intimidate the local tribes. In the future, offensives would be rare and conducted only by the *comitatenses* under the command of the emperor or a close relative. Still, there are no indications of any major change in Roman strategic thinking at this time. Diocletian's and Constantine's primary goal, like Hadrian's and the Antonines', still was to keep the barbarians on the far side of the Empire's frontiers. This strategic priority was never far from the mind of any third-century emperor. But Diocletian succeeded because the tetrarchy for a few decades ended the enfeebling and distracting civil wars and placed the full resources of the Empire back under the control of one man. Constantine's civil wars disrupted this peace, but when they ended the Empire was again united under a single strong ruler capable of returning Roman strategy to its age-old imperatives.

It is, in fact, the permanent establishment of the *comitatenses* that is the most crucial strategic change during the period. Rome had never had an established strategic reserve, which is what the *comitatenses* was clearly intended to be. One could make some claim that the ten cohorts of Praetorian Guard could be considered the Principate's strategic reserve. But while these splendid-looking formations may have been the prettiest and best-turned-out cohorts in the Roman army, they were seldom soldiers, in any serious sense of the word. They could, of course, bully the civilian population, but as we have seen, if they pushed too hard they could soon find themselves on the losing end of a series of brutal street battles. The Roman mob once aroused could be fearful to behold, but it is doubtful it could ever have made a stand against a legion just returned from the frontiers. Moreover, the praetorians' pathetic attempts to stand against the frontier legions during times of civil war could not have given any emperor much faith in their combat abilities. In the end, Constantine contemptuously dismissed them. A claim could also be made that Legio II Parthica, stationed just outside Rome by Severus, acted as a strategic reserve. But in practical terms it was not particularly effective in that role, since it was too far from the frontier zones. Thus, its employment in any crisis zone would take many weeks or months.

As discussed earlier in this work, Rome's true strategic reserve remained the troops along or close to the frontier. It was these troops who could move quickly along the Danube and the Rhine to any theater while also using these rivers to transport the tons of supplies needed to maintain an army on the move. In fact, by using the Danube to reach the Black Sea ports, legions in Gaul could get to Antioch in almost the same time it would take to move a legion from Italy. By keeping the *comitatenses* close to the frontier zones, Rome was getting the best of all worlds. The *comitatenses* kept much of the same strategic mobility along the river lines as any legion garrisoning the *limes*. But because it possessed more cavalry than the armies of the Principate, it had the operational maneuverability to react to and contain any enemy force already within the province or even dioceses. And because the *comitatenses* was still preponderantly a heavy infantry force, it had the weight to stand toe to toe with an enemy battle line in a set-piece battle.

Many historians have argued that this change made large-scale warfare and battles something only the field army engaged in. But this had always been the case. The difference was that before the establishment of the *comitatenses*, it took months to gather such a force. In the fourth century the field army was always present, trained, and ready to go into action. It was also more effective than the hastily assembled armies of the Principate, for as anyone with military experience knows, a force that has operated together for long periods creates bonds between leaders and units. It is this faith in each other's capabilities, born of long tradition, that allows a veteran army to hugely outclass any pick-up force. The question, therefore, is whether the *comitatenses* weakened the *limes*, as the troops used to man it were permanently unavailable to garrison the frontier fortifications. In strategic terms, this is always going to be a trade-off. But given the increased number of fortifications, their increasing strength, their new defensive orientation, and the addition of troops as a result of Diocletian's increasing the size of the army, it is safe to say that the *limes* were as strong as ever. Still, as the tribes continued to amalgamate, the barbarian threat also grew, and one also has to account for the fearsome Goths entering the Danube basin. Still, the *limes* were never meant to be impenetrable barriers to large-scale barbarian invasions. The increased strength of the *limes* fortifications was able to maintain the status quo, but a large-scale invasion, of which the barbarians were now more capable than ever, would surely break through the frontier zone. This is what made the *comitatenses* indispensable. In the past Rome would have needed time to assemble a field force and then deploy it to the impacted area. In the future, even after the additions of supporting forts in the interior and walled cities to delay and channel invaders, the field army would have to arrive quickly. This was possible only if it remained a permanent force.

Too often a focus on Rome's military forces has led to an unfortunate tendency to ignore what truly made Rome a great military power: its cities and the communications links that netted them together. The Roman Empire in the fourth century still maintained an unparalleled level of basic infrastructure that allowed it to move troops and resources to any point of the Empire at speeds unequaled until the modern era. It was Rome's ability to build, sustain, and move its armies rapidly over strategic distances that made it the ancient world's greatest power. We should also not forget the crucial importance of economic wherewithal, since that is what paid for military forces and infrastructure—and the regeneration of armies during times of crisis and disaster. Other ancient powers had demonstrated an ability to build huge armies, but these were almost always temporary forces that were mostly disbanded at the end of the fighting season. Even the Sassanids had immense trouble sustaining their field armies over multiple seasons, not to mention years. Rome, on the other hand, was able to sustain its multiple *comitatenses* with a strength of 35,000 to 50,000 men each, continuously, for over a century. One just has to consider the immense amount of food and fodder such a force would require every year—many times what any single province could produce—to get some idea of the huge logistical and administrative tasks involved in maintaining the *comitatenses*. It was the ability to pay for, organize, and manage this burden year after year that made Rome a fearsome military power.

Much of the administrative burden necessary to maintain these forces was eased by Diocletian's and then Constantine's separation of command duties from administrative duties. Military leaders would train their forces and command them in the field, but their pay, care, and most other needs were now handled by the civilian administration within a province. This did not simplify the tasks involved, but it placed them in the hands of those most suited to them. The permanent creation of the *comitatenses* also required the extension of communication lines and logistical facilities within the areas where these forces were stationed. However, most of this work was done over time, and by the start of the fourth century it was substantially completed.

By the fourth century the *comitatenses* were always attached to the emperors or their Caesars. Regional temporary field armies, when they existed, were hastily formed in times of crisis and disbanded once the crisis had passed. Thus, the imperial field army was the core of the emperor's military power, and it had to be watched very closely, because anyone who commanded a field army could potentially raise the flag of revolt. This was somewhat alleviated by the dual military-administrative command structure: soldiers might love their commander, but they knew their pay and food now came from a separate imperial administrator. Still, it was the various field armies, each commanded by a son of Constantine, that turned upon each other in the next decades and nearly collapsed Rome's entire defensive edifice.

Throughout the third and fourth centuries the performance in battle of the field armies was at least equal to, and in many cases superior to, the Principate's legions. Their continued dominance reflected their ability to move quickly and effectively inside and beyond the frontiers, a lasting capacity to defeat enemies in pitched battles, and the maintenance of the highest standard of technical equipment, engineering, and professional drill.[7] The late imperial army was as professional as any that had gone before it, and the popular notion that the field army was little better than a force of marauding barbarians must be vanquished. Moreover, the Roman Empire as a whole did not become more militarized, nor did a militarized bureaucracy take over the Empire. Rather, it had a very civilian-oriented bureaucracy taking over many routine military functions.

When Constantine died, the Empire was rapidly restoring its economic power, and its military power was as great as ever. Admittedly, the threats that nearly collapsed the Empire during the Crisis of the Third Century had not been eliminated, and a strong case could be made that they were even more dangerous in the early fourth century. But the Empire had caught its breath and rebuilt its strength, and it was now more than ready to meet any external challenge. Constantine's military reformations likely gave the Empire its best chance of preserving its territory and prestige.[8] Unfortunately, ultimate success and the continued survival of the Empire rested upon its internal stability. To sustain itself, Rome had to avoid civil war and the ensuing internal fragmentation that would make the resources of one portion of the Empire unavailable to other provinces that might come under assault. In short, Rome had to avoid the enervating effects of civil war. Doing so, however, proved impossible.

The Romans were not stupid and they could see clearly the damage their multiple suicide attempts were inflicting upon the Empire, as well as it prospects against outside invaders. So, why did successive rulers continue to divide the Empire into separate governing sections and thereby set the conditions for persistent bouts of civil war? The reason lies with the geographic scope of the Empire coupled with new threats beyond the frontiers made effective command and control from a central location impossible. The system required multiple poles of power, but there was no cost-free method of doing this. The Romans had a structural problem that required duplicate imperial courts. These were established despite emperors having extensive and often personal knowledge of the likely effects.

CHAPTER 16 | Four Battles and a Divorce

CONSTANTINE WAS DEAD, but his successor had not been decided. Even as Constantine's body lay in state, powerful forces, likely orchestrated by Constantine's son Constantius, were working to bring the army to stand behind the succession of the three sons of Constantine.[1] As Eusebius tells us, "As soon, however, as the soldiery throughout the provinces received the tidings of the emperor's decease, they all, as if by a supernatural impulse, resolved with one consent, as though their great emperor had been yet alive, to acknowledge none other than his sons as sovereigns of the Roman world."[2] The three sons of Constantine—the new Augusti—then launched a lightning purge of half brothers, cousins, and assorted other threats to the dynasty. Only two of Constantine's nephews—one of whom, Julian, later became emperor of Rome—were spared, but even they were kept in relative seclusion and their interests limited to academic pursuits. The purge—or, in Gibbon's words, "the slaughter of the Flavian race"—finally ended after consuming the man who probably did the most to secure the brothers' succession, Flavius Ablabius. After that the three Augusti met in Pannonia to divide their inheritance. Constantius retained the whole of the east with the addition of Thrace; Constans received Illyricum, Italy, and Africa; and Constantine, the oldest brother, was given Gaul, Spain, and Britain. All three promptly undertook the now nearly requisite military campaigns meant to legitimize their rule and add glory to their names. Constantius secured a Roman-friendly ruler in Armenia, Constans attacked the Sarmatians on the far side of the Danube, and Constantine won or claimed to have won a victory against the Alemanni on the Rhine.[3]

The choice of campaigning areas at least put on display the primary strategic concerns of the Empire, but as these actions were undertaken primarily for reasons of imperial prestige, they were never pursued to the point where they had a decisive long-term result. In fact, these attacks likely stirred up more future trouble than Rome had the resources to deal with. This is particularly true when the Empire was once again divided. Instead of bringing the full weight of Roman power to bear on any single strategic problem, resources were dissipated in three unrelated offensive enterprises. The return of divided rule, without a patently dominant Augustus, not only wasted resources but also brought back the instability of the years between Diocletian's abdication of power and Constantine's ascent to one-man rule. It was not long, therefore, before the brothers were at each other's throats.

In 340 Constantine led his legions out of Gaul and crossed the Alps to invade Constans's territory in Italy. Constans, or his generals, reacted quickly, sending a force of handpicked Illyrian troops to delay Constantine and promising to follow soon with a larger force. The Illyrians, however, proved more than enough, destroying a significant portion of Constantine's army in a carefully set ambush at Aquileia. Constantine was killed, leaving Constans as the Western Empire's sole ruler.[4] There appears to have been little trouble over Constans's absorption of his brother's domains, and he spent most of the next decade in Trier—the seat of his family's power—in northern Italy. We know that he conducted at least three major campaigns along the Rhine during those years, and there may have been others. He also appears to have had significant successes against the Franks in the north, and Ammianus informs us that the Alemanni feared only Constans and the later emperor, Julian.[5]

But campaigns are costly, and without recourse to the financial might of the unified Empire, the expense of war fell primarily upon Gaul. The civilian animosity this created would have mattered little, but Constans, despite his victories, was also losing the respect of the army. Eventually the combination of civilian and military discontent was too much, or, as Zonaras explains: "Then, after he [Constans] had plunged into depraved loves and a perverted mode of life, he was plotted against and wretchedly destroyed by Magnentius." Recognizing his vulnerability as a usurper, Magnentius, who had commanded Constans's best and most loyal imperial guard units—the Herculians and Jovians—moved quickly to consolidate his hold on power. Only when he began to move east into the Balkans to rally the Danubian legions to his cause did he first stumble.

In the meantime, Constantius was waging a prolonged defensive war against Sapor II. His father had not left him in an enviable position. The treaty of 298 between Galerius and Narses had kept the peace for a generation, but its harsh terms sowed the seeds for renewed conflict. By the time of Constantine's death, the Roman and Sassanid Empires were once again on the brink of war. Constantius was still dealing with the details of his father's funeral arrangements when Sapor II invaded Roman territory. Sapor II could not have been oblivious to Constantine's preparations for invading the Sassanian Empire and probably hoped his assault would forestall a Roman invasion. No matter what Sapor's aims, he first had to capture the fortified city of Nisibis along with the fortified towns in its vicinity. Since Severus's reign, a full legion had been stationed in Nisibis, which would sit athwart Sapor's supply lines, as well as his line of retreat if he was to advance beyond the frontier. Thus, Nisibis had become the key to Rome's frontier defense. As Sapor knew this, he expected that any attack on Nisbis would draw the entire Roman army forward for a climactic battle near the city.

But Constantius, in what for a Roman emperor was an extraordinary decision, adopted a defensive strategy, one in which the army, with its central base at Antioch, would maneuver behind the fortified frontiers to hold the enemy in place. This was even more remarkable: the contemporary *Itinerarium Alexandri*, which surely reflects the mood of the times, compares him to Alexander the Great and Trajan.[6] Plainly, Constantius was expected to take the army Constantine bequeathed him and launch a grand assault upon the Sassanians. According to the *Itinerarium*, Constantius possessed an army about equal in size to that of Alexander, which means it was small. But it also claims that Constantius's force was better trained than Alexander's, which is at the very least a debatable assessment. In any event, Sapor, after taking the time to divert a river and launch at least one massive assault on Nisibis's walls, was forced to give up the siege.

Either his losses in the siege were extraordinarily high—possibly due to disease—or his attentions were diverted elsewhere, because for the next several years there was no major Persian assault along the Roman frontiers. Only when Constantius captured a small Persian town and transported its population to Thrace did Sapor rouse himself to raise a large enough army to launch an invasion. This resulted in the Battle of Singara (344), the only major battle in over a decade of conflict. After a nearly twenty-mile forced march, the Romans caught Sapor's army napping. Eschewing a pause to refresh themselves, as Constantius wished, the lead formations launched an immediate assault on the Persians, dragging the rest of the army into the fray. When Sapor saw the size of the Roman army, he retreated toward the Tigris, leaving his son in charge of the army. It was nightfall before the Romans battered their way into the Persian camp, capturing Sapor's son—whom they tortured to death—along with the Persian treasury. Victory, however, had been costly, and Constantius's army was in no condition to launch a pursuit of the routed Persians or to take advantage of the victory through a strategic offensive. For this Constantius was condemned by his many enemies, who, because there was no lasting result from the battle, portrayed it as a defeat.[7]

Still, Constantius stuck with his strategy and refused to allow his main field army to stray beyond the frontier line. He even held it in reserve when Sapor later besieged Nisibis in 346 and again in 350. In both cases Nisibis held, stopping Sapor from penetrating the Roman frontiers. Whether it was by conscious design or by force of circumstance—one suspects the latter—Constantius had discovered the key to maintaining the frontiers of the Empire while economizing on how much of his military and treasure was expended.[8] One suspects that this was not the kind of war he wanted to fight, for Constantius would surely have felt the need to prove himself a worthy successor to Constantine by acquiring military glory. Moreover, he must have been aware of how the criticisms of his defensive policies were undermining his reputation, which was the foundation of any emperor's power. If this erosion went too far, it was only a matter of time before a usurper appeared.

But Constantius was dealing with two strategic handicaps that curtailed the options available to him. First, he only controlled the Eastern Empire, meaning that the tremendous financial and military resources of the West were denied to him. This situation is a foreshadowing of later events, when the Empire was permanently split and neither half was able to muster the Empire's full resources to meet the multiple crises that finally ended the Western Empire's existence. Constantius's second concern likely arose after the Battle of Singara. That fight had been very costly, with the brunt of the losses being inflicted on Constantius's elite troops. Although he had won, it was at best a pyrrhic victory. Another such battle would have seen his army ruined, leaving nothing to stop Sapor from plunging deep into the Eastern Empire's vitals. Moreover, Constantius knew that no Roman emperor was long for this world if he is without an army at his back.

In 350 Sapor's unrelenting pressure along the frontier eased as the Persian army marched east to confront a new enemy—barbarian incursions. It was not a moment too soon, for Constantius desperately needed to turn his attention to the west, where the usurper Magnentius had replaced his brother Constans and was rapidly consolidating his power. But, in what was a blessing in disguise, another usurper, Vetranio, arose in the Balkans. It is not clear whether he ever meant to challenge Constantius, and he may even have coordinated his activities with the rightful emperor. What he did do was demonstrate once again that an emperor ignored the various field armies—the *comitatenses*—only at great peril. Constans had spent much of his time in the Balkans and had neglected the army in Gaul, which eventually overthrew him. With the army in Gaul now running things in Rome, the Balkan forces were looking for their own champion. Constantius was occupied in the east, so Vetranio stepped into the breach. The practical effect of his usurpation was to deny Magnentius control of Rome's army in the Balkans.

In a move that was too smooth not to have been orchestrated, the Balkan army—the Illyrian legions—switched sides as soon as Constantius and his eastern veterans approached. Both armies assembled on a great field where Constantius addressed them. The acclamations began as soon as he finished: "Away with these upstart usurpers! Long life and victory to the son of Constantine! Under his banners alone we will fight and conquer."[9] Vetranio immediately abdicated and was sent into retirement with a government pension—not the typical fate of a failed usurper.[10]

Dealing with Vetranio, even in an unscripted way, had been an easy matter; Magnentius would be a much more difficult and prolonged affair. Even after Sapor II marched away, the Eastern Empire remained restive; it could easily become another danger for Constantius if neglected too long. Experience taught that if an emperor was forced to absent himself from restive regions, it was best to put matters in the hands of a relative. But the wholesale slaughter of anyone who could contest the rule of Constantine's sons left only two candidates: Gallus and Julian. Because both had been kept far from the Empire's political centers, they had never been prepared to rule. Constantius, overlooking Gallus's obvious incompetence for the role, elevated him to the rank of Caesar and left him in the competent hands of his *magister equitum*, Ursicinus.

Unwilling to wait for the combined force of the eastern and Illyrian legions to descend on him, Magnentius launched a preemptive attack into the Balkans. For a time Magnentius proved himself the better general. But Constantius was the better politician, and he convinced one of Magnentius's senior officers, a Frank named Silvanus, to betray him and take a large portion of the Western army into Constantius's camp. Eventually the two armies met at Mursa (modern Osijek, Croatia) on September 28, 351. This was one of the great but almost forgotten battles of the era, as Zosimus reports: "a battle was fought as had not occurred before in the course of this war, and great numbers fell on both sides."[11] The fighting began in the late afternoon and was fierce on both sides. Julian says that Constantius's left outflanked Magnentius, and his phalanx was overwhelmed.[12] According to Zosimus, no quarter was asked or given. Eventually it was Constantius's mail-clad cavalry that tilted the balance. After repeated charges against fanatical resistance, Magnentius's line broke and ran, pursued by the deadly mounted archers of the Eastern army. When it was over, 54,000 Romans lay dead on the field, and likely thousands more were wounded. Two-thirds of Magnentius's army was annihilated, along with as much as half of Constantius's force. Losses were so heavy that Constantius required more than a full year to recruit and train new forces before he felt strong enough to follow his opponent into Italy. It is hard to overstate the extent of the strategic disaster that unfolded on the plains of Mursa. Three Roman field armies had been wrecked. These were not hastily raised armies or forces comprised of second-rate troops. Rather, they were the elite of each of Rome's *comitatenses* and as such nearly irreplaceable.

Unfortunately, the magnitude of this loss did not divert Constantius from his priority of winning the war. And, as always, when a Roman emperor considered his strategic priorities, unless he was immediately beset by barbarian hordes, destroying usurpers was always at the top of the list. Thus, Constantius offered the German tribes across the Rhine large bribes to raid Gaul. The Germans acted without hesitation, easily piercing the denuded frontier fortifications to wreak devastation across large swaths of the undefended province. Still, Constantius did not invade Italy and finish off Magnentius until 353, when he destroyed the usurper's hastily raised army at Mons Seleucus.

Magnentius committed suicide, but that did not stop Constantius from undertaking a widespread purge of his supporters. Here it is worth noting the hidden impact of usurpation and civil war. Every usurper had followers, often spread throughout the Empire. Whenever there was a new usurper, nearly all of the Roman elites, from obscenely rich senators to more humble members of local administrative councils, had to choose sides. This greatly raised the stakes of political rivalries and the costs of a poor decision. Only one side could win a civil war, and the results were felt across the Empire. In the case of Magnentius, the Roman Senate, which had supported his assumption of the purple, immediately began making expansive offers to the victor in the hope of allaying his wrath. But all across the Western Empire, those who supported the House of Constantine were now in a position to destroy their rivals with the full support of the state. In his great work on the Peloponnesian War, Thucydides lays out the results of such a switch in local power in the city-state of Corcyra and then expands his observations to the rest of Greece. It is fair to believe that much the same was happening throughout the Roman Empire at the end of many of its civil wars, so it is worth reading these passages in their entirety:

> Meanwhile they killed any of their enemies whom they caught in the city. On the arrival of the ships they disembarked those whom they

had induced to go on board, and dispatched them; they also went to the temple of Herè, and persuading about fifty of the suppliants to stand their trial condemned them all to death. The majority would not come out, and, when they saw what was going on, destroyed one another in the enclosure of the temple where they were, except a few who hung themselves on trees, or put an end to their own lives in any other way which they could. And, during the seven days which Eurymedon after his arrival remained with his sixty ships, the Corcyraeans continued slaughtering those of their fellow-citizens whom they deemed their enemies; they professed to punish them for their designs against the democracy, but in fact some were killed from motives of personal enmity, and some because money was owing to them, by the hands of their debtors. Every form of death was to be seen; and everything, and more than everything, that commonly happens in revolutions, happened then. The father slew the son, and the suppliants were torn from the temples and slain near them; some of them were even walled up in the temple of Dionysus, and there perished. To such extremes of cruelty did revolution go; and this seemed to be the worst of revolutions, because it was the first. . . . Thus revolution gave birth to every form of wickedness in Hellas. The simplicity which is so large an element in a noble nature was laughed to scorn and disappeared. An attitude of perfidious antagonism everywhere prevailed. . . . At such a time the life of the city was all in disorder, and human nature, which is always ready to transgress the laws, having now trampled them under foot, delighted to show that her passions were ungovernable, that she was stronger than justice, and the enemy of everything above her. If malignity had not exercised a fatal power, how could any one have preferred revenge to piety, and gain to innocence? But, when men are retaliating upon others, they are reckless of the future, and do not hesitate to annul those common laws of humanity to which every individual trusts.[13]

It does not take much imagination to grasp how localized turmoil, such as that at Corcyra, could destroy a region's economy and political stability while leaving hatreds that could carry down for generations. But to fully comprehend the vast strategic shock of Rome's civil wars, one must contemplate the impact of similar events taking place across the *entire* Roman Empire at the end of *every* civil war. It is too easy to think about ancient wars as only impacting the armies involved and the lands they trod upon. But civil wars are of a very different nature, and the terrible impacts of such conflicts almost always spread far and wide, potentially encompassing the entire Empire. Thus, while examining the damage civil wars inflicted on the Roman military power remains crucial to understanding immediate strategic options, anyone trying to fully grasp Rome's strategic choices over a prolonged period must also take account of how the underlying foundations of Roman power were eroded by constant internal political disorder within every town and city, and even across much of the countryside.

While Constantius was securing his hold on the Western Empire, his cousin Gallus was busily establishing his own base of power in the east. Without going into the several years of court intrigue involved in this high-stakes power struggle, it is worth noting that the Empire remained politically divided until 354, when Constantius finally orchestrated Gallus's deposition and execution. But the unification of the Empire was barely completed before its fabric was again torn. This time it was the Frank, Silvanus, who, after switching sides just before the Battle of Mursa, had been rewarded with command in Gaul. In 355 at Cologne Silvanus declared himself emperor and began mustering his Rhine legions. Constantius sent Ursicinus, who had commanded Gallus's military forces and was now being held under close watch in Milan, north to undermine Silvanus's power and, Constantius hoped, kill him. Ursicinus, along with a small group of Roman officers, including the historian Ammianus, accomplished their mission, and Silvanus was murdered while attending church services. His hold on the prize had lasted only a month.

Constantius had lingered too long in Italy, and it was time to return his attention to the Balkans and the east, where troubles were piling up. Sarmatian and Quadi barbarians were rampaging through Pannonia and Upper Moesia, while the frontier with Persia was becoming increasingly restive. But before he could depart, Constantius needed a figurehead to rule the west, someone incapable of seizing power himself but able through his mere presence to keep others from rallying to the banners of a more competent general or prefect. Despite his experience with Gallus, he selected his remaining cousin, Julian.

Constantius did not think much of his choice, who had grown up a virtual prisoner and when released from close confinement had immediately headed to Athens to undertake a deep study of philosophy and religion. There he cast off Christianity and dedicated himself to the ancient gods, an apostasy that he wisely kept hidden from Constantius. He was still engrossed in his studies when the summons from the imperial court arrived. Despite some lingering misgivings, Constantius elevated Julian to the rank of Caesar and sent him to Gaul. Wary still over creating a new power center, and as a precaution against Julian's having any independent thoughts, the new Caesar was presented with a list of detailed instructions, written in the emperor's own hand, that went so far as to detail what was to be set before him at mealtime—forbidding such things as pheasant and insisting on the coarse rations of a common soldier.[14]

In Gaul, Julian soon found himself embroiled in war, for the denuding of the frontiers to fight civil wars had not gone unnoticed by the Alemanni, nor by the Franks, whose raiding parties pushed deep into Gaul, where they were soon followed by migrating settlers. By the time Julian arrived, the Rhine defenses were shattered. According to Ammianus, the Roman fortresses and forts of Cologne, Mainz, Worms, Speyer, Saverne, Brumat, and Strasbourg were all held or destroyed by the Alemanni. All that was left for Julian to base his operations around was a single tower near Cologne and two smaller forts near Remagen and Koblenz. Undeterred, Julian, in a series of rapid campaigns, in 356 regained much of what had been lost and began the process of either exterminating the Alemanni or moving them back to the right bank of the Rhine. Although Julian traveled with the military expeditions that accomplished these missions and directed some of the low-level fighting, the actual planning and execution of the campaigns were undertaken by more experienced Roman generals such as Ursicinus and later Marcellus.

One may also wonder about to the extent of Julian's victories, since he clearly did not finish the removal of the barbarian settlers and was still busily working to reestablish and man frontier outposts when his main army went into winter quarters. Moreover, he was forced to make terms with the Franks in northern Gaul without ever defeating them in battle. Evidently Julian considered his forces incapable of defeating two barbarian forces. Moreover, the portion of the army he kept with him that winter was besieged at Senon, near Verdun.[15] The siege lasted only a month before the invaders withdrew to sit out the winter.[16] But it is worth taking a moment to contemplate how low the state of Roman arms had fallen that a field army under the direct command of a Roman Caesar could be penned up and held captive within a city's walls. For this insult to Roman dignity, Julian blamed his general, the *magister equitum* Marcellus, whom he accused of failing to bring the rest of the army to his aid. Eventually the affair was brought before Constantius, who, after being convinced that Julian was entirely loyal to himself, dismissed Marcellus from the army.[17] Marcellus was replaced by the older and more docile Severus, whom Julian had no problem overshadowing and controlling.

Julian, while professing his loyalty to the emperor, nonetheless began working in earnest to secure an independent power base. He now had a province and, with Marcellus and Ursicinus out of the way, an army of his own.

What he lacked was a reputation that would bind his army to him and make him more attractive to the legions beyond his immediate control. That would come the following summer at Strasbourg. In 357 Constantius ordered another offensive against the Alemanni. This time, an army commanded by the *magister peditum* Barbatio, who replaced Silvanus, was tasked to march through what is now Switzerland and then along the right bank of the Rhine, while Julian was to take his smaller army down the left bank of the Rhine to meet Barbatio's force.[18] This pincer, as Ammianus describes it, "should be driven into straits as if with a pair of pliers by twin forces of our soldiers and cut to pieces."[19] The Roman plan collapsed when Barbatio's force—possibly only the vanguard—was ambushed and forced to retreat to its starting location. This left Julian's smaller force isolated and with two options: retreat back upon his fortresses or accept an open battle against a force that possibly outnumbered his own by as much as three to one.[20] Julian, however, must also bear some of the blame for his predicament. His advance to meet Barbatio had been conducted with unusual slowness, since he took time to eliminate small barbarian groups that likely posed little threat as he marched. He also held up his army to rebuild the fortress at Saverne, which, once completed and manned, would have dominated the Alsace region and blocked Alemanni movements into Gaul. It was this threat that the Alemanni could not ignore.

With Barbatio in full retreat, the Alemanni high king, Chonodomarius, supported by no fewer than six lesser kings, turned the full power of the temporarily united Alemanni upon Julian.[21] As the various Alemanni contingents massed at Strasbourg, Julian advanced to meet them. At midday, after an exhausting six-hour march, his forces came upon the well-rested Alemanni. Julian feared his men were too tired to engage in a pitched battle and implored them to wait in a fortified camp until morning. But they implored him to attack. One can feel the frustration of troops who had spent years trying to pin down small war bands now being denied the chance to destroy the assembled might of their enemies. From their perspective, Roman armies on open plains almost always won pitched battles against barbarians. And before them stood the largest conglomeration of their enemies that had been seen in generations. They must have worried that the Alemanni would come to their senses during the night and melt away. Julian's pleas for a delay were met by growls, gnashing teeth, and the soldiers "striking their spears and shields together" as the army clamored for battle.

If the din of the soldiers' shouts and beating of shields did not convince Julian, the words of his praetorian prefect, Florentius, finally did. He warned that while battling such a large number of barbarians was risky, the greater risk was that they would scatter. Florentius's fear was not that the enemy would depart to cause mischief elsewhere, but that the soldiers would not endure being denied a victory they believed was within their grasp and would then take recourse in "the final extremity."[22] There was no hiding the meaning of "final extremity"; Julian would be overthrown, and the army would create a new Caesar, one who would bring them victories.

The two armies drew up less than a mile from Strasbourg's ruined walls, probably near modern Oberhausbergen. The Roman left flank was under the command of the capable *magister equitum* for Gaul, Severus, while almost all of the imperial cavalry—with the light cavalry in the front and the heavy, mail-armored cataphracts behind—was on the right flank, commanded by Julian. A corps of mounted archers were also placed on the right flank, while the Roman heavy infantry filled the center. It was the infantry's job to hold off the masses of barbarians until the cavalry had won its battle on the right and turned into the flanks and rear of the Alemanni.

Chonodomarius had hidden an ambushing force in the marshes on his right, in front of Severus's troops, but it was mostly pushed aside before the main battle began. On his left he placed his cavalry, but knowing it could not stand up to the shock of Julian's cataphracts, he took a page from Julius Caesar, who, when outclassed by Pompey's cavalry at Pharsalus, had supported it with hidden infantry.[23] As the Alemanni infantry moved into position to the right of their cavalry, they began yelling at the princes and nobles to dismount and fight with them. Their point was to ensure that if the battle was lost, the chiefs, princes, and other nobles could not easily escape but would have to take the same chances as any other warrior. When Chonodomarius heard the soldiers' cries, he immediately leaped from his horse and joined the front line of troops. He was soon joined by the rest of the Alemanni nobility.[24] The net effect of this display of courage was that no one was left in a position to direct the course of the battle once engaged.

When all was set, the trumpeters blew the call to battle, launching the Roman heavy cavalry into an ill-considered charge. In the ensuing melee, Chonodomarius's placement of infantry within his own cavalry's ranks soon paid off: the infantry began spearing the unprotected bellies of the horses and toppling the cataphracts, who became easy prey once dismounted. Panic ensued when one of Julian's cavalry tribunes fell. The day was saved by the solidarity of the legions, who one imagines lowered their spears as the panicked cavalry rushed back upon them. After all, when it comes to crashing through the ranks of unbroken infantry, the intention of the rider counts for nothing: no horse will ever charge a thicket of spear points no matter what encouragement is offered. Forcing the cavalry to retreat along the battle line before turning and resuming their flight to the rear had two very salutary effects. First, the need to rein in before impacting with the infantry would have greatly slowed the retreat and given the leaders a chance to gain at least minimal control of the retreating force. Second, the logical place to continue the retreat was at the end of the infantry line, which would have acted as a natural funnel into which almost the entire cavalry force would have flowed. There they found Julian, holding aloft his "purple ensign of a dragon, fitted to the top of a very long lance and spreading out like the slough of a serpent." Julian was personally stopping passing tribunes and forcing them to rally their troops.[25] Thus, "sheltered in the bosom of the legions," the cavalry halted, reorganized, and prepared to reenter the fray.[26]

In the meantime the Alemanni, cheered by the rout of the Roman cavalry, rushed forward. But the Roman line, anchored by the elite Cornuti and Bracchiati regiments, remained firm. As the Germans approached, both regiments began their famous war cry—the *barritus*. The Alemanni's maddened charges made no impression on the tightly formed Roman shield wall, "which protected our men like a tortoise-formation"—the famous testudo formation.[27] The opponents seem to have been evenly matched, and the battle was drawn out and exhausting. In the last extremity, the Alemanni drew together a large mass of relatively fresh soldiers and charged through their own lines to strike the weary Romans. They hit with enough force to buckle and likely disintegrate a couple of Roman regiments. In any ancient battle, a broken line almost always presaged of disaster. In this case, however, even though the Roman line had split and the Alemanni were pouring through the breach, the remaining regiments fighting on both sides of the gap continued their desperate struggle. This tells us quite a bit about the quality and discipline of the legions even at this late date.

Julian, who had already taught himself much about the conduct of a battle, was prepared for the calamity befalling him. As more and more Alemanni pushed into the gap and surged forward, they ran headlong into Julian's reserve—the household troops of the Primani legion, manned by the vicious Batavian cohorts. These elite troops were massed before the Romans' fortified camp, which one assumes was bristling with archers and missile artillery. According to Ammianus, the Primani stood in closely packed ranks and held "their ground fast and firm, like towers."[28] The German breakthrough was halted, as line after line of frenzied Alemanni crashed upon the disciplined Primani: "they fell in uninterrupted succession, and as the Romans now laid them low with greater confidence, fresh savages took the places of the slain; but when they heard the frequent groans of the dying, they were overcome with panic and lost their courage."

Julian now ordered a general advance, which broke the will of the fatigued Alemanni troops. Their lines broken, the Alemanni "made haste with all speed to get away." For a losing army, this was always the most dangerous phase of a battle, when the defeated troops were forced to run before the bloodlust of the victors. This is when the losers, their unprotected backs exposed and denuded of the protection of a cohesive line, take most of the battle's casualties and their army is irretrievably smashed and dispersed. It is this kind of unrelenting pursuit that explains the huge difference in losses between the victors and the losers in ancient battles. At Strasbourg at least a third of the shattered Alemanni perished in the fighting and the pursuit. Their leader, Chonodomarius, was run to ground and sent to Constantius, who was still in Milan. He later died in "senile decay," imprisoned within the squalor of a camp for Alemanni prisoners.[29] Those who did not surrender and could not run fast enough were mercilessly pursued by Roman cavalry and infantry all the way to the Rhine. Many were cut down as they ran, and large numbers drowned attempting to swim across the river while being struck by Roman missiles or weighed down by their armor.

Ammianus reports that six thousand Alemanni were dead on the field and that "heaps of dead, impossible to reckon, were carried off by the waves of the river.[30] The Roman loss was slight, just 243 men, including four tribunes.[31] The battle was such a resounding success that his army proclaimed Julian as Augustus and insisted he assume the purple. Julian wisely refused, rebuking them by claiming they were thoughtless in offering such an elevation of his position and telling them he neither deserved nor expected such an honor. To appease their disappointment, for soldiers gained much by being in the victorious cohorts of a successful Augustus, he assembled the army and began distributing rewards.

The battle was a turning point for Julian's relationship with Constantius. Julian had proven himself a capable soldier, able to hold the frontier without assistance from the *comitatenses*, while also demonstrating that he was not a threat to Constantius's own position as Augustus. Over the next two years Julian carefully followed Constantius's instructions and edicts to the letter while building a base of support deep within Gaul. Nor did Julian neglect the army, which, like all Roman armies, gave its utmost loyalty to aggressive and victorious generals. Consequently, for the next two years Julian led the army on successive campaigns, first to break the power of the Franks, who had moved west of the Rhine, and then to smash the remnants of the Alemanni confederation. When he was done, he controlled a prosperous Gaul and had a large, loyal, and experienced army at his back. Now was the time to turn his attention to the overthrow of his cousin and the assumption of the title of Augustus that he had ostentatiously refused in the immediate wake of the Battle of Strasbourg.

Constantius was likely aware of his cousin's growing ambitions, but as the moment of crisis approached, his attention was drawn eastward.[32] Sapor was once again on the march, having done little to conceal his intentions. He even had the temerity to send a note to Constantius in 359 demanding his birthright, which he believe consisted of everything controlled by the Persian Empire when it was ruled by Cyrus the Great. His writ therefore extended to the River Strymon in Macedonia, but in a gesture of munificence he said he would settle for the Roman-controlled provinces of Armenia and Mesopotamia. Sapor concluded his letter with a warning that if his just requests were rebuffed, he would gird himself with all of his strength and "hasten to come on."[33]

When he was rebuffed, Sapor lost no time in making good on his threats. Despite his warnings, the Roman commanders along and behind the frontiers were unprepared for the swiftness and power of the attack. This surely had much to do with Constantius's preoccupation with religious matters, for he was in the midst of another great council of bishops when he would have better served the Empire by securing the eastern frontier. This preoccupation of the emperors, from Constantine forward, was the true danger Christianity held for the security of the Empire, rather than the supposedly enervating influences that a peaceful religion had on the legions, who manifestly maintained a zeal for combat until the final collapse. Surely Julian's Christian troops pleading with him to lead them into battle against the Alemanni did not lack for martial ardor. But even if one discounts the claims of Christian authors of the period in favor of other (admittedly scant) sources, it still shocks the senses to see how much attention emperors and their retinues gave to matters of faith and doctrine at a time when the frontiers were being assailed from every quarter.

Roman salvation came only from an accident of war. Sapor had learned during the desultory years of fighting since the Battle of Singara that the only way to defeat the Romans was to invest and then bypass the frontier fortresses so that his armies could immediately plunge deep into the Eastern Empire's vitals without wasting most of the campaigning season on perilous sieges.[34] By causing as much devastation as possible over a wide area or by threatening Antioch, Sapor hoped to force an unprepared Roman army to rush into battle. This represented a major strategic change of direction in Sassanid planning, one the Romans would have been hard-pressed to counter. But as his army invested Amida, a bolt fired from the fortress walls killed the son of Grumbates, king of the Chionitae, one of Sapor's most powerful allies. After two days of mourning, Sapor was ready to move on, but Grumbates refused to march unless his son was avenged in blood by the seizure of Amida, and Sapor could not advance without his sizable contingent of troops (Figure 16.1).

Left no choice, Sapor ordered an assault, but Amida was not a push-over. Normally, the city was garrisoned by V Parthica and a large force of local auxiliaries, but as Sapor approached it was reinforced by six additional legions.[35] When a series of furious assaults was repulsed with heavy losses on both sides, Sapor settled in for a lengthy siege.[36] There was evidently some debate between Constantius's two leading military commanders, Ursicinus and Sabinianus, as to whether to march the eastern army to the relief of the city, but in the end the army stayed where it was. Ammianus claims that this was a result of petty jealousies between the two commanders as well as Constantius's wariness over allowing Ursicinus, who would lead the expedition, to gain further glory. He was viewed as a man who, once he had an army under his control, would try and wrest the Empire from Constantius.

The more likely reason for the lack of a Roman response was that Amida was doing exactly what it was supposed to do. Constantius was unable to call on the power of the entire Empire, since Julian refused to send him and troops, claiming the western army would rebel if forced to march east.

FIGURE 16.1 Walls of the Amida Fortress, Diyarbakir

Neither could any troops could be spared from the recently restored but still restive Danubian frontier. Constantius must also have felt great reluctance to risk his field army against the full might of the Sassanids, particularly because seven of his best legions were penned up in Amida.

Moreover, Amida was doing good service holding Sapor's army in place as the campaign season waned. The tide of Sapor's supposedly irresistible advance was being broken upon the walls of Amida. In this regard, Amida was acting similarly to the German army surrounded in Stalingrad in World War II. If the city had fallen early, massive Soviet armies surely would have rushed as far as Rostov and beyond, collapsing all of Army Group South and possibly the Germans' entire position in the Soviet Union. Amida was being sacrificed to save the Eastern Empire. But from a Roman viewpoint, the city's fall was uncertain, and there were good reasons to believe it could withstand Sapor's siege without the assistance of the field army.

Amida did eventually fall, but it had held for seventy-three days and cost Sapor the flower of his army: reportedly thirty thousand Persians had died before the walls.[37] Also, the campaigning season was coming to an end, and the amount of time even a ruler as powerful and respected as Sapor could hold the multiethnic Sassanid army together was coming to an end. He had no choice: he had to march his army back east, away from the rich Roman provinces. But a gap had been punched in the Roman lines: the walls of Amida were dismantled, and two lesser fortresses—Singara and Bezabde—had also fallen. Rome had also lost six legions, and although these were no longer the huge legions of the Principate, their loss must have been keenly felt, as was the loss of the thousands of trained auxiliaries that perished at their side. The fact that Sapor had strongly garrisoned Bezabde before departing was a sure indication that the Sassanids planned to return the following spring.[38]

To fend off such an attack, Constantius required access to the full resources of the Empire. Hence, he sent messages to Julian demanding that every spare man and unit be sent east as rapidly as possible. Julian, however, had other plans, which were visibly long in preparation.[39] In 360, at the supposed behest of his soldiers, he declared himself Augustus, making himself equal to Constantius in the east. In 361 he began marching his army east, finally ready to contest control of the Empire with his cousin. As Julian's army descended out of the Black Forest and rapidly overran the Balkans, Constantius could only look on helplessly from Edessa, where his army was waiting for Sapor to renew his attack. This is one of the few times in the history of the Empire that an emperor placed the threat of an attack from the other side of the frontiers ahead of the challenge of a usurper.

By the time it became clear that Sapor was not going to restart his offensive—supposedly due to bad omens, but one suspects other unknown motivations—the campaigning season was almost over. Still, Julian posed a risk that Constantius could not afford to ignore any longer. He mustered his forces and prepared for a march that would take most of the fall. Once again Julian's luck held: before the two armies met, he received news that Constantius had succumbed to a fever. Julian now controlled the whole of a unified Roman Empire, except for some holdouts in the Italian city of Aquileia. He spent the first few months of his reign conducting the by-now-ritual purges, this time done through the quasi-legality of the Tribunals of Chalcedon, where cases dealing with members of Constantius's court, as well as the generals thought to have opposed him, were tried. More crucially, from a historical viewpoint, Julian renounced Christianity in favor of the old pagan gods—forever earning the appellation "Apostate" after his name. Although historians have made much of Julian's apostasy, its strategic impact was nil. By this time Christianity had embedded itself deeply within the fabric of Roman society and administration, and it would have taken a long and focused effort to wrest away the church's accumulated power within and over Roman society. Unfortunately, for those still clinging to the old gods, Julian's hold on power was not destined to be a long one. Moreover, his decision to reestablish paganism appears to have had no discernible impact upon the Empire's military forces.

In May 362 Julian moved to Antioch to begin preparations for bringing what amounted to the full deployable might of the Roman Empire to bear on Persia. He had arrived in the Balkans with the elite of the Western armies, where he had gathered to his standard the best of the Danubian legions and now had the loyalty of Constantius's field army. Sapor must have been aware of the magnitude of Rome's preparations, so, with serious trouble brewing on his own northern and eastern frontiers, he offered Julian a truce.[40] Julian, however, set on securing his hold on power the old-fashioned way—through offensive conquest—disdainfully rejected Sapor's olive branch. Ammianus tells us he decided upon war because he was inflamed by a longing for it after months of inactivity, and because he wanted the glory of the surname Parthicus added to his own as the conqueror of Persia. Both were noble but unwise ambitions for a Roman emperor.[41]

Still, many of his advisors cautioned against a costly and dangerous invasion. These generals would have to be won over by better arguments than victory would add to the emperor's glory, and besides, Julian already had a formidable military reputation. Julian was certainly aware of the effectiveness of Constantius's policy of entrapping Sapor's huge armies within the frontier fortifications and keeping him away from the economically vital provinces along the coast. But as successful as this defensive posture had been, it also had severe drawbacks. For one, it was costly; it also kept the field army pinned to the Persian frontier and unable to help when crises manifested elsewhere. Worse, Sapor had been patiently eroding the strength of the frontier fortresses for half a decade. It was only a matter of time until the defenses completely collapsed and the Sassanid army poured through unhindered, with a secure supply line back to their Persian bases.

Nonetheless, Julian believed that further conquests would not only add to his glory but also demonstrate to the world the continuing superiority of Roman arms. There were also major strategic gains to be had from a successful invasion. For over a hundred years the Sassanid Empire had been a constant threat to Rome's eastern provinces, one that far exceeded that of the previous Parthian Empire. Although Rome had had successes in a series of wars against the Sassanids, the overall situation was a prolonged strategic stalemate that constantly diverted Roman attention from other threats and consumed vast resources. Rome's major strategic hurdle, at least since Trajan's reign, was that the Roman Empire had already reached its maximum governable extent. As we can see from the huge difficulties Rome faced managing the current halves of the Empire, there was little chance that it could absorb and govern the vast expanse of the Sassanid Empire. If the conquest and assimilation of the Sassanid Empire were beyond Rome's capabilities, was there a justification for war beyond the possibility of adding some additional territory to act as buffers along the frontiers? There likely was, for Julian had a trump card residing in his own court: Sapor's brother, Ohrmazd, had been exiled and living among the Romans for four decades.[42] A letter written by Libanius after the campaign indicates that Ohrmazd was an integral part of Julian's campaign planning: "We hope that our emperor will bring the current ruler, handing the kingdom over to one who was exiled."[43] It appears that Julian's aim was not conquest but regime change, substituting one brother for another who was more favorable to a permanent accommodation with Rome.

Julian planned to send one army under a distant relative, Procopius, into Armenia to join forces with the Armenian king, Arsaces. They were then to act as a feint, drawing off Sapor's main army. Given that Armenia had been the central theater of war for over a century, Sapor had no problem believing this was Julian's primary offensive move for the season. He also viewed it as a limited-risk attack whose goal was to achieve limited gains. This, from Sapor's viewpoint, was a wise move, since Julian would be foolish to risk more so early in his reign. He misread his man. Julian was all too willing to risk all on a single roll of war's iron dice. Moreover, with the combined power of Rome's three major field armies wielded into a single force, he had the power to accomplish his goals.

When the majority of Sapor's army headed north toward Armenia, Julian departed Antioch with his main army, planning to follow the Euphrates through what is now Iraq to the Sassanid capital of Ctesiphon. Many scholars and strategists, then and since, have commented on the brilliance of Julian's overall plan, only to find fault with its execution. But the plan actually had numerous flaws. Foremost amongst them was its predictability; after all, he was following the same routes used by Trajan and Severus. Also, once he started on his campaign, which included a thousand supply ships, he had no choice but to continue down the Euphrates River. But because he was facing enemies far more determined than the Parthian generals of the past, this large supporting fleet became a major handicap. Facing generals who were even more ruthless then those of the past, Julian had no ready answer when they began cutting the dykes and canals surrounding Ctesiphon. The earlier Persian generals had never chosen to ruin their own agricultural regions in pursuit of victory. Moreover, as soon as Sapor realized he had been duped, he would return with his main army, which would then be sitting athwart Julian's communications lines and his only route of escape. If this happened, Julian had only two recourses: lure Sapor's army into a decisive battle or capture Ctesiphon in hopes the shock of losing the capital would collapse Sapor's hold on power. The first option was the more difficult: he could not force Sapor into a battle he did not wish to fight, and the Sassanid field army could retreat before him indefinitely. As for the second option, its promise may have been destroyed by an almost inconceivable error: no one had thought to pack a siege train sufficient to take a city in those thousand support vessels.[44] Thus, when Julian arrived before the Sassanid capital after an uneventful march down the Euphrates, he found the region flooded, denuded of food and forage, and the Sassanids waiting behind sturdy defenses made impregnable to an army without siege engines. Worse, as he milled about trying to find a solution to problems of his own making, Sapor's army returned to Mesopotamia, threatening to trap the entire Roman army far from the succor of Roman fortresses.

During the march, Julian had let his soldiers feast on the enemy's fields, abounding in fruits of every kind, but when they were satiated, he ordered the remaining fields, crops, and infrastructure burned. Living off the land allowed him to conserve the food stored on his riverine armada, but it also ensured he could not return the way he had come in the event of a reverse. And that reverse was upon him. Unable to take Ctesiphon by storm and unable or unwilling to settle in for a long siege, Julian was in trouble. Sapor's army was known to be on the march toward his rear, and an unassailable fortress was to his front. With no local foodstuffs available, his army would soon exhaust his shipborne supplies. Consequently, tarrying in hopes that Sapor elected to risk a decisive battle meant his army would soon starve. Out of options, Julian ordered a retreat up the Tigris River. For reasons not fully explained, he also ordered that the fleet and everything still aboard the vessels be burned.[45] This was another unforced error, as the army now set out on a long march supplied only by what the soldiers and surviving mules could carry. The impact on Roman morale was catastrophic.

Before them was a devastated landscape that could provide little sustenance during their long march. All around them were Persian and Saracen light horsemen who picked off stragglers and made foraging nearly impossible. Despite the setbacks and privations, Roman discipline held, and the army trudged north, watching for the expected arrival of Sapor's main field army. Sapor evidently offered battle, and at least one major assault was beaten back with great loss, but not so great that his army was imperiled.[46] After the battles, the Romans rested in place for the duration of a three-day truce. In that time they exhausted what was left of their food.[47] Despite the frightful state of his army, Julian scorned any discussion of peace, and at the end of the truce he ordered the army to continue its march. Sapor contented himself with a strategy that had wrecked Roman armies in the past, opting to harry it along its line of march and deny it any chance of resupply. It was only a matter of time until the Roman force began to disintegrate and would no longer be a match for Sapor's troops. On the tenth day of the march disaster struck, drawing the moment of the Roman army's final collapse much nearer. Julian, rushing to the point of a Persian harassing attack, recklessly neglected to don any armor. As he was rallying his retreating troops, a Persian spear struck his side and buried itself in his liver—a mortal wound.[48]

At first it was impossible to choose a successor. The House of Constantine was at an end, and the generals could not agree on which one of their own should replace the dead emperor. This was to be expected in an army that was essentially a fusion of the Gallic, Danubian, and Eastern field armies in which none of the officers of these respective forces trusted the others. Their only common bond was Julian, and he was gone. Unwilling to select a senior officer who would have a solid power base of his own, the generals settled on a junior officer, Jovian. Few, however, are likely to have considered Jovian's elevation as the ultimate answer. For most, it was merely a stopgap to get them through an emergency. It could all be fixed or redone later once the army was safely back at Antioch.[49]

The army trudged north but could not cross the raging Tigris while being so closely watched by Sapor's army. At Dura the Romans paused for several days, giving Sapor time to tighten the ring around the demoralized Roman army. Fixed to its position and with starvation taking hold, the army edged toward destruction. Salvation came from an unexpected quarter when Sapor offered to allow the army to cross unmolested and depart Persian territory in return for Rome's transfer of all the lands Diocletian had gained and then some:

> Now the king [Sapor] obstinately demanded the lands which (he said) were his and had been taken from him long ago by Maximianus; but, in fact, as the negotiations showed, he required as our ransom five provinces on the far side of the Tigris: Arzanena, Moxoëna, and Zabdicena, as well as Rehimena and Corduena with fifteen fortresses, besides Nisibis, Singara and Castra Maurorum, a very important stronghold. And whereas it would have been better to fight ten battles than give up any one of these, the band of flatterers pressed upon the timid emperor, harping upon the dreaded name of Procopius, and declaring that if he returned on learning of the death of Julian, he would with the fresh troops under his command easily and without opposition make himself emperor.[50]

Jovian acceded to all of these demands, which also included a promise that for the duration of the truce—thirty years—he would not support Arsaces in Armenia, which doomed that state to Sassanid control. After crossing the Tigris, Jovian moved the army to Nisibis, where the fortress city that had withstood sieges in 337, 346, and 350 was handed over to Sassanid control. Jovian, however, would be dead by the end of the year, likely as a result of an accident, though Ammianus indicates there were suspicions of foul play.[51]

It is impossible to overestimate the strategic impact of Jovian's surrender. In a single instant, the frontier fortresses that had protected the Eastern Empire for generations ceased to serve Rome and were handed over to the enemy. The defenses were not just ruptured—they vanished. A rupture in the system could be fixed once the Sassanid army returned home after the campaigning season, but the elimination of the East's entire defensive infrastructure was irreparable. With the frontier defenses gone, Rome's first line of defense against invasion was now the field army, followed by the walls of the Eastern Empire's great cities. As bad as this was, Jovian's election had another major impact, barely noticed at the time. As Kulikowski points out, Jovian's selection by the competing high command of Rome's various armies heralds a new dynamic that would soon dominate the politics of the

Empire: from this point forward, emperors became increasingly insignificant, as they were dominated by the generals who controlled the armies.

In many ways, the political situation was beginning to look something like the days of the late Republic and the early Empire. The Senate could posture and rant, but whoever had the loyalty of the army held ultimate power. The Republican Senate had transferred control of the legions to the generals, but Augustus had concentrated ultimate military authority under himself. And so it had remained for over three centuries. If you were a general who wanted to command armies against the expressed desire or wishes of the ruling emperor, you first needed to establish yourself as an Augustus. But from Jovian's elevation until the final collapse in the west, emperors were mostly a collection of puppets controlled by their great generals. The power of these generals, in turn, rested on the regional armies, which were increasingly in competition with each other for ever-scarcer resources and funding. This was the inevitable outcome of Diocletian's and Constantine's administrative regional reforms, which had created a new, vastly expanded administrative structure that, when not commanded by a strong emperor, tended to award power to regional and provincial elites, who increasingly placed local issues ahead of imperial concerns.[52]

Jovian's untimely death left the generals of the assembled armies in the same quandary they had faced upon the death of Julian, this time without the pressure cooker of having Rome's combined field armies on the verge of being wiped out. After considering and rejecting several senior candidates, they settled on a tribune, Valentinian. As he had no independent power base, he too was a compromise candidate, incapable of threatening the prerogatives of either the commanders of various regional political elites or the generals. The soldiers, however, were not pleased. Fearing further dissension among their generals and having no desire to be led into mutual slaughter in another series of civil wars, they demanded that a co-Augustus be chosen. Valentinian consulted with his generals, one of whom advised, "If you love your relatives, most excellent emperor, you have a brother; if it is the state that you love, seek out another man to clothe with the purple."[53] Displeased with this advice, he appointed his brother Valens as his co-emperor. In the spring of 366 the two emperors divided the spoils: Valentinian would command the two great prefectures of the Western Empire, and Valens would control the Eastern Empire.[54] Soon after Valens was emplaced, the brothers faced their first major challenge. Procopius, a distant and the final member of Constantine's dynasty, the same man whom Julian had entrusted with the feint toward Armenia during his failed invasion of the Sassanid Empire, raised the flag of revolt.

Valens asked his brother for help. However, plagued by renewed Alemanni attacks across the Rhine and under the sway of his generals, Valentinian refused to march, often stating that "Procopius was only his own and his brother's enemy, but the Alemanni were enemies of the whole Roman world."[55] For several months it appeared as if Procopius's bid for power would succeed as Valens bided his time and gathered his forces. When reinforcements made their way up from Antioch, Valens felt strong enough to advance on the usurper. Procopius's end was anticlimactic: his generals deserted him, taking their troops with them.[56] Valens had Procopius executed, but found himself ever more under the control of his own generals.

The Goths had sent three thousand of their warriors to assist Procopius, arriving after the usurper was defeated, so Valens decided it was necessary to remind the Goths of the might of Roman arms. For the next three years he conducted mostly fruitless campaigns on the north side of the Danube. In the first year's campaign the Goths simply melted into the mountains and refused battle. In the second year a season of miserable weather made it nearly impossible for the Roman field army to maneuver.[57] Finally, after three years of campaigning, in 369 he brought the Gothic king Athanaric to battle. As was usually the case, the Goths were no match for the Romans in a set-piece battle, but for unknown reasons Valens, after winning a great victory, did not press his military advantage.[58] After all, he had what he needed—a military triumph that he could proclaim to the Roman people.

In the meantime, Valentinian was occupied with finishing the work Julian had left undone when he marched east. For five years he busily dispatched generals to destroy dangerous barbarian incursions in Britain and along the northern Rhine while continuing to strengthen the fortresses along the Saxon shores and rebuilding the Rhine frontier fortifications.[59] As Ammianus states, "No one, not even one of his persistent detractors, will reproach him with lack of ingenuity in behalf of the state, especially if one bears in mind that it was a more valuable service to check the barbarians by frontier defenses than to defeat them in battle."[60] Although Valentinian preferred a strategy based on the frontier defenses and cunning diplomacy, he also understood the need for propaganda victories that could be attained only by offensive action beyond the frontiers. Consequently, he personally led two major expeditions across the Rhine, ostensibly to punish the Alemanni for their raiding and attacking the fortress city of Mainz (Moguntiacum), but probably more crucially to bolster his personal military image. At one point, after foolishly setting out to conduct a personal reconnaissance, he and his few companions were ambushed. Only the speed of his horse and the sacrifice of his entourage saved him.[61] Soon afterward a fierce battle ensued—the

Battle of Solicinium—in which the Romans were victorious after a frontal assault had pushed the Alemanni into the jaws of a pincer, as Valentinian's reserves moved forward to outflank the barbarian position.[62] Satisfied that he had restored peace and gained sufficient glory for himself and young Gratian, Valentinian returned to Gaul. For the next several years the emperor undertook a major construction program all along the Rhine frontiers, sometimes supervising the construction himself. At one point he decided to build a new fort on the far side of the river, probably as a base for future expeditions. The Alemanni, after pleading to no avail for the work to be halted, attacked and wiped out the engineers.[63] In 368 Valentinian reacted with a combination of diplomacy and offensive action. He contacted the Burgundians in hopes that by exploiting their rivalry with the Alemanni he could induce them to join the Roman field army in a joint operation.[64] The Burgundians sent their warriors out, but when they arrived at the rendezvous, the Romans were not there:

> And so they halted for a time, but when Valentinian did not appear on the appointed day, as he had agreed, and they saw that none of his promises had been fulfilled, they sent envoys to the emperor's camp, demanding that support be given them for their return to their homes, in order that they might not expose their unprotected rear to the enemy. And when they perceived that by subterfuges and delays their request was practically denied, they went off from there in sorrow and indignation. And their kings, on learning what had happened, furious at being mocked, killed all their prisoners and returned to their native lands.[65]

The loss of the Roman hostages was probably felt, but the chance to have the two great barbarian kingdoms at each other's throats while the Romans watched without participating was no doubt too good an opportunity to pass up. As it was, the Burgundian advance had so disordered Alemanni defensive arrangements that Theodosius, Valentinian's *magister equitum*, was able to attack out of Raetia with tremendous effect.[66] In the wake of that attack, Valentinian offered peace to the high king of the Alemanni, Macrianus Marcian. After protracted discussions near Mainz, Macrianus agreed to a peace, which he adhered to until he was killed fighting the Franks. Having had success against the Alemanni Theodosius was sent to quell an uprising in Africa, and after nearly two years of hard fighting he broke the revolt in 374. Theodosius was now the most successful Roman general since Constantine, and his popularity was starting to rival that of the emperor. This, of course, was a very dangerous position for any Roman general to find himself in, particularly one who inspired the envy of his colleagues. It was therefore no great surprise when in 376 he was secretly investigated and then executed in Carthage.

Valentinian needed peace on the Rhine because in 374 a new military threat arose on the Danube. The Quadi, who had been at peace with the Empire since Constantius II's reign, were angered by the construction of a Roman fortress on their side of the Danube and the murder of their king, Gabinius, who had entered a Roman camp to discuss peace. So the Quadi crossed the Danube and began ravaging Pannonia. Two legions—the Pannoniaca and the Moesaica—were roughly handled by the invaders, forcing Valentinian to concentrate the field army and prepare for a major campaign in 375.

Valentinian broke the field army into two parts, personally leading one half across the Danube at Aquincum (Budapest) and plunging deep into Quadi territory. For two months Roman field armies did what they always did in enemy territory—destroyed everything in sight and killed or enslaved as many of the locals as possible. At the same time, Theodosius—the twenty-seven-year-old son of the *magister equitum* Theodosius—leading another Roman column, smashed a Sarmatian force that was advancing to support the Quadi. Not long afterward the Quadi sued for peace. When their leaders were brought before Valentinian, they begged forgiveness, but they then had the temerity to mention the Roman provocations that caused them to opt for war. Valentinian flew into a stroke-inducing rage. Just a few hours later he was dead.

The Danubian generals, acting in unseemly haste, acclaimed the dead emperor's four-year-old son Valentinian II emperor. The Gallic generals were furious and initially refused to acknowledge Valentinian's elevation. After all, they had the dead Valentinian's teenage half brother, Gratian, under their control at Trier. Moreover, they had the Pannonian legions on hand to enforce their choice. Civil war was avoided when Valens sent an envoy, the philosopher Themistius, to negotiate the disposition of his nephews. After a series of retirements and executions, where both the Gallic and Balkan high commands disposed of their opponents in each other's camp to feel safe, Themistius negotiated a final settlement. Gratian assumed control of the Western Empire and began appointing Gallic and Balkan generals to important positions. No one was fooled by Gratian's apparent initiative. He may have held the title of emperor, but the generals—those that survived the mutual purge—held the power. The child Valentinian II was made a junior partner in the Western Empire, where he remained under the close control of his generals until his dead body was discovered hanging in his room in 392.

Valens, who had brokered the peace, had no choice but to accept Gratian's and Valentinian II's rise, as he had bigger problems to worry about.

Sapor, now in his seventies, had little to concern himself with on his western border since he had made peace with Jovian. For one, the great cities and fortifications that had both defended the Roman frontiers and acted as support bases for invasions into Persia were now all in his hands. Moreover, in the years after Jovian's death, the Roman military was fully occupied by the Goths and Alemanni. Despite Rome's promise not to involve itself in Armenia, the region remained, as it had been for centuries, a bone of contention between the two empires. But Rome's barbarian distractions opened a window for Sapor's advances. First he had the pro-Roman ruler Arsaces invited to negotiate with his envoys. When he arrived, Arsaces was blinded and later tortured to death, allowing Sapor to place his own choice on the throne. Sapor had made his first move in what was an unambiguous attempt to rule Armenia as a Sassanid province.

In 370 Valens, having secured peace on the Danube, moved his imperial court to Antioch and took in Arsaces' son, Pap. With Roman support, Pap returned to Armenia, but he was forced to retreat when Sapor led an invasion army to expel him. But Persian armies still suffered from a lack of staying power, and Sapor returned to Persia after only a few months. Pap returned to Armenia, executed the Sassanid governors, and unwisely sent their heads to Sapor. It was an incitement to a full-fledged invasion, and Sapor prepared to oblige him. For almost all of the next decade Valens was forced to remain in Antioch, since each year the Persians threatened a major invasion not just of Armenia but also of Rome's eastern provinces. The reasons for Sapor's reticence are unknown, but it is likely that the Sassanid Empire was suffering internal turmoil as aspirants for the aging ruler's throne jockeyed for position. At the same time, the Sassanids were not immune from the tumult the Huns had unleashed throughout the steppes to their north, including Hunnic expansion into the Sassanid province of Bactria.

In the spring of 377 matters came to a head. Sapor declared the Jovian peace a dead issue, as most of its signatories were now dead. In reply, Valens issued an ultimatum stating that Sapor's claims were unjust and that Armenia must remain independent. Sapor, who had settled affairs along his frontier, now turned his full attention to Armenia and Rome. Throughout 377 both sides mustered their forces for a showdown to decide not only the fate of Armenia, but also the control of all that was lost by Jovian.

It was not to be. Just as Valens began his final preparations, news of a disaster on the Danube reached him. A hasty peace was arranged with Sapor, and Valens departed to take command of a new war against the Goths.

CHAPTER 17 | The Gothic Challenge

T HE REASONS FOR the new Gothic eruption are found well to the east, where new climatic conditions and a population explosion on the steppes set the stage for the Huns to make their first major appearance on the world stage. The Huns, whose domains lay beyond the Sea of Azov, were superb horsemen and fierce fighters. But that could be said of all the steppe people, or at least their warriors. What set the Huns apart was the invention of a new composite bow that allowed them to shoot remarkable distances with unprecedented penetrating power. Moreover, they could shoot accurately without ever having to dismount. Moving west, the Huns defeated and absorbed all the bordering tribes who proved unequal to the ferocity of their assaults. In Ammianus's words:

> This race of untamed men, without encumbrances, aflame with an in-human desire for plundering others' property, made their violent way amid the rapine and slaughter of the neighboring peoples as far as the Halani, once known as the Massagetae.[1]

The Hunnic advance was finally halted for a time when they came up against the Tervingi Goths. Under their king, Athanaric, the Tervingi waited behind a strong defensive position north of the Black Sea, along the Dniester River. The Huns had already defeated the Greuthungi Goths, who had also fallen back upon the Dniester. The two Gothic branches did not, however, unite against a common foe. Instead, the Tervingi were left alone to face the Hunnic force, while the Greuthungi, perhaps too battered to be of much help, disappear from our sources until they showed up along the Danube in 377. Had the Tervingi been able to hold their fortified line, it is likely the Huns would have been forced to break up in search of food and pasture. How this might have changed the course of history is unknowable. In any event, a savage night attack broke the Gothic line and would likely have brought an end to the Tervingi entirely if the Huns had not halted their advance to satisfy their appetite for loot.

The Goths made a strategic retreat of about two hundred miles, stopping atop the old *limes transalutanus* that had defended the Carpathian passes when Dacia was an imperial province. As discussed previously, here is one of the great what-ifs of Rome's strategic arrangements. One can only guess the impact on the Empire's future if the Romans had manned and maintained the *limes transalutanus*, with a supporting road system and a network of fortifications and fortified settlements arranged in depth beyond it. With Dacia as a buffer and able to absorb and settle migratory tribes who then could have assisted in their own defense, the Huns might have been halted far short of the Danube. The problem, of course, was a matter of logistics. It was much easier to support the frontier garrisons and the field army when they were close to a major river.

It hardly mattered. The Gothic move was too late, and the old Roman defenses could not be repaired and expanded in time to meet the next Hunnic advance. Wary of Roman arms and unwilling to break his previous promise to Valens to never again enter Roman territory, Athanaric appears to have taken some of his people into the safety of the Carpathian Mountains. But the bulk of the tribe followed two new leaders, Alavivus and Fritigern, who sent envoys to Valens pleading for permission to cross the Danube and promising to obey Roman laws and to provide recruits for the Roman army.[2] Valens, with his limitless need for soldiers, during a recruiting campaign to man the army facing the Persians, accepted the Gothic offers. The Tervingi were permitted to cross, although the other major Gothic branch, the Greuthungi—now also on the Danube—were forbidden to do so. Without asking for permission, the Greuthungi soon crossed anyway, joined by some of the local tribes.[3]

Winter was closing in, and the Goths began crossing the Danube and moving into the Empire. So far there was only one thing unique about what was happening, and it does not appear that the Romans took much notice of it at the time. In the past, large groups of migrants entering the Empire were quickly broken up and moved to distant corners, far from their kin on the other side of the frontiers. This time, however, the Goths asked for a portion of Thrace to be handed over to them to settle as a group. It is worth noting that the Tervingi had already displayed a degree of political organization capable of holding a large society together to coordinate a widespread resistance to the Huns, to survive a tribal split when Athanaric departed with his followers, and to sustain a coordinated migration of approximately—if Eunapius is to be believed—as many as 200,000 persons over several hundred miles.[4] They then calmly settled along the Danube and sustained themselves over several months of negotiations with Roman authorities.

Rome was not dealing with a desperate horde. Rather, it allowed into the Empire a militarily dangerous, efficiently organized society capable of taking coordinated action if they were not handled with care. What was called for was a deft touch, much political wisdom, and the massing of sufficient forces to intimidate the newcomers and enforce the will of Rome. What happened, instead, was a comedy of errors ending in catastrophe. The first rule of any migration into Roman territory was that the newcomers be disarmed, and this was certainly Valens's intention. Those who enlisted in the army could be rearmed from Roman arsenals at a later date, once they were far from their kin. The planned disarmament was the first Roman failure: many of the Goths and probably all of the warriors crossed with their arms. The disarmament having failed, the next element of the process—recruiting as many Goths as possible into the army and moving them to distant postings—had little chance of success and does not appear to have been a priority. Finally, while the Goths awaited resettlement, it was the job of the local administrators to shelter and feed them. Through a combination of venality, incompetence, and greed, the Roman commanders on the spot—Lupicinus, the *comes rei militari*, and Maximus, probably the *dux* of Moesia—decided that they had been given a wonderful opportunity to enrich themselves. They placed an oppressive tax on the food that had been sent to feed the Goths. As Gibbon relates, "The vilest food was sold at an extravagant price; and, in the room of wholesome and substantial provisions, the markets were filled with the flesh of dogs, and of unclean animals, who had died of disease."[5] Soon the Goths were bartering their children as slaves in return for food. As Gothic restlessness increased, Lupicinus ordered the Goths to move toward Marcianopolis, where the garrison could be added to the frontier troops who were guarding their encampment. When the frontier troops departed to escort the Tervingi, the suddenly denuded frontier was wide open for the Greuthungi Goths to cross the Danube into Thrace unopposed. There were now two huge bands of Goths within the Empire, both hungry, armed, and dangerous.

Lupicinus, trying to forestall a full-scale Gothic revolt, invited the Gothic chieftains Alavivus and Fritigern to a banquet at his Marcianople (modern Devnja, Bulgaria) headquarters. While dinner was being served to the ruling elites, the starving Goths fought a pitched battle with the townsfolk over access to food. Lupicinus, either in a panic or in a move he had already planned, ordered the murder of Gothic leaders' guards, and Alavivus and Fritigern were taken hostage. When the Goths threatened to storm the walls if their leaders were not released, Lupicinus released Fritigern, who had claimed he could calm the enraged Goths.

Instead of settling the Goths, Fritigern told them that the Romans had no plans to honor their agreements and led them in a series of raids throughout the countryside. Realizing that he had mismanaged the crisis from the start, Lupicinus reverted to the Roman playbook—mass what troops are available and march to battle as soon as possible. Most of the time this rapid action was successful. But on some occasions, such as the 9 CE disaster in Teutoburg Wald, it led to disaster. This was one of those occasions. Lupicinus's army gathered about nine miles from the city and marched against the Gothic encampment. Without bothering to form up, the Goths swarmed out of their camp and dashed upon the Roman shields. It was all over in a few minutes. The Roman force was surrounded, overwhelmed, and exterminated, leaving the frontier denuded of troops and the Balkan provinces exposed to the Gothic ravages.[6] Fritigern's Goths armed themselves with captured Roman weapons and armor and ranged as far as Adrianople, two hundred miles distant. At the same time they increased their numbers dramatically as other Goths already admitted to the Empire, as well as thousands of slaves, flocked to the invaders' banners.

Valens, as soon as he had concluded arrangements with Sapor, rushed north, sending ahead two of his best generals, Profuturus and Traianus, to muster any remaining troops and try to contain the Goths. At the same time Gratian, who was beginning to comprehend the magnitude of the problem, sent two of his best generals, Frigeridus and the *comes domesticorum* Richomeres, east to help as best they could. Their instructions were to help the Eastern Empire's forces if possible, but above all to make sure the Goths were contained in Thrace and Moesia and the troubles did not spread westward. We have previously seen how the generals surrounding Valentinian refused to let him help Valens against Procopius's attempted usurpation. One suspects, therefore, that they recognized the complete collapse of the Danubian frontier as a much more serious threat to their own domains and well-being. Dynastic squabbling may not have been able to hold their attention, but the collapse of the frontier focused them. Frigeridus soon fell ill, leaving Richomeres to command the western army reinforcements, which were mostly legions scraped up from the Rhine frontier and Pannonia.

Valens's generals were not up to the task, and by apparently common consent Richomeres took command of Rome's Balkan army. He camped his recuperating troops near Salicles—"By the Willows"—only a few miles from the main Gothic army.[7] For some time the two armies watched each other as the Goths sheltered behind their wagon fort and called in their raiding parties. This was playing Rome's game, since the Roman logistical system could supply their army's needs while the Goths would soon exhaust whatever meager amounts of food they had collected. Eventually the Goths considered themselves as strong as they would ever be and advanced on the Roman position. The subsequent battle was bloody but indecisive, only ending when night fell. Both armies stood to their arms all night, and the Romans were shocked to find the Goths still on the field in the morning. Ammianus describes a second daylong battle in which the Romans suffered serious losses but also inflicted many casualties upon the Goths.[8]

The damaged Gothic force retreated into the safety of the Haemus Mountains, while the Roman army marched south to Marcianople. By this time Gratian's general, Frigeridus, had recovered his health and had advanced with some additional legions to Beroea, which he fortified. Here he wiped out a large band of Gothic raiders led by Farnobius, sending the survivors to work the fields of Italy as slaves. But his job was apparently to guard Pannonia, not to help clear the rest of the Balkans of the Gothic menace.

That winter Richomeres returned to Gaul while Valens sent reinforcements along with his best general, the *magister equitum* Saturninus, to command the remaining imperial forces. Saturninus penned the Goths up in their mountain holdouts, hoping to starve them sufficiently to attempt an advance through an opening he had left in his defenses, whereupon he planned to annihilate them in the open fields to the north. Instead, the Goths allied themselves with a newly arrived combined Hunnic-Alan force and moved south to Thrace. Here the barbarians were able to make good use of the undefended Roman road network to raid as far as the shores of the Bosporus and even approach Constantinople itself.

The crisis was now at a point where both Valens and Gratian planned personally to take the field. As the two Augusti gathered their forces, Saturninus won a series of small battles against the Gothic raiders, which only served to alert Fritigern to the growing danger and order his forces to concentrate near Cabyle. From there the Goths marched toward Adrianople, where Saturninus's army was camped.

Gratian's plans to help catch the Goths in a pincer between the Roman field armies were delayed when an Alemanni tribe, the Lentienses, observing that the frontier was only weakly held owing to Gratian's concentration of forces in Pannonia, crossed the Rhine in large numbers. Ammianus claims that between forty thousand and seventy thousand of these Alemanni struck

Raetia, forcing Gratian to recall the legions he had already sent east.[9] The Lentienses invasion was contained and then destroyed, but instead of heading east immediately, Gratian took his army across the Rhine to inflict greater damage upon the Alemanni. His likely intent was to cow them sufficiently that they did not consider another assault while the field army was in the east. Over fifteen hundred years later, what possible necessity required such a move cannot be judged. Only in hindsight can we see how it led to disaster, for the diversion cost Gratian several weeks of campaigning time, whereas, had that time been put to better use marching east, Valens and the eastern field army would have been saved and the Goths destroyed.

Throughout the winter and spring of 378 Roman forces continued to stream through Constantinople. Valens arrived in May 378. An Arian Christian in a Nicene city, he was not a favorite of the populace. Moreover, the city was suffering from riots over the lack of food, since little was making its way in from the ravaged hinterlands. After just a week in Constantinople, Valens moved his headquarters to one of his summer palaces along the road to Adrianople. Fritigern, despite still not having much of his cavalry on hand, moved his army to Nike, just a few miles from Adrianople. Valens now heard from Gratian, who informed him that he was in Sirmium with his army and preparing to move further east. Gratian also boasted of his victories over the Alemanni, which his generals had won for him, and inflamed the jealousy of Valens, who had spent nearly a decade facing the Persians without garnering the glory of military victory. Even his earlier success against the Goths was now being made a mockery of by the massive Gothic forces destroying vast swaths of his domains.

Without his cavalry, Fritigern's Goths were at a severe disadvantage against the concentrated Roman field army. He therefore sent a Christian presbyter to ask the emperor to confer Thrace upon the Goths in return for lasting peace.[10] Valens, desirous of a much-needed military victory and believing intelligence reports stating that the Goths numbered only ten thousand, scorned the offer and advanced his army of between twenty and forty thousand men toward the enemy. Once at Adrianople, Valens fortified his position and, now seeing the size of the Gothic host, settled in to await the arrival of Gratian's field army. Richomeres, arriving with the vanguard of the western army, begged Valens to wait until the main army, now only a few days away, arrived. A lengthy debate now ensued among the Roman commanders as well as some high-ranking courtiers. The question was whether the Eastern Empire's army should stand the defensive or march out and attack the Goths without waiting for Gratian's force. The sensible choice was to wait: the Goths were no match for the combined forces of both halves of the Empire. And although some generals pleaded for that course, Valens was of a mind to attack. Aggressive, ruthless offensive action had always been the hallmark of successful Roman emperors. Gratian had proven he had the mettle for ruthless attacks and hard fighting, but Valens had not yet gained such a reputation. Still, from a strategic standpoint, it was an error for Valens to bet the Empire's future on a single roll of the dice, when just a few days' wait would have heavily tilted the odds in Rome's favor.

In the end, the generals were stalemated in their respective opinions. In stepped the courtiers, who were only too ready to impress upon on the emperor how weak he would appear if his nephew were to share or, worse, claim the credit for defeating the Goths. From the start, Valens had been in favor of an immediate assault, and it did not take much of an appeal to his vanity for that course to carry the day. According to Ammianus, "The fatal insistence of the emperor prevailed, supported by the flattering opinion of some of his courtiers, who urged him to make all haste so that Gratian might not have a share in the victory which (as they represented) was already all but won." Valens ordered the army to march.

Having decided to attack, the eastern emperor further demonstrated his unsuitability for command by leaving his logistics train, as well as his treasury, back in Adrianople. The soldiers who had marched before dawn would now be forced to go the day without food. Furthermore, the generals, probably piqued over being outvoted by courtiers with no military experience, failed to make provisions for water along the line of march. The August heat soon exhausted an army forced to march eight miles in full armor. By the time they caught sight of the Goths' fort, the soldiers were ready to drop from thirst. The harrowing march was made much worse by the Goths, who burned brush all along the march route, enveloping the gasping Romans in smoke. As Ammianus reports, Fritigern now played for time, in hopes his cavalry would return soon, by sending envoys to discuss peace while the imperial army was being slowly broiled in the hot sun. Why Valens allowed these negotiations to continue into the afternoon while his army's fighting capacity rapidly withered will always be a mystery. The Goths, on the other hand, rested within and near their fortified lagger, drinking and eating their fill as they awaited the Roman advance.

The battle was finally brought on when two of the army's most elite units, the Scutarii and the Sagitarii, advanced without orders. This opening skirmish was observed by two chiefs of the Greuthungians, Alatheus and Saphrax, who had just arrived on the edge of the battlefield with the Gothic cavalry, joined by a band of Alans. Their impetuous charge into the flank of the advancing Romans sent the Sagittarii and Scutarii flying back toward the advancing Roman line. In their wake came the Gothic cavalry, pressing their attack into the Roman flanks and compressing the solid Roman lines so that it was difficult for the soldiers to wield their weapons. With the decline in tactical discipline that coincided with Constantine's death and the loss of so many veteran troops in the civil wars that followed, Roman infantry had become dependent upon the psychological bond of close physical proximity to their fellow soldiers. Long gone were the days when hard training and ruthless discipline allowed the tactically flexible formations of Constantine's era. The tactical formations of the late Roman armies were virtually solid blocks that were difficult to maneuver, nor did they allow individual soldiers much room to move. The result was a disaster for Roman arms:

> On every side armor and weapons clashed, and Bellona, raging with more than usual madness for the destruction of the Romans, blew her lamentable war-trumpets; our soldiers who were giving way rallied, exchanging many encouraging shouts, but the battle, spreading like flames, filled their hearts with terror, as numbers of them were pierced by strokes of whirling spears and arrows. . . . And because the left wing, which had made its way as far as the very wagons and would have gone farther if it had had any support, being deserted by the rest of the cavalry, was hard pressed by the enemy's numbers, it was crushed, and overwhelmed, as if by the downfall of a mighty rampart. The foot-soldiers thus stood unprotected, and their companies were so crowded together that hardly anyone could pull out his sword or draw back his arm. Because of clouds of dust the heavens could no longer be seen and echoed with frightful cries. Hence the arrows whirling death from every side always found their mark with fatal effect, since they could not be seen beforehand nor guarded against. But when the barbarians, pouring forth in huge hordes, trampled down horse and man, and in the press of ranks no room for retreat could be gained anywhere, and the increased crowding left no opportunity for escape, our soldiers also, showing extreme contempt of falling in the fight, received their deathblows. . . . Finally, when the whole scene was discolored with the hue of dark blood, and wherever men turned their eyes heaps of slain met them, they trod upon the bodies of the dead without mercy. Now the sun had risen higher and . . . scorched the Romans, who were more and more exhausted by hunger and worn out by thirst, as well as distressed by the heavy burden of their armor. Finally, our line was broken by the onrushing weight of the barbarians.[11]

Toward the end Valens was forced to seek shelter within the Mattiarii's formation. This was one of the field army's regular line units, so we can assume that the imperial bodyguard, along with other elite forces, had already been massacred. As the slaughter continued, Valens's generals Victor, Richomeres, and Saturninus attempted to bring the auxiliaries, who made up half the army and had been left in reserve, into the fray. But it was obvious to these soldiers that the battle was already lost, and they just melted away. In the end, Valens's generals also fled the field, leaving the remainder of the army to be butchered. Valens himself had fallen during the battle, and his body was not recovered.[12] With him had fallen at least two-thirds of a Roman field army—perhaps more than thirty thousand men. As Themistius wrote of that day—August 9, 378—five years after the event: "Thrace was overthrown, Illyricum was overrun, armies vanished altogether, like shadows."[13]

This was a disaster; the loss of Valens's army extinguished almost all of Rome's military power in the east. All that remained were the garrisons of the cities and forts, and even these had been weakened when soldiers were withdrawn from them to feed the field army's needs. The Roman defeat was not caused by superior Gothic cavalry overrunning Roman infantry. Rather, it reflected mistakes made by the Roman commanders. The Battle of Adrianople may have ushered in a period when cavalry dominated the battlefield, but that domination was the result of a lack of discipline among the infantry that prevented them from standing firm in the face of cavalry charges. Horses will not charge into a line of infantry that stands firm; no horse is that valorous. But without cohesion, an infantry formation is a mob and will always fall prey to a rapid cavalry charge.

Adrianople taught those succeeding Valens in the east the crucial lesson of the fragility of military power. And on that lesson the survival of the Empire depended for the next millennium. Thus, the strategic approach for the remainder of the Eastern Empire's existence emphasized the diplomatic and manipulative aspects of foreign policy. For most of their rulers, at least after Justinian had frittered away the army's strength trying to rebuild the Empire of Trajan's time, war was resorted to only when no other choice existed, and the survival of the Empire depended on military force alone. But both in terms of the resources available and in their understanding of the relative strategic weakness of their power, they used force with the utmost discretion.[14]

CHAPTER 18 | Adrianople's Aftermath

U PON LEARNING OF the disaster at Adrianople, Gratian turned the
western field army around and returned to Sirmium to contemplate his
options. One Roman field army was destroyed and the second, with him in
Sirmium, would soon be needed back in Gaul, where the Alemanni were already beginning to stir. But if he left immediately, the unrest in the Balkans
would spread. Thrace and Moesia were already lost to the Empire, and much
of the Balkans had been consumed by chaos for three years. The Eastern
Empire still possessed sufficient strength to hold onto most key cities,
and Fritigern had not even been able to take Adrianople after the battle.
Similarly, the Goths were stymied by the walls of Constantinople, as well
as by the fortifications of many towns and cities throughout the Balkans.
Fritigern, knowing that the Goths did not have the expertise or equipment
required to press a siege, had previously said that he "kept peace with walls."
His experiences after the Battle of Adrianople only confirmed his opinion.

It was the massive building of walls and fortifications that took place
during and after the Crisis of the Third Century that was the salvation of the
Eastern Empire. The barbarians could devastate the countryside, limit movement along roads, and deny central imperial authorities the income from the
ravaged provinces, but they were incapable of conquest. Without control of
the cities, the Goths could not establish their own permanent settlements or
collect taxes. All they could do was plunder. But plundering provided only
a onetime windfall and, in reality, damaged the Goths' long-term economic
prospects. Moreover, the network of cities and towns provided the secure bases

required for the inevitable Roman counterattack. When that counterattack was prepared, it was the fortifications of the cities and towns that kept the Goths in the Balkans and away from the vital tax-producing centers of the Empire. And it was these untouched revenue-producing provinces that ensured Roman strategic resilience in the face of yet another great military disaster.

The true consequence of Adrianople was that it locked in place the separation that arose when Constantine's sons decided to divide the Empire between them and then fought a series of civil wars to bring it back together. In the meantime they had done little to assist each other against outside threats. Of course, it had long been understood that the Empire was too big to be run by just one man. This realization had been the basis for the tetrarchy, but even the tetrarchy had had a single senior emperor to rule the others. Constantine must have thought that a similar arrangement would be made upon his death. Unquestionably, he did not intend for his sons to fight a series of crippling civil wars after he died. Moreover, there were always centrifugal forces trying to break the Empire up or tear parts of it away. One has only to look at the Empire at the time of Aurelian, when he was forced to use military force to bring the Gallic and Palmyran Empires back into the fold. Still, few at the time considered such divisions permanent, outside of those elites trying to break away.

But after Adrianople the Empire was for all practical purposes permanently divided, although not in any manifestly political way, since there remained two Augusti who were communicating with each other. What changed was that only rarely would either half of the Empire be willing to help the other. And even when they did, the help was rarely of meaningful size or long maintained. Gratian's army marching to help Valens marked the last time an eastern or western Roman field army marched to the assistance of the other. When his army marched back west, it heralded a break that doomed the consolidated Empire that had existed since the reign of Augustus. Moreover, as the Eastern Empire's economy became increasingly gold based, even while the Western Empire stayed entirely silver based, an unbreachable economic divide was created. In short, for the Empire to remain whole, each side needed to be able to draw upon the resources of the other in times of crisis. After Adrianople, doing so remained theoretically possible, but in fact it was now unrealistic for either half of the Empire to count on help from the other. This, and not some notion that Adrianople marked the beginning of cavalry's ascent over infantry on the battlefield, or that the Romans lost their battlefield edge over barbarians, was what made Adrianople a turning point in world history.

Realizing that he could not adequately rule both halves of the Empire, Gratian appointed Theodosius, who just a few years earlier had smashed a Sarmatian force in Raetia, as his co-Augustus. Now thirty-three years old, Theodosius likely came to power thanks to a coup effected by the eastern generals, who had no intention of playing second fiddle to the generals who dominated Gratian's court. Gratian therefore accepted Theodosius's rise to the purple because he was given no other choice. But from a selfish perspective, things were so bad in the east that a long series of continued failures was expected. Hence, as Gratian saw things, it was better to have Theodosius held responsible for failures rather than himself.

For two years Theodosius employed his meager forces in a series of minor battles that did much to attrit Gothic combat power. That, coupled with the Goths' inability to take fortified locations, denied them new plunder and soon had them looking for more fertile regions to pillage. By 380 there were two main groups of Goths in the Balkans. One, still led by Fritigern, decided to march south into Thessaly and Macedonia, while the other struck out west toward Pannonia, which was part of Gratian's Western Empire. This latter group was engaged by the western field army and halted. Gratian then bought peace by allowing the invaders to take up permanent residence in portions of Pannonia and Upper Moesia.[1]

For his part, Theodosius attempted to block Fritigern's forces in Macedonia. A sharp battle was fought, and the greatly outnumbered Roman force, filled with new and barely trained recruits, suffered heavy losses. Zosimus reports that the emperor barely escaped with his life and that if the Goths had followed up on their battlefield success, they would have gained much, including the capture of Theodosius.[2] Instead, they settled down to become masters of Macedonia and Thessaly but once again left the towns uninjured.

The Roman cause was greatly aided when the old king, Athanaric, who had originally brought his followers to the Carpathians, finally made his way across the Danube. Theodosius, despite being so sick that his courtiers anticipated his death, went out to meet him along the road to Constantinople. He and many of his followers were brought into the great city and treated with every honor. Athanaric was reportedly so awed by what he saw that he promised to make peace and support the Romans as best he could. Unfortunately, he died only two weeks later. But the state funeral that Theodosius provided—possibly already arranged for his own expected demise—so impressed the Goths that large numbers of the Tervingi agreed to go into Roman service.

By now the Goths were running out of new sources of attainable booty, and with no other strategy beyond plunder, they were looking for alternatives to constant raiding. Theodosius, likely buoyed by his agreement with Athanaric's followers, was also pondering a broader peace. In court, his adviser, Themistius, was already stating that it was better to fill Thrace with Gothic farmers than Gothic dead.[3] Consequently, Theodosius sent his *magister militum*, Saturninus, to negotiate peace terms. What exactly was agreed to is lost in the mists of time. But what is certain is that the Goths ceased their raiding and that none of the leaders—who had brought the Empire to its knees—were ever heard from again. Probably an agreement was made to settle the Goths in areas where they already were in large numbers and let them remain under the command of their own chiefs. Judging from the number of Goths that later served in Theodosius's wars, there was probably also an agreement for Goths to serve as soldiers when called upon. There had, of course, been large numbers of barbarians in Roman service for centuries. What made this arrangement different was that the Goths agreed to fight only as separate national units and under their own commanders. They were, in reality, allies of Rome—the *foederati*. Consequently Rome regained control of its Danube frontier, as demonstrated when a chief named Odotheus led a large force of recently arrived Goths across the Danube. He was handily beaten in a combined riverine and land battle by the Roman commander on the scene, Promotus. When Theodosius arrived later, he went to look at the large number of prisoners and began bribing them to join his army, with which he soon expected to march west.[4]

While Theodosius regained control of the Balkans, Gratian was mostly content to enjoy a life of imperial luxury in Milan. Only in 382 was he again convinced to go on campaign, this time against an Alemanni force that was raiding Raetia. Personally untested in war, the co-emperor did not make a great impression on the army and further angered them when he showed favoritism to a band of three hundred Alan archers whom he designated his personal bodyguard. Before the campaign could be concluded, Magnus Maximus, the *comes* in Britain, who was jealous of Theodosius's rise, arranged for his men to declare him emperor. Following the old Roman rule that engaging a usurper trumped all other concerns, Gratian ended his campaign in Raetia and marched the field army north to engage Maximus. Maximus, in turn, took most of the forces in Britain with him to the Continent, where he soon gained the loyalty of the legions along the Rhine. The Gallic legions in the interior, however, stayed loyal to Gratian. It took several days of maneuvering and skirmishing around Paris to convince them of Gratian's military ineptitude. With no desire to be led to slaughter by an incompetent, the Gallic field army switched sides. Deserted by his army, Gratian fled, but he was soon discovered and executed. Overwhelmed by problems in the Eastern Empire and uncertain of his field army's fighting capacity, as well as of the wisdom of marching west and leaving a frontier so recently pacified open to new assaults, Theodosius was forced to formally accept Maximus's rise to the purple.

Valentinian II was still in Italy, and upon Gratian's death he was technically the senior Augustus, but as he commanded no serious military forces, he was more tolerated than feared. His long-term position vis-à-vis Maximus was untenable. But at first Maximus made no attempt to cross the Alps, tacitly approving of Theodosius's assuming seniority and becoming the arbiter between the two western emperors.[5] But in 386 Maximus had had enough of the charade and crossed the Alps in force, sending Valentinian II fleeing east to Theodosius's court in Thessalonica. Unfortunately for Maximus's long-term prospects, Theodosius was well positioned for war. Sapor's death in 379 threw the Persian Empire into turmoil and civil war until Sapor III established himself on the throne. Needing time to recover from civil wars and to deal with the barbarians plaguing Persia's northern frontiers, Sapor III was willing to make peace with Rome. Thus, in 386 Theodosius made peace with the Sassanids, agreeing to surrender two-thirds of Armenia to Persian control. As noted, in 386 Theodosius's army had also destroyed a Gothic offensive across the Danube. This had reinforced the morale of the army and given a clear demonstration of the fact that the rebuilt eastern field army was now a cohesive, well-trained force. Thus, when Maximus made his move, Theodosius's eastern frontier was peaceful, the Danube was quiet, and he had an army ready to garner further victories.

Despite having made the first move by invading Italy, Maximus was caught flatfooted by the speed of Theodosius's counterattack. In the summer of 388 Theodosius sent his army forward, quickly capturing Maximus's forward bases and pushing across the Alps to fall upon Aquileia before Maximus could establish the city's defenses. Maximus was captured in Aquileia while sitting on his throne doling out money. One suspects therefore that the city fell to a coup de main.[6] Maximus was arrested and quickly executed, and Valentinian was soon returned to Rome and restored to his position as western emperor. He was, however, an emperor without real power, as Theodosius demonstrated by transferring the best units in the western field army to the east.

Before returning to the east, Theodosius sent the western field army, under the *magister militum* Flavius Arbogast, into Gaul to defeat Maximus's son and conduct a campaign against the Franks. After this Arbogast became the true power in the west, and when, after four years of insults to his authority, Valentinian tried to remove him, Arbogast tore up his dismissal notice in the presence of the impotent emperor, claiming that only Theodosius had the power to remove him. This is a strong demonstration of how the generals supposedly serving the emperors were now making the rules. Soon afterward the humiliated Valentinian was found dead, probably by his own hand. Arbogast was too senior a general to make a bid for the purple—the other generals would have seen him as a danger to their positions and prerogatives. Moreover, Theodosius would never have accepted a successful and powerful general as his co-Augustus. Thus, after several fruitless months of negotiations, Arbogast made a pliable teacher of rhetoric, Eugenius, emperor, without the approval or support of Theodosius.

Desperate for support, Eugenius turned away from Christianity, hoping to bring the still mostly pagan Roman Senate into his camp. He even restored the Altar of Victory to the Senate's chambers and threatened the powerful bishop of Milan, Ambrose, with having his palace turned into a stable and his priests forced into the army.[7] Although the ensuing struggle has been painted by generations of historians as the final stand of paganism against Christianity, it was really just another in a long line of power struggles between the regimes controlling each half of the Empire who could no longer establish sufficient common ground to coexist, never mind render each other mutual aid.

With his frontiers still quiet, Theodosius marched east with the entire eastern field army, reinforced by a large contingent of Goths fighting under their own chiefs. Their advance through Pannonia was unopposed, and, inexplicably, they also passed unmolested through the Alps. The two armies eventually met at the Frigidus River on September 5, 394.[8] The exact location of the battle is unknown; locations in the Isonzo Valley and Slovenia have been suggested. Later Christian writers state that before the battle, Arbogast and Eugenius placed statues of the old gods Jupiter and Hercules before the army, while the Christians were protected by military flags with the Chi-Rho symbol emblazoned on them—the *labarums*—which had become the Christian talisman of choice since Constantine first took it into battle. Just in case the *labarum* was not enough, Theodosius began the battle by sending his Arian Goths forward. In savage fighting, ten thousand of them were killed, including one of their kings, Bacurius. These losses mark the beginning of the breakdown of the Roman-Gothic peace, since many Goths, including their future leader, Alaric, believed that the Romans had allowed the Goths to be slaughtered in order to reduce any threat they might pose in the future. The first day's fighting was a bloody draw, probably with Arbogast having a bit better of it. To ensure a victory the next day, Arbogast sent a large force around Theodosius's flank in the dark with instructions to cut off the eastern army's escape route and fall on their rear once the fight was renewed in the morning. Unfortunately for Arbogast's cause, for a large financial consideration, that force deserted to Theodosius and was found fighting in his army the next day.

The second day's fighting was proving just as indecisive when a seasonal wind known as the bora began blowing. This wind, which easily reaches sixty or more miles an hour, was blowing directly into the faces of Arbogast's soldiers. In an instant, the advancing western field army was being pushed back by the wind on their shields, even as they were blinded by sand and dust. Moreover, their arrows and missiles were being caught in the wind and blown backward, a disaster for any late Roman army, since firepower was now just as crucial as the shock infantry in deciding a battle. In just a few minutes the western army broke and ran for their camp, with Theodosius's eastern troops hard on their heels. The camp was immediately stormed; Eugenius was taken alive and quickly executed. Arbogast had fled, but after a few days eluding patrols he took his own life. Theodosius was now the sole ruler of the entire Roman Empire.

CHAPTER 19 | Denouement

WHATEVER PLANS THEODOSIUS had for the Empire will forever be unknown; he died in Milan on January 17, 395, only a few months after the Battle of the Frigidus. He left behind two young sons. One, Honorius, ruled in the west, where he was dominated by his *magister peditum*, Flavius Stilicho. In the east, his other son, Arcadius, was almost of an age to rule on his own, but he too was dictated to by one of his generals, Rufinus, the praetorian prefect. Rufinus, however, was murdered within the year, and power devolved to one of Theodosius's courtiers, the eunuch Eutropius. Between both sides was a large force of disgruntled Visigoths—a tribal amalgamation of the Tervingi and Greuthungi that took place at some point after the Battle of Adrianople—under their new leader, Alaric.

Stilicho, who was with the emperor when he died, claimed that on his deathbed Theodosius had asked him to act as guardian over both his sons. But this claim could not be enforced in the east unless Stilicho was ready to employ military force. First, though, he needed to deal with the more immediate problem of the Visigoths, who were still expecting substantial rewards for their role in winning the Battle of the Frigidus, particularly for their young leader, Alaric, who anticipated promotion to *magister militum*.[1] When none of these rewards was forthcoming, Alaric, taking advantage of the fact that the eastern field army was still in Italy, marched on Constantinople. Rufinus at first tried to personally negotiate with Alaric, but this just led to accusations that he was being self-serving. Because most of the eastern army, or at least its elite units, were still in the west, Rufinus had no stick in the event his offer of carrots failed. So, unless Stilicho marched east with the field army, the Visigoths could do as they pleased.

This Stilicho was ready to do, for a victory over the Visigoths would secure his position in the west and considerably strengthen it in the east. According to the court poet and panegyrist Claudian, Stilicho had Alaric's Visigothic army trapped in an unenviable position. But before he could finish the barbarian force off, a letter from Arcadius ordered him to return the troops from the eastern army to Constantinople and withdraw the rest of the western army from the eastern provinces. Stilicho, without a murmur of complaint, accepted Arcadius's demands and brought his army back to Italy.[2] If Claudian's narrative is true, then Stilicho's action is one of the greatest strategic errors in Rome's long history. First we must acknowledge that Claudian may have been stretching the truth. He was paid to praise Stilicho, and his work is littered with over-the-top verses.

Thus, there is a good possibility that Stilicho's war against the Visigoths had bogged down, and Arcadius's letter provided just the excuse he needed to extricate himself from a politically damaging stalemate. But if the Goths were trapped and on the verge of destruction, Stilicho's actions are incomprehensible. It was the toleration of the Goths on the Roman side of the Danube that was the principal and immediate cause of the fall of the Western Empire.[3] Truly, what was the point of the *limes* system if the barbarians were already deep within the Empire? Theodosius's settlement with the Goths after the disaster at Adrianople was a matter of necessity. But Alaric's raiding voided the 382 settlement at a time when Rome was strong enough to destroy the cancer within. All it took was a moment of concerted action by both halves of the Empire. Lacking that, Stilicho was still in a position to ignore Arcadius's order and hold the combined field army together until Gothic power was broken. His failure to do so is an inexcusable error and can be considered the foundational strategic error that doomed the Empire.

When Rufinus went out from Constantinople to greet the returning eastern troops, the soldiers hacked him to death; he had obviously overestimated his popularity with the rank and file. But his death did nothing to enhance Stilicho's power in the east, for another courtier, Eutropius, took control of the weak Arcadius. Stilicho moved west with his army and is next heard from inspecting the Danube frontier. In the meantime Alaric marched south, sacking towns and cities all along his route of march deep into the Peloponnese. With a rebuilt western army, one thoroughly dependent on barbarian recruits, Stilicho crossed the Adriatic and, supposedly, once again trapped Alaric's army, only to allow him a free passage to Epirus with all of his plunder. This time Arcadius declared Stilicho a public enemy, once again forcing Stilicho's departure from the Balkans. Arcadius then appointed Alaric to the rank of *magister militum per Illyricum*, making him the highest-ranking

Roman official in the Balkans. Alaric now had access to all of the region's cities, including their arms factories and arsenals. For the next several years he remained quiet as he rebuilt his forces and armed them at Rome's expense, with Roman equipment.

No sooner had Stilicho returned to the west when North Africa rose up in a revolt led by Count Gildo and supported by the eastern emperor and Eutropius. Because North Africa supplied most of Rome's wheat, this was a mortal threat to the western regime, and Stilicho reacted accordingly. After securing a short-term supply of wheat from Sicily and Sardinia, he dispatched an elite force built from the handpicked best of the field army's elite regiments. Command of this force was given to Gildo's brother, Mascezel, who hated Gildo for executing his wife and children a few years earlier. There was no fighting because Gildo's army turned on him and killed him. Still, the threat to Rome's richest provinces and its grain supply should have awoken Rome to Africa's crucial strategic importance. Unfortunately, the lesson appears not to have sunk in.

In the east a Hunnic raid coming out of the Caucasus and into Armenia was thrown back by a revitalized eastern army, which pursued the Huns across much of Armenia, inflicting enough damage that the theater remained free of barbarian incursions until 425. Eutropius himself had taken the field, and after his success he thought he was in a strong enough position to have himself made consul in 399. This was a step too far for any eunuch to contemplate, and the general revulsion of the population opened a window for Eutropius's enemies to attack. After much political turmoil and a few executions, Arcadius's wife, Eudoxia, and her allies dominated the court and the emperor until her death four years later.

In the summer of 401 Alaric moved north and entered Italy. His timing could not have been better: Stilicho and the western field army were north of the Alps fighting off an invasion of Alans, Suebi, and Vandals. Aquileia, the great fortress city of northern Italy, quickly fell, and soon the Visigoths, who appear to have been trying to march west into Gaul, were at the gates of Milan—the emperor Honorius's court. Stilicho, counting on Milan to hold out much longer than Aquileia, tarried to finish his fight in Raetia before heading south. At his back was the veteran field army, reinforced by troops stripped from Britain and the Rhine frontier. The two armies met at Pollentia on Easter Sunday 402, where, after a hard struggle, the Romans won a significant if not decisive victory. Stilicho once again offered terms allowing the Visigoths to march east back to Illyricum. When Alaric instead turned his army north towards the alpine passes, Stilicho, who was likely trailing the Visigothic force, inflicted two more defeats on them at Hasta and Verona, forcing the barbarians eastward.

The troops that were stripped from the frontiers never returned. This, along with the movement of the imperial court from Milan to Ravenna, signaled that the Empire was now prioritizing the immediate defense of Italy rather than the frontiers. This strategic shift is just one of the consequences of having to worry about a large barbarian force permanently settled within the Empire, but likely the most significant. The result of this change of Rome's strategic outlook was predictable: in 405 a large force of Ostrogoths and some allied tribes led by Radagaisus smashed across the denuded frontier into Pannonia and then across the Alps into northern Italy. This force of probably 100,000 persons and over 20,000 warriors was too large for Stilicho's field army to take on with any confidence of success.[4] It was therefore allowed to move and plunder northern Italy until the lack of logistical support began to bite. Unable to find enough food for all, the barbarian army soon broke apart, much of it leaving Italy with its collected plunder. The forces that were left, which remained significant, moved to besiege Florence.

With thirty regiments of the field army reinforced by Alans and Huns, Stilicho marched to relieve the city. His arrival caught the barbarians, who had had an easy six months of it, by surprise. The Ostrogoths were easily defeated and pushed into the heights of Fiesole, where they were blockaded. Cold and starvation soon had their effect, and Radagaisus's army was cut to ribbons trying to make its escape. Radagaisus himself was captured and executed, but approximately twelve thousand of his warriors were integrated into the Roman army, many of them relocated with their wives and families. After this victory Stilicho was at the height of his power. Unfortunately for Rome, his ascendancy lasted but a brief time.

While he was still the man of the hour Stilicho decided it was time to take on the Eastern Empire again, this time by demanding that most of Illyricum be attached to the domains of the Western Empire. To accomplish this he made a deal with Alaric, who, in return for the title *comes et magister militum per Illyricum*, a cash bounty, and the promise of Roman troops was to gather his force in Epirus and be ready to attack the east. Stilicho's intent was probably some combination of securing the Empire's best recruiting grounds for the west and ending the Visigothic threat by keeping them busy fending off the Eastern Empire's inevitable counterattack. Whatever his reasons, it was another tremendous strategic blunder. Even if everything had worked out and Illyricum had been secured for the west, the most enduring impact would have been a likely renewal of civil war between the two halves of the Empire. What was needed was reconciliation, or at least watchful coexistence, while the west turned its full attention back to securing the northern frontiers and recovering from the damage of multiple invasions. Neither happened, and once again the consequences were not long in coming.

Two simultaneous crises struck the Empire in 406. First, Britain, forgotten by the imperial center and under continuous attack, revolted. The island's remaining soldiers declared three persons emperor in rapid succession. Ultimately Constantine won out, and in 407 he led his limited forces across the Channel into Gaul. The Roman forces, still garrisoning the province, immediately declared for him, as did most of Spain. But before he could advance across the Alps to meet the Roman field army in Italy the Rhine frontier collapsed.

This collapse, the second great disaster of that year, struck on the last day of 406 when an amalgamation of barbarian tribes—Vandals, Alans, and Suebi—struck across the frozen Rhine near Mainz. A federated force of Franks tried to stop the advance, but they were quickly defeated and pushed aside. The remainder of the defenses, such as they were, were rapidly overrun, and the invaders advanced inland. This force cut a wide swath of destruction across Gaul from the Rhine to the foothills of the Pyrenees. A force of Burgundians and Alemanni took advantage of the collapsing frontier and also burst across the upper Rhine, capturing and sacking a number of cities before settling down along the Roman side of the frontier. Constantine's army appears to have done little to meet either threat as it advanced on the Alps to engage Honorius's field army.

As had been almost universally true for the entire span of the Empire's existence, the imperial court prioritized the usurper over all other threats. Honorius therefore sent Sarus, a Gothic general in imperial service, to meet and defeat Constantine before he could reach the alpine passes. Sarus did manage to defeat the usurper's vanguard but was then in turn defeated when Constantine's main force came up. Sarus retreated into Italy, but Constantine did not follow. Instead, he fortified the passes, and by May 408 was ruling much of Britain, Spain, and Gaul from his new capital at Arles.

In the meantime Alaric, tired of waiting for his payment and for the promised Roman reinforcements to show up, marched north. Once he reached the Italian border, he demanded payment for his time in Epirus. At first the proud Roman Senate refused to pay, and Honorius agreed with them. But Stilicho, understanding that with two crises to deal with already Rome did not need to add a third, pressured the Senate and court to pay up. They finally agreed to give Alaric four thousand pounds of gold, but the cost to Stilicho's prestige was huge. When added to his apparent inability to crush the usurper and the loss of much of northern and western Gaul to barbarian invaders, Stilicho, after over twenty years at the top, was suddenly vulnerable. When Arcadius died in 408, Stilicho made a final, fatal error. Honorius had wished to go to Constantinople to secure the rights of his nephew, the infant Theodosius II. Stilicho talked him out of the long and dangerous trip and offered to go in his place. Rumors were soon abroad that Stilicho was planning to place his own son on the throne, planting seeds of doubt in Honorius as to the loyalty of his over-mighty field marshal.

Stilicho's power was broken when a visit by Honorius to the field army occasioned an eruption of violence against Stilicho's supporters. Stilicho surrendered when told his life would be spared. But soon after his capture that judgment was reversed, and Honorius ordered his execution. Zosimus tells us that his followers were ready to resist, but "Stilicho deterred them from the attempt by all imaginable menaces, and calmly submitted his neck to the sword."[5] Most of Stilicho's strongest supporters were soon rounded up, tortured, and led to the executioner. But Honorius had made one great mistake during the purge: he allowed his soldiers to attack the families of the Goths in Roman service, including those twelve thousand Gothic soldiers who had only recently been integrated into the Roman army from the remains of Radagaisus's defeated Ostrogoths. Writes Zosimus:

> But as if all these circumstances were not sufficient to satisfy the evil genius that held mankind in bonds of wickedness, and confounded all things through the neglect of sacred observances, the former disasters were heightened by an additional one, which thus happened. The soldiers who were in the city, on hearing of the death of Stilicho, fell upon all the women and children in the city, who belonged to the barbarians. Having, as by a preconcerted signal, destroyed every individual of them, they plundered them of all they possessed.[6]

The incensed Goths—Zosimus tells us they were thirty thousand in number—deserted the Roman army and joined Alaric in the hopes that he would wage war on Rome. They were not disappointed, for with Stilicho dead, Honorius reneged on the promised four thousand pounds of gold. At first Alaric offered to take a lesser sum and to retreat into Pannonia. His offer was not accepted, so he took the only course open to him: he summoned his brother-in-law, the Ostrogoth Ataulf, and marched on Rome. There was no Roman army worthy of the name in Italy, so by early fall the Gothic army settled in for an extended blockade of the eternal city. With no relieving army in sight, the starving population soon gave in. Alaric agreed to lift the blockade in return for five thousand pounds of gold, thirty thousand pounds of silver, four thousand silk robes, three thousand scarlet fleeces, and three thousand pounds of pepper.[7] By December, a hugely enriched Gothic army had moved its encampments to Etruria.

In 409 a new government in Rome—under Jovius, the newly appointed praetorian prefect of Italy—began a new round of negotiations. At first Alaric demanded an annual payment of gold and grain, as well as lands in Ventia, Noricum, and Dalmatia for use as permanent Gothic settlements. Honorius rejected these demands, prompting Alaric to rouse his army for a return to Rome. Before doing so, he moderated his demands, asking only for lands in Noricum and as much grain as the emperor thought reasonable. These demands were also rejected, and Alaric began the second siege of Rome. After breaking off talks with Ravenna, Alaric began negotiating with the Roman Senate. His request was simple: depose Honorius and elect a new emperor. The senators refused at first, but empty stomachs soon forced them to accept reality. Alaric selected the elderly Priscus Attalus as emperor and moved his army away from Rome. To survive, Attalus had to control Africa's grain and tax payments, but the governor, Heraclian, remained loyal to Honorius. A small Roman force was sent to Africa, and Alaric, his pet emperor Attalus, and the Visigothic army marched on Ravenna. Honorius at first sent Jovius out to negotiate, but when Jovius changed sides the emperor was on the verge of fleeing to Constantinople. But he changed his mind when four thousand elite eastern soldiers arrived to reinforce Ravenna's garrison. This force restored morale in the city, but the paucity of the force indicates how reluctant the east remained to aid its western counterpart.

When word came that Heraclian had destroyed the force Attalus had sent to Africa, it sparked new hope among the court in Ravenna as all of Alaric's plans fell apart. Alaric had gained nothing all year. Honorius had successfully played for time, hoping that the Visigothic army would start to break up and offer opportunities to be defeated in detail, as what happened to Radagaisus's barbarian army. After deposing Attalus, who was no longer of any use to him, Alaric agreed to a new round of talks. These had just begun when Sarus, whose army was supposedly watching for Constantine's approach from Gaul, suddenly attacked a band of Goths commanded by Ataulf.

Alaric saw treachery and marched back for a third siege of Rome. His army was before the walls only a short time when, on August 24, 410, someone inside Rome's walls threw open the Salarian Gate. The Visigothic army marched in unopposed. For the first time in over eight hundred years an enemy army trod the streets of Rome. For three days the Visigoths burnt, raped, and pillaged before heading south with their loot. Alaric intended to take either

Sicily or Africa, but when his fleet was destroyed in a storm, the Goths again trudged north. Along the way, Alaric died and was replaced by Ataulf.

Word of Rome's sack spread, shaking the Empire. As Jerome, a father of the Christian church, wrote, "In one city the whole world perished." The historian Procopius presents an unusual report about Honorius's reaction to the news when he mistakenly thought he was hearing a report that his favorite chicken, named Rome, had died:

> At that time they say that the Emperor Honorius in Ravenna received the message from one of the eunuchs, evidently a keeper of the poultry, that Rome had perished. And he cried out and said, "And yet it has just eaten from my hands!" For he had a very large cock, Roma by name; and the eunuch comprehending his words said that it was the city of Rome which had perished at the hands of Alaric, and the emperor with a sigh of relief answered quickly, "But I, my good fellow, thought that my fowl Roma had perished." So great, they say, was the folly with which this emperor was possessed.[8]

But what was the strategic impact of Rome's fall? Honorius still ruled in Ravenna, and Constantinople was not touched. Even the western field army, such as it was, remained in the field, but near the alpine passes, safely out of harm's way. Alaric and his army had the enjoyment of sacking a city—the mythical core of the Empire—that had been thwarting Gothic ambitions, but those ambitions were no closer to being realized than ever. The Goths were still roaming Italy without a settled homeland of their own and running out of places capable of providing enough food. The true impact of Rome's fall was to announce to the world that the Rome of the fifth century was not the Rome of legend. It could be vanquished.

At Ravenna, a new power behind the throne emerged from the ensuing political chaos: Flavius Constantius, of whom little is known before his emergence as a power player in 410. After bringing down the previous administration surrounding Honorius, he was promoted to *magister utriusque militae*, a position that gave him command of all of the forces left to the Empire. For the next decade he ruled the remains of the Western Empire with all of the power and energy of Stilicho but with infinitely more strategic wisdom. Ignoring the wandering Goths, he focused his attention on Constantine. From a long-term strategic viewpoint, this is one of the few times that focusing on the usurper made sense. Rome had already been sacked, and the Goths were now aimless and growing increasingly dispirited. They could do little more damage in Italy. On the other hand, removing Constantine would return a good portion of the Gallic tax revenues to Honorius and open up other prospects in Spain and beyond.

While Honorius and his court were focused on the threat Alaric posed, Constantine had not been idle. After defeating Sarus's forces and sending them reeling back into Italy, Constantine sent his son, Constans, to Spain. There Constans rapidly defeated the Roman forces commanded by several of Honorius's cousins. He then returned to Constantine in Arles, leaving his father's *magister militum* Gerontius in Spain. As he was returning, Constans left the passes over the Pyrenees unguarded, allowing the Suebi, Alans, and Vandals to move into Spain. This was another massive strategic blunder, as these tribes soon removed Spain and its resources from imperial control forever, except for a few short years. Moreover, the jump from southern Spain to North Africa was an easy one, and it was only a matter of time before one or another of these tribes made the leap.

Constans had only been in Arles a short time before Constantine ordered him back to Spain. In the meantime, Constantine, whom Honorius had elevated to co-emperor in 409, entered Italy in 410. Ostensibly, he was there to help Honorius at the behest of Roman officials looking to replace Honorius. But almost immediately he sensed treachery and returned to Gaul. Upon his return he learned that back in Spain Gerontius had rebelled against him, made his own son, Maximus, emperor, and defeated and then killed Constans. In 411 Gerontius marched on Arles at the same moment Constantius marched out of Italy with the imperial field army. There was no battle: Gerontius's army deserted to Constantius as soon as the legitimate forces of the emperor Honorius approached. Gerontius was killed or committed suicide in Spain, while his son fled to the protection of the barbarians. Constantius then placed Constantine under siege in Arles and waited for starvation to take its toll. When a small relieving army was destroyed, Constantine surrendered, but not before he became a priest. Unfortunately for him, taking holy orders did not save him from the executioner or from having his head displayed on a pike in Ravenna.

Constantius returned to Italy and saw Ataulf and his Visigothic army march north toward the alpine passes. By 412 the Goths were in Gaul, where they joined forces with a new usurper, Jovinus, who appears to have made his headquarters in Mainz. Jovinus not only had the support of much of Gaul's Gallo-Roman nobility but also was allied with the tribal confederations of the Alemanni, Alans, and Burgundians. This is another clear demonstration of how Rome's focus on the security of Italy and its incapacity to defend the provinces was altering centuries of political arrangements. Plainly many of the Gallo-Roman nobles must have come to accommodations with the barbarian invaders, to the extent that they were resisting the reimposition of imperial authority. We are now witnessing the barbarian tribes taking an active political role in the fate of the Empire and their willingness to work with the resident Roman elites to accomplish their own political goals.[9] Still, such a large group of Romans joined with a barbarian coalition was always going to be unwieldy and difficult to manage. Cracks soon appeared, particularly after Jovinus declared his brother, Sebastianus, emperor, over Ataulf's objections. In response, Ataulf pulled the Goths out of the alliance, depriving Jovinus of his largest and most seasoned band of warriors Without the Goths, Jovinus was doomed, and his surrender was soon forthcoming. His head too was sent south to decorate the streets of Ravenna, and his Gallo-Roman supporters were hunted down for quick trials and slow executions.

In return for their support, the Visigoths were promised food, which was never delivered, as Heraclian, still commanding in North Africa, took his turn to revolt, which cut off Rome's grain shipments. The revolt was soon crushed, but the damage was done. The Gauls, feeling betrayed, moved into Narbonne, where they fought Constantius's forces near Marseille in 413 but failed to capture the port city. Ataulf now decided to play his two trump cards. During the sack of Rome, the Goths had taken two important persons. One was Attalus, the man Alaric had made an emperor and then deposed. He was once again raised to the purple in hopes of drawing support away from Honorius. The other was Honorius's sister, Placidia, whom Ataulf now married, without any objections from her. Ataulf was now playing a very different game, trying to bind the Visigoths and the Romans under a single ruler. All he needed was a son, whom Placida soon provided. The baby, Theodosius, was a direct threat to the future of the Theodosian dynasty, as well as Constantius's own imperial ambitions, since he too wanted Placidia's hand.

Unfortunately for Ataulf, the Goths still had one great strategic weakness: they could not stay in one place long before exhausting the food supply. Consequently, Constantius opted not to engage the Goths in a dangerous battle but instead blockaded them by land and sea until the desperate Goths marched into Spain and occupied the region around Barcelona. Attalus, the man who was twice made emperor by the Goths, was left behind to the untender mercies of Honorius. Placidia and her son went to Spain, where the infant died. Constantius followed close behind, keeping up the pressure, until the greater part of the Goths turned on their leader, realizing that Ataulf's vainglory was keeping them from a permanent settlement with Rome. In a series of coups, Ataulf was killed, as was his successor, until power fell to Wallia, who promptly handed over Placidia in return for grain. The Goths were also required to join in a military alliance to retake Spain.

For half a decade the tribes that had smashed across the Rhine in 406 had been settled in Spain, where they laid claim to the revenues that would have gone to the imperial treasury. That was about to change, as a Romano-Gothic army, which had been fighting each other for nearly a decade, was turned loose on the Vandals, Alans, and Suebi. Hydatius outlines the results of the three-year conflict in his *Chronicle*:

> All of the Siling Vandals in Baetica were wiped out by King Wallia. The Alans, who were ruling over the Vandals and Sueves [Suebi], suffered such heavy losses at the hands of the Goths that, after the death of their king, Addax, the few survivors, with no thought for their own kingdom, placed themselves under the protection of Gunderic, the king of the [Hasding] Vandals, who had settled in Gallaecia.[10]

With the bulk of Spain retaken and the remaining barbarians in the Spanish provinces reeling, Constantius became concerned at how rapidly the Goths were destroying the various barbarian tribes and occupying Spain for themselves. He therefore recalled the Gothic armies and agreed to resettle their entire population in Aquitaine, where they would have their own land and be able to sustain themselves with the region's plentiful supply of food.

By any measure, Constantius's achievement was stunning. How had he done it? First, although the west's territorial losses had been great, North Africa, with its abundant grain and immense tax revenues had, except for one brief spell, remained loyal to Honorius. As in the worst days of the Crisis of the Third Century, Rome continued to hold the most vital revenue-producing portion of the Western Empire—Rome's "tax spine." Revenues from these untouched provinces paid for the fleet and the army, while their grain kept Italy fed, with enough left over to use as a diplomatic tool. Constantius employed his small army to good effect, first to harry the Goths out of Italy and then by combining it with the fleet in a combined operation to defeat first Constantine, then the great coalition of Jovinus, and finally the Goths. Constantius fought when he had to but preferred to use maneuver and the blockading power of the fleet to win victories while conserving his precious forces. Finally, he spared his army major losses by engaging a recent foe, the Visigoths, to attack and retake much of Spain in the name of Rome.

Despite Constantius's successes, the Western Empire remained fragile. Britain and its revenues were lost forever. Although those areas of Gaul that were controlled by the usurper Constantine were now sending their tax revenues to the imperial treasury, those from much of Gaul were also lost forever. After all, it is difficult to believe that the Goths paid any taxes on their Aquitaine lands, nor did the Alemanni and Burgundians who dominated the lands along both sides of the upper Rhine, while the Franks were making deep inroads in the north. Moreover, many of the provinces that returned to the imperial orbit, including Spain, had suffered so much damage that the imperial treasury had to settle for a mere fifth of the revenues paid before the invasions of 406. Honorius also had to agree to reduce Italy's tax burden by four-fifths for an unspecified period.

Peter Heather's close study of the *Notitia Dignitatum* reveals how much damage the Western military had suffered since 395. In that year there had been 157 regiments in the field army, a total that rose to 181 in 420. Perhaps as many as ninety-seven of these regiments had been raised after 395, leaving only eighty-four that survived the entire twenty-five-year span. That meant that close to half of the entire western army had been lost, with the Roman army of the Rhine suffering the most, having lost over 60 percent of its original regiments. But these numbers do not tell the full story. Even the regiments that had survived must have taken frightful losses; the only difference was that they were able to recruit replacements before they reached the point where it would be more economical to disband them and start over. What can be surmised with some certainty is that the Roman army was much more brittle than its numbers and recent successes indicated. This is demonstrated by Constantius's reluctance to risk battle unless necessary.

Finally, at several points in this work references have been made about the forces that were fragmenting the Empire even as the whole remained under imperial authority. The immediate impact of this fragmentation was felt in the reduction in long-distance trade within the Empire as regions, provinces, and communities became increasingly autarchic. However, the invasion of 406 and its aftermath demonstrated the real strategic danger of economic fragmentation, for the local elites soon made common cause with the invading barbarians. At the start of the Crisis of the Third Century, the imperial center was responsible for provincial security, and it still had a vital role in every province's economic well-being. Moreover, the center provided provincial political leadership in the form of constantly rotating governors and their staffs. By the fourth century, not only was the central government no longer crucial to economic success, but its increasingly heavy tax demands were harming the economy. Moreover, Diocletian's and Constantine's administrative reforms had established a core of long-serving professional administrators in each region who were capable of independent governance without guidance or control from the center. By 406 all that Rome was providing to the provinces was security, and when the Rhine invasions made it clear that Rome's protection was no longer assured, local elites, unable to move their land-tied wealth, were forced to make accommodations with whatever military power was present. For the moment, Constantius's rapid reassertion of central authority and the presence of a rejuvenated if still brittle field army had reversed the process. Still, the willingness of the locals to break away from Rome had been revealed, and the impulse to do so again, if similar conditions prevailed, remained.

Among Constantius's rewards for having saved the Empire was his eventual elevation to the rank of Augustus; also, and more crucially for a man with dynastic ambitions, he was given the hand of Placidia. It was not a happy match, but in 419 the marriage produced an heir, Valentinian, who joined his sister, Honoria, born a year prior. When the eastern emperor refused to recognize the infant's titles and therefore his eventual right to rule, Constantius began readying the field army for another round of civil war. His death in September 421 ended preparations for war, but it also set off a new round of intermural fighting to fill the power void at the center of the western court. Placidia was on the losing side of the ensuing drama: she and the infant Valentinian were forced to seek refuge in Constantinople.

When Honorius died, in 423, events proceeded at a furious pace. The eastern emperor, Theodosius, was now the sole emperor of the Roman Empire, and his delay in naming a western emperor made it clear he intended to continue in that role. But delay also created opportunities for the western court to install their own candidate. Castinus, an inept general but a devious politician, accepted the support of the rising Aetius to place a civilian official, Joannes, on the throne. The new emperor's only apparent talent was his ability to follow Castinus's orders. Theodosius now belatedly recognized Constantius's elevation to Augustus, and Placida's to Augusta, making her son, Valentinian III, the rightful heir. He then ordered his general, Ardaburius, and his son, Aspar, to lead the eastern field army into Italy. Castinus and Joannes could not count on the field army's loyalty against Placida and the rightful heir, so they sent Aetius to the Huns to beg for help.

Before any help could arrive, Ardaburius was captured, but Joannes failed to order his immediate execution. Instead, he was permitted to move about within Ravenna, where he immediately started sowing dissension throughout the court. It was an easy job, for another supporter of Placidia, Boniface, had installed himself in Africa and cut off Italy's grain supply. As always, famine quickly concentrated the minds of court officials as to where their true interest lay. The gates of Ravenna were thrown open, and Aspar walked in and captured John, who was tortured and executed. Castinus was given easier treatment and merely sent into exile. That left only one powerful supporter of John to deal with—Aetius. He, however, required careful handling, for he had reappeared in Italy with a reported sixty thousand Hunnic warriors at his back.

Aetius, as a young man, had been held hostage by the Huns for several years. He seems to have gotten to know many of their key leaders and was able to summon large forces of Huns to do his bidding for unnamed rewards. Aetius was thus the Empire's most powerful individual. Joannes was dead, so it was in everyone's best interest to reach an accommodation. The Huns were bought off for an unspecified amount of gold, and Aetius was made the *comes et magister militum per Gallias* in Gaul, with a mandate to push back the Visigoths, who had tried to profit from the turmoil at the imperial center by seizing Arles.

A new strategic stage was now being set. Placidia was regent, and from that position she would match wits and balance the respective power of the West's three most powerful generals—Felix, Aetius, and Boniface. Felix, *magister militum praesentalis*, commanded the western field army in Italy, which for the most part had sat out the recent turmoil. In Gaul Aetius quickly took hold of the Gallic field army, while Boniface, always the most loyal of Placidia's supporters, continued to hold sway in Africa. But other players in the unfolding drama were waiting in the wings. They included the Vandal leader Geiseric, who possessed one of the best military minds produced by the barbarians. Geiseric's Vandals controlled southern Spain and were poised to jump into Africa. Franks and Saxons were also restive all along the lower Rhine, as were the Alemanni and Burgundians along the central and lower Rhine. And, most terrible of all, the Huns had finally moved into Europe to occupy the Great Hungarian Plain in force. All they lacked was a leader to hold the various Hunnic factions together long enough to lead their powerful masses deep into the Empire. Attila would be that leader.

Felix moved first, accusing Boniface of disloyalty to Valentinian and ordering his return to Italy. Obedience was tantamount to suicide, so Boniface wisely refused the summons. Felix then dispatched a portion of the field army to Africa, but it was easily defeated. At this point Aetius decided to take a role in the dispute. He had had already built a military reputation by rapidly defeating Theodoric's Goths at Arles and driving them back into Aquitania. He also had some success against the Franks in 428, defeating their king, Chlodio, and restoring parts of the Rhine frontier to Roman control. For these victories he was promoted to a position just below Felix in rank and transferred to Italy. Both the promotion and the transfer demonstrate his growing favor with Placidia. Her support, coupled with the prestige of being viewed as a victorious general, positioned Aetius to challenge Felix. The details of these events are lost to history, but Felix was soon arrested and executed.

Now there were two. But before the inevitable struggle for ultimate power could take place, Boniface was distracted by a new threat. Taking advantage of the chaos caused by Boniface's having to employ his limited forces to defeat Felix's invasion, Gaiseric led as many as eighty thousand Vandals— probably a third or more of them fighting men—into North Africa. In 430 the Vandals moved into Numidia and defeated Boniface, who retreated into Hippo. In that city an aging Augustine had just published, in 426, *The City of God*, which was to have a profound impact on Christian thinking for the next fifteen hundred years. The siege went on for over a year before Gaiseric was forced to lift it to confront a relieving eastern army commanded by Aspar. In mid-432 Gaiseric smashed the combined forces of Boniface and Aspar and took Hippo unopposed.

Boniface and much of his remaining force were recalled to Italy by Placidia, who had no interest in being ruled by Aetius. This was part one of Rome's greatest strategic error; it allowed the Vandals to secure their beachhead in Africa. Although the Vandals were busy securing Numidia for the next couple of years, they were now established beside the most vital provinces of the Empire. The correct strategic action, and one that was recognized at the time, was to rally all available forces to destroy the Vandals or at least evict them from Africa. Instead, the Roman leadership in the West opted for another round of civil war.

After his victory over Felix, Aetius's power at court dwindled, and Placidia decided to send him north, where he once again had some military successes in Raetia and Noricum and may even have reestablished Roman control along the upper Danube. When news reached him of Boniface's return to Italy and his promotion to *magister militum praesentalis*, Aetius abandoned the frontiers and marched into Italy. In 432 he and Boniface met near Rimini, where Aetius's army was defeated, but Boniface was mortally wounded, supposedly in direct combat with Aetius. The post of *magister militum praesentalis* now went to Boniface's son-in-law Sebastianus, whose first order of business was to try and have Aetius assassinated.

Aetius fled to the Huns and soon returned to Italy with a Hunnic force large enough to encourage Sebastianus to flee to Constantinople in precipitate haste. Aetius had now defeated all of his rivals, leaving Placidia little choice but to make him *magister militum praesentalis*. Valentinian remained emperor, but Aetius now controlled the Western Empire.

Aetius's first important strategic act was to agree with Constantinople to maintain Aspar's forces in North Africa for a prolonged period. After their defeat outside of Hippo in 431, Aspar's army was not strong enough to risk another set-piece battle, but it was able to delay and harass a renewed Vandal advance, which eventually brought Gaiseric to the negotiating table. A treaty was signed in February 435 in which the Vandals were handed most of Mauretania and parts of Numidia. But the treaty allowed Aetius and Aspar to protect the most vital two provinces in North Africa, Proconsularis and Byzacena.

This treaty for a time secured Aetius's southern flank, allowing him to turn his full attention to the north. His priority was securing the Rhine frontier, which he accomplished with Hunnic support. There was, however, a huge strategic cost to involving the Huns in another Roman war. Instead of the traditional payment of gold and silver for their services, the Huns wanted land, specifically in Pannonia. The sources are silent on the reasons for the change in Hunnic demands. They are equally silent on why Aetius agreed to them. The Huns were already acknowledged as the most dangerous barbarian group Rome had ever faced, so it was strategic folly to allow them uncontested control of territory on the south side of the Danube barrier. Everything Aetius and other Roman emperors and generals had ever done to defend the Danubian *limes* and secure the direct avenues of approach into Italy and Gaul evaporated the instant Aetius handed Pannonia to the Huns. It is not possible that Aetius was unaware of the strategic problems he was storing up, for memories of the results of allowing Alaric's Goths to control of much the same area remained fresh. Finally, any hope of strategic military coordination between the two halves of the Empire was now ruined, as a Hunnic army was now athwart the primary land communications route.

Aetius enjoyed further success, this time against the Burgundians on the central Rhine. Once again Hunnic support was deemed essential when in 437 a combined Roman-Hunnic force launched a devastating assault that broke the back of the Burgundians for a generation. As many as twenty thousand Burgundians were killed, and the survivors were settled near Lake Geneva as Roman *foederati*. About this same time, while Aetius was trying to secure the Gallic interior against Bagaudae rebels, the Goths rose again. This time they marched south and east and laid siege to Narbonne. Mustering a force large enough to counter this massive Gothic invasion proved beyond Rome's means, and the Huns were called upon once again. Even with Hunnic support, the war against the Goths dragged on for three years before they were pushed back into Aquitaine, having suffered ruinous losses, whereupon they reaffirmed the treaty of 418.

Aetius's achievements in this decade were prodigious. With Hunnic aid, the Franks and Alamanni were pushed back beyond the Rhine, the

Burgundians were smashed beyond recovery, and the Bagaudae rebel bands were quieted if not destroyed. Finally, after three years of grueling warfare, the Visigoths had been beaten into submission. This, in turn, opened a path to employing diplomacy backed with military threats to return much of Spain to imperial control.[11]

By all appearances the Western Empire had once again weathered the storm. The patient was still weak but no longer appeared terminal. What was needed was time to complete the recovery. It was not to be. Without warning, a new storm delivered a fatal blow to the Empire's hopes. In the fall of 439, four years after signing a peace with Aspar, the Vandals, still led by Gaiseric, burst upon the North African provinces still held by Rome. In an orgy of carnage and bloodshed, they advanced upon Carthage. They were barely resisted, and before long North Africa was lost. With it went most of the Roman navy, which was captured in North Africa's ports. In a twinkling Rome lost its richest provinces as well as naval control of at least the western Mediterranean. The Vandals broke the Mediterranean infrastructure of the west, depriving Rome of its crucial source of food, breaking the Carthage-Rome tax spine, and dooming the Western Empire. The population of the city of Rome fell precipitously after the mid-fifth century and dropped more than 80 percent in the following century. With the loss of Africa, Rome's fiscal system collapsed just when the Empire needed vast amounts of cash to purchase as many troops as it could.[12]

The failure to foresee the damage that Geiseric's seizure of Carthage would inflict upon the Empire as a whole is arguably the main strategic error of the imperial government in the fifth century.[13] The breaking of Rome's tax spine tore out the economic machinery of the Western Empire.[14] Without economic resources, not even the most brilliant strategic conception could be enacted. After five hundred years of adhering to a simple strategic formulation, Rome, in the mid-fifth century, had forgotten its cardinal tenet: defend at all costs the rich economic core of the Empire. Without North Africa the Empire was essentially doomed to a slow but inevitable death.

An argument could be made that Aetius, whose power base was in Gaul, could not afford to ignore that region's troubles in favor of securing North Africa. But that argument is hard to justify in strategic terms, for the loss of North Africa ensured that Gaul could not be held for long. The Roman provinces on the European continent remained a long way from being able to bear the tax burdens of previous decades, and until they could do so, North Africa had been paying to maintain the Empire. Moreover, North Africa was still Rome's breadbasket, and although the Vandals were convinced to keep making grain shipments for a few years, this was no longer a tax. In fact, the tax revenues had reversed. Instead of Rome taxing North Africa, the shipments of grain became a commercial transaction in which Rome had to use revenues gathered elsewhere to pay the Vandals. Moreover, these shipments were always at the mercy of the Vandals and could be cut off at any time. When Gaiseric finally decided to do so, the pain in Rome and Italy was immediate. Without a secure supply of food Rome could barely function. But Gaiseric increased the pain when he took Sardinia in the 460s and began to ravage the coast of Sicily, the major alternative grain supplier to Italy.[15] Rome could have afforded the loss of Gaul—as it had during the Crisis of the Third Century—but there was no recovery possible from the loss of North Africa.

The loss of North Africa focused the minds of Rome's leadership. A joint campaign including forces from both halves of the Empire was planned, and the armies assembled in Sicily. Owing to logistical problems, the combined force was not ready until 441. Most of the eastern troops, however, had been drawn from the Danube frontier, where they had been closely watching the Huns, who were now approaching the high-water mark of their power under two new leaders—Attila and his brother, Bleda. The two brothers had spent years forcing the surrender of most of the other tribes north of the Danube in an attempt to create the largest barbarian confederation yet assembled. The departure of much of the eastern army from the Danube had not gone unnoticed, and the brothers were quick to pounce. In 441, the Huns crossed the Danube in force, quickly capturing Viminacium and Margus while driving raiding parties deep into the Balkans.

Word of the Hunnic attack was only the final straw in an unfolding breakup of the two field armies in Sicily, who never trusted one another. The Eastern forces were soon recalled to deal with the Balkan crisis, ending any possibility of retaking Africa in the short term. Although many expeditions were later planned and some executed, it was not until nearly a century later, in 534, that Belisarius, acting for the Eastern Empire, reconquered the provinces. The failure of the planned expedition in 442 forced Rome to make a treaty with Gaiseric, in which the provinces originally given to the Vandals in 425 were returned to Rome—as the Vandals had abandoned them in favor of richer pickings—but the richest provinces taken in 429 were ceded to the Vandals. Worse, the Suebi, long contained in northwestern Spain, took advantage of Rome's fixation with North Africa to seize most of the Iberian Peninsula, further eroding the Western Empire's tax base.

If the Western Empire had been forced to deal with a huge Hunnic assault in the 440s in addition to the catastrophes in North Africa and Spain, it would certainly have collapsed a generation earlier than it did. Thankfully for the west, Attila's immediate attention was focused on the Eastern Empire, where he was set on extorting as much gold as possible from Theodosius II. The Huns had made their first direct threats on the Eastern Empire in 435, when they extorted a tribute of 350 pounds of gold and additional payments for the return of captured Roman soldiers. After the first payment, the Huns returned to the Hungarian Plain, and Theodosius lost no time massively strengthening the walls around Constantinople and building the city's first sea wall. The Huns then turned on the Sassanids until in 440 they were defeated in Armenia. Unable to make progress against Persia, their attention was returned to the Eastern Empire just as it began to strip troops off the frontiers to help invade North Africa.

The return of the eastern army, coupled with a huge recruitment drive, emboldened Theodosius to resist Attila's demands for more gold and to prepare for war. The war did not take place immediately—both sides took their time setting the conditions for victory, which for Attila meant having Bleda killed, making Attila himself sole ruler of the Hunnic Empire.[16]

Attila struck in 447, first unleashing his armies on the hapless border troops and then rapidly pushing into the Balkans. His armies easily overran the recently strengthened and reinforced fortress at Ratiaria, before advancing along the Haemus Mountains to finally meet the Thracian field army, commanded by Arnegisclus. The Roman army was probably reinforced by the army in Illyricum as well as the forces directly commanded by the emperor—the *praesental* army. This huge force indicates that the Eastern Empire was risking much on a single battle. If its army was destroyed, there would be nothing left in the Balkans capable of slowing down a renewed Hunnic advance. Strategically, this was probably worth the gamble, since much of the Balkans was already ruined and would take decades to fully recover. A decisive victory would have bought those decades. Moreover, the walls of Constantinople, recently strengthened in the wake of a powerful earthquake, remained impregnable. And no barbarian army was going to risk being wiped out by starvation and disease in what would have been a multi-year siege, assuming the Huns could acquire the necessary fleet. Having advanced out of his headquarters at Marcianople with almost every soldier available in the Balkans, Arnegisclus gave battle on the river Utus. There is no detailed record of the battle, but it was hard fought and lasted almost all day. Eventually the Romans were overwhelmed, and Arnegisclus fell in battle. The Huns swept south, brutally sacking as many as a hundred cities as they marched. The diplomat Priscus later traveled through these ruined cities and tells us: "When we arrived at Naissus we found the city deserted, as though it had been sacked; only a few sick persons lay in the churches. We halted at a short distance from the river, in an open space, for all the ground adjacent to the bank was full of the bones of men slain in war."[17] Attila's Huns only returned to the Danube after Theodosius II agreed to buy them off. The Huns were given six thousand pounds of gold immediately and promised an additional twenty-one hundred pounds every year. Furthermore, a buffer zone of a five-day march from the Danube was created, which had the practical effect of ensuring that future invaders would never again be hampered by a fortified line or have their logistics threatened by a powerful Danubian fleet. From now on the strategic defense of the east relied on the walls of Constantinople and the financial wherewithal of Anatolia, Syria, and Egypt.

In 450 Theodosius died and was replaced by Marcian, who promptly cut off the Huns' annual subsidy. This was a calculated gamble. Attila might march into the Balkans again, but he would gain little. Cities that had been so recently sacked had little to offer to anyone sacking them a second time. All Attila could accomplish in the Balkans was exhausting his horses and men without any hope of a big payday. Because there was no way to get past the walls of Constantinople, the Huns were barred from the rich Syrian provinces. Attila knew this and was probably already planning to direct his army toward the west, even before Marcian cut off his gold payments. To keep things diplomatically tidy though, he would need a pretext to invade a Western Empire to which the Huns had until recently been closely allied.

The royal family soon provide him with one. Honoria, the emperor Valentinian's sister, was with child, conceived with her unsuitable mate Eugenius, who was promptly executed. Honoria was locked away and then betrothed to a Roman senator in whom she had no interest. Finding no allies among the Roman elite, Honoria wrote to Attila proposing marriage and offering half the Western Empire as a dowry if he would ride to her rescue. Thus, in or about 450, Attila made a formal demand for Honoria's hand and threatened war. What we should make of this is hard to know. The story appears in a wide variety of sources, and the fact of Honoria's disgrace seems securely enough established. The likelihood is, however, that Attila (having probably exhausted the possibilities of immediate gains in the east) was heading west without any encouragement from the naïve Honoria.

After preparing the ground in the west with a series of diplomatic maneuvers and demands while also papering over outstanding issues with Constantinople, Attila was ready to march. He had exploited every possible opening to provoke a conflict while trying to ensure that his enemies would not form a coalition against him. For instance, in his final diplomatic flurry he wrote letters both to the emperor in Ravenna and to Theodoric I, the

Visigothic king. He told the emperor he was coming to attack the Goths, while he told the Goths he was attacking the imperial forces and asked each to help him defeat the other. Jordanes tells us that "beneath his ferocity, [Attila] was a subtle man, and fought with craft before he made war."[18]

Attila's army crossed the Rhine around Mayence, in Belgica, where they first sacked Metz and Trier in April of 451 before turning towards Orleans and placing a force of Alans, who were holding the city, under siege. So far the Roman army had not been heard from. Most likely, in the face of a threat of unimaginable strength, it was taking time to put together a coalition that could match the Huns on an open battlefield. But by summer 451 Aetius—now fighting against his previous Hunnic ally—had completed that task and was advancing rapidly on Orleans with the combined Roman armies of Italy and Gaul along with allied forces from the Alans and Burgundians, as well as a huge force of Visigoths led by Theodoric. In mid-June the Romans reached Orleans and pursued Attila's withdrawing Huns 150 miles east to Troyes. Here, on the Catalaunian Fields (Campus Mauriacus), the two armies collided in what is often referred to as the Battle of Châlons.

This is the last great battle fought by the Western Roman Empire and is included in Creasy's famous list of the world's most decisive battles. It is therefore worth quoting our best source, Jordanes, at some length.

> The armies met, as we have said, in the Catalaunian Plains. The battlefield was a plain rising by a sharp slope to a ridge, which both armies sought to gain; for advantage of position is a great help. The Huns with their forces seized the right side, the Romans, the Visigoths and their allies the left, and then began a struggle for the yet untaken crest. Now Theodoric with the Visigoths held the right wing and Aëtius with the Romans the left. They placed in the center Sangiban (who, as said before, was in command of the Alani), thus contriving with military caution to surround by a host of faithful troops the man in whose loyalty they had little confidence. For one who has difficulties placed in the way of his flight readily submits to the necessity of fighting.
>
> On the other side, however, the battle line of the Huns was arranged so that Attila and his bravest followers were stationed in the center. In arranging them thus the king had chiefly his own safety in view, since by his position in the very midst of his race he would be kept out of the way of threatening danger. The innumerable peoples of the diverse tribes, which he had subjected to his sway, formed the wings. . . .

So then the struggle began for the advantage of position we have mentioned. Attila sent his men to take the summit of the mountain, but was outstripped by Thorismud [King Theodoric's son] and Aëtius, who in their effort to gain the top of the hill reached higher ground and through this advantage of position easily routed the Huns as they came up.

At this point Jordanes digresses into a long speech by Attila as he tried to raise the spirits of his army after this initial setback, in which they lost the most dominating feature on the battlefield. Much of this speech is spent insulting the fighting capacity of the Romans, no doubt unfairly considering the damage they did to his army over the next few hours. One must assume that the Romans wasted no time rolling masses of their artillery onto the just-conquered heights, from which they could dominate the entire Hunnic line. This likely explains the demoralization Attila was attempting to overcome by his speech.

And although the situation was itself fearful, yet the presence of their king dispelled anxiety and hesitation. Hand to hand they clashed in battle, and the fight grew fierce, confused, monstrous, unrelenting—a fight whose like no ancient time has ever recorded. There such deeds were done that a brave man who missed this marvelous spectacle could not hope to see anything so wonderful all his life long. . . .

Here King Theodoric, while riding by to encourage his army, was thrown from his horse and trampled underfoot by his own men, thus ending his days at a ripe old age. But others say he was slain by the spear of Andag of the host of the Ostrogoths, who were then under the sway of Attila. This was what the soothsayers had told to Attila in prophecy, though he understood it of Aëtius. Then the Visigoths, separating from the Alani, fell upon the horde of the Huns and nearly slew Attila. But he prudently took flight and straightway shut himself and his companions within the barriers of the camp, which he had fortified with wagons. A frail defense indeed; yet there they sought refuge for their lives, whom but a little while before no walls of earth could withstand.

At dawn on the following day, when the Romans saw the fields were piled high with bodies and that the Huns did not venture forth, they thought the victory was theirs, but knew that Attila would not flee from the battle unless overwhelmed by a great disaster. Yet he did nothing cowardly, like one that is overcome, but with clash of arms sounded the trumpets and threatened an attack. He was like a lion pierced by hunting spears, who paces to and fro before the mouth of his den and dares not spring, but ceases not to terrify the neighborhood by his roaring. Even so this warlike king at bay terrified his conquerors.

Therefore the Goths and Romans assembled and considered what to do with the vanquished Attila. They determined to wear him out by a siege, because he had no supply of provisions and was hindered from approaching by a shower of arrows from the bowmen placed within the confines of the Roman camp. But it was said that the king remained supremely brave even in this extremity and had heaped up a funeral pyre of horse trappings, so that if the enemy should attack him, he was determined to cast himself into the flames, that none might have the joy of wounding him and that the lord of so many races might not fall into the hands of his foes.[19]

Besieged within his wagon lagger, Attila pondered the Huns' first great military defeat. His initial reaction, as Jordanes says, was to kill and immolate himself, but he was talked out of this course. A short stalemate ensued, but, Jordanes points out, an army as large as Attila's could not stay in one place for long before it began to starve. Soon the Hunnic force was retreating east, and Aetius was content to let them do so. The Huns continued to ravage Roman territory as they retreated, for little could be done to hinder them. Afterward the Goths returned to their base in Aquitaine to select a new king and recover from their not insubstantial losses. Aetius's great coalition quickly dissolved.

Attila's first invasion had been repulsed, but in 452 he and the Hunnic horde were back. This time the blow fell on Italy. The great fortress at Aquileia held out for a time, but after one final great attempt the walls were stormed and the city taken. The Hunnic horde pushed west across northern Italy and the Po Plain. One after another great city fell to Hunnic storms. Padua, Mantua, Vicentia, Verona, Brescia, and Bergamo were all lost, with only the former imperial capital at Milan requiring a lengthy siege. At this point Pope Leo came forth from Rome to convince Attila to turn around and to spare Rome. Soon thereafter Attila did so, and for centuries the papacy has claimed the credit for Rome's salvation from the "scourge of God." The truth is more prosaic. After a series of hard marches, long sieges, and the costly storming of numerous city walls, the Hunnic army was depleted. It was also running out of food, and our sources tell us that it was suffering greatly from disease, the great killer of all besieging armies. Taken together, the Huns had no choice but to retreat to the Hungarian Plain for a period of recuperation.

In 453, while moving through Pannonia, Attila took another wife. After a night of festivities, the man who made both the Eastern and Western Empires tremble burst a blood vessel and died in his sleep. His sons immediately engaged in a vicious struggle for power that ended in the Battle of Nedao in 454, where his eldest son, Ellac, was killed. This Hunnic civil war, coming atop the losses of two campaigns in the west, weakened the Huns' power sufficiently for their many captive nations to rise against them. The Hunnic yoke was thrown off and in a historical instant, the Hunnic Empire disintegrated into constituent parts, with Gepids, Goths, Rugi, Heruls, and Suebi all asserting their independence.[20] With the end of the Hunnic threat, Valentinian III no longer needed Aetius, whose power he had grown to resent. In September of 454 Valentinian assassinated Aetius personally, but the emperor himself was murdered in early 455 by two of Aetius's bodyguards, who resented the loss of their patron.

With Aetius went the Roman army. Only the overriding threat of Attila had brought the barbarian tribes together with the Romans in a grand coalition. With that threat gone, all of these tribes began to agitate for a greater role in running the Empire, as well as autonomy in the regions they controlled. Moreover, the imperial army had mostly dissolved after Attila departed, since there were no longer any funds to pay it. Without the North African revenues, as well as the taxes from the regions occupied by various barbarian proto-states, the imperial government could no longer fund an army capable of any serious effort. In other words, it could no longer fund a strategy. As I spelled out earlier in this work, strategy always rests on three pillars—ends, ways, and means. Rome no longer had the means, which is the foundational underpinning of everything one may wish to accomplish on a strategic scale.

Unable to check the expansion of the various barbarian proto-states, there was no choice but to invite their participation in the Empire's body politic. This process began almost immediately after Valentinian III's murder when his self-declared replacement, Petronius Maximus, sent Avitus to Theodoric II's court to convince him of the benefits of a long-term alliance with Rome. He was still en route when word came that Petronius had been killed during the Vandals' sack of Rome. It was the second sack in as many generations, and the Vandal army had marched into Rome virtually unopposed. When it was done, the Vandals returned to North Africa with unimagined riches, along with Valentinian's wife and daughter. It would not be long before Avitus was nominating his own candidate for emperor.

Taking advantage of the renewed confusion, Avitus had himself declared emperor, with the backing of the Gallo-Roman nobles, the Visigoths, and the

Burgundians. But he held no influence in Rome, where the army, commanded by Ricimer and Majorian, refused to recognize his elevation to the purple, as did the Eastern Empire. In 456 Avitus advanced into Italy but was defeated at Placentia. He soon resigned, became a bishop, and died a few weeks after the battle, presumably murdered. From this point forward there is a succession of emperors all empowered and controlled by Ricimer, who was content to remain the power behind the throne without the trappings and dangers of being emperor himself. Ricimer may have had a force powerful enough to control Italy, but he remained powerless to act beyond Italy's borders. Just as Petronius had discovered, Rome could only influence its former provinces by bringing various barbarian groups into ever-changing coalitions. Gaining barbarian participation always came at a cost, which was taken out of a radically smaller and decreasing economic and territorial base. In truth, Rome rarely gained anything from these associations. For instance, as Peter Heather points out, when Rome enlisted the Visigoths to retake Spain from the Suebi and then return it to imperial control, Theodoric II's troops operated on their own, "ransacking northern Spain, including its loyal Hispano-Romans, of all the wealth they could force their victims to produce."[21] Spain was wrecked, and there was no return of revenues to the imperial tax base. For Rome, this was all take and no give.

Majorian, after gaining the support of other generals and Leo I in Constantinople, replaced Avitus. A successful general in his own right, he was not Ricimer's puppet, and the two appear to have worked closely together over the next several years to restore the Empire's stability. Some progress was made in Gaul, but when Majorian attempted to retake North Africa, his army was given a serious drubbing. This provided Ricimer with sufficient cause to have him deposed and executed. Majorian was replaced by Libius Severus, who tried to buy Gothic support by handing them Narbonne, which caused a revolt of the Gallo-Roman nobility under Aegidius in 463. This revolt was only contained through Aegidius's assassination while he was negotiating with Geiseric to ally against Ricimer. Severus, after failing to gain the support of the Eastern Empire, met an unhappy end, probably poisoned by Ricimer.

The next western emperor, a joint pick of Leo and Ricimer, was the eastern general Anthemius. After securing the support of the Goths, Burgundians, and the Gallo-Roman nobility, he turned his attention to North Africa. A huge expedition sailed in 468, but it was greeted by Vandal fire ships and destroyed, with great loss of life. Rome's last chance of the Western Empire's retaking North Africa sank with the fleet. Victory would have removed the Vandals from an overcrowded game board and assured the emperor prestige;

most vitally, the rump Empire would have regained its richest provinces. With money and time, all things were possible. But defeat only hastened the end. By 470 what was left to the imperial center was no longer worth fighting over. Instead, the leaders of the various barbarian tribes began to fight over those parts of the old Empire that still had some value. In 470 Euric, king of the Visigoths, launched a series of assaults that by 475 gave him control of most of Gaul and northern Spain. In the northwest, the Franks also continued their steady expansion. Most interestingly, the Burgundians, under their king, Gundobad, helped Ricimer remove Anthemius, and they themselves became kingmakers after Ricimer's death.

In the end, the commander of the diminished imperial army in Italy, Orestes, proclaimed his son, Romulus, emperor. With no funds left in the treasury and no sources of new funds available, the army fell into unrest. In 476 the barbarian warlord Odoacer, who was also a subordinate officer in the imperial army, had Orestes murdered, whereupon the army declared him king—not emperor—of Italy. Odoacer then marched on Ravenna, captured the young Romulus Augustulus ("little Augustus"), and sent him to live, with a pension, in Campania. Soon thereafter an embassy from the West arrived in Constantinople, where it handed over to the eastern emperor the imperial insignia. The message was clear: the Western Empire no longer existed.

Conclusion

THE ROMAN EMPIRE in its totality lasted five hundred years, while the Eastern Empire, going it alone after the fifth century, retained much of its glory and power for centuries after the west's fall. Because the Empire lasted for so long and its demise was accompanied by such a spectacular shattering of Western civilization, explaining Rome's fall has occupied the minds of historians since Gibbon penned his famous work in the late eighteenth century. But for those seeking lessons on how to avoid a similar fate, it is more profitable to examine how Rome managed to survive for five centuries despite numerous enemies and environmental challenges. After all, Rome fell only after it was unwilling or unable to obtain the resources and sustain the strategies that had maintained the empire's power and glory for all that time.

At the core of these strategies were three elements: securing the economic foundations of the Empire, maintaining a military force second to none, and having a seemingly inexhaustible supply of soldiers. These core principles were so intertwined as to present a chicken-and-egg problem. The military was required to protect the economy, but a strong economic base was the underpinning of military power. None of these could be long sustained without a large and growing population, for warm bodies are a precondition of both military and economic power—they provide the soldiers for one and the labor for the other.

From the first Rome clearly understood the benefits of a seemingly inexhaustible manpower base. In fact, the early Republic's expansion was always geared toward enhancing its future combat power, by integrating subjugated

Italian populations into its military structure while adding their farms to Rome's agricultural base. How important a huge population base was to Roman ambitions, even its survival, was made clear when Rome engaged in the Punic Wars against what was then the greatest economic power in the Mediterranean, Carthage.[1] Even after Hannibal had inflicted several crushing defeats, including the near annihilation of two consular armies at Cannae, Rome still possessed the manpower to continue challenging Hannibal in Italy while simultaneously waging war in Spain and the Baltics. For Carthage, manpower was always in short supply, and they were constantly forced to pay exorbitant costs for Spanish and North African mercenaries.

Rome never lost its manpower advantage. For several hundred years none of its enemies could ever match its numerical superiority. Even the Persians, who probably had a roughly comparable number of troops within their Empire, could never match Roman numbers in their primary theaters of war. Any Persian force formed within the interior of the Empire would have to march for months, much of it through desiccated wasteland, just to arrive at the Roman frontiers. The Romans, however, were within short marches of the Empire's richest and most populous provinces. Moreover, reinforcements could pour in from all sides, as sea transport greatly eased the process of massing and supplying armies at any threatened point.

Rome's other major foe—the barbarians across the frontier zones—never came close to matching Roman numbers, although they could from time to time gain local superiority. But even when they could bring a formidable force onto the battlefield, they could not sustain its momentum, as they did not possess the logistical infrastructure to feed their massed soldiers for very long. Only when they penetrated and settled deep in the Empire, where they could exploit Rome's infrastructure for their own use, did the balance of power irrevocably change. Allowing the barbarians to settle in large swaths of the Empire was one of Rome's greatest strategic errors, for it deprived the Empire of men and resources while enriching its enemies.

Economic power—Rome's second strategic pillar—gave the Empire advantages its enemies could not hope to duplicate. Starting with the Augustan Age and the end of decades of civil war, the Pax Romana provided the perfect environment for the rapid and sustained growth of the economy. It was this foundational wealth that maintained Rome's military at mobilization levels that would have bankrupted any other power. Not until the modern age could any state once again afford to keep such a large military establishment on a permanent basis. A growing economic base also served to soothe and stabilize conquered populations, greatly easing their peaceful integration into the Empire.

As long as Rome sustained a flourishing economy, it could confront any challenge confident of eventual success. Wealth equaled resilience, which allowed Rome to overcome even the most severe reverses. Even at the height of the Crisis of the Third Century, Rome never lost its hold on the Empire's economic core. Although much outside this core was lost—including all of Gaul and most of the Roman east—Italy, Spain, and, most crucially, the rich provinces of western North Africa were untouched. In Africa, only Egypt was torn away from the Empire, and that for only a short time. By mustering the full financial wherewithal of its economic core, Rome was able to rebuild its armies and outlast its foes.

The destruction of Roman economic power was a consequence of several factors. The first was the continuous series of civil wars that plagued the post-Principate Empire. These wars destroyed large amounts of economic infrastructure, and this was no longer repaired or replaced in full—the next round of fighting would see it destroyed once again. Consequently, the economic infrastructure in large swaths of the Empire returned to its pre-Augustan state. Moreover, each civil war further damaged the fabric of Roman society and eroded civic trust. And as any economist will tell you, trust is the bedrock of trade. Where trust does not exist, trade stops, with huge negative economic consequences. Serial civil wars also tore at the Roman fisc as the economy strained to support multiple field armies and to rebuild forces destroyed during internecine conflicts. All of this came on top of the damage caused by invaders taking advantage of Rome's internal distractions. As both barbarian tribes and the Persians ripped away an increasing number of formerly tax-producing provinces from Rome's control, the overall level of resources available to the state correspondingly decreased.

Finally, the Roman army was fragmented and allowed to deteriorate. There is no reason to repeat the prolonged deterioration that this book has covered in detail. But it is worth noting that the impact of the collapse of Roman combat power relative to the threats it faced was catastrophic. As the European Union has discovered, soft power has severe limits when it is not backed up by the military power to intimidate or coerce, whatever a state's overall financial power. Rome built an empire on the backs of its legions and maintained it through their intimidating power, and it was the legions that held it against all challengers for centuries. When the legions were no longer up to the task or were busy killing one another, the consequences were predictable. The result, however, was likely hastened by the splitting of the Empire's economic and particularly its military power in the late fourth century. One of the secrets of the Empire's longevity was that when any one part of the Empire was threatened, it could count on the resources of the whole to help overcome the crisis. When the forces of either the eastern or western halves of the Empire curtailed or refused to support the other, the result was a series of unredeemed military disasters. It is mere speculation as to whether the Empire had the resources to withstand the hammer blows besetting it at the end. But the Western Empire certainly could have endured for decades longer and hoped for better days ahead if they could have counted on soldiers of the east to help hold the Empire's economic core.

There are great lessons here for modern strategists. If a great power neglects any one of these elements—maintaining a large and productive population, substantial economic power, and a large and effective military establishment—or even prioritizes one far above the others, it has set itself upon a path of strategic irrelevance and possible ruin. One does not have to look back in history as far as the Roman Empire to find abundant evidence for this proposition. At the start of the modern era Great Britain was at best a peripheral power. But toward the end of the seventeenth century it began to emerge as the most powerful state in Europe and was well on its way to becoming a transcontinental power. By the second decade of the eighteenth century the Royal Navy ruled the world's seas, its treasury was bankrolling the armies of every other European power, its own army was strong enough to face down Napoleon at Waterloo, and it was in possession of a globe-spanning empire.[2]

How?

First, it implemented a new system of taxation and debt management—the English Financial Revolution—that provided the state with financial wherewithal far surpassing that of any other European power.[3] The huge amounts of capital created by these financial reforms not only paid for Great Britain's unsurpassed military force but was also available for employment by private firms and investors to propel a nascent Industrial Revolution into hyperdrive. Thus, although Great Britain's population was small compared to that of its rivals, it was the most productive on the globe. In summary, Britain rose to world dominance on the back of a productive population, a powerful military establishment, and the strongest economic base in the world—the same formula that made Rome a great and unrivaled power. Only when other European powers learned and adopted the secrets of Britain's transformation did they begin to rival its global primacy. When these powers turned upon each other in two destructive and mutually exhausting world wars—reminiscent of Rome's civil wars—they opened the door to the rise of a new power on the global stage: the United States.

America, through the foresight of Alexander Hamilton, adopted almost all that was good in the British financial system. It then employed the huge amounts of excess capital provided to pay for its own industrial revolution and continental expansion. Meanwhile the nation opened itself to unprecedented levels of immigration that it undertook to educate, train, and employ. In just a single century the United States was a global economic power with a large and incredibly productive population. The first two elements of great-power status were in place to provide the foundation for the rapid rise of American military power during World War II, which has been sustained ever since.

In the past two decades America has seen the rise of China, which has clearly adopted a formula that harks back to the Roman Empire to propel its rise to great-power status. A huge and well-educated population has been suddenly made significantly more productive as a result of financial and economic reforms. In combination, these factors first propelled China to the ranks of an economic superpower, surpassing Japan and rivaling America and the European Union. Now that economic power is being employed to enlarge and modernize the Chinese military, which is already a peer competitor to that of the United States.

Fortunately, the formula for competing with China is well known, and it is one the United States has pursued for over two centuries. It remains to be seen if America has the will to sustain the policies that led to its current global position. If it does, then the twenty-first century will be another American century, which will benefit not just America but the entire world. Rome's ultimate collapse demonstrates that success is not guaranteed. Even the most powerful state can quickly come to ruin if it fails to adapt its strategies as the challenges it faces change. Rome stands as a beacon of what is possible when a state gets its strategy right, as well as a stark warning of the consequences of failing to do so.

NOTES

Introduction

1. Edward N. Luttwak, *The Grand Strategy of the Roman Empire: From the First Century A.D. to the Third* (Johns Hopkins University Press, 1976). A lightly edited edition was released in 2016.
2. Anyone who delves deeply into the works of those historians who have dedicated their professional lives to the study of ancient economies, particularly Rome's, cannot help but be impressed by how much consensus there is on the larger topic. While there remains much for the historians to argue over for another century, I am convinced that there is a broad enough consensus on major points for me to reliably include discussions of economics throughout this work.
3. There are, of course, scholars, such as A. D. Lee, Michael Whitby, Karl Strobel, Adrian Goldsworthy, Hugh Elton, and many others, who have produced masterful works on the Roman army and its war, from which I have profited enormously. My contribution in this area is in applying a wide knowledge of the entire scope of military history to the study of Roman military affairs.

Chapter 1

1. For a brilliant survey of strategic thinking through the ages, see Beatrice Hauser, *The Evolution of Strategy: Thinking War from Antiquity to the Present* (Cambridge University Press, 2010).
2. Daniel J. Hughes and Harry Bell, *On Strategy* (1871), as translated in *Moltke on the Art of War: Selected Writings* (Presidio Press, 1993), 124

3. The Marine Corps War College Strategy Primer (Marine Corps University Press, 2020). See https://www.usmcu.edu/Portals/218/MCWAR%20Strat egy%20Primer_web.pdf.

4. See https://www.jcs.mil/Portals/36/Documents/Doctrine/pubs/jp3_0ch1. pdf?ver = 2018-11-27-160457-910.

5. Aristotle, *Rhetoric*, Book 1, Part 4.

6. During this discussion, I will routinely refer back to three scholars—C. R. Whittaker, Benjamin Isaac, and Susan Mattern—who have provided the foundation of the current historical consensus on Rome's strategic planning capacity. Moreover, their work underpins much of our current understanding of the Roman Empire, particularly in the East.

7. Aristotle, *Rhetoric*, Book 1, Part 4.

8. Clausewitz, *On War*, famously defined the nature of war as primordial violence, hatred, and enmity (the people); the play of chance and probability (the military), and subordinated to policy which makes it subject to reason (the government). See Carl von Clausewitz, *On War*, ed. and trans. Michael Howard and Peter Paret, ind. ed. (Princeton University Press, 1984), 89.

9. The dominant role of institutions and a legal framework capable of enforcing contracts and private property rights has been recognized as the key determinant in long-term economic growth at least since Douglas North won the Nobel Prize for his work on the topic. The number of publications that explore this topic is overwhelming, but a good place to start is Douglas C. North, *The Rise of the Western World* (Cambridge University Press, 1976).

10. Edward N. Luttwak, *The Grand Strategy of the Roman Empire: From the First Century A.D. to the Third* (Johns Hopkins University Press, 1976). A slightly revised edition was released in 2016.

11. Brian Campbell, "The Army," in *The Cambridge Ancient History*, vol. 12, *The Crisis of Empire, A.D. 193–337*, ed. Alan K. Bowman, Averil Cameron, and Peter Garnsey (Cambridge University Press, 2009), 114.

12. In this chapter I will be expanding on the commentary of Kimberly Kagan and Everett Wheeler. See Kimberly Kagan, "Redefining Roman Grand Strategy," *Journal of Military History* 70, no. 2 (2006): 333–362; Everett Wheeler, "Methodological Limits and the Mirage of Roman Strategy: Part I," *Journal of Military History* 57, no. 1 (1993): 7–41; and Everett Wheeler, "Methodological Limits and the Mirage of Roman Strategy: Part II," *Journal of Military History* 57, no. 2 (1993): 215–240.

13. Susan P. Mattern, *Rome and the Enemy: Imperial Strategy in the Principate* (University of California Press, 1999), 21.

14. Benjamin Isaac, *The Limits of Empire: The Roman Army in the East* (Clarendon Press, 1990), 399–400.

15. For a thorough commentary on the state of the field in reference to Rome's geographical knowledge, see Daniel Raisbeck, "Grand Strategy in Antiquity: The Case of Imperial Rome," in *Reflections on Macedonian and*

Roman Grand Strategy, ed. Fred Naiden and Daniel Raisbeck (Universidad Gran Colombia, 2019), forthcoming. Also see Serena Bianchetti, Michele Cataudella, and Hans-Joachim Gehrke, eds., *Brill's Companion to Ancient Geography: The Inhabited World in Greek and Roman Tradition* (Brill, 2015).

16. Vegetius, *De Re Militari*, 3.6.4 (emphasis added); as quoted in Mattern, *Rome and the Enemy*, 28.

17. The standard work on the Antonine Itinerary remains Otto Cuntz, *Itineraria Romana* (B. G. Teubner, 1929). Also see Nicholas Reed, "Pattern and Purpose in the Antonine Itinerary," *American Journal of Philology* 99, no. 2 (1978): 228–254.

18. For an exhaustive study of the Tabula Peutingeriana see Richard J. A. Talbert, *Rome's World: The Peutinger Map Reconsidered* (Cambridge University Press, 2010). The map can be viewed in detail at https://peutinger.atlantides. org/map-a/.

19. For Strabo, see Duane W. Roller, *The Geography of Strabo* (Cambridge University Press, 2014). This is an abridged translation, but the notes are valuable. Also see Daniela Dueck, *Strabo of Amasia: A Greek Man of Letters in Augustan Rome* (Routledge, 2011). A complete translation of Strabo's work can be found at http://penelope.uchicago.edu/Thayer/E/Roman/Texts/Strabo/ home.html. For Ptolemy, see Edward Luther Stevenson, *Geography of Claudius Ptolemy* (New York Public Library, 1932); J. Lennart Berggren and Alexander Jones, *Ptolemy's Geography: An Annotated Translation of the Theoretical Chapters* (Princeton University Press, 2002); and https://digitalmapsoftheancie ntworld.com/ancient-maps/ptolemys-map/. For the Map of Agrippa, see the description given by Pliny (*Natural History*, 3.17); see also Claude Nicolet, *Space, Geography and Politics in the Early Roman Empire* (University of Michigan Press, 1991); and finally, J. J. Tierney, "The Map of Agrippa," *Proceedings of the Royal Irish Academy: Archaeology, Culture, History, Literature* 63 (1962–1964): 151–166.

20. Mattern, *Rome and the Enemy*, 41.

21. See Gábor Timár, Sándor Biszak, Balász Székely, and Gábor Molnár, "Digitized Maps of the Habsburg Military Surveys," in *Preservation of Digital Cartography*, ed. Markus Jobst (Springer, 2010), 273–283; see https://www. researchgate.net/publication/227254186_Digitized_Maps_of_the_Habsbur g_Military_Surveys_-_Overview_of_the_Project_of_ARCANUM_Ltd_ Hungary.

22. David Chandler, *The Campaigns of Napoleon* (Scribner, 1966), 371.

23. Vegetius, *De Re Militari*, 3.7.

24. Frederick II, *Military Instruction from the Late King of Prussia to His Generals*, trans. Lieut. Colonel Foster (Sherborne, 1818), 61.

25. https://taskandpurpose.com/military-tech/navy-aircraft-carrier-history/.

26. See https://fas.org/sgp/crs/natsec/RL32411.pdf.

27. <IBT>Paterculus, *Roman History*</IBT>, 2.109.1.

28. Ibid., 2.109.2–5. See also Dio, *Roman History*, 55.29 (emphasis added).

29. Paterculus, *Roman History*, 2.106.2–3.

30. A case could be made for George Washington's having achieved a similar result during the Yorktown campaign.

31. Ronald Syme, "Military Geography at Rome," *Classical Antiquity* 7, no. 2 (1988): 227–251. Syme repeatedly makes the case that Rome was rarely if ever defeated because of a lack of geographical knowledge. Rather, defeats were a consequence of arrogance, obstinacy, and miscalculations. This article also provides an excellent summary of Roman geographic knowledge as known from the extant sources.

32. Benjamin Isaac, "The Meaning of the Terms *limes* and *limitanei*," *Journal of Roman Studies* 78 (1988): 125–147; Benjamin Isaac, *The Limits of Empire* (Oxford University Press, 1993); and C. R. Whittaker, *Frontiers of the Roman Empire* (Johns Hopkins University Press, 1994).

33. David Cherry, "The Frontier Zones," in *The Cambridge Economic History of the Greco-Roman World*, ed. Walter Schiedel, Ian Morris, and Richard P. Saller (Cambridge University Press, 2007), 720–721.

34. Publius Aelius Aristides, *The Roman Oration*; see https://www.bradford-del ong.com/2017/11/aelius-aristides-the-roman-oration-it-is-a-time-honored-custom-of-travelers-setting-forth-by-land-or-sea-to-m.html.

35. Appian, *Roman History*, preface, 1.7.0 (emphasis added).

36. Herodian, *History of Rome*, 2.11.5.

37. Zosimus, *New History*, 2.34.1–2 (trans. G. J. Vossius, 1814). A copy can be found at Livius.org.

38. For an interesting take on Zosimus's biases, sources, and similarity to and reception by more recent historians, see Walter Goffart, "Zosimus, the First Historian of Rome's Fall," *American Historical Review* 76, no. 2 (1971): 412–441.

39. Isaac, *Limits of Empire*, 409.

40. Whittaker, *Frontiers of the Roman Empire*, 139.

41. For an interesting appraisal of how the Romans viewed the frontiers, as opposed to how many historians have interpreted the evidence, see Geoffrey Greatrex, "Roman Frontiers and Foreign Policy," in *Aspects of the Roman East: Papers in Honour of Professor Fergus Millar*, ed. Richard Alston and Samuel Lieu (Brepols, 2007), 103–173.

42. Isaac, *Limits of Empire*, 411; Dio, *Roman History*, 66.9.6.

43. Isaac, *Limits of Empire*, 411.

44. For a through discussion of the use of natural obstacles during the period, see Mark W. Graham, *News and Frontier Consciousness in the Late Roman Empire* (University of Michigan Press, 2006).

45. Whittaker, *Frontiers of the Roman Empire*, 91.

46. Mattern, *Rome and the Enemy*, 21.

47. Dio, *Roman History*, 56.28.2.

48. See <IBT>Wheeler, "Methodological Limits and the Mirage of Roman Strategy: Part II,"</IBT> 231–234, for a brief but pointed detailing of the evidence for such an apparatus.

49. Ibid., 232.

50. Tacitus, *Annals*, 1.11.7. An earlier version of this inventory was known to exist in 23 BCE; see Suetonius, "Augustus," 28.1: "when he went so far as to summon the magistrates and the senate to his house, and submit an account of the general condition of the empire."

51. Tacitus, *Annals*, 4.5.

52. James Thorne, "Battle, Tactics, and the Limites in the West," in *The Companion to the Roman Army*, ed. Paul Erdkamp (Wiley-Blackwell, 2007), 229.

53. David Potter, "Measuring the Power of the Roman Empire," in *East and West in the Roman Empire of the Fourth Century: The End of Unity*, ed. Roald Dijkstra, Sanne van Poppel, and Daniëlle Slootjes (Brill, 2015), 26–48.

54. Interestingly, the *Notitia Dignitatum* records a number of forts as being in barbaric areas, that is, lying within barbarian territory and outside the Empire. This is fairly clear evidence that the Romans possessed an excellent idea of where their frontiers ended and where barbarism began.

55. Wheeler, "Methodological Limits and the Mirage of Roman Strategy: Part II."

56. David Cherry, "The Frontier Zones," in *The Cambridge Economic History of the Greco-Roman World*, ed. Walter Schiedel et al. (Cambridge University Press, 2007), 721.

Chapter 2

1. Gundula Lidke and Sebastian Lorenz, *The Bronze Age Battlefield in the Tollense Valley—Conflict Archaeology and Holocene Landscape Reconstruction*; see https://pdfs.semanticscholar.org/063e/80e4ac8fdeb88105dc4a86cef032b b78b3af.pdf?_ga=2.175628642.1786001317.1586113397-24107569.158 6113397.

2. Isotope studies demonstrate that many of the battle's participants were drawn from hundreds of miles distant. T. Douglas Price et al., "Multi-Isotope Proveniencing of Human Remains from a Bronze Age Battlefield in the Tollense Valley in Northeast Germany," https://link.springer.com/article/ 10.1007/s12520-017-0529-y.

3. Many of the skeletons that have been found exhibit evidence of healed wounds, presumably from previous battles.

4. Andrew Curry, "Slaughter at the Bridge: Uncovering a Colossal Bronze Age Battle," *Science*, March 24, 2016, https://www.science.org/content/article/ slaughter-bridge-uncovering-colossal-bronze-age-battle.

5. Detlef Jantzen et al., "An Early Bronze Age Causeway in the Tollense Valley, Mecklenburg–Western Pomerania—The Starting Point of a Violent

Conflict 3300 Years Ago?" *Bericht der Romisch-Germanischen Kommission* 95 (2018), https://journals.ub.uni-heidelberg.de/index.php/berrgk/article/view/44423/37892; and G. Lidke and S. Lorenz, "The Bronze Age Battlefield in the Tollense Valley—Conflict Archaeology and Holocene Landscape Reconstruction," DEUQUA Spec. Pub. 2 (2019): 69–75, https://doi.org/10.5194/deuquasp-2-69-2019.

6. Tacitus comments on the Baltic amber trade in *Germania*: "They even explore the sea; and are the only people who gather amber . . . they gather it in the rough; bring it unwrought; and wonder at the price they receive" (45). Given that the Germans had been trading in amber for well over a thousand years prior to Tacitus's writings, one suspects they were not awed at the prices they received. Perhaps they were overcharging the Romans by a significant amount and were surprised to find Romans paying above-market prices.

7. Joachim Krüger, F. Nagel, Sonja Nagel, and Detlef Jantzen, "Bronze Age Tin Rings from the Tollenese Valley in Northeastern Germany," *Praehistorische Zeitschrift* 87, no. 1 (2012): 29–43, https://www.researchgate.net/publication/250308166_Bronze_Age_tin_rings_from_the_Tollense_valley_in_North eastern_Germany.

8. Robert Drews, *The End of the Bronze Age: Changes in Warfare and the Catastrophe ca. 1200* (Princeton University Press, 1993); and Eric H. Cline, *1177 B.C.: The Year Civilization Collapsed* (Princeton University Press, 2014).

9. Kenneth Kitchen, *Pharaoh Triumphant: The Life and Times of Ramesses II, King of Egypt* (Aris & Phillips, 1982), 40–41.

10. Barry Cunliffe, *Europe between the Oceans, 9000 BC–AD 1000* (Yale University Press, 2008), 237; and Trevor Bryce, *The World of the Neo-Hittite Kingdoms: A Political and Military History* (Oxford University Press, 2012).

11. A. Bernard Knapp and Sturt W. Manning, "Crisis in Context: The End of the Late Bronze Age in the Eastern Mediterranean," *American Journal of Archaeology* 120, no. 1 (2016): 99–149.

12. David Kaniewski et al., "The Sea Peoples, from Cuneiform Tablets to Carbon Dating," *PLoS ONE*, https://www.ncbi.nlm.nih.gov/pmc/articles/PMC 3110627/.

13. Marc Van De Mieroop, *A History of Ancient Egypt* (Wiley-Blackwell, 2011), 251.

14. Herodotus, *Histories*, 1.104.

15. Ibid., 1.106.

16. Ibid., 1.212.

17. Ibid., 4.83–144.

18. For our purposes we will stay with the traditional dates for the rise and fall of the Roman Empire, which began in 27 BCE, when Augustus was made "first citizen" and awarded the *proconsular imperium*, and ended in the West in 476 CE, when Romulus was deposed by Odoacer.

19. Livy, *History of Rome*, 5.37.

20. Ibid., 5.41.

21. Ibid., 5.48.

22. Ibid., 5.49.

23. Plutarch, *Parallel Lives*, "Camillus," 5.29.

24. Ibid., "Marius," 11.8. The first to use the term *Furor Teutonicus* was the Roman poet Lucan: Lucanus, *Pharsalia*, 1.255–256.

25. Plutarch, *Parallel Lives*, "Marius," 20.3.

26. Ibid., "Caesar," 15.5. These numbers are certainly exaggerated, but they do give one an idea of how ferocious the multiyear struggle was and how dangerous the barbarians could be if they were ever united. The closest the Celts ever came to such a unification was before the walls of Alesia in 52 BCE, where Caesar came within a hair's breadth of seeing his army exterminated in a hard-fought battle that finally broke the barbarians' military power. For an excellent analysis of all of the demographic numbers used in Caesar's Gallic campaigns, see David Henige, "He Came, He Saw, We Counted: The Historiography and Demography of Caesar's Gallic Numbers," *Annales de démographie historique* 1, *Le mariage, règles et pratiques* (1998): 215–242; see https://www.persee.fr/docAsPDF/adh_0066-2062_1998_num_1998_1_2 162.pdf.

Chapter 3

1. Polybius, *The Histories*, 9.10.11.

2. For an excellent source on the Roman Republic's economic change during the period in which its Mediterranean empire was built, see Philip Kay, *Rome's Economic Revolution* (Oxford University Press, 2014). See also David B. Hollander, *Money in the Late Roman Republic* (Brill Academic, 2007).

3. Kay, *Rome's Economic Revolution*, 37–39.

4. Ibid., 42.

5. Pliny, *Natural History*, 33.55.

6. As done by Kay: As we know the weight of Roman coins and the ratio of gold to silver during the period (1:10), and the conversion ratio of sesterces to denarii, the treasury at this time contained 14,624,400 denarii in gold, 1,853,800 denarii in silver, and 1,533,850 denarii in coin; for a grand total of 18,012,130 denarii. See Kay, *Rome's Economic Revolution*, 22.

7. Pliny, *Natural History*, 33.56.

8. Ibid.

9. The actual mathematical number in talents is a bit lower, but I have adjusted upward to reflect higher pay for centurions and legates, and to reflect the requirement to pay specialists a bit extra. Kay comes up with a similar number when he discusses Scipio bringing 400 talents in silver with him to Spain to pay the four legions present there. As these legions were in all likelihood extremely depleted from battle, Scipio probably brought more than enough to make good on the troop's arrears, as well

as to pay for the undertaking of a campaign. See Kay, *Rome's Economic Revolution*, 24.

10. Of course, paying the army was far from the only cost Rome had to budget for. Tenny Frank, *Economic Survey of Ancient Rome* (Johns Hopkins University Press, 1933), placed the total Roman budget during this period at about 55 million denarii.

11. Plutarch, *Parallel Lives*, "Caesar," 33.

12. Pliny, *Natural History*, 33.56.

13. Lucan, *Pharsalia*. See https://www.loebclassics.com/view/LCL220/1928/volume.xml.

14. I am accepting the calculations (conversions) in Tenney Frank, "The Sacred Treasure and the Rate of Manumission," *American Journal of Philology* 53, no. 4 (1932), 360–363, http://penelope.uchicago.edu/Thayer/E/Journals/AJP/53/4/The_Sacred_Treasure_and_the_Rate_of_Manumission*.html.

15. Suetonius, *The Lives of the Twelve Caesars*, XXI, http://www.fordham.edu/halsall/ancient/suetonius-julius.html (accessed March 29, 2009).

16. Tenney Frank, *An Economic Survey of Ancient Rome*, vol. 1 (Johns Hopkins University Press, 1959), 320–345. According to Frank, during the civil war Caesar raised approximately HS600 million from requisitions of silver and gold from Spain. For perspective, the HS600 million revenue in 50 BCE was equal to about 600 million grams silver or some 6.4 million troy ounces. This would be equivalent to about 23,000 Athenian talents (829.5 ounces per talent).

17. Suetonius, *Lives*, "Caesar," 38.1.

18. Ibid., 54.3.

19. Appian and Dio present different numbers (I have used Appian's; see Appian, *Civil Wars*, 4.5). Syme believes both sets of numbers are exaggerated; see Ronald Syme, *The Roman Revolution* (Oxford University Press, 1939).

20. Appian, *Civil Wars*, 4.3.

21. R. Morris Coats and Gary M. Pecquet, "The Calculus of Conquests: The Decline and Fall of the Returns to Roman Expansion," *Independent Review* 17, no. 4 (2013): 517–540.

22. Appian, *Civil Wars*, 4.100.

23. Ibid., 4.120.

24. Ibid., 5.6.

25. For an economic analysis see Leander Heldring, James A. Robinson, and Sebastian Vollmer, "The Long-Run Impact of the Dissolution of the English Monasteries" (August 2015), https://cpb-us-w2.wpmucdn.com/voices.uchicago.edu/dist/f/1135/files/2018/06/paper_submission_version-2fy89hl.pdf.

26. Diodorus Siculus, *The Library of History*, 17.20–22. For a full accounting of the Persian treasure looted by Alexander, see Frank L. Holt, *The Treasures of Alexander the Great: How One Man's Wealth Shaped the World* (Oxford University Press, 2016).

27. The Romans did debt-finance the building of a fleet. See Polybius, *The Histories*, 1.59: "The treasury was empty and would not supply the funds necessary for the undertaking, which were, however, obtained by the patriotism and generosity of the leading citizens. They undertook singly, or by two or three combining, according to their means, to supply a quinquereme fully fitted out, on the understanding that they were to be repaid if the expedition was successful." This, however, was not truly what modern economists consider debt financing, which had to wait until the Dutch and English Financial Revolutions of the sixteenth and seventeenth centuries. See James Lacey, "The Financial Revolution," in *Makers of Modern Strategy* (Princeton University Press, forthcoming 2022).

28. See: Robin Waterfield, *Dividing the Spoils: The War for Alexander the Great's Empire* (Oxford University Press, 2011).

29. For an analysis of great state competitions and conflicts demonstrating how this fact has been borne out over three thousand years of history, see James Lacey, *Great State Rivalries: From the Classical World to the Cold War* (Oxford University Press, 2017).

30. This is akin to the modern broken-windows fallacy, where one can stimulate economic activity by breaking and then replacing every window in the country. But once you have finished replacing the windows, the result simply reestablishes the foundational wealth of the economy to what it was prior to breaking all the windows. In short, despite the frenzy of economic activity, there has been no economic advance.

31. This flies in the face of Moses Finley's assertion that there was very little technical innovation or economic progress in the ancient world. See M. I. Finley, "Technical Innovations and Economic Progress in the Ancient World," *Economic History Review*, n.s., 18, no. 1 (1965): 29–45. His argument was taken up by a number of medievalists who wished to demonstrate that their own chosen period of study was rife with technological innovations that owed very little to preceding ones. For a convincing counterargument, one that underpins my own beliefs, see Andrew Wilson, "Machines, Power and the Ancient Economy," *Journal of Roman Studies* 92 (2002): 1–32. Also see Paul Erdkamp, "Population, Technology and Economic Growth in the Roman World," in Paul Erdkamp, Koenraad Verboven, and Arjan Zuiderhoek, *Capital, Investment and Innovation in the Roman* World (Oxford University Press, 2020), 39–67.

32. Wilson, "Machines, Power and the Ancient Economy."

33. Mark Merrony, *The Plight of Rome in the Fifth Century* (Routledge, 2017).

34. Tacitus, *Annales*, 1.10.

35. It is not until the reign of Domitian that we see a large increase in legionary pay. Before this, pay was often increased through gifting of donatives at irregular intervals. Caligula, for instance, gave every solider 300 sesterces (about half a year's pay) upon his ascent to the throne, while his less secure

successor Claudius presented the army with 31,000 talents—enough to pay all of Rome's legions for a decade.

36. For information on the role of timber in the Roman economy, see Robyn Veal, *The Politics and Economics of Ancient Forests: Timber and Fuel as Levers of Greco-Roman Control*, in P. Derron (ed.), *Economie et inégalité: Ressources, échanges et pouvoir dans l'Antiquité classique* (Hardt Foundation, 2017), https://www.repository.cam.ac.uk/handle/1810/267207. The definitive work on the topic remains Russell Meiggs, *Trees and Timber in the Ancient Mediterranean World* (Oxford University Press, 1983). For recent evidence of the importance of timber and long distance trade, see M. Bernabei, J. Bontadi, R. Rea, U. Büntgen, and W. Tegel, "Dendrochronological Evidence for Long-Distance Timber Trading in the Roman Empire," *PLoS ONE* 14, no. 12 (2019): e0224077, https://journals.plos.org/plosone/article?id=10.1371/journal.pone.0224077. For further information on the impact of fisheries on the Roman economy, see Andrew Wilson, "Fishy Business: Roman Exploitation of Marine Resources," *Journal of Roman Archaeology* 19, no. 2 (2006):; Annalisa Marzano, "Fish and Fishing in the Roman World," *Journal of Maritime Archaeology* 13 (2018): 437–447, https://doi.org/10.1007/s11457-018-9195-1; Tonnes Bekker-Nielsen, "Fish in the Ancient Economy," in *Ancient History Matters: Studies Presented to Jens Erik Skydsgaard on his Seventieth Birthday*, ed. Karen Ascani, Vincent Gabrielsen, Kirsten Avist, and Anders Holm Rasmussen (L'Erma di Bretschneider, 2002), 29–37.

37. Pliny, *Natural History*, 33.97.

38. Strabo, *Geography*, 3.2.10. The author uses Polybius as his source.

39. The cost of paying and sustaining a legion had more than doubled since the cost during the Punic Wars, mostly as a consequence of Caesar's doubling legionnaire pay. Pliny, *Natural History*, 33.21.

Chapter 4

1. I am dating recorded history as beginning approximately with the published works of Herodotus.

2. For an summary outline of NSC-68's history and impact, see https://history.state.gov/milestones/1945-1952/NSC68; for a copy of the document, see https://fas.org/irp/offdocs/nsc-hst/nsc-68.htm.

3. For a brief summary and copy of the Four Freedoms speech, see https://www.fdrlibrary.org/four-freedoms.

4. While taxation was the surely the underlying grievance, the death of Herod the Great and the removal of his strong hand provided the opening for the Jewish revolt. His son, Herod Archelaus, who took control of Judaea and Samaria after his father's death, proved incapable of crushing the rebellion. See Josephus, *Antiquities of the Jews*, 17.10.

5. Josephus does not identify the three legions involved, but III Gallica, VI Ferrata, X Fretensis, and XII Fulminata were all under Varus's command at the time.

6. Josephus, *Antiquities of the Jews*, 17.10.9–10.

7. The following reconstruction is my own. It is based on evidence provided by ancient writers and recent archaeological excavations of the Teutoburg Wald battle site. See Dio, *Roman History*, Book 56, chaps. 18–24; Velleius, *Roman History*, Book 2, chaps. 117–120; Tacitus, *Annals*, 1.60–62, and Florus, *Epitome of Titus Livy*, 2.30. This reconstruction was also informed by two modern works: Adrian Murdoch, *Rome's Greatest Defeat: Massacre in the Teutoburg Forest*, 1st ed. (Sutton, 2009), and Peter S. Wells, *The Battle That Stopped Rome* (New York, 2003). Of these, Velleius's *Roman History* must be given the greatest credit. Although it was written twenty years after the battle, he was the only ancient source who actually talked to survivors. Moreover, he was a Roman general with extensive combat experience in Germania.

8. The sources do not discuss this phase of the battle. However, the author believes that it is a fair reconstruction, for it is certain that the Romans repulsed the first attacks. Also, there is a recorded instance of ambushed legions behaving in precisely this manner when Caesar's army was attacked by the Nervi in 57 BCE.

9. This phase of the fight is also not mentioned in the ancient sources, but recent archaeological finds indicate there was a hard fight at the wall.

10. Archaeological digs show evidence of dead Romans on the German side of the wall.

11. Varus's subordinate, Vala, had led the cavalry in a breakout. Tradition holds that this was a cowardly attempt to escape that left the infantry exposed. However, the cavalry was more of a hindrance than a help in this fight, and it is just as likely that Varus ordered them to flee in order to save something from the disaster engulfing his army. In any case, they did not make it: German horsemen ran the Roman cavalry to ground and annihilated it.

12. Only a small force based at Aliso, near modern Haltern, commanded by Cadencies (an experienced veteran and likely the *primus pilus*—commander of a legion's first cohort—of the XIX Legion) managed to cut its way through enemy territory back to the safety of Gaul.

13. Tacitus, *Annals*, 1.60–61.

14. Suetonius, *The Twelve Caesars*, trans. Robert Graves, rev. Michael Grant (Penguin Classics, 1979).

15. Suetonius, "Tiberius," 16.1–2.

16. Ibid., 16.1. While Tiberius appears to have had fifteen legions at his disposal, with all of their auxiliary forces, most of the fighting was done by five legions assigned to the region, reinforced as necessary during the rougher parts of the three-year conflict.

17. For the most through surviving accounts of the war, see Dio, *Roman History*–55.29–34, and Velleius, *Roman History*, 2.110–117.

18. Dio, *Roman History*, 55.31.

19. Velleius, *Roman History*, 2.110.1–6. Such numbers from ancient writers are always suspect. But clearly they raised a large enough host that Tiberius thought it prudent to concentrate his own force of ten legions and auxiliaries—nearly 100,000 men—in a central location.

20. Ibid., 2.110.6.

21. Ibid., 2.112.3.

22. Tacitus, *Annals*, 1.69.1.

23. For those interested in a more detailed treatment of Germanicus and his military career, see Adrian Goldsworthy, *In the Name of Rome: The Men Who Won the Roman Empire* (Weidenfeld & Nicolson, 2003), 237–262.

24. Tacitus, *Annals*, 2.26.

25. James Lacey and Williamson Murray, *Moment of Battle: The Twenty Clashes That Changed the World* (Bantam Books, 2013).

26. Virgil, *Aeneid*, 6.1151–1154.

27. Dio, *Roman History*, 56.33.5.

28. For an excellent outline of the debate, see Josiah Ober, "Tiberius and the Political Testament of Augustus," *Historia: Zeitschrift für Alte Geschichte* 31, no. 3 (1982): 306–328. It is more recently discussed in David J. Breeze, *The Frontiers of Imperial Rome* (Pen and Sword, 2011), 14–19.

29. Modern historians have followed P. A. Brunt's lead, and it is now generally accepted that Dio created a fiction that Augustus was always oriented toward peaceful solutions. Dio, who was always opposed to expansion, was perfectly willing to create a pacific Augustus as an exemplar for future emperors. See P. A. Brunt, *Roman Imperial Themes* (Oxford University Press, 1990), 96–109, and P. A. Brunt, "Reviewed Work: *Die Aussenpolitik des Augustus und die Augusteische Dichtung* by Hans D. Meyer," *Journal of Roman Studies* 53 (1963): 170–176.

30. Alison Cooley, *Res Gestae divi Augusti*, edition with introduction, translation, and commentary (Cambridge University Press, 2009).

31. Augustus, *Rae Gestae*, 26.6–7. See P. A. Brunt and J. M. Moore (trans.), *Res Gestae divi Augusti* (Oxford University Press, 1967), https://droitromain.univ-grenoble-alpes.fr/Anglica/resgest_engl.htm.

32. Brunt, *Roman Imperial Themes*. Brunt has argued that although the Romans had a very good idea of the geography of the Empire and beyond the frontier for several hundred miles (much further than the Eastern Empire), they may not have had any idea how much further the world extended beyond that zone, making it feasible that Augustus, and others, believed that with one great push beyond the existing frontiers they could occupy the world.

33. C. M. Wells, *The German Policy of Augustus: An Examination of the Archaeological Evidence* (Oxford University Press, 1972).

34. J. C. Mann, "Power, Force, and the Frontiers of the Empire," *Journal of Roman Studies* 69 (1979): 179.

35. Edward Gibbon, *The History of the Decline and Fall of the Roman Empire*, ed. David P. Womersley, vol. 1 (New York, 1996), 1–2 (emphasis added).

36. Wells, *The German Policy of Augustus*, 246.

37. Arthur Ferrill, *The Fall of the Roman Empire: The Military Explanation* (Thames and Hudson, 1986), 23. Ferrill uses Th. Mommsen, "Das römische Militärwesen seit Diocletian," *Hermes* 24, no. 2 (1889): 195–279, https://www.jstor.org/stable/4472189?seq=1#metadata_info_tab_contents.

38. Ferrill, *The Fall of the Roman Empire*, 23.

39. James Thorne, "Battle, Tactics, and the Emergence of the Limites in the West," in *The Companion to the Roman Army*, ed. Paul Erdkamp (Wiley-Blackwell, 2007), 228.

40. That the Romans could think in such strategic terms is clearly attested to in Tacitus, *Annals*, 4.5 (quoted at length earlier in this volume).

41. I will readdress this topic later in this work when I examine the policies of Diocletian and Constantine.

Chapter 5

1. Theodor Kissel, "Road Building as a Munus Publicum," in *The Roman Army and the Economy*, ed. Paul Erdkamp (J. C. Gieben, 2002), 127–160.

2. Ibid., 130. This is based on the calculation given of HS100,000 per mile. Kissel gives a total of one quintillion, which is off by at least an order of magnitude once the cost per mile is multiplied by 56,000 miles.

3. Ann Kolb, "Army and Transport," in *The Roman Army and the Economy*, ed. Paul Erdkamp (J. C. Gieben, 2002), 161–166.

4. Paul de Soto, "Network Analysis to Model and Analyze Roman Transport and Mobility," in *Finding the Limits of the Limes*, ed. Philip Verhagen et al. (Springer, 2019): 271–289. https://link.springer.com/chapter/10.1007/978-3-030-04576-0_13.

5. Suetonius, "Augustus," 49.3.

6. Pliny the Younger, *Letters*, 10.46–47.

7. Aelius Aristides, *Or.*, XXVI: To Rome, as quoted in Simon Corcoran, "State Correspondence in the Roman Empire: Imperial Communication from Augustus to Justinian," in *State Correspondence in the Ancient World: From the New Kingdom Egypt to the Roman Empire*, ed. Karen Radner (Oxford University Press, 2014), 173–209 (emphasis added).

8. Richard Duncan-Jones, *Structure and Scale in the Roman Economy* (Cambridge University Press, 1990), 360–363.

9. David J. Breeze, *The Frontiers of Imperial Rome* (Pen & Sword, 2011), 6.

10. Tacitus, *Annals*, 4.5 (emphasis added).

11. There is also evidence that Caligula built several bases in the lower Rhine region during a visit in 39–40 CE. These, however, cannot be considered part of any systemic strategic thinking, as the entire military expedition into the region appears farcical. At one point he appears to have declared war on the sea, and after arraying his legions and all of their artillery for an attack, he suddenly orders the legionaries to start collecting seashells and fill their pockets with them, calling them his spoils of war (Suetonius, "Caligula," 46).

12. Breeze, *The Frontiers of Imperial Rome*.

13. Adrian Goldsworthy, "War," in *The Cambridge History of Greek and Roman Warfare: Rome from the Late Republic to the Late Empire*, vol. 2, ed. Philip Sabin et al. (Cambridge University Press, 2007), 112.

14. David J. Breeze, "The Value of Studying Roman Frontiers," *Theoretical Roman Archaeology Journal* 1, no. 1 (2018): 1, http://doi.org/10.16995/traj.212.

15. Of course, some walls (such as those of prisons) are built to keep people in, but their geopolitical purpose is to keep enemies at bay. An obvious exception is the Berlin Wall of the twentieth century, one of the few border walls ever built to keep a population in.

16. Arrian, *Circumnavigation of the Black Sea*, 6.2.9; as quoted in Breeze, *The Frontiers of Imperial Rome*, 25.

17. Ammianus, *The Roman History*, 31.6.4.

18. The idea of a fortress line was given a bad connotation in the minds of many strategists by the supposed failure of France's Maginot Line in 1940, which the Germans bypassed by attacking through the Ardennes and into Belgium. This, of course, totally misses the Maginot Line's rationale. It was never meant as a wall to hide behind. Rather, it was meant to secure the German frontier and act as a pivot for the main French armies advancing to confront the German invasion of Belgium. In this, the Maginot Line succeeded; the faults that led to rapid French defeat lay elsewhere.

Chapter 6

1. See Dio, *Roman History*, 55.25.1–3, for the start of this new fund. See Augustus, *Rae Gestae*, 17, for the amount. This fund was maintained both by regular payments from the emperor and by new taxes on inheritances and auctions.

2. Augustus, *Rae Gestae*, 3.

3. Ibid., 16.

4. Tacitus, *Annals*, 1.17.

5. Ibid., 4.5.

6. The great expansion of the number of legions during and after the tetrarchy is addressed later in this work.

7. For a more detailed description of the organization and command structure of the legions, see: Kate Gilliver, "The Augustan Reform of the Imperial

Army," in *A Companion to the Roman Army*, ed. Paul Erdkamp (Wiley-Blackwell, 2011), 183–197. Other works that were instrumental in preparing this chapter include Nigel Pollard, "The Roman Army," in *A Companion to the Roman Empire*, ed. David Potter (Wiley-Blackwell, 2010), 207–227; Lawrence Keppie, "The Army and the Navy," in *The Cambridge Ancient History*, 2nd ed., vol. 10, *The Augustan Empire, 43 B.C.–A.D. 69*, ed. Alan K. Bowman, Edward Champlin, and Andrew Lintott (Cambridge University Press, 1996), 371–396; Mark Hassall, "The Army," in Alan Bowman et al., *The Cambridge Ancient History*, 2nd ed., vol. 11, *The High Empire, A.D. 70–192*, ed. Peter Garnsey, Dominic Rathbone, and Alan K. Bowman (Cambridge University Press, 2000), 320–343.

8. Suetonius, *Lives*, "Claudius," 10.1–2.

9. Ibid., 10.4.

10. Tacitus, *Annals*, 12.69.

11. *Historia Augusta*, "Pertinax," 14.6.

12. Dio, *Roman History*, 74.16.

13. Ibid., 75.1.

14. Ibid., 77.15.3.

15. Brian Campbell, *Warfare and Society in Imperial Rome, c. 31 BC–AD 280* (Routledge, 2002), 119.

16. Josephus, *The Wars of the Jews*, 3.70–76 (emphasis added). Read all the way through to 3.109 to get Josephus's complete appraisal of the Roman army of his time.

17. Caesar, *The Civil Wars*, 3.93.

18. In this author's opinion, the closest Hollywood ever came to depicting a Roman battle correctly was in the HBO series *Rome*, with the battle scene in the movie *Gladiator* placing a close second, at least until it was allowed to degenerate into a swirling mass of individual combats.

19. Appian, *Civil Wars*, 3.68 (emphasis added).

20. Caesar, *Gallic Wars*, 7.86–88.

21. For an excellent and thorough analysis of Roman battle, see Philip Sabin, "The Face of Roman Battle," *Journal of Roman Studies* 90 (2000): 1–7.

22. For specifics of Roman weapons and battle formations see James Thorne, "Battle, Tactics, and the Emergence of the Limites in the West," in *The Companion to the Roman Army*, ed. Paul Erdkamp (Wiley-Blackwell, 2007), 218–233.

23. Lawrence Keppie, *The Making of the Roman Army: From the Republic to the Empire* (University of Oklahoma Press, 1984), 173–74.

24. Ibid., 173–182. Also see Vegetius, *De re militari*, 2.12 for a discussion of the Roman rank system and how centurions were promoted to higher levels.

25. Kate Gilliver, "The Augustan Reform and the Imperial Army," in *The Companion to the Roman Army*, ed. Paul Erdkamp (Wiley-Blackwell, 2011), 186.

26. There were also mixed cohorts of infantry and cavalry, but their numbers appear to have been small.

27. Gilliver, "The Augustan Reform and the Imperial Army," 193.

Chapter 7

1. Sextus Pompey's naval power was broken by Augustus's top general, Agrippa, at the Battle of Naulochus in 36 BCE (Appian, *Civil Wars*, 5.104–108).

2. Graham Webster, *The Roman Imperial Army of the First and Second Centuries A.D.*, 3rd ed., introd. Hugh Elton (University of Oklahoma Press, 1998), 158.

3. D. B. Saddington, "*Classes*: The Evolution of the Roman Imperial Fleets," in *A Companion to the Roman Army*, ed. Paul Erdkamp (Wiley-Blackwell, 2011), 209.

4. Robert Gardiner (ed.), *Age of the Galley: Mediterranean Oared Vessels since Pre-Classical Times* (Conway Maritime Press, 2004), 78.

5. Tacitus, *Histories*, 1.58.

6. Saddington, *Classes*, 213.

7. J. W. Hayes, "Carausius, Admiral and British Monarch (A.D. Century III): His Life and Times," *Journal of the British Archaeological Association* 33, no. 2 (1927): 357–374, https://www.tandfonline.com/doi/abs/10.1080/00681288.1927.11894413?journalCode=yjba18.

8. For an excellent examination of Rome's northern fleets, see Christoph Rummel's unpublished dissertation "The Fleets of the Northern Frontier of the Roman Empire from the 1st to 3rd Century," http://eprints.nottingham.ac.uk/27819/. For an examination of Rome's Black Sea fleet, see Everett Wheeler, "Roman Fleets in the Black Sea: Mysteries of the 'Classis Pontica'," *Acta Classica* 55 (2012): 119–154.

9. For detailed examinations of each of these fleets and their operations, see Michael Pitassi, The *Navies of Rome* (Boydell Press, 2009); Michael Pitassi, *The Roman Navy: Ships, Men and Warfare, 350 BC–AD 475* (Seaforth, 2012); James J. Bloom, *Rome Rules the Waves: A Naval Staff Appreciation of Ancient Rome's Maritime Strategy, 350 BCE–500 CE* (Pen and Sword, 2019); William L. Rodgers, *Naval Warfare under Oars, 4th to 16th Centuries: A Study of Strategy, Tactics, and Ship Design* (Naval Institute Press, 1983); and Chester W. Starr, *The Roman Imperial Navy, 31 B.C.–A.D. 324* (Cornell University Press, 1941).

10. During this period the various fleets also played an important role in Roman politics. For instance, in 69 CE, Vespasian's march to ultimate power was greatly aided by the *Classis Pontica*, and a good case can be made that the tide turned in his favor when the praetorian fleet at Ravenna declared its support for his cause. In fact, the civil wars of 69 CE—the Year of the Four

Emperors—started when Nero suborned the prefect of the Misene fleet to murder his mother, Agrippina.

11. Stanford University's ORBIS project—the Stanford Geospatial Network Model of the Roman World—makes it easy for anyone to plot out travel times within the Roman Empire, using any mode of travel at various points in the year. The study also makes it possible to study the cost of travel and transport from points throughout the Empire. A study of the site's maps and research would be well worth any reader's time. See https://orbis.stanf ord.edu/.

12. Zosimus, *New History*, 1.42–1.43.2.

13. The dating of these events in the extant sources is extremely confusing. See David S. Potter, *The Roman Empire at Bay*, AD 180–395, 2nd ed. (Routledge, 2014), 259–264, to make some sense of it all.

14. Pitassi, *The Roman Navy*, 15.

15. Ibid., 16.

Chapter 8

1. It is beyond the scope of this work to examine the political maneuvers employed by Augustus, over a period of decades, to emplace himself as sole ruler, establish a dynasty, and bring the last vestiges of the Roman Republic to an end. See Werner Eck, *The Age of Augustus* (Wiley-Blackwell, 2007); Adrian Goldsworthy, *Augustus: First Emperor of Rome* (Yale University Press, 2015); Karl Galinsky, *The Cambridge Companion to the Age of Augustus* (Cambridge University Press, 2005); and Ronald Syme, *The Roman Revolution*, rev. ed. (Oxford University Press, 2002).

2. The funds for these settlements came from Augustus's own funds and a new tax on the manumission of slaves.

3. *Historia Augusta*, "The Life of Hadrian," Part 2, 15.11–13 (emphasis added).

4. Strabo, *Geography*, 17.3.25. This portion of Strabo's work lays out in some detail how Augustus organized the Empire's provinces, as well as the ranks of the men he sent to govern them.

5. Tacitus, *Annals*, 1.2.1. See also J. A. Crook, "Augustus: Power, Authority, Achievement," in *The Cambridge Ancient History, 2nd ed., vol. 10, The Augustan Empire, 43 B.C.–A.D. 69,* ed. Alan K. Bowman, Edward Champlin, and Andrew Lintott (Cambridge University Press, 1996), 113–146. For a good summary of Augustus's path to ultimate power, see Erich S. Gruen, "Augustus and the Making of the Principate," in *The Cambridge Companion to the Age of Augustus*, ed. Karl Galinski (Cambridge University Press, 2005), 33–51.

6. Brian Campbell, *War and Imperial Society* (Routledge, 2002), 7.

7. Virgil, *Aeneid*, 6.1151–1154.

8. Dio, *Roman History*, 56.30.4.

9. Ibid.

10. Suetonius, "Tiberius," 21; Dio, *Roman History*, 56.31.1.

11. For a full analysis of the events surrounding Agrippa's death see M. P. Charlesworth, "Tiberius and the Death of Augustus," *American Journal of Philology* 44, no. 2 (1923): 145–157, https://www.jstor.org/stable/pdf/289 557.pdf.

12. Tacitus, *Annals*, 1.7.

13. Ibid., 1.8.

14. Suetonius, "Tiberius," 24.1.

15. A second eagle was recovered in the following year's campaign. The third eagle was not recovered until 41 CE, during Claudius's reign (Dio, *Roman History*, 60.8.7).

16. Tacitus, *Annals*, 2.17.

17. Ibid., 2.16.

18. Ibid.

19. Ibid., 2.17–18.

20. Ibid., 2.20–21.

21. Ibid., 2.26.

22. For an excellent study of the politics and ideology driving these events, see D. S. Potter, "Political Theory in the 'Senatus Consultum Pisonianum'," *American Journal of Philology* 120, no. 1 (1999): 65–88.

23. Tacitus, *Annals*, 6.31.

24. Ibid., 6.32. "The man [Vitellius], I am aware, had a bad name at Rome, and many a foul story was told of him. But in the government of provinces he acted with the virtue of ancient times. He returned, and then, through fear of Caius Caesar and intimacy with Claudius, he degenerated into a servility so base that he is regarded by an after-generation as the type of the most degrading adulation. The beginning of his career was forgotten in its end, and an old age of infamy effaced the virtues of youth."

25. Suetonius, "Vitellius"; Josephus, *Antiquities*, 18.4.3.

26. S. J. V. Malloch, "Gaius on the Channel Coast," *Classical Quarterly* 51, no. 2 (2001): 551–556.

27. Suetonius, "Caligula," 46. See also David Woods, "Caligula's Seashells," *Greece & Rome* 47, no. 1 (2000): 80–87.

28. Suetonius, "Claudius," 10.

29. T. E. J. Wideman, "Tiberius to Nero," in *The Cambridge Ancient History*, 2nd ed., vol. 10, *The Augustan Empire, 43 B.C.–A.D. 69*, ed. Alan K. Bowman, Edward Champlin, and Andrew Lintott (Cambridge University Press, 1996), 229.

30. At the start of his reign, Claudius received the title of imperator, as a result of his generals punishing two German tribes for unknown offenses. Although Dio points out the title was well merited, the fighting was such a minor affair that it is unlikely that many agreed with him at the time. In Dio's

words: "This same year, however, Sulpicius Galba overcame the Chatti, and Publius Gabinius conquered the Chauci and as a crowning achievement recovered a military eagle, the only one that still remained in the hands of the enemy from Varus' disaster. Thanks to the exploits of these two men Claudius now received the well-merited title of imperator" (Dio, *Roman History*, 60.8.7).

31. Dio, *Roman History*, 60.2.6.
32. David Braund, "Apollo in Arms: Nero at the Frontier," in *A Companion to the Neronian Age*, ed. Emma Buckley and Martin Dinter (John Wiley & Sons, 2013), 83–101.
33. Strabo, *Geography*, 4.5.3 (emphasis added).
34. Suetonius, "Nero," 18.
35. Poison cannot be proven, but every available ancient source points the finger squarely at Agrippina, except for Josephus who calls it a rumor. Moreover, the timing of the murder, at a time when the one man who may have stopped her, Narcissus (a freedman and Claudius powerful personal secretary— *ab epistulis*), was absent from Rome, is too exquisite to be coincidental (Wideman, "Tiberius to Nero," 41).
36. Dio, *Roman History*, 62.18.3.
37. Tacitus, *Annals*, 14.31. Dio adds a financial reason for the start of the war, claiming that Romans such as Seneca were calling huge loans made to the Britons and using the army to enforce their claims (*Roman History*, 62.2.1).
38. Tacitus, *Annals*, 14.32.
39. Braund, "Apollo in Arms: Nero at the Frontier," 86.
40. After hearing of Paulinus's victory at the Battle of Watling and knowing he was disgraced for not allowing his legion to partake in the glory of such an overwhelming victory, he literally fell on his sword (Tacitus, *Annals*, 14.37).
41. Dio, *Roman History*, 62.8. 2–3.
42. Tacitus, *Annals*, 12.51. Tacitus relates that when his pregnant wife began to fall behind, rather than let her be captured by his enemies, Radamistus stabbed her and threw the bleeding body into the Araxes. She survived and was brought to Tiridates' court, where she was apparently well-treated.
43. Ibid., 13.35.
44. Ibid., 15.18.
45. Ibid., 15.25.
46. Ibid., 15.25.
47. Ibid., 15.26.
48. Suetonius, "Nero," 13.
49. Ibid.
50. Miriam Griffin, "The Flavians," in *The Cambridge Ancient History*, 2nd ed., vol. 11, *The High Empire, A.D. 70–192*, ed. Alan K. Bowman, Peter Garnsey, and Dominic Rathbone (Cambridge University Press, 2000), 41.
51. Dio, *Roman History*, 62.23.5.

52. It cannot be proven, but the timing of this campaign indicates that the Roman troops involved were from the same legions that had been wrecked under Paetus during the fighting in Armenia. Clearly, they had not yet been able to make good their losses of trained leaders, or to recuperate sufficiently that they could be trusted on an independent campaign.

53. The best detailed description of these campaigns remains Josephus's *War of the Jews:* http://penelope.uchicago.edu/josephus/.

54. Tacitus, *Histories*, 1.79.

55. Ibid. (emphasis added).

56. Of course, the Persian Cataphracts had been employed with great effect against Rome's legions for centuries before Adrianople was fought. Moreover, using Adrianople as a set-in-stone marker for a transition that unfurled in fits and starts for centuries is not without controversy.

57. Strabo, *Geography*, 7.147.

58. Herodotus, *The Histories*, 5.3.

59. Tacitus, in Book 2 of the *Annals*, has a detailed description of how Augustus and Tiberius handled Thrace and its kings. (2.64–67). Also see Dio, *Roman History*, 59.12 for a brief mention of Caligula's handling of the region.

60. Another king, Decebalus, would unite the Thracian (Dacian) tribes north of the Danube at the end of the first century, and prove a daunting foe for the Emperor Trajan's legions.

61. Suetonius, "Caligula," 35; Dio, *Roman History*, 60.8.

62. Griffin, "The Flavians," 39.

63. Luttwak, *The Grand Strategy of the Roman Empire*, 24–26.

64. Ibid., 26.

Chapter 9

1. See: Gwyn Morgan, *69 A.D.: The Year of the Four Emperors* (Oxford University Press, 2007); Kenneth Wellesley, *Year of the Four Emperors* (Routledge, 2000). For the ancient sources see Dio, *Roman History*, 63.22–66.2; Plutarch, *Lives of Galba and Otho*; Suetonius, "Galba," "Otho," "Vitellius," and "Vespasian"; and Tacitus, *Histories*, Books 1–5.

2. Dio, *Roman History*, 63.24. Dio's version of events appears to show that Rufus was bringing the Rhine legions to support the revolt against Nero. But the Rhine legions could not bear the sight of the armed Gauls before them, and their hatred brought on a battle the leaders did not desire. If true, this indicates that the Rhine legions were never as loyal to Nero as many assumed.

3. Suetonius, "Galba," 16.1–2. Nymphidius Sabinus was the praetorian prefect who turned the guard against Nero, but when he tried to make himself emperor, the praetorians killed him.

4. Tacitus, *Histories*, 2.42.1.

5. Ibid.

6. Ibid., 2.43.1.

7. Ibid., 2.44.1.

8. Ibid., 3.13.

9. Ibid., 3.21.

10. Ibid., 3.22.

11. Ibid., 3.24.

12. Ibid., 3.25.

13. See John Nicols, "The Emperor Vespasian," in *A Companion to the Flavian Age of Imperial Rome*, ed. Andrew Zioss (Wiley Blackwell, 2016), 62–75.

14. Ibid., 67.

15. Dio, *Roman History*, 67.11.1–2.

16. Ibid., 67.2.1.

17. Ibid., 67.3.3–4.

18. James Thorne, "Battle, Tactics, and the Emergence of the *Limites* in the West," in *The Companion to the Roman Army*, ed. Paul Erdkamp (Wiley-Blackwell, 2007), 219.

19. Alesandro Galimberti, "The Emperor Domitian," in *A Companion to the Flavian Age of Imperial Rome*, ed. Andrew Zioss (Wiley-Blackwell, 2016), 97.

20. Dio, *Roman History*, 62.4.5–6.

21. Tacitus's work *Agricola* deals primarily with these campaigns: https://sour cebooks.fordham.edu/ancient/tacitus-agricola.asp.

22. Tacitus, *Agricola*, 30 (emphasis added). There is some historical dispute as to whether Calgacus truly existed, or is a fiction created by Tacitus to give focus to his narrative. If he did not exist, then the quote is all the more damning in its judgment on Roman warfare, as it springs from the mind of a Roman senator, who was likely not alone in his thinking on the topic. This, however, does not mean Tacitus was condemning this style of warfare. After all, Rome's imposition of a what we now call a Carthaginian peace was a long-standing and venerable tradition in Roman policy circles.

23. Ibid., 34. The remark about fifty years obviously references when the Romans first sent forces to Britain on a permanent basis.

24. Ibid., 36.

25. Ibid., 37. It is worth noting Tacitus's close relations with Agricola, which may have colored some aspects of the historian's narrative.

26. There may have been some fighting in the area as early as 81, just as Domitian took the throne. See Everett L. Wheeler, "Rome's Dacian Wars: Domitian, Trajan, and Strategy on the Danube, Part II," *Journal of Military History* 74, no. 4 (2011): 1185–1227.

27. Dio, *Roman History*, 67.6.1.

28. The sources for Rome's Dacian Wars are notoriously sparse. For a good summary of the extant material, see Wheeler, "Rome's Dacian Wars," 209.

29. Dio, *Roman History*, 67.10.

30. Ibid.
31. Another good reason to do away with the client system whenever it was practicable.
32. Tacitus, *Agricola*, 45.1.
33. Alesandro Launaro, "The Economic Impact of Flavian Rule," in *A Companion to the Flavian Age of Imperial Rome*, ed. Andrew Zioss (Wiley-Blackwell, 2016), 97.
34. R. Bruce Hitchner, "The Advantages of Wealth and Luxury: The Case for Economic Growth in the Roman Empire," in *The Ancient Economy: Evidence and Models*, ed. J. G. Manning and Ian Morris (Stanford University Press, 2005), 207–222.
35. Tacitus, *Histories*, 4.74, as quoted in Hitchner, "The Advantages of Wealth and Luxury," 210.
36. Dennis P. Kehoe, "The Early Roman Empire: Production," in *The Cambridge Economic History of the Greco-Roman World*, ed. Walter Scheidel, Ian Morris, and Richard Saller (Cambridge University Press, 2007), 543.
37. Keith Hopkins places the excess GDP over subsistence level at approximately one and a half times, while R. W. Goldsmith places it closer to three times. The estimates of most other analysts have fallen somewhere between these two extremes, and most place it at two times. That means only half of the Empire's overall GDP was required to keep the population alive and thriving. The remainder, a colossal sum by ancient standards, was theoretically available for other uses. For purposes of comparison, even if Roman tax collectors only picked up half of this surplus, a Roman emperor would have at his disposal close to ten times the revenue Herodotus tells us was available to Darius at the height of the Persian Empire. For a discussion of various Roman GDP estimates, see Kehoe, "The Early Roman Empire: Production," 543–569.
38. This is based on A. J. Parker, *Ancient Shipwrecks of the Mediterranean and the Roman Provinces* (Oxford University Press, 1992). There have been several studies since the publication of Parker's monograph that have added to the number of wrecks discovered but have not much impacted the ratios involved. See also Justin Leidwanger, *Roman Seas: A Maritime Archaeology of Eastern Mediterranean Economies* (Oxford University Press, 2022).
39. Joseph R. McConnell et al., "Lead Pollution Recorded in Greenland Ice Indicates European Emissions Tracked Plagues, Wars, and Imperial Expansion During Antiquity," *PNAS* 115, no. 22 (May 29, 2018), 5726–5731; first published May 14, 2018; https://doi.org/10.1073/pnas.1721818115.
40. Military construction on the frontier along with military pay would also have worked to transfer silver from the Empire's economic center to the poorly developed edges of the Empire, where it would have fueled explosive growth on both sides of the frontier.

41. Tacitus, *Annals*, 13.54.

42. The actual quote is "This is a first-class case of man's monument to stupidity." Patton supposedly made the remark when he saw France's Maginot Line in 1944: see Paul D. Harkins, *When the Third Cracked Europe: The Story of Patton's Incredible Army* (Stackpole, 1969).

Chapter 10

1. For most of what the ancient sources tell us about Nerva, see Dio, *Roman History*, 68.1–4, and Aurelius Victor (attrib.), *Epitome de Caesaribus*, http://www.roman-emperors.org/epitome.htm.

2. Dio, *Roman History*, 68.3.

3. For example, see Pliny the Younger, *Panegyricus*.

4. Dio, *Roman History*, 68.4.

5. Ibid., 68.7.

6. Ibid.

7. Ibid., 68.6.

8. Ibid., 68.7.

9. Herodotus, *Histories*, 4.93.

10. Meda of Odessos, daughter of the Thracian king Cothelas. She reportedly killed herself when Phillip was murdered so that she could follow him to Hades.

11. Dio, *Roman History*, 68.8.

12. The Dacian army, with its Roxolani and Bastarnae (Sarmatian tribes) allies, were trapped near the city of Nicopolis, and the Dacian-Sarmatian army was destroyed at the Battle of Adamclisi. All that is known about the battle comes from a victory monument Trajan later had constructed at the site, the Troaeum Traiani.

13. Dio, *Roman History*, 68.9.

14. Ibid., 68.10.3–4.

15. Once again, we know virtually nothing about the particulars of the campaign, as Dio spent much more time marveling about a stone bridge Trajan had his chief engineer, Apollodorus of Damascus, build than he did in giving readers a campaign narrative.

16. Dio, *Roman History*, 68.14.

17. The only historical record of the sieges is Trajan's Column.

18. This vast treasure was used to refill the Roman treasury and finance a major building program that included a new port at Ostia. It also financed celebratory games in which 10,000 gladiators fought (one can suppose there were a number of newly captured Dacians in that number) and 11,000 beasts were killed. According to a sixth-century chronicle by Loannus Lyndus, citing a source contemporary to Trajan, the Romans netted 180 tons of gold

and 360 tons of silver from the Dacian horde. See J. Carcopino, *Les étapes de imperiasme romain* (Hachette, 1961)

19. The Romans later built a new city of the same names about thirty miles from the original.

20. Luttwak, *Grand Strategy of the Roman Empire*, 101.

21. It was toward the end of the Dacian conflict that A. Cornelius Palma Frontonianus, legate of Syria, annexed Arabia after a show of force that involved little or no fighting, transforming the Nabatean kingdom from one of the last of the client states into a Roman province (Dio, *Roman History*, 68.14).

22. Once again, the historian is plagued by a lack of sources. All we have in terms of a contemporary record of the campaign are coins for dating, a small number of fragments written by Arrian, and some small portions of Dio's history preserved by Xiphilinus. For the most complete account of Trajan's Parthian War, see F. A. Lepper, *Trajan's Parthian War* (1948).

23. Dio, *Roman History*, 68.19.

24. C. S. Lightfoot, "Trajan's Parthian War and the Fourth Century Perspective," *Journal of Roman Studies* 80 (1990): 115–126.

25. Dio, *Roman History*, 68.18.2.

26. Ibid., 68.26.

27. Ibid., 68.29.

28. Ibid., 68.29.3.

29. According to Orosius (*Against the Pagans*, 7.12.6–8): "Then in an incredible movement at one time, as if carried away by madness, the Jews flared up in different parts of the world. For throughout Libya they waged the fiercest warfare against the inhabitants: the land was so desolated by the killing of the people . . . that if Hadrian afterwards had not collected and sent colonists there from elsewhere the country would have remained completely empty. . . . However, in Alexandria they were overcome and wiped out in pitched battle. And in Mesopotamia by order of the emperor war was directed against the rebels. Thus many thousands of them were killed in the blood-bath." Also see Eusebius, *Ecclesiastical History*, 4.2, and Dio, *Roman History*, 68.32, for further details (Dio's version is particularly lurid).

30. Dio, *Roman History*, 68.30.2.

31. Ibid., 68.75.9.

32. Ibid., 68.30.3.

33. Miriam Griffin, "The Flavians," in *The Cambridge Ancient History*, 2nd ed., vol. 11, *The High Empire, A.D. 70–192*, ed. Alan K. Bowman, Peter Garnsey, and Dominic Rathbone (Cambridge University Press, 2000), 126.

34. *Historia Augusta*, "Hadrian," 6.2.

35. Aurelius Victor, *Epitome: Book of the Caesars*, 14. See http://www.roman-emper ors.org/epitome.htm.

36. *Historia Augusta*, "Hadrian," 5.

37. Dio gives us the names—Palma, Celsus, Nigrinus, and Lusius (*Roman History*, 69.2.5). We know that at least Palma—Aulus Cornelius Palma—was a military commander, as it was he who had overrun Arabia Nabataea, while Trajan was fighting in Dacia. He and Lucius Publius Celsus were, according to the *Historia Augusta*, reputedly personal enemies of Hadrian.

38. Dio, *Roman History*, 69.2.5.

39. Ibid., 69.8.

40. *Historia Augusta*, "Hadrian," 10.

41. Dio, *Roman History*, 69.9. (emphasis added).

42. An adaption of a phrase in Vegetius's *De Re Militari*: "Igitur qui desiderat pacem, praeparet bellum" (Therefore let him who desires peace get ready for war).

43. R. A. Birley, "Hadrian to the Antonines," in *The Cambridge Ancient History*, 2nd ed., vol. 11, *The High Empire, A.D. 70–192*, ed. Alan K. Bowman, Peter Garnsey, and Dominic Rathbone, (Cambridge University Press, 2000), 137.

44. *Historia Augusta*, "Hadrian," 5.

45. Ibid., 12.6.

46. These fortifications were likely a reaction to increasing numbers of tribal penetrations, particularly by the Alani, with the support of Pharasmanes, king of Iberia (in the Caucasus) and likely also Parthian encouragement. Arrian had beat off many of previous such incursions, but was probably happy to have had a fortified frontier as a pivot to operate in in the larger Alani attacks into Cappadocia in 135. (Dio, 69.15; See also: Arrian: Expedition Against the Alan, 1–31.)

47. Birley, "Hadrian to the Antonines," 142.

48. Michael Kulikowski, *The Triumph of Empire: The Roman World from Hadrian to Constantine* (Harvard University Press, 2016), 25.

49. Dio, *Roman History*, 69.13.2.

50. Ibid., 69.14.1–2. See also Eusebius, *Ecclesiastical History*, 4.6.1–4.

51. Kulikowski, *The Triumph of Empire*, 32.

52. Ibid., 26.

53. Publius Aelius Aristides, *The Roman Oration*. See https://www.bradford-del ong.com/2017/11/aelius-aristides-the-roman-oration-it-is-a-time-honored-custom-of-travelers-setting-forth-by-land-or-sea-to-m.html.

54. As quoted in David J. Breeze, *The Frontiers of Imperial Rome* (Pen and Sword, 2011), 181.

55. As quoted in Birley, "Hadrian to the Antonines," 153.

56. Luttwak, *The Grand Strategy of the Roman Empire*, 126.

57. Appian, *Roman History*, Preface, 1.7.0 Also quoted on p. 20 of this work.

58. Luttwak, *The Grand Strategy of the Roman Empire*, 126.

59. Aurelius Victor, *Epitome de Caesaribus, 16*.

60. *Historia Augusta*, "Marcus Aurelius," 8.7.

61. Dio, *Roman History*, 71.2.

62. Ibid. There is speculation that could have been the lost Legio IX Hispania, which was last known to be in York during Trajan's reign, but in the 165 CE list of legions it does not exist.

63. *Historia Augusta*, "Marcus Aurelius," 8.12.

64. Ibid., 8.13. See also *Historia Augusta*, "Verus," 6.9.

65. The *Historia Augusta* has a length list of lurid examples of his sternness as a disciplinarian, including his policy of cutting off the hands of many deserters and breaking the legs and hips of others.

66. *Historia Augusta*, "Avidius Cassius," 4.3.

67. Kulikowski, *The Triumph of Empire*, 48. See also Birley, "Hadrian to the Antonines," 160–165, for a recounting of this conflict.

68. The *Historia Augusta* ("Marcus Aurelius," 14.1) states only that "the Victuali and Marcomanni throwing everything into confusion, *but other tribes, who had been driven on by the more distant barbarians and had retreated before them, were ready to attack Italy if not peaceably received*" (emphasis added).

69. *Historia Augusta*, "Marcus Aurelius," 13.1.

70. Ibid., 14.6.8.

71. Ibid., 21.6.6–7. According to Dio (*Roman History*, 10.2–3): "Many of the Germans, too, from across the Rhine, advanced as far as Italy and inflicted many injuries upon the Romans. They were in turn attacked by Marcus, who opposed to them his lieutenants Pompeianus and Pertinax; and Pertinax (who later became emperor) greatly distinguished himself. Among the corpses of the barbarians there were found even women's bodies in armor. Yet, though a mighty struggle had taken place and a brilliant victory had been won, the emperor nevertheless refused the request of the soldiers for a donative, declaring that whatever they obtained over and above the regular amount would be wrung from the blood of their parents and kinsmen."

72. As this work is being written, the world is experiencing the impact of the COVID-19 pandemic. As terrible as the losses have been from this disease, in relative terms, it has killed only a small fraction of the number of people the Roman Empire lost as a consequence of the Antonine Plague. Even so, containing the spread of COVID-19 forced much of the global economy to close, with economic impacts that will take a generation to recover from. One can use this lived experience as a mental template to get some grasp of the economic impacts a plague would have on a preindustrial society.

73. As we will detail later, prices in the Roman Empire were unusually resistant to actions that would spark inflation in many other societies and eras in history.

74. According to the *Historia Augusta*: "When he had drained the treasury for this war, moreover, and could not bring himself to impose any extraordinary tax on the provincials, he held a public sale in the Forum of the Deified Trajan of the imperial furnishings, and sold goblets of gold and crystal . . . even flagons made for kings, his wife's silken gold-embroidered

robes, and, indeed, even certain jewels which he had found in considerable numbers in a particularly holy cabinet of Hadrian's. This sale lasted for two months, and such a store of gold was realized thereby, that after he had conducted the remainder of the Marcomannic war in full accordance with his plans" (*Historia Augusta*, "Marcus Aurelius," 17.4–5).

75. Dio, *Roman History*, 72.3.

76. Albino Garzetti, *From Tiberius to the Antonines: A History of the Roman Empire, AD 14–192* (Meuthen LTF, 1960), 480–490.

77. Ammianus, *The Roman History*, 29.6.1.

78. The fighting carried out by Marcus in Italy mentioned above was against settlers, not an organized military force. Moreover, the sources are exceedingly difficult to interpret. This battle could easily have taken place in northern Illyricum or southern Pannonia.

79. Birley, "Hadrian to the Antonines," 172.

80. This, of course, was always the weakness of any large barbarian raid. Unless the army was accompanied by families with plans to stay and settle the land, there was a limit to how long it could continue to fight far from home. With no logistical support coming from their own territories, they had to live off the land. But the Romans were masters of slowly hemming in such incursions, leaving the barbarians few options: fight a massed Roman army or make a break for home. Either choice was fraught with peril.

81. *Historia Augusta*, "Marcus Aurelius," 21.10.

82. Kulikowski, *The Triumph of Empire*, 55.

83. Dio, *Roman History*, 72.8.

84. The XII Fulminata never left Cappadocia, although it likely sent vexillations to the Danube. The conservator of Dio's work, Xiphilinus, inserts his own thoughts in the epitome's next section to make a case for Christ's intervention (Dio, *Roman History*, 72.9).

85. For a detailed study of the "rain miracle" and all of its implications, see Péter Kovács, *Marcus Aurelius' Rain Miracle and the Marcommanic War* (Leiden, 2009).

86. Kulikowski, *The Triumph of Empire*, 56.

87. Dio, *Roman History*, 72.16.

88. Ibid., 72.11.

89. Kulikowski, *The Triumph of Empire*, 58.

90. Dio, *Roman History*, 72.27.

91. Ibid., 72.27.2. Dio informs us that he was finished off by a decurion (a commander of a Roman cavalry squadron).

92. There are claims that she committed suicide rather than face trial for having tried to make arrangements with Cassius at the start of the revolt. As Dio says of that incident: "Seeing that her husband had fallen ill and expecting that he would die at any moment, [she] was afraid that the throne might fall to some outsider, inasmuch as Commodus was both too young and also rather

simple-minded, and that she might thus find herself reduced to a private station. Therefore she secretly induced Cassius to make his preparations so that, if anything should happen to Antoninus [Marcus Aurelius], he might obtain both her and the imperial power" (Dio, *Roman History*, 72.22–23). It still remains more likely that she died of natural causes.

93. Dio, *Roman History*, 72.33.

94. Ibid., 72.34.

95. Ibid., 73.1.

96. *Historia Augusta*, "Commodus," 1.7–8.

97. Dio, *Roman History*, 72.35.4.

98. From time to time a brave historian has tried to rehabilitate Commodus's reputation. These attempts are, however, sparse, and they mostly fail, because they primarily rest upon the fact that he was mostly hated by the senatorial class, who wrote the histories. The fact that most senators, including his biographers, detested him does not, however, mean they are lying about his character. After all, they had to have had a reason to detest him. Dio did remain popular with the soldiers and the average Roman citizen. How could he not be? He paid the soldiers well and required little fighting from them, and the citizenry was pleased to have an emperor who spent lavishly.

99. As quoted in John Rae's *Life of Adam Smith* (Macmillan, 1895): "One day Sinclair brought Smith the news of the surrender of Burgoyne at Saratoga in October 1777, and exclaimed in the deepest concern that the nation was ruined. 'There is a great deal of ruin in a nation,' was Smith's calm reply." His meaning, of course, was that it would take more than just a few military reverses to destroy the country.

100. Kulikowski, *The Triumph of Empire*, 60. Herodian of Antioch adds a bit to this tale, stating the barbarians were not so much beaten as bought off: "The barbarians are by nature fond of money; contemptuous of danger, they obtain the necessities of life either by pillaging and plundering or by selling peace at a huge price. Commodus was aware of this practice; since he had plenty of money, he bargained for release from care and gave them everything they demanded" (Herodian, *History of the Roman Empire*, 1.6.9).

101. Kenneth Harl, *Coinage in the Roman Economy: 300 B.C. to A.D. 700* (Johns Hopkins University Press, 1996), 120.

102. *Historia Augusta*, "Commodus," 13.5.6.

103. Dio, *Roman History*, 73.8.

104. *Historia Augusta*, "Commodus," 17.2; Dio, *Roman History*, 22.4.

105. Herodian, *History of the Roman Empire*, 1.7.

Chapter 11

1. Herodian, *History of the Empire*, 2.5.1.

2. C. Velleius Paterculus, *Roman History*, 2.111.1.

3. Dio, *Roman History*, 74.17.5.
4. Herodian, *History of the Empire*, 2.13.10.
5. Ibid., 2.14.7.
6. Of course, the comparisons are inexact, but they make a point.
7. Herodian, *History of the Empire*, 2.15.4.
8. *Historia Augusta*, "Albinus," 7.4.
9. Herodian, *History of the Empire*, 3.5.1–8.
10. Ibid., 3.2.10.
11. Ibid., 3.3.1–2.
12. Dio's version of the battle is a bit different, crediting a cavalry attack in Niger's rear and the impact of a heavy storm that was blowing in the faces of Niger's forces (Dio, *Roman History*, 75.7).
13. Herodian, *History of the Empire*, 4.4.5.
14. Brian Campbell, "The Severan Dynasty," in *The Cambridge Ancient History*, 2nd ed., vol. 12, *The Crisis of Empire, A.D. 193–337*, ed. Alan K. Bowman, Peter Garnsey, and Averil Cameron (Cambridge University Press, 2009), 5.
15. Dio tells us that Severus needed to cross to Euphrates and conducted substantial operations in the vicinity of Nisibis, but these did not amount to much, as he had to rapidly curtail them to deal with Albinus. He did, however, gain a good deal of practical experience in the logistic requirements of fighting a war in such an arid environment.
16. Dio, *Roman History*, 75.11.14.
17. Potter, *The Empire at Bay*, 108.
18. Herodian, *History of the Empire*, 3.7.2.
19. Dio, *Roman History*, 76.6; *Historia Augusta*, "Severus," 10.7–11.7; Herodian, *History of the Empire*, 3.7.1.8.
20. Edward Gibbon, *The Decline and Fall of the Roman Empire*, vol. 2 (B. F. French, 1830), 63.
21. *Historia Augusta*, 12.1.
22. See pp. 297–298 of this work for Thucydides' account of how damaging such civil conflict could become.
23. Campbell, "The Severan Dynasty," 6.
24. Dio, *Roman History*, 66.10.1.
25. Ibid., 76.10.3.
26. Herodian, *History of the Empire*, 3.7.4.
27. II Parthica moved to a base on Alban mountain near Rome. Here it could work as a strategic reserve, while also acting as a counterweight to the Praetorians, if they were ever again to behave in the manner they were accustomed to before Severus remade the organization.
28. Dio, *Roman History*, 75.3.2–3.
29. Potter, *The Empire at Bay*, 112.
30. Isaac, *Limits of Empire*, 257.
31. Potter, *The Empire at Bay*, 114.

32. Kulikowski, *The Triumph of Empire*, 93.

33. Caracalla's birth name was Lucius Septimius Bassianus. Severus later changed it to Marcus Aurelius Antoninus in an attempt to manufacture a union of his family with that of Antoninus Pius and Marcus Aurelius. The name Caracalla was attached to him from the Gallic hooded tunic that he habitually wore.

34. Kulikowski, *The Triumph of Empire*, 97.

35. Dio, *Roman History*, 77.15.1.

36. Ibid., 77.14.

37. Ibid., 77.14.7.

38. Ibid., 77.15.2.

39. Potter points out that based on wheat prices in Egypt, which had doubled over the previous century (an inflation rate of well under 1 percent a year), there was likely substantial inflation of foodstuff in other parts of the Empire also. But Potter also points out the legions were insulated from these cost increases, as they got their food for free, and by this point were no longer paying for their own equipment. One should also note that just because the legions were spared the inflationary cost of food does not mean the Empire's treasury was not impacted.

40. Potter, *The Empire at Bay*, 126.

41. Ibid., 125.

42. Ibid., 128.

43. Herodian, *History of the Empire*, 4.4.7.

44. Dio, *Roman History*, 78.3.1–2. There is room in the sources to argue over what was promised to who. What is not in doubt is that Caracalla bankrupted the Roman treasury through payments to the praetorians and the legions for their blessing upon his right to rule.

45. Ibid., 78.9.4.

46. Campbell, "The Severan Dynasty," 18–19.

47. Dio, *Roman History*, 78.22.1–3.

48. Ibid., 79.1.

49. Herodian, *History of the Empire*, 4.10.2–4.

50. Ibid., 4.11.8.

51. Ibid., 4.151–3.

52. Dio, *Roman History*, 79.27.

53. Ibid., 79.37.

54. Ibid., 80.13.2

55. *Historia Augusta*, "Elagabalus.," 16.5. Dio has a bit different version of events: "Later he again formed a plot against Alexander, and when the Pretorians raised an outcry at this, he went with him to the camp. But he then became aware that he was under guard and awaiting execution . . . so he made an attempt to flee, and would have got away somewhere by being placed in a chest, had he not been discovered and slain, at the age of

eighteen. His mother, who embraced him and clung tightly to him, perished with him; their heads were cut off and their bodies, after being stripped naked, were first dragged all over the city, and then the mother's body was cast aside somewhere or other, while his was thrown into the river" (Dio, *Roman History*, 80.20).

56. Herodian, *History of the Empire*, 6.9.3.
57. Ibid., 6.1.1.
58. Dio, *Roman History*, 80.3.1.
59. Ibid., 80.4.2.
60. Ibid., 80.4.1.
61. Herodian, *History of the Empire*, 6.2.3–4.
62. Zonaras, *The History of Zonaras,* 12.15.
63. Herodian, *History of the Empire*, 6.5.1–6.
64. Ibid., 6.5.9–10.
65. The Roman propaganda machine also went into overdrive to portray Alexander's expedition against the Persian menace as a great success. Sources such as Aurelius Victor, Eutropius, Jerome, and Zonaras all state that Alexander won a great victory, although Zonaras (*History of Zonaras*, 12.15) tempers this with a mention of heavy Roman losses. From this point, the *Historia Augusta* becomes increasingly less trustworthy, as we can see its description of the campaign and Alexander's role: "In this battle he himself commanded the flanks, urged on the soldiers, exposed himself constantly to missiles, performed many brave deeds with his own hand, and by his words encouraged individual soldiers to praiseworthy actions. At last he routed and put to flight this great king, who had come to the war with seven hundred elephants, eighteen hundred scythed chariots, and many thousand horsemen" (*Historia Augusta*, "Alexander," 55.1–2). Unfortunately for Alexander, his soldiers knew the truth.
66. Herodian, *History of the Empire*, 7.2.
67. Ibid., 7.9.

Chapter 12

1. David Potter points out that this is utterly without support in any known Persian text of the period; see David Potter, "The Transformation of the Roman Empire: 235-337," in *A Companion to the Roman Empire*, ed. David Potter (Wiley-Blackwell, 2010), 157–158. If one were to speculate, the former ruling Parthian dynasty, the Arsacids, who were seeking refuge within the Empire, had good reason to attribute such ambitions to their Sassanid successors.
2. Herodian, *History of the Empire*, 6.2.2. This does not imply that the Parthians did not employ their Achaemenid past in both propaganda and threats (see Tacitus, *Annals*, 6.37), but there are no indications that the reconquest of the Achaemenid Empire was ever part of Parthian policy. For a discussion

of this topic see Beate Dignas, Engelbert Winter, *Rome and Persia in Late Antiquity: Neighbors and Rivals* (Cambridge University Press, 2010), 13–17.

3. For a more complete commentary on Sassanid-Roman relations see Richard N. Frye, "The Sassanians," in *The Cambridge Ancient History*, 2nd ed., vol. 12, *The Crisis of Empire, A.D. 193–337*, ed. Alan K. Bowman, Averil Cameron, and Peter Garnsey (Cambridge University Press, 2005), 461–480.

4. Kyle Harper recently created a sensation in the field with his book *The Fate of Rome: Climate, Disease, and the End of an Empire* (Princeton University Press, 2017). The popularity of his work, not to mention its ambitious scope, naturally attracted many alternative viewpoints (for a comprehensive example see John Haldon, Hugh Elton, Sabine R. Huebner, Adam Izdebski, Lee Mordechai, and Timothy P. Newfield, "Plagues, Climate Change, and the End of an Empire: A Response to Kyle Harper's *The Fate of Rome* (2): Plagues and a Crisis of Empire," *History Compass*, 2018;e12506, https://doi.org/10.1111/hic3.12506. It is far beyond the scope of this work to enter into this debate. Instead I will provide the big and mostly agreed-upon trends and then present my own analysis of the strategic impacts. In outlining these trends I am relying on Michael McCormick, Ulf Büntgen, Mark A. Cane, et al., "Climate Change during and after the Roman Empire: Reconstructing the Past from Scientific and Historical Evidence," *Journal of Interdisciplinary History* 43, no. 2 (2012): 169–220.

5. For a comprehensive examination of the impact of the last mini–Ice Age see Geoffrey Parker, *Global Crisis: War, Climate Change and Catastrophe in the Seventeenth Century* (Yale University Press, 2013).

6. The globe has been in another such warming period since the end of the last mini–Ice Age in approximately 1850. This book takes no position on the extent to which humans may have accelerated as well as increased the amount of warming in the current period.

7. Ulf Büntgen, "2500 Years of European Climate Variability and Human Susceptibility," *Science* 331, no. 6017 (February 4, 2011): 578–582, doi: 10.1126/science.1197175. For the past few decades there has been an increasing trend to discuss this period in terms of a "transformation" instead of what it really was: a total civilizational collapse. We will come back to this debate later, but I will be following in the wake of more recent scholarship of professors such as Peter Heather, Chris Wickham, and Bryan Ward-Perkins, who present clear and convincing evidence that if this was a "transformation" it was the most destructive one in human history.

8. McCormick, "Climate Change during and after the Roman Empire," 169–220. Later in his article there is an interesting commentary on food production during the third century: "After 155 AD when the Empire struggled to face mounting political, military, and economic challenges, the best harvests became substantially more infrequent and the worse ones more common. The written records suggest that unusually favorable climate

conditions for Egyptian food production prevailed throughout the first two centuries of the Roman Empire, whereas the conditions underpinning food production appear to have been consistently less good from 155 to 299 AD."

9. David Harms Holt, "Did Extreme Climate Conditions Stimulate the Migrations of the Germanic Tribes in the 3rd and 4th Centuries AD? An Examination of Historical Data, Climate Proxy Data, and Migration Events" (Ph.D. diss., Deaprtmment of Geography, University of Arkansas); David Harms Holt, "Germania and Climate Variability in the 3rd and 4th Centuries A.D.: A Methodological Approach to Dendroclimatology and Human Migration," *Physical Geography* 32, no. 3 (2011): 241–268; doi: 10.2747/0272-3646.32.3.241; McCormick, "Climate Change during and after the Roman Empire": "[On the Asian steppes] the first half of the third century was wetter than average, and the second half was marked by drought conditions from about 242 to 293. . . . But the crucial development was the severe drought of the fourth century that lasted nearly forty years, one of the worst in 2000 years" (190).

10. Walter Scheidel, "Disease and Death in the Ancient City of Rome," working paper, https://www.princeton.edu/~pswpc/pdfs/scheidel/040901.pdf.

11. Kyle Harper has created an internet database of the source record for pestilence within the Roman Empire; see https://www.kyleharper.net/uncate gorized/database-of-pestilence-in-the-roman-empire/.

12. Pliny, *Natural History*, 19.1, records travel speed approximately that fast: Cadiz to Ostia in just seven days, and Ostia to Africa in just two days.

13. Eutropius, *Breviarium*, 8.12.

14. As quoted in Rebecca Fleming, " Galen and the Plague," in Caroline Petit, *Galen's Treatise Περὶ Ἀλυπίας (De indolentia) in Context* (Leiden: Brill, 2018), 219–244, doi: https://doi.org/10.1163/9789004383302_011. Jerome's *Chronicle*—the *Chronicon* or *Temporum liber* (Book of Times)—was written about 380 CE. It was a history from Abraham to Jerome's own day. Jerome's work was a translation and revision of Eusebius of Caesarea's *Chronicon*.

15. Jerome, *Chronicle*.

16. R. P. Duncan-Jones, "The Impact of the Antonine Plague," *Journal of Roman Archaeology* 9 (1996): 108–136, doi:10.1017/S1047759400016524. See https://anaskafh.files.wordpress.com/2020/07/the_antonine_plague_revisi ted.pdf.

17. Kyle Harper, "Pandemics and Passages to Late Antiquity: Rethinking the Plague of *c.* 249–270 Described by Cyprian," *Journal of Roman Archaeology* 28 (2015): 223–260.

18. Harper, *The Fate of Rome*, 137.

19. As quoted in ibid., 138.

20. *Historia Augusta*, "Claudius," 11.3–4. In Zosimus's version this event reads as follows: "Egypt being thus reduced by the Palmyrenians, the barbarians, who survived the battle of Naissus between Claudius and the

Scythians, defending themselves with their carriages which went before them, marched towards Macedon, but were so distressed by the want of necessaries, that many of them and of their beasts perished with hunger. They were met likewise by the Roman cavalry, who having killed many of them, drove the rest towards Mount Haemus; where being surrounded by the Roman army, they lost a vast number of men" (*New History*, 1.45.1–2).

21. *Historia Augusta*, "Claudius," 12.1. Zosimus mentions these invasions but not the pestilence (*New History*, 1.46).

22. For a more through discussion of the changes within barbarian tribal structures since Tacitus's *Germania* was written, see Malcolm Todd, "The Germanic People and Germanic Society," in *The Cambridge Ancient History*, 2nd ed., vol. 12, *The Crisis of Empire, A.D. 193–337*, ed. Alan K. Bowman, Averil Cameron, and Peter Garnsey (Cambridge: Cambridge University Press, 2005), 440–460.

23. Peter Heather, *The Fall of the Roman Empire: A New History of Rome and the Barbarians* (Oxford University Press, 2006), 84–94. This was an eye-opening book for me and the work that convinced me that a new examination of Roman strategy was necessary. Throughout the rest of this work, I am following in Heather's footsteps whenever I discuss the impact the barbarians had on Rome in its last centuries.

Chapter 13

1. It has become fashionable in recent decades to question if there truly was a crisis in the third century. According to Averil Cameron, "There is a kind of consensus today that the concept of crisis is somehow no longer appropriate, and that instead we should use terms which are relatively value-free, such as 'change' or 'transformation'"; quoted in Wolf Liebeschuetz, "Was There a Crisis of the Third Century?," in *Crises and the Roman Empire: Proceedings of the Seventh Workshop of the International Network Impact of Empire (Nijmegen, June 20–24, 2006)*, ed. Olivier Hekster, Gerda de Kleijn, and Daniëlle Slootjes, Impact of Empire 7 (Leiden, 2007), 11–20. I am not one to argue against a "valueless" approach to the study of history. But any time a state or empire goes through over fifty rulers in as many years, breaks into three major entities, suffers several catastrophic military defeats, and has its economy ruined by rapid inflation, I think we can safely use the word "crisis" without too much fear of contradiction.

2. Much of the historiography of the third century comes from later sources. It is beyond the scope of this book to deeply examine this histography, but the historian feels the loss of Dio, and even the flawed Herodian. We are now forced to rely on the works of Zosimus and Zonaras, written in the sixth and twelfth century, respectively. For a good description of the historiographical problems, see Potter, *The Empire at Bay*, 228–232. For a more detailed study

see John Marincola, *A Companion to Greek and Roman Historiography* (Wiley-Blackwell, 2010).

3. We know nothing about this battle, as it is only mentioned by Ammianus as one of the great victories the Romans had over the Persians (*Res Gestae*, 23.5.17). Considering the extent of Roman reverses after this battle was fought, one may wonder whether it was as decisive a battle as Ammianus would have us believe.

4. This battle is not mentioned in any Roman sources and is only found in Persian inscriptions. Sapor claims that his army killed Gordian in this battle, but it is a certain fact that the emperor died in Zaitha.

5. Zosimus's account cannot be given any credence: "Observing that abundance of military provisions was supplied, while the emperor was staying about Carrhae and Nisibis, he [Philip] ordered the ships that brought those provisions to go further up the country, in order that the army, being oppressed with famine, might be provoked to mutiny." (*New History*, 1.18.3). That a general could order that food be sent away from a famished Roman army and survive beggars belief.

6. Ibid., 1.22.1–2.

7. John Drinkwater, "Maximinus to Diocletian and the 'Crisis'," in *The Cambridge Ancient History*, 2nd ed., vol. 12, *The Crisis of Empire, A.D. 193–337*, ed. Alan K. Bowman, Peter Garnsey, and Averil Cameron (Cambridge University Press, 2005), 38–39.

8. Our understanding of the campaigns of 251 CE have been hugely enhanced by now fragments of Dexippus's history. See Fritz Mitthof, Jana Grusková, and Gunter Martin, *Empire in Crisis: Gothic Invasions and Roman Historiography* (Vienna, 2020). Crucially, the battlefield at Abrittus has been discovered and it is clear that Decius had only three legions with him; see Radoslavova, Dzanev, and Nikolov, *Archaeologica Bulgarica* 15, no. 3 (2011): 23–49, http://www.archaeologia-bulgarica.com/wp-content/uploads/2016/01/PDF_website_Archelogia_Bulgarica_3_2011.pdf.

9. Zonaras, *Extracts of History*, 12.20. Decius's son, Herennius Etruscus, may have been killed in an earlier skirmish, as we find this from Jordanes: "In the battle that followed they [Goths] quickly pierced the son of Decius with an arrow and cruelly slew him. The father saw this, and although he is said to have exclaimed, to cheer the hearts of his soldiers: 'Let no one mourn; the death of one soldier is not a great loss to the republic', he was yet unable to endure it, because of his love for his son. So he rode against the foe, demanding either death or vengeance, and when he came to Abrittus, a city of Moesia, he was himself cut off by the Goths and slain, thus making an end of his dominion and of his life" (Jordanes, *The Origins and Deeds of the Goths*, 13.103).

10. Zonaras (*Extracts of History*, 12.20) claims that it was Gallus who convinced Cniva to establish his defense in the swamp where Decius would be easy to

defeat, whereas according to Zosimus (*New History*, 1.23.2), "Gallus, who was disposed to innovation, sent agents to the barbarians, requesting their concurrence in a conspiracy against Decius. To this they gave a willing assent, and Gallus retained his post on the bank of the Tanais."

11. Ammianus, *Res Gestae*, 31.5.15.
12. Alleksander Burshce, "The Battle of Abrittus, the Imperial Treasury and Aurei in Barbaricum, *Numismatic Chronicle* 173 (2013): 151–170; https://www.academia.edu/13213004/The_Battle_of_Abrittus_the_Imperial_Treasury_and_Aurei_in_Barbaricum_Numismatic_Chronicle_173_2013_s_151_170.
13. Ammianus, *Res Gestae*, 23.5.3. There is some confusion over the dating of this event.
14. Drinkwater, "Maximinus to Diocletian and the 'Crisis'," 40–41.
15. Potter, *The Empire at Bay*, 250.
16. Kulikowski, *The Triumph of Empire*, 159.
17. Julius Caesar, *Gallic Wars*, 2.20–21 (emphasis added).
18. There are various traditions as to how Valerian met his end. According to Lactantius *(De mortibus persecutorum*, 5), Sapor used him as a stepping stool to help mount his horse, and then had him flayed, his skin dyed with vermilion, and hung on a palace wall; Aurelius Victor (*Liber de Casearibus*, 32.5) claims he was hacked to death immediately after his capture. Most sources, however, just say he grew old in ignominious solitude.
19. Potter, *The Empire at Bay*, 252.
20. Zosimus, *New History*, 1.39.2.
21. Christopher Malland and Caillan Daavenenport, "Dexippus and the Gothic Invasions: Interpreting the New Vienna Fragment ("Codex Vindobonensis Hist. Gr. 73," Ff. 192 v–193 R)," *Journal of Roman Studies* 105 (2015): 203–226, accessed March 20, 2021, http://www.jstor.org/stable/26346898.
22. Drinkwater, "Maximinus to Diocletian and the 'Crisis'," 48.
23. Potter, *The Empire at Bay*, 266.
24. Michael Kulikowski sees in this triumvirate of Claudius, Placidianus, and Heraclianus, a coordinated military junta that worked together to depose Gallienus and then each took one of the Empire's multiple fronts as their own responsibility. The evidence for this is scant, but the idea is intriguing, and judging by the frantic pace of obviously planned activity in the first weeks of Claudius's reign, he certainly must have been planning Gallienus's overthrow and subsequent actions for some time. See Kulikowski, *The Triumph of Empire*, 171–172.
25. Zosimus, *New History*, 1.43.2. For a more fanciful, but entertaining account of Claudius's achievement see the *Historia Augusta* ("Claudius," 6–9.)
26. Drinkwater, "Maximinus to Diocletian and the 'Crisis'," 49–50.
27. Alaric Watson, *Aurelian and the Third Century* (Routledge, 1999), 61.
28. Zosimus, *New History*, 1.44.1–2.

29. This is the first mention of the Vandals anywhere close to the Roman frontier zone in our sources. It is likely that this is just a giant warband that had heard, even hundreds of miles distant, that there were treasures to be had within the Roman Empire, and there was never a better time in which to stake a claim to them. Once this force was repulsed it would many decades before the migrating Vandals started placing sustained pressure along the frontiers. Until then, Rome was always much more concerned with the tribes of the Alemanni confederations, the Quadi, the Sarmatians, and the newly arriving tribes that were welding themselves into a Gothic proto-state.
30. *Historia Augusta*, "Aurelian," 21.1–4.
31. Potter, *The Empire at Bay*, 268.
32. Ammianus, *Res Gestae*, 30.8. For a more florid telling of this event, see the *Historia Augusta*, "Aurelian," 21.5–9.
33. *Historia Augusta*, "Probus," 9.5.
34. Ibid., "Aurelian," 22.5.
35. Ibid., 23.2.
36. Zosimus, *New History*, 1.50.3–4.
37. Ibid., 1.52.2–3.
38. Ibid., 1.53.1–4.
39. Zenobia's ultimate fate is unknown. According to Zosimus, she "died of disease or want of food," and her son and closest advisers were all drowned somewhere near Chalcedon (*New History*, 1.59.). Other traditions have her chained and put on display in Antioch and then paraded in a Roman triumph (John Malalas, *Chronographia*, 12.30), while the *Historia Augusta* claims that after his triumph in Rome, Aurelian allowed her to live in a villa with her children ("Aurelian," 30.2). And Zonaras claims she later married a Roman nobleman (*Extracts of History*, 1.28). Many modern historians believe that Zonaras got it right, as it appears there were persons in the fourth century claiming her as an ancestor.
40. For a fuller discussion see Watson, *Aurelian and the Third Century*, 94.
41. Potter, *The Empire at Bay*, 294.
42. Gregory of Tours, *History of the Franks*, 3.19, https://sourcebooks.ford ham.edu/basis/gregory-hist.asp. See also Watson, *Aurelian and the Third Century*, 94.
43. Potter, *The Empire at Bay*, 274. For an excellent paper on the economics of Aurelian's reforms, see Merav Haklai-Rotenberg, "Aurelian's Monetary Reform: Between Debasement and Public Trust," https://www.academia.edu/5914954/Aurelians_Monetary_Reform_Between_Debasement_and_Public_Trust.
44. Zosimus, *New History*, 1.62.1–2.
45. Ibid., 1.63.1–2.
46. As Zosimus points out, "The former of these [Probus] governed all Syria, Phoenicia, Palestine, and Egypt; but the latter [Florian] was in possession of

all the countries from Cilicia to Italy; besides which the homage of all the nations beyond the Alps, the Gauls, Spaniards, Britons, and Africans was paid to him" (*New History*, 1.64).

47. Jona Lendering, "The Gallic Empire," https://www.livius.org/articles/conc ept/gallic-empire/.

48. The remaining siege works are an outstanding example of how Rome conducted a siege; see G. Davies, "Cremna in Pisidia: A Re-Appraisal of the Siege Works," *Anatolian Studies* 50 (2000): 151–158.

49. Probus, for instance, during his march to Antioch, was forced to stop in Asia Minor to have his troops root out and destroy Isaurain bandits and other local troublemakers. For more on the Bagaudae, see J. F. Drinkwater, "Peasants and Bagaudae in Roman Gaul," *Echos du monde classique: Classical Views* 28, n.s. 3, no. 3 (1984): 349–371, https://www.muse.jhu.edu/article/655801; and C. Minor, "Bacaudae: A Reconsideration," *Traditio* 51 (1996): 297–307, doi:10.1017/S0362152900013465.

50. The *Historia Augusta* informs us that there were many other problems with barbarians newly settled within the Empire: "Having made peace, then, with the Persians, he returned to Thrace, and here he settled."

51. *Historia Augusta*, "Probus," 18.1–2.

52. Ibid., 16.1.

53. There are reports at this time of revolts in Syria, led by the governor Saturninus, in Cologne, and also in Britain. All were put down rather easily, but they attest both to a widespread disgruntlement with Probus, as well as a continuing instability throughout the Empire, as the Aurelian Depression persisted; see *Historia Augusta*, 18.1–8.

54. Alan K. Bowman, "Diocletian and the First Tetrarchy, AD 284–305," in *The Cambridge Ancient History*, 2nd ed., vol. 12, *The Crisis of Empire, A.D. 193–337*, ed. Alan K. Bowman, Peter Garnsey, and Averil Cameron (Cambridge University Press, 2005), 71–72.

55. Potter, *The Empire at Bay*, 285.

56. Bowman, "Diocletian and the First Tetrarchy," 73.

57. Bill Leadbetter, *Galerius and the Will of Diocletian* (Routledge, 2009), 89.

58. Bowman, "Diocletian and the First Tetrarchy," 73.

59. Eutropius, *Breviarium*, 9.24, http://www.tertullian.org/fathers/eutropius_br eviarium_2_text.htm.

60. According to Eutropius (*Breviarium*, 9.25), "But having soon after collected forces in Illyricum and Moesia, he fought a second time with Narses . . . in Greater Armenia, with extraordinary success. . . . After putting Narses to flight, he captured his wives, sisters, and children, with a vast number of the Persian nobility besides, and a great quantity of treasure; the king himself he forced to take refuge in the remotest deserts in his dominions.

61. According to Potter (*The Empire at Bay*, 293), the provinces turned over were Ingilene (centered on the city of Egil); Sophanene, bounded to the west by

the Tigris and in the south by the Batman River; Arzanene; Corduene; and Zabdicene.

62. For an excellent review and an assessment of this conflict and the Peace of Narses, including extensive quotes from our best source for events, Peter the Patrician, see Dignas and Winter, *Rome and Persia in Late Antiquity*, 122–130.

63. Almost immediately after the victory over the Persians, Galerius departed with the Danubian field army to fight off a Sarmatian assault. The evidence is that he won a decisive enough victory in late 298 or early 299 to quiet that frontier for a time.

64. Drinkwater, "Maximinus to Diocletian and the 'Crisis'," 60.

65. It is beyond the scope of this work to reproduce the finding of the numerous archaeological field surveys conducted in recent decades, all demonstrating the extent of the economic collapse, as well as attempts of the economy to right itself from 300 CE to the final collapse. For an excellent and exhaustive examination of the evidence, see Michael McCormick, *Origins of the European Economy: Communications and Commerce, AD 300–900* (Cambridge University Press, 2002), and Chris Wickham, *Framing the Early Middle Ages: Europe and the Mediterranean, 400–800* (Oxford University Press, 2005).

66. Drinkwater, "Maximinus to Diocletian and the 'Crisis'," 62.

67. Ibid., 63.

68. For an excellent economic analysis of Roman inflation during the third century, see Pródromos-Ioánnis Prodromídis, "Another View on an Old Inflation: Environment and Policies in the Roman Empire up to Diocletian's Price Edict," monograph, Centre of Planning and Economic Research, Athens, Greece.

69. Drinkwater, "Maximinus to Diocletian and the 'Crisis'," 62.

Chapter 14

1. For a detailed narrative of the administrative structure of the Empire after Diocletian's reforms, see J. H. G. W. Liebeschuetz, *From Diocletian to the Arab Conquests* (Variorum, 1990), section X.

2. Alan K. Bowman, "Diocletian and the First Tetrarchy, AD 284–305," in *The Cambridge Ancient History*, 2nd ed., vol. 12, *The Crisis of Empire, A.D. 193–337*, ed. Alan K. Bowman, Peter Garnsey, and Averil Cameron (Cambridge University Press, 2005), 74–76.

3. David S. Potter, "The Transformation of the Empire: 235–337 CE," in *A Companion to the Roman Empire*, ed. David S. Potter (Wiley-Blackwell, 2005), 166.

4. Elio Lo Cascio, "The New State of Diocletian and Constantine: From the Tetrarchy to the Reunification of the Empire," in *The Cambridge Ancient History*, 2nd ed., vol. 12, *The Crisis of Empire, A.D. 193–337*, ed. Alan K.

Bowman, Peter Garnsey, and Averil Cameron (Cambridge University Press, 2005), 180. The Italian diocese was split into two vicariates: one for the northern regions; the other in the south was assigned to a separate *vicarius*. His power over Rome itself is still disputed.

5. Ibid.

6. Hugh Elton, "Military Forces," in *The Cambridge History of Greek and Roman Warfare*, vol. 2, ed. Philip Sabin, Hans van Wees, and Michael Whitby (Cambridge University Press, 2007), 273.

7. For a discussion of the state of the *limes* when Diocletian took power as well as his later improvements, see Pat Southern and Karen R. Dixon, *The Late Roman Army* (Yale University Press, 1996), 23–32.

8. Although enlarging the army and rebuilding the frontier defenses was the government's largest expense, Diocletian also undertook a massive building campaign, including multiple palaces for each tetrarch, a new senate building, and the massive baths of Diocletian in Rome. Moreover, there was the expense of a new and immense administrative system that needed to be paid for.

9. Lo Cascio, "The New State of Diocletian and Constantine, 170–179.

10. Hugh Elton, *The Roman Empire in Late Antiquity: A Political and Military History* (Cambridge University Press, 2018), 123, and Michael Kulikowski, *The Tragedy of Empire: From Constantine to the Destruction of Roman Italy* (Belknap Press of Harvard University Press, 2019), 54.

11. Kulikowski, *The Tragedy of Empire*, 54.

12. For a more complete discussion of the third-century economy, particularly the onset and impact of economic fragmentation, see Mireille Corbier, "Coinage," in *The Cambridge Ancient History*, 2nd ed., vol. 12, *The Crisis of Empire, A.D. 193–337*, ed. Alan K. Bowman, Peter Garnsey, and Averil Cameron (Cambridge University Press, 2005), 393–439.

13. A great deal of myth surrounds this event; see Leadbetter, *Galerius and the Will of Diocletian*, 158, for a short collection of some of these stories, including claims that Galerius deliberately sent Constantine into dangerous situations that he not only survives but in which he earns great distinction, as well as the romance of Constantine galloping at a furious pace across the Empire and killing the post horses at each stop so that he cannot be pursued.

14. Zosimus, *New History*, 2.9.2.

15. According to Zosimus, Galerius had at first thought to take the field himself against Maxentius, but "on his arrival in Italy, he found the soldiers about him so treacherous, that he returned into the east without fighting a battle" (ibid., 2.10.3).

16. Potter, *The Empire at Bay*, 349–350.

17. Ibid., 351.

18. Lactantius, *On the Deaths of the Persecutors*, 48.

19. Zosimus, *New History*, 2.15.1.

20. Gibbon, *The Decline and Fall of the Roman Empire*, vol. 1, chap. 14.

21. Ibid.

22. Potter, *The Empire at Bay*, 357.

23. Zosimus, *New History*, 2.16.1.

24. Lactantius, *On the Deaths of the Persecutors*, 44.5.

25. Zosimus, *New History*, 2.18.4.

26. Ibid., 2.19.3.

27. Charles Matson Odahl, *Constantine and the Christian Empire* (Routledge, 2004), 145.

28. Zosimus, *New History*, 2.22.3–7.

29. Potter points out that after the defeat of Licinius, Fausta, and Crispus spent almost all of their time in the west, while Constantine was in the east. He calls attention to the probability that the three were forming a second center of political power that could rival and one day contest control of the Empire with Constantine. See Potter, *The Empire at Bay*, 382.

30. This work does not accept Gibbon's belief that the rise of Christianity, with its belief in a better life after death, promoted indifference to earthly life among Roman citizens and weakened their desire to sacrifice for the Empire. There is scant evidence that any significant number of the Empire's citizens decided to forgo making their current environment more hospitable in favor of a monkish life as they awaited the next life. Nor is there any evidence that the ideal of Christian pacifism diminished Rome's traditional martial spirit. As long as there were funds available, Rome never had a problem finding soldiers to do the fighting.

31. Odahl, *Constantine and the Christian Empire*, 201.

32. Kulikowski, *The Triumph of Empire*, 273.

33. Potter, *The Empire at Bay*, 447.

Chapter 15

1. Brian Campbell, "The Army," in *The Cambridge Ancient History*, 2nd ed., vol. 12, *The Crisis of Empire, AD 193–337*, ed. Alan K. Bowman, Peter Garnsey, and Averil Cameron (Cambridge University Press, 2005), 122.

2. Nigel Pollard, "The Roman Army," in *A Companion to the Roman Empire*, ed. David S. Potter (Blackwell, 2006), 206–227.

3. Zosimus, *New History*, 2.34.

4. See p. 21 of this work.

5. Zosimus, *New History*, 2.34.1–2. Much of this passage is quoted earlier in chap. 1.

6. Potter, *The Empire at Bay*, 449.

7. Karl Strobel, "Strategy and Army Structure between Septimius Severus and Constantine the Great," in *A Companion to the Roman Army*, ed. Paul Erdkamp (Blackwell, 2007), 267–325.

8. Brian Campbell, "The Army," in *The Cambridge Ancient History*, 2nd ed., vol. 12, *The Crisis of Empire, AD 193–337*, ed. Alan K. Bowman, Peter Garnsey, and Averil Cameron (Cambridge University Press, 2005), 130.

Chapter 16

1. For a through account see R. W. Burgess, "The Summer of Blood: The 'Great Massacre' of 337 and the Promotion of the Sons of Constantine," *Dumbarton Oaks Papers* 62 (2008): 5–51.
2. Eusebius, *The Life of the Blessed Emperor Constantine*, 4.68, https://sourcebooks. fordham.edu/basis/vita-constantine.asp.
3. David Hunt, "The Successors of Constantine," in *The Cambridge Ancient History*, vol. 13, *The Late Empire, A.D. 337–425*, ed. Averil Cameron and Peter Garnsey (Cambridge University Press, 1997), 5.
4. Zonaras, *Extracts of History*, 13.5.
5. Ammianus, *Res Gestae*, 30.7.5: "the Alamanni, who were raising their heads higher after learning of the death of the emperor Julian, who was absolutely the only one whom they feared after the death of Constans."
6. Waldemar Heckel, *Alexander the Great: Historical Sources in Translation* (Blackwell, 2004).
7. For a detailed reconstruction of the battle based on the scant primary source material available, see John S. Harrel, *The Nisibis Wars: The Defense of the Roman East, AD 335–363* (Pen and Sword, 2016), 77–81.
8. For an excellent collection of source material arranged to tell something akin to a narrative history, see Michael H. Dodgeon and Samuel N. C. Lieu, eds., *The Roman Eastern Frontiers and the Persian Wars, AD 226–363: A Documentary History* (Routledge, 1994).
9. As quoted in Edward Gibbon, *The Decline and Fall of the Roman Empire*, vol. 1 (B. F. French, 1830), 337. See also Julian's *Orations,* 1.30–32. A different version is given by Zosimus (2.44.4): "When the soldiers heard this, having been previously corrupted by valuable presents, they cried out, that they would have no mock emperors, and immediately began to strip the purple from Vetranio, and pulled him from the throne with the determination to reduce him to a private station. Constantius would not suffer them to injure him, and therefore sent him into Bithynia, where he allowed him a competency for life. He had not remained there long without employment before he died."
10. For an analysis of the concept of usurpation in the fourth-century Roman Empire, see Alan E. Wardman, "Usurpers and Internal Conflicts in the 4th Century A.D.," *Historia: Zeitschrift für Alte Geschichte* 33, no. 2 (1984): 220–237.
11. Zosimus, *New History*, 2.50.4.
12. Julian, *Orations*, 1.37.

13. Thucydides, *History of the Peloponnesian War*, 3.82–84.

14. Ammianus, *Res Gestae*, 16.5.3.

15. Here I accept Drinkwater's opinion that he did not winter in Sens, which is still found in most narratives of the period. See John F. Drinkwater, *The Alamanni and Rome, 213–496: Caracalla to Clovis* (Oxford University Press, 2007), 220. Drinkwater makes the case that the Alemanni were not truly as dangerous as Julian and his supporters portrayed them. One wonders than how they managed to capture and destroy so much of Rome's Rhine defenses. Even after being stripped of troops, to reinforce the field army and engage in the emperors' continuous civil wars, these defenses would still have been a formidable obstacle that would have taken a large and very dangerous Alemanni force to overcome.

16. Ammianus, *Res Gestae*, 16.2–4.

17. Ibid., 16.7.

18. Drinkwater makes the case that Julian's only motive for attacking the Alemanni was to enhance his military reputation; he doubts that they provided any serious threat to the empire. To come to this conclusion, he has to overlook that the offensive was ordered by Constantius, who had no interest in seeing Julian gain a reputation that would draw others into his orbit. Moreover, these supposedly hapless allies had just recently collapsed the Roman frontier defenses, besieged a Roman Caesar, and, during this campaign, handled Barbatio's force roughly enough to force it to retreat to its starting point.

19. Ammianus, *Res Gestae*, 16.11.3.

20. The number of participants in ancient battles is always a matter of debate. Often the numbers are so ludicrously inflated that they can easily be dispensed with. In this case, the most historians agree the Roman numbers of 13,000 is likely accurate but dispute the 35,000 Ammianus attributes to the Alemanni. I believe the figure of 35,000 presented for the Alemanni is credible. It would be hard to claim a victory of the proportions Julian did, if he had merely dispersed a force not much larger than his own. Moreover, the fact that the Alemanni were generally quiet for over generation afterward leads one to believe they suffered a shattering defeat.

21. Ammianus names Vestralpus, Urius, Ursicinus, Serapio, Suamarius, and Hortarius as initially coming together (*Res Gestae*, 16.12.1) and being later joined by Vadomarius—apparently against his will (ibid., 16.12.17)—along with ten princes and a long train of nobles (ibid., 16.12.26).

22. Ibid., 16.12.13.

23. Drinkwater presents a radically different reconstruction of the Battle of Strasbourg as well as the events leading up to it. In his reconstruction, he creates a battle that finds no support in Ammianus's work or in Julian's *Orations*. One supposes that, because versions presented by the ancient historians run counter to his narrative of barbarian weakness and general

harmlessness, he feels compelled to create a new version (Drinkwater, *The Alemanni and Rome*, 229–252). But if modern historians are allowed to present versions of history that run directly counter to extant sources, then we must give up the quest of understanding history and admit we know nothing. The ancient sources can be interrogated, but they cannot be ignored. For a detailed analysis of Ammianus's work from a language and style perspective, see R. C. Blockley, "Ammianus Marcellinus on the Battle of Strasburg: Art and Analysis in the 'History'," *Phoenix* 31, no. 3 (1977): 218–231.

24. Ammianus, *Res Gestae*, 16.12.34.

25. Ibid., 16.12.39.

26. Ibid., 16.12.37.

27. Ibid., 16.14.44.

28. Ibid., 16.12.49.

29. Ibid., 16,12.63.

30. Ibid.

31. Ibid.

32. This account passes over the nearly three years (357–359) Constantius spent campaigning along the Danube against the Quadi and the Limigantes. After the huge losses at the Battle of Mursa, the frontier garrisons could no longer hold the line.

33. Ammianus, *Res Gestae*, 17.5.8.

34. We are informed that this new approach was not a product of Sapor's genius, but was based on the recommendations of a high-level Roman deserter.

35. Ammianus, *Res Gestae*, 18.9.3.

36. Ammianus is, as for so much of this period, our best and most reliable source. In this case, he was actually in Amida during the siege and barely escaped with his life after the fortress-city finally fell. He retells the story in book 19 of his history.

37. Ammianus, *Res Gestae*, 19.9.9.

38. After Sapor departed, Constantius brough his field army forward to besiege Bezabde, but he failed to take the city. His army went into winter quarters in Antioch, leaving the Sassanid bridgehead unmolested for the winter. Sapor did return in 360 but limited his offensive to taking a few border fortresses. One can do no more than guess at why he was so reluctant to press his advantage. Still, he was slowly eroding the frontier networks upon which Roman strategy was based.

39. See Potter, *The Empire at Bay*, 493, for an analysis of the evidence for Julian's extended preparation.

40. The Sassanid provinces of Sogdiana and Bactria were being overrun by steppe nomads, possibly forerunners of the Huns, who would plague the Roman Empire in coming decades.

41. Ammianus, *Res Gestae*, 22.12.1.

42. Kulikowski, *The Tragedy of Empire*, 30.

43. Potter, *The Empire at Bay*, 504.

44. Many secondary sources state that Julian did not bring a siege train with him. But Ammianus, who was with the expedition, clearly tells us this was not true.

45. Ammianus informs us that this was a grave error and one Julian regretted almost as soon as the order was given, for he soon ordered the fires extinguished. But the conflagration had already progressed too far and could not be put out. Other sources claim that the boats could not be brought up the swift-flowing Tigris, and even Ammianus says it would have taken twenty thousand men to do so. Another reason for the order to burn the ships was that Julian, unable to capture Ctesiphon, had elected, like Alexander, to march east toward Susa and expected to be able to live off the unspoiled lands deep in the Sassanid territories. As there were no east-flowing rivers, the fleet was of no use to him in this endeavor. One wonders whether Julian was so unwise as to consider such a major operation without well-laid plans or preparations. In any event, his explorations east appeared to have been halted within a couple of days, when his army had become lost as a result of the misdirection of local guides.

46. Ammianus, *Res Gestae*, 25.1. For a recent biography of Julian, see H. C. Teitler, *The Last Pagan Emperor: Julian the Apostate and the War against Christianity* (Oxford University Press, 2020).

47. Ammianus, *Res Gestae*, 25.2.1.

48. For contesting versions of Julian's death, see http://ccat.sas.upenn.edu/rak/courses/735/Historiography/julian.html.

49. For a full recent account of Jovian's brief reign, see Jan Willem Drijvers, *The Forgotten Reign of the Emperor Jovian (363–364): History and Fiction* (Oxford University Press, 2022).

50. Ammianus, *Res Gestae*, 25.7.9. For Sapor, this was a great trade-off. He was allowing a broken and defeated army to escape. But in return he was getting the entire Roman defensive system handed over to him without the expense of blood and treasure it would have cost to take these locations by siege.

51. Ibid., 25.10.13.

52. Kulikowski, *The Tragedy of Empire*, 33.

53. Ammianus, *Res Gestae*, 26.4.1.

54. This basically followed the division of prefectures made by Constantine, one being Gaul, Britain and Spain, and the second consisting of Italy, Africa, and Illyricum.

55. Ammianus, *Res Gestae*, 26.5.13.

56. Zosimus, *New History*, 4.8.2.

57. Ammianus, *Res Gestae*, 27.5.2.

58. Ibid., 27.5.6.

59. Ibid., 27.5.5. "In the following year, having attempted with equal energy to invade the enemy's territory, he was prevented by extensive floods of the Danube and remained inactive, near a village of the Carpi in a permanent camp which he had made, until the end of autumn. And since he was cut off by the extent of the waters from doing anything, he returned from there to Marcianopolis for winter quarters."

60. Ibid., 29.4.1.

61. Ibid., 27.10.10–11.

62. Ibid., 27.10.12–15.

63. Ibid., 28.2.5–10. Only their leader, Syagrius, survived to bring the news to court. He was cashiered and banished from court for having survived the annihilation of his command.

64. Ammianus tells us that most of this rivalry revolved around the ownership of highly productive salt pits. Because this salt was of great use within the empire, it provides another demonstration of the crucial importance of interlocking economies even during times of turmoil (Ammianus, *Res Gestae*, 28.5.11). Little had changed in this regard since Tacitus wrote about the Hermunduri and the Chatti going to war over salt centuries before (Tacitus, *Annals*, 13.57.1).

65. Ammianus, *Res Gestae*, 28.5.11–13.

66. Ibid., 28.5.11–14. Theodosius had recently been promoted to the rank of *magister equitum* for service in Britain, where in 367 he had returned Britain to Roman rule after its garrisons had been shattered by combined raids of Franks, Saxons, and Picts. After his success against the Alemanni, he was sent to quell an uprising in Africa; two years of hard fighting later, in 374, Theodosius broke the revolt. He was now the most successful Roman general since Constantine, and his popularity was starting to rival that of the emperor. In 376 he was secretly investigated and then executed in Carthage.

Chapter 17

1. Ammianus, *Res Gestae*, 31.2.12. Also see John Mathews, *The Roman Empire of Ammianus* (Michigan Classical Press, 2008), and Otto J. Maenchen-Helfen, *The World of the Huns: Studies in Their History and Culture* (University of California Press, 1973).

2. Kulikowski makes a good case for this Gothic collapse's having been spread over several decades, rather than its being the result of one coordinated Hunnic offensive. The case for either circumstance cannot now be proven, as our only source for these events is the last part of Ammianus's history. See Michael Kulikowski, *Rome's Gothic Wars* (Cambridge University Press, 2008), 127–128. See also Peter Heather and John Matthews, *The Goths in the Fourth Century* (Liverpool University Press, 1991), for the most useful collection of literary and archaeological material on Gothic society.

3. Peter Heather, *Empires and Barbarians* (Oxford University Press, 2010), 151.
4. Given the losses the Goths suffered in the next six years of war, their starting numbers must hâve been substantial. They did, of course, get continuous reinforcements from beyond the Danube, but when one considers that these two would include a substantial number of women and children, the 200,000 number is supportable.
5. Edward Gibbon, *The History of the Decline and Fall of the Roman Empire,* ed. J. B. Bury with an introduction by W. E. H. Lecky, vol. 4 (Fred de Fau, 1906), 71.
6. Ammianus, *Res Gestae*, 31.5.9.
7. The location is unknown today, but according to the Antonine Itinerary it is between Tomi and Salmuris.
8. Ammianus, *Res Gestae*, 28.7.10–16.
9. This would have been a combat host as great as or greater than what the Goths had at Adrianople. One would be on safe ground assuming that the Alemanni invasion, which was an opportunistic adventure, was a mere fraction of this claim. One could only guess at the tally, but given the known circumstances and the speed with which this invasion was put together, the barbarian force would be lucky to have numbered as many as ten thousand men. The speed of the Alemanni's destruction would also point to a lower number.
10. Ammianus, *Res Gestae*, 31.12.8.
11. Ibid., 31.7.10–16.
12. Some sources report that he was felled by an arrow on the battlefield. Zosimus, however, states: "The barbarians resolutely opposed them, and gained so signal a victory that they slew all, except a few with whom the emperor fled into an unfortified village. The barbarians, therefore, surrounded the place with a quantity of wood, which they set on fire. All who had fled thither, together with the inhabitants, were consumed in the flames, and in such a manner, that the body of the emperor could never be found" (Zosimus, 423.2).
13. As quoted in Kulikowski, *The Gothic Wars*, 143.
14. Some of this analysis can be found in my earlier work: James Lacey, *Moment of Battle: The Twenty Clashes That Changed the World* (Random House, 2011).

Chapter 18

1. Zosimus, *New History*, 3.34.2.
2. Ibid., 4.31.1–4.
3. "For just suppose that this destruction was an easy matter and that we possessed the means to accomplish it without suffering any consequences, although from past experience this was neither a foregone nor likely conclusion, nevertheless just suppose, as I said, that this solution lay within

our power. Was it then better to fill Thrace with corpses or with farmers? To make it full of tombs or living men? To progress through a wilderness or a cultivated land? To count up the number of the slaughtered or those who till the soil? To colonize it with Phrygians and Bithynians perhaps, or to live in harmony with those we have subdued?" (Themistius, *Orations*, 16).

4. Zosimus, *New History*, 4.38.1–39.5.
5. Potter, *The Empire at Bay*, 551.
6. Zosimus, *New History*, 4.46.3.
7. John Curran, "From Jovian to Theodosius," in *The Cambridge Ancient History*, 2nd ed., vol. 13, *The Late Empire, A.D. 337–425*, ed. Averil Cameron and Peter Garnsey (Cambridge University Press, 1998), 110.
8. Literally "Cold River" or "Frigid River."

Chapter 19

1. Zosimus, *New History*, 5.5.4.
2. Claudian, *Against Rufinus*, 2, https://penelope.uchicago.edu/Thayer/E/Roman/Texts/Claudian/In_Rufinum/1*.html.
3. Gibbon, *The Decline and Fall of the Roman Empire*, XXVI.
4. For a defense of this number, see Peter Heather, *The Fall of the Roman Empire: A New History of Rome and the Barbarians* (Oxford University Press, 2006), 198. Zosimus place the number of invaders at 400,000, but such a massive force is not credible (Zosimus, *New History*, 5.26.4).
5. Zosimus, *New History*, 5.34.5.
6. Ibid., 5.35.5.
7. Ibid., 5.41.4.
8. Procopius, *History of the Wars*, trans. H. B. Dewing, 7 vols. (Harvard University Press and Wm. Heinemann, 1914), 2:11–23, https://sourcebooks.fordham.edu/ancient/410alaric.asp.
9. R. C. Blockley, "The Dynasty of Theodosius," in *The Cambridge Ancient History*, 2nd ed., vol. 13, *The Late Empire, A.D. 337–425*, vol. 13, ed. Averil Cameron and Peter Garnsey (Cambridge University Press, 1998), 130.
10. As quoted in Heather, *The Fall of the Roman Empire*, 241.
11. Ibid., 418.
12. Chris Wickham, *The Inheritance of Rome: Illuminating the Dark Ages, 400–1000* (Viking Penguin, 2009), 78.
13. Ibid.
14. The Eastern Empire's survival was only possible because Constantinople stood as a bulwark against any barbarian incursions across the Dardanelles. As such, the rich provinces in Anatolia, Syria, Palestine, and Egypt were unmolested. Upon this wealth, Constantinople would survive for another thousand years, despite losing much of it during the great Arab invasions of the seventh and eighth centuries.

15. Chris Wickham, *Framing the Middle Ages: Europe and the Mediterranean, 400–800* (Oxford University Press, 2005), 87.

16. Many histories, following the ancient historian Theophanes, discuss two wars in the years after 442. This position has been demolished, and it is now certain that there was only one more great conflict in 447. For a discussion see Heather, *The Fall of the Roman Empire*, 306–313.

17. Priscus, Fragment 8, https://people.ucalgary.ca/~vandersp/Courses/texts/pris fr8.html.

18. As quoted in Peter Heather, "The Western Empire, 425–76," in *The Cambridge Ancient History,* 2nd ed., vol. 14, *Late Antiquity: Empire and Successors, A.D. 425–600,* ed. Averil Cameron, Bryan Ward-Perkins, and Michael Whitby (Cambridge University Press, 2007), 17.

19. Jordanes, *Getica*, XXXVII–XL, https://people.ucalgary.ca/~vandersp/Cour ses/texts/jordgeti.html#attila.

20. Heather, "The Western Empire, 425–76," 18.

21. Ibid., 22.

Chapter 20

1. See P. A. Brunt, *Italian Manpower, 225 B.C.–A.D. 14* (Oxford University Press, 1971).

2. There are many excellent works on this process and the history of the period, but the place to start is John Brewer, *The Sinews of Power: War, Money, and the English State, 1688–1783* (Harvard University Press, 1988).

3. P. G. M. Dickson, *The Financial Revolution in England: A Study in the Development of Public Credit, 1688–1756* (Routledge, 2016).

FOR FURTHER READING

Early on in the writing of this I decided to rely on the ancient writers as much as possible. But as mentioned in the introduction, what I bring to the study of Roman strategy is expertise in military affairs and strategic studies. It is therefore vital to temper what I was reading in the ancient texts with the scholarly interpretations and context of dedicated scholars of Roman history. This is particularly true with texts such as the *Historia Augusta*, which appears to weave a fair amount of fiction in with historical fact. Still, if one wants to comprehend Roman policies and actions as the Romans understood them, then reading the ancient sources is a must. Moreover, although modern historians have mined these sources for generations, few have employed them to shed light on Roman strategy. For those seeking to dig deeper into Roman strategic thinking, then, the ancient texts still have much to reveal. Moreover, almost all of these texts are translated into English and available online.

The crucial sources for the Empire's first century remain Tacitus (*Agricola*, *Germania*, the *Histories*, and the *Annals*), Suetonius (*The Twelve Caesars*), and Dio Cassius (*Roman History*, much of it in fragments). From the start of the second century until the Crisis of the Third Century historians still look to the often untrustworthy *Historia Augusta* (multiple unknown writers), and the somewhat more accurate Herodian (*Roman History*) covering from the reign of Marcus Aurelius to the start of reign of Gordian III.

When examining the period between the accession of Nerva to the Battle of Adrianople, Ammianus Marcellinus (*Res Gestae*) remains the foundational source. Ammianus's history is supplemented by the remaining works of Aurelius Victor, Eutropius, and Festus. Zosimus (*New History*) is also crucial for the period of 238 until the start of the final crisis in 410, as he employs ancient histories that are available only in fragments today, including those of Dexippus, Eunapius, and Olympiodorus.

Any study of Roman strategy should start with the first work to specifically address the topic, Edward Luttwak's *Grand Strategy of the Roman Empire*, followed by the works that are most employed by those taking a contrary view to Luttwak: C. R. Whittaker's *Frontiers of the Roman Empire*, Benjamin Isaac's *The Limits of Empire: The Roman Army in the East*, and Susan Mattern's *Rome and the Enemy: Imperial Strategy in the Principate*. These works can be immensely supplemented by Fergus Millar's magisterial three volumes, *Rome, The Greek World*, and *The East*. It is of course impossible to understand how the Roman Empire was held together without grasping how its military power was organized and employed. The following books were instrumental in informing this work: Paul Erdkamp's *The Companion to the Roman Army*; Brian Campbell's *War and Imperial Society* and *The Roman Army: 31 B.C.–A.D. 337*; David J. Breeze's *The Frontiers of Imperial Rome*; Lawrence Keppie's *The Making of the Roman Army: From the Republic to the Empire*; Graham Webster and Hugh Elton's *The Roman Imperial Army of the First and Second Centuries A.D.*; A. D. Lee's *Warfare in the Roman World* and *Warfare in Late Antiquity*; Adrian Goldsworthy's *Roman Warfare* and *The Complete Roman Army*; and Hugh Elton's *Warfare in Roman Europe, AD 350–425* and *Frontiers of the Roman Empire*. Those looking for more information on the role of the Roman fleets can reference Michael Pitassi's *The Roman Navy: Ships, Men and Warfare, 350 BC–AD 475*; William L. Rodgers's *Naval Warfare under Oars, 4th to 16th Centuries: A Study of Strategy, Tactics, and Ship Design*; and Chester G. Starr's *The Roman Imperial Navy, 31 B.C.–A.D. 324*.

This book has made a point of emphasizing the vital importance of Rome's economy as the foundation of its power. In recent decades there has been an outpouring of publications on various facets of ancient economies, building on the earlier works of M. Rostovtzeff, M. I. Finley, and A. H. M. Jones. Among the many books consulted for this work, readers will profit from Philip Kay's *Rome's Economic Revolution*; Walter Scheidel, Ian Morris, and Richard P. Sallers's *The Cambridge Economic History of the Greco-Roman World*; Walter Scheidel and Sitta von Reden's *The Ancient Economy*; and J. G. Manning and Ian Morris's excellent *The Ancient Economy: Evidence and Models*. Finally, see Richard Duncan-Jones's *The Economy of the Roman Empire: Quantitative Studies* and *Structure and Scale in the Roman Economy*.

A narrative explanation of Roman strategy cannot be written without referencing the works of other historians of the period. But for anyone with an interest in the history of Rome, the *Cambridge Ancient Histories* (vols.

10–14) are an unsurpassed resource and should be the starting point for any serious examination of the period. In addition to the Cambridge volumes, the works that most informed this book are Ronald Syme's *The Roman Revolution*; David S. Potter's *A Companion to the Roman Empire* and *The Roman Empire at Bay, AD 180–395*; Michael Kulikowski's *The Triumph of Empire* and *The Tragedy of Empire*; Beate Dignas and Engelbert Winter's *Rome and Persia in Late Antiquity: Neighbours and Rivals*; Kyle Harper's *The Fate of Rome: Climate, Disease, and the End of an Empire*; A. D. Lee's *From Rome to Byzantium, AD 363 to 565: The Transformation of Ancient Rome*; Peter Heather's *The Fall of the Roman Empire: A New History of Rome and the Barbarians* and *Empires and Barbarians: The Fall of Rome and the Birth of Europe*; and John F. Drinkwater's *The Alamanni and Rome, 213–496: Caracalla to Clovis*.

ACKNOWLEDGMENTS

My first thanks must go to my wife, Sharon, without whose support it would have been impossible to finish this book. Not only did she provide much-needed encouragement throughout the research and writing of this book, but she also made sure that I was loved and properly nourished. I also need to thank my editor Stefan Vranka, who was a true believer in this book from the start. I also want to thank Zara Cannon-Mohammed, Barbara Norton, and James Fraleigh for their fantastic work of editing this volume and seeing it through production. Thanks also go to my agent, Eric Lupfer, who made an idea into reality. Finally, I want to thank Professors Williamson Murray, David Potter, and Peter Heather who all made many valuable suggestions on the original draft manuscript. Any remaining errors are, of course, entirely my fault.

INDEX

For the benefit of digital users, indexed terms that span two pages (e.g., 52–53) may, on occasion, appear on only one of those pages.
Note: Figures are indicated by *f* following the page number